Dudley Rutherford

12.05

ROMANCING ROYALTY

365 Devotions to Draw You Closer to King Jesus

by

Dudley C. Rutherford

Joy Comes in the Morning Productions,
Porter Ranch, California

Romancing Royalty
Published by Joy Comes in the Morning Productions

© 2005 by Joy Comes in the Morning Productions
International Standard Book Number: 0-9764289-1-1

Scripture quotations are from:
The Holy Bible, New International Version
© 1973, 1984 by International Bible Society,
used by permission of Zondervan Publishing House

Printed in the United States of America

For information:
JOY COMES IN THE MORNING PRODUCTIONS
19700 RINALDI STREET
PORTER RANCH, CA 91326

DEDICATION

*This book is dedicated to Dr. Scott Bauer
who lived every day drawing nearer to Jesus
than he had the day before.*

Today he lives at Jesus' side.

(see pages 604-607)

ACKNOWLEDGEMENTS

First and foremost, I want to thank my father, H. Dean Rutherford, of Fresno, CA, for the inspiration and development of many of these devotions and the writing of most of the prayers. He has the unique gift of powerfully communicating God's truths whether in writing or by preaching. He kept me on track and did not let this project lose any steam.

I want to thank the numerous contributors for their gift of insight. This book truly is a collaboration of writers, leaders, mentors, speakers, preachers, pastors, teachers, coaches, men, women and even children (see page 130).

I do want to send a word of appreciation to Murry Whiteman who helped design the cover of this book. We both knew intuitively that the single rose laid across the crown of thorns was a vivid reminder of how much Jesus loves us.

Lastly, I am compelled to express my gratitude to Kari Macer, my personal assistant, who must be part angel for never complaining and only complying when, at the last second, I throw unrealistic timetables her way. Thank you Kari, for your diligence and your loyalty.

PREFACE

Jesus is in love with you!

In fact, this very moment Christ is scouring the earth searching for a bride. The Savior intensely desires to be married to you. He has a gold covenant ring He wants to place on your finger. His intentions are pure and honorable. He will be eternity's best provider and protector. Jesus is the paragon of staunch, unswerving faithfulness. He earnestly seeks your heart and your hand in marriage.

Oh, dear friend, we can assure you, He will not turn you down because of your past. He has proven His passion at Calvary. There He poured out His regal, royal, red blood for His betrothed. It's engagement time, now! His ambition is Holy Matrimony with you alone. What will you do with His magnificent offer? Will you spurn again His gentle offer of divine grace?

Every false religion on earth is a story of man seeking God. Christianity is the story of God seeking and wooing mankind. Let Him be your lover today and always. The rich reward for Romancing this Royalty is an eternal honeymoon, an unending rendezvous with the Prince of Glory. Just imagine, Jesus and you, together, spending endless years of foreverness!

Our prayer is that some of the carefully chosen phrases of this book will tempt you to respond more deeply to His life-changing entreaties.

H. Dean Rutherford   Dudley C. Rutherford

ROMANCING ROYALTY

January 1

But I trust in you, O LORD; I say, "You are my God." My times are in your hands; deliver me from my enemies and from those who pursue me. (Psalm 31:14)

And God said, "Let there be lights in the expanse of the sky to separate the day from the night, and let them serve as signs to mark seasons and days and years." (Genesis 1:14)

Meditation   Dudley C. Rutherford

R.G. Lee eloquently said, "Jesus was born in the saddest hour of history. Born when the scepter of power was frozen by the tyranny of impeached civilizations. When religion was clasping hands with idolatry. Born when the world crisis had come upon the Jewish race as they slept in robes of beautiful Jewish prophecy."

But Christ's humble, lowly birth in that ancient land has made Bethlehem more famous than a thousand New Yorks. I wanted to say at the very beginning of this New Year that the birthday of Jesus splits time in two around His cradle. This Jesus, whom neither calendars, clocks or historians took note of, has bent the dateline of all the nations around His lowly manger.

Others have tried to do what Jesus did. The Greeks thought they could date time from the founding of their Olympic games. The Romans tried to date time from the founding of their imperial city. Justinian tried to mark the beginning of time from certain tax levies. La Place, from the conjunction of certain planets. The French were sure they could date it from their revolutions. But they all failed. What the Jews, Greeks, Romans and French could not do, Jesus did. He did it without a vote or command, without some legislative edict. This timeless Christ had Christianized the calendars of the world. No one in this world writes a letter, or signs a deed, or reads a newspaper, or turns on a computer without that birthday of Christ at the top of the page. Happy New Year to you in the name of Jesus!

First Days of the Year

Prayer

Thank You, Lord, for inventing time and for dating time from Your lowly birth. It helps me to remember that You are the reason for everything in life that is important. You mark not only the beginning of the calendar, but also the beginning of true happiness, true joy and salvation itself. Help me to make every day of this New Year count and invest it in Your Kingdom and in my future. I'm excited to reach that land where we will need no clocks or calendars. I put my trust into Your hands. In Christ's name, I pray. Amen.

Questions

- According to Psalm 31, whose hands hold all the times?

- Name some people who tried to set the calendar of years.

- What can you do to make this year your best ever?

Journal

January 2

"Did God really say, 'You must not eat from any tree in the garden'? You will not surely die," the serpent said to the woman. "For God knows that when you eat of it your eyes will be opened, and you will be like God, knowing good and evil." (Genesis 3:1b, 4, 5)

Meditation   *Dudley C. Rutherford*

We discover in the book of beginnings the spoken words of our Creator, our biological parents and even the enemy of our souls. Although there was a pristine quality to the creation story, everything changed when the serpent appeared on the scene. The words the devil spoke clearly revealed his deceptive nature. What God plainly stated to Adam and Eve, the devil blatantly twisted and challenged. And isn't this the same tactic he has continued to use with every son and daughter born on the earth? He has always lied and led us to believe that we didn't really need God in our lives... that we could manage quite well on our own.

Even though the devil had a 100% success rate with humanity, the tide forever changed when he tried those same lies on the "last Adam," the "Only Begotten Son of God." Ironically, the first Adam was in a lush garden, yet he didn't refuse the fleshly craving that allowed him independence from God. The last Adam was in a state of utter starvation, yet He did not indulge in any source of life outside of God Himself. Fortunately for us today, Jesus rejected the lies the devil spoke to Him. For herein we find our only hope: "The first man Adam became a living being; the last Adam, a life-giving Spirit."

Thank You, Jesus

Prayer

Lord and Creator of the universe, thank You for sending Jesus to destroy the work of the devil. When the difficulties we face threaten to bring us down, please help us recall that our struggle isn't against flesh and blood, but against the principalities and powers in the heavenly realm. We ask for the life-giving Spirit of Jesus to fill our hearts, so we will have the strength to overcome the evil one. We confess today that we don't want to live independently of You, for You alone are the true source of life! In Jesus' name I pray. Amen.

Questions

- How were "the lust of the flesh, the lust of the eyes, and the boastful pride of life" all facets of Adam and Eve's temptation in the Garden of Eden?

- How does the last book of the Bible describe the devil? (Revelation 12:9)

- In John 10:10, do you recognize the stark contrast between what the devil comes to do and what Jesus comes to do?

Journal

_____

_____

_____

_____

_____

> *Do your best to present yourself to God as one approved, a workman who does not need to be ashamed and who correctly handles the word of truth. (II Timothy 2:15)*

Meditation   *Ben Merold*

We must know the Bible if we are to handle it correctly. It is the "word of truth" and knowledge of it will come only by prayerful study. The following illustration shows the importance of the Bible in the daily life of a Christian.

I was visiting with a young attorney and his wife, and our conversation seemed to focus on the importance of daily devotions. The young man commented, "I can always tell when my wife has let down on her quiet time of Bible reading and prayer, because she will start to become anxious and irritable."

When his wife looked at him rather sharply, he quickly added, "And I presume it is the same with me when I let down on my Bible reading and prayer time."

I laughed inwardly, but I retained that simple story in my memory because it impacted my life. I remembered hearing the great motivational speaker Zig Ziglar refer to what he called "stinkin' thinkin,'" and I concluded that his descriptive terminology for a bad attitude often develops because we are out of communion with God.

I can be busy in the work of the church and still drift into negative thought patterns of anxiety and irritation. Every time I find myself victimized by "stinkin' thinkin,'" it seems to coincide with a letdown of Bible reading and prayer. I believe it will be the same with you.

Prayer

Dear Father in Heaven, I come to You in Jesus' name to thank You for every gift and blessing. I especially thank You for the gift of Your Word, the Bible and for the privilege of prayer. I ask that the Holy Spirit, who inspired the Scriptures, will inspire me as I read them. I pray for growing understanding of Your "word of truth" to better control my thoughts and my attitude. Help me to be sensitive to Your command and promises so that my life can be a positive witness for Jesus Christ. In His name, I pray. Amen.

Questions

- How much time did you give to Bible study and prayer in the last seven days?

- Did your Bible reading bring conviction about any sin or area of weakness in your life?

- Did you receive any answers to prayer? Have you prayed persistently?

Journal

_____

_____

_____

_____

■ January 4

*He answered: "Love the Lord your God with all your heart and with all
your soul and with all your strength and with all your mind"; and, "Love
your neighbor as yourself."*
(Luke 10:27 - as quoted from Deuteronomy 6:5 & Leviticus 19:18)

Meditation   *Dudley C. Rutherford*

You have just tuned in to another exciting episode of the first-century
game show, "Who Wants to Stump the Son of God?" An expert in the law
has asked the question that has been on the minds of nearly everyone who
has ever been born: "What do I have to do to live forever?" Sensing the
lawyer's enthusiasm to reveal his own intelligence, Jesus employs His famous
technique of reversing the question. Having studied far more than the Top
Ten list of commandments, the lawyer impressively quotes passages found in
two different Old Testament books. Jesus immediately agrees with the prize-
winning answer and follows up with His own quotation: "Do this and you
will live." And that, my friend, is where the game ends and reality begins.

For Jesus explicitly taught that loving the Lord your God is not only an internal,
vertical experience but devotion to God is also revealed both externally and
horizontally, in the way we treat the people we meet along the pathway of our
lives. We certainly cannot plan to live forever, if we do not choose to minister to
the wounded and dying of this world. If we have the eyes to see and ears to hear,
they are everywhere! "Little children, let us not love with word or with tongue,
but in deed and truth."

Where Reality Begins

Prayer

Almighty Father, I confess that many times I have the attitude of this first-century lawyer, rather than that of Your Son, Jesus Christ. I open my mouth to eagerly quote the correct words, but I do not open my heart to meet the very real needs of those around me. Through the power of Your Spirit, I ask that You give me a sensitive heart, so that I will never miss the opportunity to show Your compassion to those I meet. Remind me of the words of Jesus, "Do this and you will live." In His name, I pray. Amen.

Questions

- Why do you think people are so interested in living forever? (See Ecclesiastes 3:11a)

- Why does God care how you treat others? (I John 4:20)

- What practical ways to "love your neighbors" did Jesus suggest in Matthew 25:34-40?

Journal

_____

_____

_____

_____

January 5

Meditation   *Dudley C. Rutherford*

Although it has been said that beauty is only skin deep, radiance is a completely different matter. Have you ever known someone who seems to emanate radiance, despite their outward appearance? Just as beauty is observed with our eyes, radiance is recognized with our spirits. Paul did not claim to be a scientist, but he accurately described us as "jars of clay." Like clay, our bodies are composed of carbon-based atoms. Even though we are depicted in such simplistic terms, the Creator of the heavens and the earth has a treasure He wants to place within each one of us. In fact, we learn from this passage that when God said, "Let there be light," He actually had a far greater objective than just illuminating this vast universe. Ultimately, His supreme purpose in creation was to make His light shine in each one of our hearts.

God didn't create you just to look at you from the outside – though many people focus their attention there. God created you to be a jar for *His radiance!* The very radiance that was seen in the face of Jesus Christ is what God desires for each of us today. May it be our ambition to say with Paul: "And we, who with unveiled faces all reflect the Lord's glory, are being transformed into His likeness with ever-increasing glory."

Prayer

Dear Father, the truth of these verses is beyond awesome. It is even more amazing to realize that You had thoughts of me all the way back to when You said, "Let there be light." I do not begin to comprehend why You care so much, but Thank You, Thank You, Thank You! Just as Jesus was the "radiance of Your glory," I ask You to fill my clay vessel with the same Light that filled Him as He lived in flesh on this earth. It will be my joy to have You glow through me forever! In Jesus' name. Amen.

Questions

- What is the Light that will continue to shine when the lights of the heavens and earth have passed away? (Revelation 22:5)

- Whose face do you need to see, so that you can begin to experience the light of God?

- What attributes of God do you see in people who reflect His radiance?

Journal

_____

_____

_____

_____

_____

Man born of woman is of few days and full of trouble. He springs up like a flower and withers away; like a fleeting shadow, he does not endure.

(Job 14:1-2)

Meditation   *Dudley C. Rutherford*

I hold in my hand a dozens red roses. Aren't they beautiful? I almost forgot to tell you, they are dead. Oh, they look alive but in reality they are as dead as dead can be. It will be just a few hours or days at most, and their colors will fade and their petals will sag and droop and fall. They will find their way to the trashcan.

God says mankind is like a flower. First we are a seed, then a plant, then a stem and then a blossom. Then we die. Flowers are here for only a short time. I don't care how young you are, or how strong you might be, or how healthy and vibrant you might feel today… someday on God's calendar, you will begin to fade. You will die, as surely as every flower dies. Your death is appointed (Hebrews 9:27).

We must live our lives for Him while there is yet time. Time is running out for all of us, even the youngest one of us. Every word of every paragraph of every page of this Bible says we are here for only a short time, and we must bloom and live our lives for Him. There is less time than we think to blossom, to spread fragrance and beauty for our wonderful Lord.

Prayer

Dear Father on high, I can tell by everything in life that I don't have forever to get my spiritual house in order. Headlines, sirens, cemeteries and a thousand other things remind me daily that I need to serve You while there is time. Help me to make the very best of every day I have left on this earth. Help me to stop acting like I am going to live on earth forever. In my dear Savior's name, I pray. Amen.

Questions

- What is certain about every flower?

- How certain are your trouble and death?

- How much time do you have left to serve the Lord?

Journal

_____

_____

_____

_____

_____

And he who searches our hearts knows the mind of the Spirit, because the Spirit intercedes for the saints in accordance with God's will. And we know that in all things God works for the good of those who love him, who have been called according to his purpose. (Romans 8:27-28)

Meditation   *Brad Small*

When our son Christopher was three years old, we had him tested for allergies. My job, as Chris's father, was to hold his body as tightly as I could. I held him tightly in my lap, face to face and chest to chest. I tucked his little arms under my arms so that he wouldn't be able to move. While I tried to keep him calm, the doctor began to place drops of serum all over his back, shoulders and arms. Next came the needle pricks. With each prick, Chris would scream and I would cry.

After what seemed like hours of this torture, the procedure was finally finished. Instead of being able to gather my son in my arms and comfort him, I had to continue to hold him securely for 15 additional minutes to prevent the serum drops from running. If the serum drops were to run, we would have to start the process all over again, so for the next 15 minutes, we both sat in the chair and cried.

Imagine the thoughts of a three-year-old: "Why is my Daddy holding me down so a stranger can hurt me?" Yet the reality is that I had to allow my son to suffer the pain, so he could get help for his allergies.

How many times do we feel like God is holding us down for someone or something to hurt us? Reality is that God walks us through pain, using the hurt to work it for our own good. We often receive the best things in life on the heels of pain and suffering.

Brad Small is the Senior Pastor of Lakeshore Church in Rockwall, TX.

Prayer

Father, grant me the ability to see Your purposes in my life. Allow me the grace to seek You in hard times and to trust You in my pain. Lord, I claim this promise that in all things You will work for my good, even when I don't see the big picture. Through Christ I choose to trust You. Amen.

Questions

- When have you been through a painful time?

- How did you see God's work in the middle of the trial?

- How did God work it out for your good?

Journal

January 8

Dear friends, let us love one another, for love comes from God. Everyone who loves has been born of God and knows God. Whoever does not love does not know God, because God is love. (I John 4:7-8)

Meditation　　　　　　　H. Dean Rutherford

Perhaps the number one word in the entire universe is "love." Millions use the word but few grasp its true meaning. The New Testament was written in *koine* Greek. The word *koine* denotes "common," because this style of Greek was the language of the common man-on-the-street during the time of Christ. *Koine* Greek became in vogue 300 years before the birth of Jesus, and soon became an obsolete language after the death of Jesus. God supernaturally invented this language so that the New Testament could be written and understood by common mankind. Let's look at the meaning of the words for "love" found in the Scripture.

Eros is the word used to describe fleshly and physical love. Our word erotic comes from that word. *Storge* is family love. *Storge* love will offer itself in death if needs be to protect its own. A very common word for love during the apostolic age was *philia*. It was the word of genuine affection – heart love. It is seen in the name Philadelphia (brotherly love). The noblest and highest form of love, however, was *agape*. William Barclay, in his description of this word, noted that, "Agape has to do with the mind: it is not simply an emotion which rises unbidden in our hearts; it is a principle by which we deliberately live." It is the kind of love we must have for all men – even our enemies (Matthew 5:44). The Christian must always act and react out of pure love. Agape love! Unquestionably, the most exhaustive treatment of what *agape* love involves is found in I Corinthians 13.

Prayer

My wonderful friend and Savior, thank You for loving me. Without You, I would never have any true understanding of real love. Forgive me for those times I've mistaken pride, patriotism, friendship, family or lust for love. I know if I place You first and foremost in my heart and keep You enthroned, I shall never have any problems with loving You or my fellow man. I renew and rededicate my life and my love to You this day. I pray all this in the name of Jesus. Amen.

Questions

- Can a person love and not know God?

- Why was the New Testament written in *koine* Greek?

- Name three different Greek words for love.

Journal

January 9

What is more, I consider everything a loss compared to the surpassing greatness of knowing Christ Jesus my Lord, for whose sake I have lost all things. I consider them rubbish, that I may gain Christ and be found in him. (Philippians 3:8, 9a)

Meditation   *Dudley C. Rutherford*

Walk into any bookstore, and it doesn't take long to discover the myriad of self-help books that are readily available. As an over-achiever in the area of self-help, the Apostle Paul could very well have been considered an expert. In fact, he spent so many years in self-development that he was even described as "faultless." Ironically, it was at the very pinnacle of human perfectionism that Paul became keenly aware he was actually missing out on life itself. He became convinced he could no longer base his life on any four- or five-step plan for Godly living. Instead, Paul focused on the passionate heart cry of God: "This is my beloved Son in whom I am well pleased, listen to Him." (Matthew 3:17)

How often we leave those awesome words in the historical setting of the first century; but God spoke them right out of the heavens for all generations and all time! Just as Paul counted everything a big, fat zero compared to "the surpassing value of knowing Christ Jesus," God aches for each of us to learn that we won't begin to experience abundant life until we "fix our eyes on Jesus!" May our hearts beat with this fervor: "...for to me to live is Christ, and to die is gain" (Philippians 1:21).

Prayer

Dear Heavenly Father, sometimes I long to hear an audible word from You; yet I must honestly confess that I haven't listened very well to what You've already said. Open my ears to hear what matters the most to You. May I grow to understand that it is not simply following the rules, but fellowshipping in the relationship that brings the biggest smile to Your face! Enable me to clearly hear and know Your beloved Son, in whom You are well pleased. May I truly gain Christ and be found in Him. I ask this in His holy name. Amen.

Questions

- Was Jesus alive in human form when Paul wrote about wanting to know Him?

- How is it possible to hear and know Jesus today?

- Is there any aspect of your life that you consider more valuable than knowing Jesus Christ in a personal way?

Journal

January 10

Then Jesus said to his disciples, "If anyone would come after me, he must deny himself and take up his cross and follow me. For whoever wants to save his life will lose it, but whoever loses his life for me will find it. What good will it be for a man if he gains the whole world, yet forfeits his soul? Or what can a man give in exchange for his soul?" (Matthew 16:24-26)

Meditation *Dudley C. Rutherford*

Jim Elliot, the martyred missionary penned these famous words: "He is no fool who exchanges what he cannot keep for what he cannot lose." Not long after he wrote this he made the exchange. He was killed in the jungles of Ecuador while preaching Jesus. He exchanged what he couldn't keep for what he could never lose! Was the exchange a good bargain?

What are some things we can't keep? Can't keep health. Can't keep your life. Sooner or later you have to leave. The strongest human on earth will soon wither away and perish. Can't keep money. It's got to be turned over to younger and more eager hands. Can't keep houses and lands. Someone else will soon live in what you call "your house." The newest car just off the production line will end up in the junkyard. Position and power can't be kept. Jim Elliot exchanged all those fading and temporal things for what? For what he could keep!

What can you keep? You can keep your soul. You can keep love, forgiveness and eternal life. You can keep salvation forever in Christ Jesus. You can keep real joy. So who is the irrational fool? It's the man or woman who trades the everlasting and eternal things of God for the fleeting fashions and pleasures of this dying world. Have you made the right exchange? Will you, would you be willing to give up those things you can't keep for what you can never lose?

The End of the Spear

Prayer

Dear God and Savior, I want to invest my life and time in those things that can never fade or pass away. Forgive me when I get to thinking that money, fashion, pride and position are things that just might last for a while. Help me to take a look around and notice the things that quickly fade from view. Help me to bet my life on Jesus Christ and His Church for which He died. Help me to exchange what I cannot keep for what I cannot lose. In the unchanging name of Jesus, I pray. Amen.

Questions

- What temporal things have many given in exchange for their souls?

- Have you checked the Internet to read about Jim Elliot? (See the movie *The End of the Spear.*)

- What exchanges have you made, and what are you willing to exchange?

Journal

January 11

> *But the cowardly, the unbelieving, the vile, the murderers, the sexually immoral, those who practice magic arts, the idolaters and all liars— their place will be in the fiery lake of burning sulfur. This is the second death.*   *(Revelation 21:8)*

Meditation   *Dudley C. Rutherford*

The word fearless ought to describe every Christian. There are 365 "fear nots" in the Bible. One for every day of the year. Paul told Timothy that God has not given us the spirit of fear (II Timothy 1:7). There's a long list of folks in our text who aren't going to escape the lake of fire. Some of those sinners we can well understand – murderers, witches, idolaters – but the dubious honor of heading this list belongs to the cowardly and unbelieving.

Are you a coward? Do you possess some measure of boldness that will allow you to talk about Jesus with your neighbors and your associates at work? Do you have the faith and resolve to bow your head before dinner in a restaurant to thank Him for the food? Are you afraid to tithe, to give God that first tenth and then trust Him to supply your needs? Are you ashamed to carry your Bible?

I hate to bring this up again but God said, "The cowardly and unbelieving shall have their part in the lake of fire." I didn't write that! I didn't make that up! I sometimes wish it wasn't there, but what can I do? Hear David say, "The Lord is my light and my salvation; whom shall I fear? The Lord is the strength of my life; of whom shall I be afraid?" (Psalm 27:1).

Prayer

Dear God, I am beginning to understand that You want me to have complete and total faith in You and Your sure Word; that there is no room or reason for fear. When I read Your Scriptures, I know I have no one to fear, no person, no force, no threat to make me afraid. My trouble comes when I stray from You and mingle in this world's culture. I want to come so close to You that never again will I fear. In Christ's blessed name, I ask it. Amen.

Questions

- What's the destiny of this list in Revelation 21?

- Spiritually speaking, what are you afraid of?

- How does Jesus erase our fear?

Journal

He was oppressed and afflicted, yet he did not open his mouth; he was led like a lamb to the slaughter, and as a sheep before her shearers is silent, so he did not open his mouth. (Isaiah 53:7)

Meditation   *Dudley C. Rutherford*

One of our basic human instincts is the instinct for survival. We generally think in terms of physical existence when we speak of survival, but consider the overwhelming desire we have to preserve our personal image and reputation. It is extremely challenging and quite unnatural to follow Jesus' example in this matter. Although He was never guilty of committing a single sin, He was forced to be on public trial for His life. When false charges were hurled against Him, "Jesus made no reply, not even to a single charge…" Instead, He "kept entrusting Himself to Him who judges justly."

While His accusers intended to destroy His reputation as the Son of God, it was through His silence that Jesus quite profoundly revealed His divine character. For who resists the urge to answer deceitful attacks, except the person who truly believes there is far more to living than just this life? This truth can also operate in our lives, when we face false accusations and respond with silence. Perhaps it is in our silence that His divine character can also be dynamically revealed in our lives. "Consider Him who endured such opposition from sinful men, so that you will not grow weary and lose heart." Surely He "will bring to light what is hidden in darkness and will expose the motives of men's hearts."

Prayer

Heavenly Father, I am thankful You have made me a partaker of Your divine nature. Although it is instinctive to verbally defend myself when people gossip and spread lies about me, I confess that You have called me to live as "aliens and strangers" during my time on this earth. Convict me today when I react to false accusations the same way everyone else in the world does. Thank You for the example Jesus showed me in His silence. May my greatest comfort come from knowing that "our lives are now hidden with Christ in You!" In Jesus' name. Amen.

Questions

- To whom did Jesus entrust Himself?

- What three-step plan helps you react to adverse comments in a Godly way? (See James 1:19, 20)

- Can you recall an occasion when the Spirit of Christ led you to take the pathway of silence in response to personally damaging accusations?

Journal

_____

_____

_____

_____

_____

Nothing impure will ever enter it, nor will anyone who does what is shameful or deceitful, but only those whose names are written in the Lamb's book of life. (Revelation 21:27)

Meditation   *Dudley C. Rutherford*

Before "once upon a time" ever introduced a story, God began thinking about a very special book. While many consider the Bible to be God's special book, there is another writing that will ultimately have greater significance for our lives. It dates "from the foundation of the world." Although you and I haven't seen it with our own eyes, Job, David, Isaiah, Daniel, Malachi and even the Apostle John were all aware of its existence.

God had great plans for this narrative to include an enormous number of people, but there was one extraordinary character God absolutely insisted on including. As the Author, God wanted His story to be about a Lamb. Not just any lamb, of course, but "a Lamb without blemish or defect." A Lamb who was willing to die.

Before the creation of the world, Jesus deliberately chose to be the Lamb of God, so that each of us could also be included in His story. To this very day, the Lamb sits next to God. Together they are listening and waiting to hear who will speak of Him and honor His name. The pen is in hand and He longs to write, for nothing impure will ever enter His Holy City, but only "those whose names are written in the Lamb's book of life."

The Lamb's Book of Life

Prayer

Father in Heaven, thank You for providing the Way to include each and every person in Your book and in Your Holy City. Thank You for sending people into my life who also love You and find great delight in talking about You and Your Son. Mercifully forgive me when I don't speak of You or honor Your name or even care if I am part of Your story at all. Instead, may I boldly honor You, so that my life clearly reveals to everyone that Your Lamb did not die in vain. I pray in His name. Amen.

Questions

- When was Jesus actually chosen to be the Lamb of God? (I Peter 1:20)

- What are some other things being written about you? (Psalm 139:16 & Psalm 56:8)

- How significant will the book of life be in the future? (Revelation 20:11-15)

Journal

There is no fear in love. But perfect love drives out fear, because fear has to do with punishment. The one who fears is not made perfect in love. We love because he first loved us. *(I John 4:18-19)*

Meditation — Jan Caldwell

We were leaving church one icy Sunday morning, and as he slipped his little hand in mine, he said, "Granny, we're good friends, aren't we? Do you know why I love you? Because Jesus loves me." At age three, my grandson understands that Jesus loves him, and because of that love, he can love others. He was born into a family filled with love. Love for each other and for him and his little brother. All too soon, the realities of the world outside his family will be forced upon him, and rarely is that a secure or loving place. But for now, he is safe in the love of Jesus and his family.

As Christians, we live in a world of "realities." Life is often difficult and sometimes cruel. We often find ourselves dodging the arrows of sin and discouragement. We need to put our hand in the Savior's hand and rest and trust in His love. For us, the real safety and security are still ahead – when we arrive at our home in Heaven. We will find safety forever in the place He has prepared for us.

Jan Caldwell is wife of John Caldwell, Senior Pastor of Kingsway Christian Church in Indianapolis, IN.

Prayer

Gentle Father, help me to be as open to Your love and leading as a little child. There is so much I can learn about You from children. Theirs is a simple faith and trust. Help me to shed Your light on the dark days that will come into their lives. Make me even more aware that only under the shelter of Your wings can I have complete safety. In Jesus' name. Amen.

Questions

- Do you pray as often as you should about your fears and insecurities?

- Do you consider daily that your security is in Christ?

- How can you allow the love of Christ to dispel the fears in your life?

Journal

January 15

Many will say to me on that day, "Lord, Lord, did we not prophesy in your name, and in your name drive out demons and perform many miracles?" Then I will tell them plainly, "I never knew you. Away from me, you evildoers!" (Matthew 7:22, 23)

Meditation   *Dudley C. Rutherford*

Although the very first word in this passage is undoubtedly the saddest, this Scripture also contains seven of the most appalling words ever spoken by Jesus: "I never knew you, depart from me…" Jesus makes it crystal clear that a day will come when each person will have a decisive, "one-on-one" session with Him. And when that day arrives, it simply won't matter how many times we said the name "Lord," or even how many times we performed incredible feats in His name. There is something else that is far more important to Jesus. *He is checking closely to see if the fruit of our lives originated in Him.*

If the confession we made and the deeds we performed were not the direct result of His life flowing in and through us, then we will have no part in His eternal life. For Jesus also proclaimed, "Now this is eternal life, that they may know You, the only true God, and Jesus Christ, whom You have sent." To really know Him is to be a member of the "great multitude that no one can count, from every nation, tribe, people and language who will stand before the throne and in front of the Lamb" to hear Jesus say seven of the most appealing words ever spoken: "Well done, my good and faithful servant!"

Prayer

Almighty God, I confess that I often live as though there will always be one more tomorrow. Please make me mindful that the "great day of the Lord" will truly come, when "we must all appear before the judgment seat of Christ." Help me grow in my understanding of what matters most to You. May my heart beat with the fervor to know You and Your Son, Jesus Christ, so that the fruit of my life will bear Your very image. It is my desire to hear You say, "Well done, My good and faithful servant." In Jesus' name. Amen.

Questions

- What is the trademark of God that must be found on the fruit of your life? (I Corinthians 13:1-3)

- How did Jesus describe eternal life? (John 17:3)

- How do you become part of the "great multitude that no one can count"? (Revelation 7:14)

Journal

January 16

But he said to them, "I have food to eat that you know nothing about. "My food," said Jesus, "is to do the will of him who sent me and to finish his work." (John 4:32, 34)

Meditation   *Dudley C. Rutherford*

Not only was Jesus tired and thirsty after walking along rugged terrain all morning, but the pain of hunger had motivated His disciples to walk to a nearby town for food. Although Jesus could have journeyed with the men to His next meal, He chose to stay behind and witness to a foreign woman. Jesus spent time telling her about Himself, letting her know that He completely understood her, and even spoke to her about worshipping His Father. As a result of this one conversation, many souls were harvested for the Kingdom. Indeed, the example of this single witness became quite impressive to the disciples.

But in the midst of this story, there was an additional lesson that initially confounded Jesus' followers. They wondered how it was humanly possible for Jesus to refuse the food they brought Him to eat. How had He received nourishment? Perhaps, like His disciples, you might consider these words of Jesus a litmus test for your efforts. After doing the work of God, do you feel burned out and depleted, or, as Jesus declares, do you actually sense an energizing that is beyond mere human explanation? When the effort to do God's work is directed and empowered by God Himself, then you can triumphantly say with Jesus, "I have a source of strength this world does not comprehend!"

Prayer

Father, thank You for permitting Your only Son to put on flesh, so I can know Your exact nature through His life. I am thankful for His example of doing Your will when He witnessed to this woman at the well. Open my eyes to see that the work You want me to accomplish is along my path each day. As I attempt to "walk as Jesus walked," I ask that You never let me be content with activity alone. May I only experience true satisfaction when I do Your work with the strength You supply. In Jesus' name. Amen.

Questions

- In John 4, what are some of the topics Jesus discussed when He witnessed to the woman?

- Will you begin a list of the people you meet in your everyday life who need to hear your witness?

- Have you ever experienced the energizing power of God that transcends mere human explanation?

Journal

January 17

I, even I, am the LORD; and besides me there is no savior.

(Isaiah 43:11)

Meditation   *Adrian Rogers*

It takes more of God's power to save a soul through the cross of Jesus than to do any other thing. God had no difficulty creating the universe. The Bible tells us that He spoke and it was so. But when God wrote salvation's story, He went to great difficulty. Let me illustrate.

What if I held a service and had the power to straighten a cripple's legs or bring sight to the blind? The next service would be standing room only. Now, I certainly want God to heal, but let me tell you something else.

What if I held a service and a little girl walked down the aisle and gave her heart to Jesus? That is a greater miracle than opening the eyes of the blind, because the Son of God had to hang on a cross in agony and blood to purchase her salvation! Jesus did not come just as a great healer or teacher; He came as a Savior.

Adrian Rogers is the former Senior Pastor of Bellevue Baptist Church in Memphis, TN.

Prayer

Dear Heavenly Father, may You awaken me each day and remind me of the greatest miracle of all miracles: that Jesus Christ came to be the Redeemer of mankind. As I busy myself with my mundane daily activities, may I never forget that I am part of a miraculous event called salvation. Thank you Lord for saving me. I once was lost but now I'm found. In Jesus' name. Amen.

Questions

- Can you recall the day you were saved?

- Reflect on the joy and emotion you experienced that day.

- When was the last time you led someone to find the grace of our Lord Jesus Christ?

Journal

_____

_____

_____

_____

January 18

So from now on we regard no one from a worldly point of view. Though we once regarded Christ in this way, we do so no longer. Therefore, if anyone is in Christ, he is a new creation; the old has gone, the new has come!

(II Corinthians 5:16, 17)

Meditation   H. Dean Rutherford

A friend of mine tells the story of a girl named Cassidy. Pain and anxiety were etched on her young face. Cassidy pulled me away from the group and begged that I say a special prayer. As she cried on my shoulder, she tearfully explained that her mother had been living on the streets, and that she had not heard from her for several days. Since arriving at the adjudicated youth center, fear for her mother's safety had dominated Cassidy's thoughts and emotions, spilling over each time we met. The more we talked, the more I learned of her mother's own indifference. For what sort of mother would introduce her 12-year-old daughter to the insidious life of drug addiction, and then place her young body on a street corner to "earn" the money needed to pay for both of their habits?

Yet in the midst of the contradictions, Cassidy began listening to stories about her Heavenly Father. Her countenance started to change, and she eagerly shared her newfound joy with many of the other young ladies at the center. Once again, God dramatically demonstrated His power to make all things new – while also reminding me of His mandate to "regard no one from a worldly point of view." We must be willing to be a bridge, and never a barrier, for "We are Christ's ambassadors, as though God was making His appeal through us."

H. Dean Rutherford is an Associate Pastor at Northside Christian Church in Clovis, CA. and the father of Dudley C. Rutherford.

Prayer

Dear God in Heaven, I confess that You alone have the power to change lives. I thank You for changing my life and then allowing me to serve as Your ambassador. May I faithfully respond to the challenge of letting You make Your appeal through me. Help me improve the way I identify people, so I will no longer be limited by a worldly point of view. May the Spirit of Jesus Christ fill my heart today, enabling me to treat people with the same care and compassion He demonstrated so many years ago. I pray in His name. Amen.

Questions

- Are you guilty of only seeing people through your natural eyes?

- Will you ask God to "open the eyes of your heart," so that you will begin to see people as He sees them?

- Have you ever been a barrier between God and another person? Ask God to give you the desire to build bridges that bring people back to Him!

Journal

All of us have become like one who is unclean, and all our righteous acts are like filthy rags; we all shrivel up like a leaf, and like the wind our sins sweep us away. (Isaiah 64:6)

Meditation   *Dudley C. Rutherford*

For those who remember the Seventies, a fashion trend began that is still in vogue today. In malls across America, people purchased jeans that had the small, white label "Calvin Klein" stitched into the waistband. Everything else about the jeans looked the same as any other pair, but people paid extra money just to have a designer label on display. Through the years, young and old alike have continued to spend excessive amounts of money on the latest, most popular designer names. Yet how many of us have given a moment's thought to the spiritual clothing we wear each day? Have we even considered that God will closely examine the label on our spiritual attire before inviting us to the marriage supper of His only begotten Son?

In the passage above, Isaiah teaches that the "Self-Made Man" line of clothing is nothing more than filthy rags. Although filthy rags aren't even acceptable merchandise for a secondhand store, our personal Designer provided the Way to wash these rags and make them white in the blood of His Lamb. Each person who hears and responds to the Gospel of Jesus Christ has the priceless privilege of changing from rags into riches! "For all of you who were baptized into Christ have clothed yourselves with Christ." We must not accept anything less than His very best. God certainly won't!

Designer Clothes

Prayer

Almighty God and Father, thank You for reminding me that my own efforts to be good enough just aren't good enough. I am eternally grateful for the One who was good enough to make the ultimate sacrifice for my filthy rags. Thank You for sending Your Son to be my Savior and to pay the price that none of us could begin to pay; just so I could be clothed in Him when I stand before Your throne. I rejoice in the free gift of eternal life I have in Christ Jesus our Lord! In His name, I pray. Amen.

Questions

- What is the only label by which you can be saved? (Acts 4:12)

- Whose label is the most important to you… honestly?

- How did Paul express himself about being spiritually clothed? (II Corinthians 5:2-4)

Journal

January 20

Jesus said to them, "I tell you the truth, unless you eat the flesh of the Son of Man and drink his blood, you have no life in you. Whoever eats my flesh and drinks my blood has eternal life, and I will raise him up at the last day. For my flesh is real food and my blood is real drink. Whoever eats my flesh and drinks my blood remains in me, and I in him."

(John 6:53-56)

Meditation   Dudley C. Rutherford

The day before Jesus uttered these words, He delighted and astounded thousands of people, feeding them on a grassy hillside along the Sea of Galilee. Although the crowd devoured as much of His miracle food as they possibly could, they desperately craved more. The next day, they crossed the sea in small boats and searched for Jesus. Upon finding Him, they continued discussing the topic of food. Jesus made many sensational statements during this conversation, but none more startling than the words of this passage. Sadly, many of His listeners refused to transition from thinking about physical food to contemplating true spiritual food, so "…many of His disciples withdrew, and were not walking with Him any more."

Suppose you were among the crowd of listeners that day. Would you have thought that the "wonder bread man" was deluded; or would you have been among the few disciples who were keenly aware that Jesus alone "had the words of eternal life"? It is not a rhetorical question, for Jesus still implores all who desire eternal life to eat His flesh and drink His blood. He invites us to feast on His life and teaching, so that our sustenance is found in Him. For truly the Scripture says, "Man does not live on bread alone, but on every Word that proceeds out of the mouth of God."

Bread From Heaven

Prayer

Dear God, thank You for sending us the True Bread from Heaven. Help me grow in my understanding of what it means to feast on the very life of Jesus. When my focused energy is only about my physical needs, I ask You to redirect my thoughts and stimulate me to hunger and thirst for Your righteousness. I confess with the disciples who have gone before me that "You alone have the words of eternal life." May I continue to come to You as the True Source and Eternal Sustainer of my life. In Jesus' name, I pray. Amen.

Questions

- What did Jesus ask us to do that helps remind us of His body and blood?

- Have you ever read the words of Jesus and sensed the powerful reality that they are "spirit and life"?

- How healthy would you be if you ate physical "bread" with the same frequency as you indulge in the True Bread from Heaven?

Journal

The Lord is my shepherd, I shall not be in want. (Psalm 23:1)

Meditation   *Barry McMurtrie*

I felt great. Freshly ordained, I called first at a huge, ugly, depressing facility that housed 700 elderly people. There was a smell about the place.

I said I was the new pastor and asked if I could have the names of people who were among my brand of Christians. She gave me 35 names but said, "You must visit Ida first."

She explained that Ida had entered the hospital at 36 years of age. She was crippled and they had nowhere to place her. She had been in this wretched place for 28 years. Her husband divorced her. She had not heard from her son in over 20 years. She had been active in the church but over the years had been forgotten.

I felt sick. I felt inadequate. I wanted to run. What could I say to someone life had punished so severely?

The nurse said, "Ida, your pastor is here."

She looked at me and said something in a voice so weak, I could not hear. I bent down. What did the woman say – the woman who had been deserted by her husband, son and church? Ida whispered, "The Lord is my shepherd, I shall not want." Humans had failed her, but God had not. Nor will He ever fail you.

Barry McMurtrie is the Senior Pastor of Crossroads Christian Church in Corona, CA.

Prayer

Dear Lord, there have been so many times when people have let me down and disappointed me. Usually when that happens, I complain and wonder why life is so unfair. May You please allow me to see and understand that God is the One who will sustain me, no matter what the circumstances. Thank You, Lord, for Ida's example. In Jesus' name. Amen.

Questions

- Have you ever been inspired by someone like Ida?

- How can you speak encouraging words to someone who is greatly suffering when life is good for you?

- Have you been through an experience where life might have crushed you, but the presence of God was so strong it brought you through?

Journal

_____

_____

_____

_____

■ January 22

For what I received I passed on to you as of first importance: that Christ died for our sins according to the Scriptures, that he was buried, that he was raised on the third day according to the Scriptures, and that he appeared to Peter, and then to the Twelve. (I Corinthians 15:3-5)

Meditation   *Dudley C. Rutherford*

Imagine a dad who takes his entire family to an ocean-side picnic. Laughter, excitement and fun abounds. Carefully, he instructs his children not to go into the water. Just as dad is putting the hamburgers on the charcoal grill, he senses his youngest son is missing. Dad instinctively rushes toward the foreboding water. As his frantic eyes scan the horizon, he spots his desperate son; the lad has been swept too far away to simply call him back to shore. This now half-crazed father computes instantly that if he is to save his boy as well as his own soul, he must dive headlong into the pitiless dark waves.

Why do we sing and praise Jesus in every sermon and in every prayer and song? Because we are the disobedient child who is lost and swept too far away to be coerced into coming back on our own. Do you get it? If we are to be saved, God has to take a chance. If we are to be rescued, the Almighty must forget His own safety. He must plunge headlong into the destructive surf of sin and human anguish. He did not simply save us; He died in the heroic effort.

Prayer

Dear Jesus, I am so glad You did not stay in Your ivory tower when I was lost. I'm glad You came down to my level and died for me. Thank You for not shouting out orders from some sterile, safe distance. Thanks for getting wet. Thanks for jumping in and risking all, that I might know the joy of salvation. I'm so glad You not only saw my coming predicament of eternal death, but that You suffered it ahead of time for me. Your awesome love demands a positive, obedient response from me, and I pray this in the name of Jesus. Amen.

Questions

- Jesus died, was buried and rose according to what?

- Why do we praise Jesus so much?

- Explain who is the lost person and who is the rescuer.

Journal

> *About the ninth hour Jesus cried out in a loud voice, "Eloi, Eloi, lama sabachthani?"—which means, "My God, my God, why have you forsaken me?" (Matthew 27:46)*

Meditation   *Dudley C. Rutherford*

I have heard many preachers explain that at this moment, God was turning His back on His only Son. Nothing could be further from the truth. Let me explain. Jesus was a rabbi, a teacher if you will. Rabbis often taught by the method of "rimitzing." *Rimitz* is a way of "alluding to" or "referring to." For example, if I said to you, "For God so loved the world that He gave..." then you, as the listener, would know I was referring to John 3:16.

Likewise, on the cross, when Jesus the rabbi said, *"My God, my God, why have you forsaken me?"* every Jewish person listening knew that Jesus was saying, "Go to the twenty-second Psalm." The very first verse says, *"My God, my God, why have you forsaken me?"* Jesus is saying, "Hey folks, one thousand years ago, David predicted all of this would happen. It might look bad, but this has been the plan all along. You see this is not a cry of defeat. It is a cry of victory. God had planned from the beginning of time that I would suffer and die by the cruel torture of the cross." Read Psalm 22 and you will understand this was all part of the plan of God, that Jesus would indeed be atonement for our sins and be the Blessed Messiah.

Prayer

Dear Father in Heaven, help me to understand that when Jesus died on the cross, He was indeed pierced for our sins. Allow me to fully understand that Jesus was the fulfillment of the Old Testament prophecies, that He is indeed the living Messiah. Lord, may You reveal to me that You did *not* turn Your back on Your Son, but that this was all part of the plan to redeem mankind. Thank You, God, for sending Jesus to bear the burden of our sin and pay the penalty. Lord, I pray I will catch a glimpse of how You carefully orchestrated the events surrounding my salvation. In Jesus' name. Amen.

Questions

- How did God orchestrate the plan of salvation?

- What does Psalm 22 say about Jesus?

- Do you really think God would turn His back on His only Son?

Journal

January 24

His master replied, "Well done, good and faithful servant! You have been faithful with a few things; I will put you in charge of many things. Come and share your master's happiness!" (Matthew 25:21)

Meditation   *Cam Huxford*

A few years ago, a missionary from Poland visited Savannah Christian Church. He talked about a Jewish family in Belarus he had led to Christ; they were so poor that a teenage girl and her grandmother had to share the same pair of shoes. At the end of the class, a 10th-grade girl took off her shoes and asked the missionary to give them to that girl who had none.

When her parents saw her after church, "barefooted and beaming," they asked her, "Where are your shoes?" Joyfully, she told them she'd given them to a girl who didn't have any. Both parents and the daughter were filled with a spirit of gladness. The daughter was glad because she had used her "stuff" to honor her Lord. Her parents were glad because of the generous, Godly heart they saw emerging in their daughter.

Has it ever occurred to you that for some people Judgment Day will be a celebration? In the famous story of our Lord that we call the Parable of the Talents, two of the proactive, joyful, responsible servants of a good master are praised and rewarded for their stewardship of their "stuff." In reality, their "stuff" didn't belong to them... it belonged to their Master. They wisely used it in a way that made their "judgment day" a time of affirmation and celebration. Good and faithful stewards are still doing the same today.

Cam Huxford is the Senior Pastor at Savannah Christian Church in Savannah, GA.

Where Are Your Shoes?

Gracious Lord, thank You for entrusting me and my family with so much of Your "stuff" to manage during my life on earth. Give me the wisdom to use my stuff in a way that will pursue Your interests on earth and make You proud of me. Help me to be "good and faithful," so that on the day when we meet face to face, I'll look forward to hearing what You say about how I managed the life You gave me. In the strong name of Jesus, I pray. Amen.

Questions

- What does it mean to be a "good and faithful servant" with your "stuff"?

- In what ways do you habitually use your "stuff" to pursue your Master's interests?

- What is the most memorable time you've used your "stuff" for your Master?

Journal

_____

_____

_____

_____

> *For we are to God the aroma of Christ among those who are being saved and those who are perishing. To the one we are the smell of death; to the other, the fragrance of life. And who is equal to such a task?*
>
> *(II Corinthians 2:15-16)*

Meditation   *Cameron McDonald*

Some years ago, I participated in a worship service that I will forever remember. I was to preach at a church in Haiti, but I had never been there and didn't know what to expect. When I arrived, I was overwhelmed by the poverty of the people.

When the time came we went to the church building. I say "building" but it was more like a huge shanty, rusted sheet metal strips standing with a rope holding them together. When the wind blew, the walls would fall in. I watched as more than a thousand Haitians packed in to worship. I couldn't understand a word they were singing, but I noticed they were immersed in the worship. They worshipped their hearts out.

Watching, I began to feel moved, but I couldn't help but be overwhelmed by the stench in the room. Even though the room was partly outdoors, the smell of dirtiness and body odor was pungent. Then it dawned on me: God was probably saying, "Man, that smells good! That smells so good; that's the best thing I have smelled in a long time! People loving other people, people together from all different walks of life, just lifting My name together." Looking back on it, I think, "Now that was worship!"

Cameron McDonald is the Preaching Associate at Shepherd of the Hills Church, Porter Ranch, CA.

Exquisite Fragrance

Father, thank You for the privilege of being the aroma of Jesus. I know that many times my life just stinks. The sin in my life smells like soured milk; it smells like an old mildewed sock. But when You smell my life, instead of soured milk, You think of a precious newborn baby; instead of a mildewed sock, You think of a newly constructed mansion. When You take a whiff of my life, You smell Jesus. Thank You, Father, that in Him we are a new creation. The old has gone, the new has come, and because of that, we no longer stink! In Jesus' name. Amen.

Questions

- What does it mean to you when you hear that to God, you are the aroma of Jesus?

- When you think about your life right now, what areas do you need to clean up?

- If you are a sweet scent rising to God, and you smell that way to other Christians, how do you smell to non-Christians?
  (Hint: Look in II Corinthians 2:14-17 for your answer.)

Journal

> *To keep me from becoming conceited because of these surpassingly great revelations, there was given me a thorn in my flesh, a messenger of Satan, to torment me. Three times I pleaded with the Lord to take it away from me. But he said to me, "My grace is sufficient for you, for my power is made perfect in weakness." Therefore I will boast all the more gladly about my weaknesses, so that Christ's power may rest on me. (II Corinthians 12:7-9)*

Meditation   *Dudley C. Rutherford*

The Lord handed the great Christian, Paul the Apostle, some terrible physical affliction. Three times he prayed for God to remove it and three times God said, "No." Paul then tells us through this second book of Corinthians why he learned to thank God for unwanted gifts. As a small boy, I remember getting two kinds of gifts for Christmas. There were "toys," and then there were "useful gifts," or "practical gifts." Sometimes Mom and Dad would give me a shirt or a pair of gloves or even a new pair of shoes. I'm telling you like it is: a package of undershirts was never a match for a baseball glove. In fact, the useful gift was almost unwanted. I had to summon a wisp of courage to say thanks to my folks. O sure, I eventually came to use the practical gifts and they usually outlasted the toys in duration.

Now that I'm grown, God is still handing me some things I cannot in the first moment appreciate. However I've lived long enough to learn that He knows what's best for me. Sometimes it's difficult to honestly say, "Thank you," but now I can for even those gifts that border on the unwanted side. I would much prefer to attend a party and feast on Mexican food than to be in a car wreck or have cancer. But God knows what I need most and what it's going to take to get me to Heaven. C.S. Lewis suggested the most often used word in Heaven will be, "Oh." "Oh, now I see." "Oh, now I know why that happened." "Oh, now it makes sense."

Prayer

Dear Lord, we've all suffered some depression and frustration in our lives. I also know that some of the most radiant lives ever lived for You have been those violently assailed with many thorns of hurt. Help me to stay in Your blessed Word long enough to learn that even sharp, bitter thorns can produce gratitude and holiness in the life of a mature servant. May I say with Paul, Your servant, "Most gladly will I glory and boast in my trials." In Jesus' blessed name, I pray. Amen.

Questions

- Why do you think God refused to answer Paul's request?

- Name some of God's useful gifts and some of His toys.

- Do you have the courage and maturity to thank Him for setbacks?

Journal

January 27

The people who survive the sword will find favor in the desert; I will come to give rest to Israel. (Jeremiah 31:2)

He made them wander in the desert forty years, until the whole generation of those who had done evil in his sight was gone. (Numbers 32:13)

Meditation   Dudley C. Rutherford

The most remarkable, compelling story in the Bible is the history of the Israelites wandering in the wilderness, yearning for the Promised Land. That drama takes up more space and spiritual mass than any other episode. God's people were in bondage for nearly 400 years. Then they began a struggle in the wilderness that would last 40 additional years, striving desperately to arrive in the Land of Promise. What makes a plot like that so great? It's the same plot of your life and mine.

We were once held in bitter bondage by Satan's snare. Jesus led us out of the land of slavery and headed us in the direction of Heaven. That's exactly where you and I are right at this moment. You and I have been delivered, but we have not yet arrived. Scholars tell us the journey could have been made in two weeks. Instead, it took 40 years. Forty years of dreariness, disappointment, desolation and danger. God wasn't trying to punish them. He was trying to discipline them, to prepare them for future battles and victories. Here is the gist, the final line, the bottom line, the last word of the lesson learned in this epic event: In spite of life's battles, hostilities and tests along the way, we can always depend on God's provision and God's presence. You can know in your deepest heart that God will bring you the final victory.

Grace in the Wilderness

Prayer

Thank You, Lord Jesus, that even in the desert Your children found the grace and guidance of God. Help me to remember, dear Lord, when the night seems dark, and the road seems steep, and light, life and music seem so far away, that Your presence shall be there to bless me. Help me to know that in the deepest desert, Your plans and purposes cannot be thwarted. As I journey through this life, help me to see Your hand of blessing, even in times of adversity. I ask these things in the name of Jesus. Amen.

Questions

- What happened to an entire generation in the wilderness?

- What was the wilderness like?

- Does God bless and provide in times of storm and desert?

Journal

> When Jesus saw this, he was indignant. He said to them, "Let the little children come to me, and do not hinder them, for the kingdom of God belongs to such as these. I tell you the truth, anyone who will not receive the kingdom of God like a little child will never enter it." And he took the children in his arms, put his hands on them and blessed them. (Mark 10:14-16)

Meditation   *Chuck Booher*

I was preaching at Kentucky Christian College on the power of prayer and the fact that God does answer prayer. One point in the sermon was that God honors the faith of a child. Sitting in the front row was Joshua Murray, who was nine years old. After the sermon, Josh went to his brother Jeremiah and asked if he had heard the sermon. Then he said, "Let's pray for Mom to get pregnant and have another child." They both loved the idea and started praying daily for this. One night as Josh and Jeremiah were praying, a student walked up to them. When she asked what they were doing, they told her. She asked if their mom and dad wanted more children. They responded, "We don't think so but did you hear Chuck's sermon?"

Lynn, their mother, was 40 years old. She and Dave love children but felt that their two were enough; they were not planning on having any other children. Their family came home from a mission trip to Venezuela and Lynn started feeling sick. She thought maybe she had gotten something over there. When the doctor examined her, he suggested they do a pregnancy test. She told him, "I don't think so; I'm 40." He did anyway and she was speechless when he told her she was pregnant.

When she told the boys, they were standing in what would one day be their sister Johanna's room. They high-fived each other. Later, we shared the news with the church. I also told them they should have some fun by standing outside the church, pointing at older ladies and act like they were praying.

Dave, Lynn and the rest of the Murray family know that God moved in response to the boys' prayers. They also know that God gave them an incredible gift in Johanna.

Chuck Booher is the Senior Pastor of Christ's Church of the Valley in San Dimas, CA.

Prayer

Lord, I pray for my faith to increase. I pray for the faith of a child. Faith that moves mountains. That calms the storms of my life. That brings powerful, wonderful answers. I want faith that can give testimony to the fact that You are a God that answers my prayers. In Christ. Amen.

Questions

- What did Jesus say about children in Mark 10:14-16?

- How often do you pray?

- Name a mountain you need God to move.

Journal

_____

_____

_____

_____

Now about the collection for God's people: Do what I told the Galatian churches to do. On the first day of every week, each one of you should set aside a sum of money in keeping with his income, saving it up, so that when I come no collections will have to be made. (I Corinthians 16:1-2)

Meditation   *Dudley C. Rutherford*

I saw a cartoon that pictured a group of serious business planners meeting around a table. One genius spoke up and said, "What we need is a brand, spankin' new idea that's been thoroughly tested." Can I say the Bible has just such an idea? It's called "tithing." May I suggest a few points about giving that I have learned over the years from being a pastor? Use the famous 10-10-80 rule! Pay God first. Pay God one dime out of every dollar. There will never be a good time, an easy time to start tithing. Even if you are wealthy, there will never be a time when you have that extra ten percent just "sitting around." And if you could give like that, it wouldn't be much of a sacrificial gift.

Make doubly sure you take it off the top and not the bottom of your income. Then put away the second tenth for your savings. Pay yourself just like you paid God. Ten percent for God and ten percent for your personal savings. Then live on the eighty percent left! This will not be a trivial task either, but the experience I've had is that all those who do this discover great blessings from God and from life. The best, happiest, most successful people I have ever known are those folks who are proper stewards of their time, talent and money. I promise you and God promises you that if you take care of that first 20% in that way, your path will be lighter and your road will be brighter. How do I know? The Bible tells me so!

Prayer

My dear wonderful God and Savior, I'm glad I'm not the first person on earth. I'm thankful that millions have lived before me and that I can profit from their lives and examples. Thank You again and again for carefully placing so much information on stewardship in Your Bible. I know I will never be at peace with You or myself, until I become a better steward of those things You have entrusted to me. I am going to begin anew today on my quest to be Your faithful steward. In the saving name of Christ, I pray. Amen.

Questions

- What is the 10-10-80 rule?

- How is it possible to rob God?

- When is the best time to step out on faith and start tithing? Why?

Journal

January 30

Come to me, all you who are weary and burdened, and I will give you rest. Take my yoke upon you and learn from me, for I am gentle and humble in heart, and you will find rest for your souls. For my yoke is easy and my burden is light. (Matthew 11:28-30)

Meditation   *Dudley C. Rutherford*

Did you know that all the water in the world can't sink a ship unless the water gets inside? And did you know the sum total of problems in the world can't sink a Christian unless the problems get inside? We need to learn to put all our cares, trials and problems at the feet of Jesus.

Toward the end of his life, the great Apostle Peter had superior advice when he wrote, "Cast all your anxiety upon Him, because He cares for you" (I Peter 5:7). Some of us are like the man carrying a big hundred-pound sack of potatoes down a dirt road. A man driving a pickup truck stops and says, "Throw your potatoes in the back and jump in. I'll give you a lift." But the man gets inside the truck and keeps the heavy potatoes on his shoulders. The driver says, "Mister, lay the potatoes down; the truck can carry that load for you." The man replies, "Look, mister, you are mighty kind. It's asking enough for you to carry me, let alone my potatoes."

I am like that sometimes. Jesus says, "Cast all your anxieties on Me," and I say, "Wait just a minute, Lord; it's asking enough that You saved me and forgave me and wrote my name in Heaven. I'm not about to ask You to carry my problems also."

Prayer

My dear broad-shouldered, divine Savior, I want to promise, from this day forward, to lay all of my burdens and worries on You. A million times over, You are bigger and stronger and wiser than I am. I'm sorry I've been so long in learning this lesson. I plead guilty of worrying when I should be relying on You. May I never forget that Your eye is on the sparrow, and I know You're watching me. I pray in Christ's name. Amen.

Questions

- Do you think it's easy or difficult to give your burdens to Jesus?

- According to Peter, how many of your burdens can you give to Him?

- Name some burdens you've yet to lay at His feet.

Journal

January 31

For great is your love, higher than the heavens; your faithfulness reaches to the skies. (Psalm 108:4)

For great is his love toward us, and the faithfulness of the Lord endures forever. Praise the Lord. (Psalm 117:2)

Meditation   *Craig Luper*

Have you ever played that silly game with a flower called "He Loves Me, He Loves Me Not?" (Or, if you're a man, "She loves me…"). The game goes like this: you pick a flower and then you begin to pluck the petals off the flower and speak out, "He loves me, he loves me not," until you get to the last one. That last petal tells the whole story of whether or not your relationship will go on or be doomed to end. You probably have done what all of us have done, and that is to get another flower so we don't end on "he/she loves me not." Go ahead, confess right now that you've done that. Confession is good for the soul. It may seem like a silly game, but I think it says a lot about the fact that all of us want to be loved.

We play the flower game with God too. We say, "He loves me," because I went to church today. "He loves me not," I cussed out my neighbor. "He loves me," I had quiet time today. "He loves me not," I thought lustful thoughts. We base God's love on whether or not we've been good, when in reality God loves us, period. As you go through this day, just thank God that He loves you. "Great is his love toward you."

Craig Luper is the Executive Pastor of Crossroads Church in Concord, NC.

Prayer

Father, I come to You not because I've been good enough, or done everything just right, but because Your great love for me draws me to You. Thank You, Father, for loving me unconditionally. I pray that You will continue to reveal Your unconditional love in my heart each and every day. As I receive Your love, Father, may I show that love to others. In Jesus' name. Amen.

Questions

- When was the last time you played the petal game with God? Did you end up loved or not loved?

- Do you honestly believe and know that God loves you unconditionally? If so, how do you know that?

- Does God love you any less or get angry with you when you've sinned?

Journal

_____

_____

_____

_____

February 1

For you know that it was not with perishable things such as silver or gold that you were redeemed from the empty way of life handed down to you from your forefathers, but with the precious blood of Christ, a lamb without blemish or defect. (I Peter 1:18-19)

You were bought at a price. Therefore honor God with your body. (I Cor. 6:20)

Meditation   H. Dean Rutherford

The salty, adult comedian tells a wrenching story he remembers from his boyhood days. He relates the fact that he had enjoyed a particularly good day shining shoes. Then went into a rundown diner and ordered supper like a king: a hamburger, fries and chili and two sodas (Amen). While he was finishing, the neighborhood drunk staggered in and ordered 26 cents worth of food. When he was finished eating, he had no money to pay, whereupon the owner knocked him down, kicked him several times and then hit him over the head with a bottle. Gregory complained, "Leave the poor guy alone. Here, I'll pay the twenty-six cents myself."

The drunk sat up and screamed at Gregory, "Keep your twenty-six cents. You don't have to pay, not now. I just finished paying for it." He continued, "If you had paid for it earlier you could have saved me a beating. I paid for it myself."

Don't try to buy or earn your way into Heaven. You owe nothing except the gratitude to love and obey! The full price has been paid for in advance. Before you were born, Jesus paid for the full price of your sin and death. If you will surrender your heart to Him in child-like faith and walk with Him, you will never owe a single penny. Your total cost of sin has been "written off" and "paid for in full" in His crimson blood.

Prayer

Most holy and gracious God, thank You for paying it all when I could pay nothing. Thank You for loving me while I am so unlovable. I know when I die that nothing will be charged to my account, because You have already paid the cost in full. I will never have to take that awful, eternal beating by Satan, for You are my protector and defender. Give me the strength and gratitude to live each day of the rest of my life for You. In Jesus name, I pray. Amen.

Questions

- Describe the price Jesus paid.

- Why are you not your own?

- Since you can pay nothing, what is your obligation?

Journal

_____

_____

_____

_____

_____

February 2

My mouth is filled with your praise, declaring your splendor all day long. (Psalm 71:8)

Meditation   David Kendrick

How many times has one heard, "I'm having a bad day!" or "This has been a rough week!" or "I am so glad this year is over!"

Each of us is prone to times of disappointment. A knock at our spiritual door may be an uninvited guest, such as failure, unexpected circumstances, a stressful situation, a difficult trial or an unanswered prayer. Our response to such a visitor may cause anxiety, despair or discouragement.

Yet Jesus gave us insight as to what we can do. Throughout the New Testament, we find Jesus using the phrase, "I praise You Father." His intent was not to heap compliments on His Father in order to build God's ego or His self-esteem, but rather to confront the negative with praise. Using the powerful weapon of daily praise invites immediate participation of our Heavenly Father into the circumstances and situations we encounter. Praise conquers uncertainty and confusion.

Praising the Lord for family, friends, church, food, shelter, health, job, freedom and, most importantly, Jesus, alters who we are. You see, praise changes one's mood, character, countenance and attitude. It allows God to usher spiritual refreshment and encouragement to our soul.

Remember, when unwelcome visitors pay a visit, apply the principle of praise. God will then answer each knock. As a result of our turning to God, He will provide us blessings of spiritual love, joy and inner peace.

David Kendrick is the Superintendent of Hillcrest Christian School, Granada Hills, CA.

Prayer

Father, I praise You because You are my Lord and King. I want to praise You no matter what takes place today, because I know You are always in complete control of my life. May I see things from Your perspective. Thank You that You have a purpose for my life and each time I praise You, I am fulfilling that purpose. In Jesus' name. Amen.

Questions

- In what areas of your life can you praise God?

- Why does God want you to praise Him?

- How can you implement praise on a daily basis?

Journal

February 3

Now there is in Jerusalem near the Sheep Gate a pool, which in Aramaic is called Bethesda and which is surrounded by five covered colonnades. Here a great number of disabled people used to lie—the blind, the lame, the paralyzed. One who was there had been an invalid for thirty-eight years. When Jesus saw him lying there and learned that he had been in this condition for a long time, he asked him, "Do you want to get well?" (John 5:2-6)

Meditation   *Carla Winters*

When we were on our Holy Land trip earlier this year, we visited these pools inside the Old City of Jerusalem. Our guide read this Scripture and posed a similar question to each of us, "Do you want to be healed?" None of us was physically disabled, but he wasn't asking us about our physical challenges. This struck me. Do I want to be healed, and what do I need to be healed from?

I certainly feel that I know where God is calling me to improve, the places where I need to be healed. But I continue to repeat old habits, sinful ways. I had to ask myself, "Do I *really* want to be healed?" It's kind of like a diet to me. It can be great to be on the journey to weight loss, but what do I do when I reach my goal? What would I have to complain about then?

Maybe, like me, you suffer from not knowing how to surrender this area of your life. Knowing how and just not doing it is the problem. Let Jesus heal you.

Carla Winters is the wife of Tim Winters, Executive Pastor at Shepherd of the Hills Church, Porter Ranch, CA.

Do You Want to be Healed?

Prayer

Father God, please reveal with certainty that one thing I need to be healed from. Lord, I know there may be many things I need help with, but I want to know that one thing You desire to change in me. Then Father, please help me make those changes, one step at a time, that would bring about Your freedom from this sin that binds me. Lord, I cannot make these changes by myself. I have tried and failed but I know that I can do all things through Your Son Jesus who strengthens me. Thank You Lord for living in me and allowing me the great privilege of being a light unto Your world through this healing and Your victory. In Jesus' precious name I pray. Amen.

Questions

- Do you want to be healed? Meditate on this, truly seeking God's answer.

- What are some of the things that might prevent you from being set free from this sin?

- How might you replace the sin with something God-honoring? (Example: someone replaces worry with singing praises to the Lord every time he or she feels the need to worry.)

Journal

■ February 4

When the perishable has been clothed with the imperishable, and the mortal with immortality, then the saying that is written will come true: "Death has been swallowed up in victory. Where, O death, is your victory? Where, O death, is your sting?" (I Corinthians 15:54-55)

Meditation   H. Dean Rutherford

We sometimes think birth is normal and death is abnormal. We feel birth is natural and death is a tragic aberration. One is as normal and natural as the other. Death is not some scary monster-trick invented by TV evangelists to frighten the timid into Godly behavior. Death is a stubborn fact of life. We don't like to talk openly about this terror, so when someone dies we simply say, "He's gone," or "He's passed away," or "He is deceased," or "He has departed." We try in vain to conceal death's finality. We dress the deceased in his fanciest clothes. Professional beauticians and makeup artists have their skillful way with the remains to create a lifelike appearance. Artificial green grass is laid over the fresh clods of dirt to divert our attention. Flowers are banked high and soft music wafts through the mourners. But alas, when the undertaker has done his best, the body is still a dead body.

The Bible says, "Man is destined to die once, and after that to face judgment…" (Hebrews 9:27). All must die, but no one needs to die unprepared. Turn your life at once to this powerful, tender Christ, to His Word, to His Church, to His plans and purposes, and that sad hour of death will be the glad hour of your life. Death will not be an ending but a beginning. Not a defeat but a victory. Talk about a sting-less death!

Prayer

My wonderful Father in Heaven, I know death is that land which no traveler can avoid. As a Christian, I look forward and anticipate that day when Your trumpet shall sound, and the dead shall be raised, and my dead mortal flesh shall finally be clothed with an imperishable body. I know that some day in this world, I shall fall asleep in Jesus and soon wake up in a paradise, with loved ones and with Him who died for me and paid the price for my eternal life. I pray these things in the name of Christ. Amen.

Questions

- How does Jesus take the sting out of death?

- How does Jesus turn the grave into a scene of victory?

- The Bible says everyone must die, and then what?

Journal

_____

_____

_____

_____

_____

My sheep listen to my voice; I know them, and they follow me. I give them eternal life, and they shall never perish; no one can snatch them out of my hand. My Father, who has given them to me, is greater than all; no one can snatch them out of my Father's hand. I and the Father are one.

(John 10:27-30)

Meditation   *Dudley C. Rutherford*

A handsome young man named George Matheson fell deeply in love and became engaged to a lovely and attractive girl. Then came the bad news. George had an eye disease and the best doctors said he would soon be blind. His bride-to-be handed him back the engagement ring, tersely telling him she did not want to live with someone so desperately dependent on her.

Loneliness is a killer and a deadly assassin. In his brokenness and blindness, George turned his life over to Christ. Through the darkness of pain, he wrote one of the phenomenal songs of all the centuries:

"O Love that wilt not let me go, I rest my weary soul in Thee; I give Thee back the life I owe, that in Thine ocean depths its flow may richer, fuller be."

In this song, George was saying, "Human love is good but it has its limits. I want to be a part of someone who never quits, never gives up or in. I want to be loved by someone whose love knows no limits and whose grace has no boundaries." Oh my friend, you can risk Jesus! You can trust the Lord! If you serve Him faithfully, there will never be a disconnect! You do your small part and He will do His. On that day on God's calendar when you are powerless and penniless and stand helpless before Him, His love will carry the day. He will save you to live with Him throughout the endless years of blissful eternity. And you will know what it means to romance the royalty of King Jesus.

Prayer

Dear God in Heaven, I want to thank You for a love that will not let me go. I know that if I give You back the life You first gave me, Your ocean of love will be even fuller and richer and will flow back into my life. The love this world has to offer is crowded and crowned with betrayal and heartbreak. It reeks of treachery and duplicity. I want to invest my time, my heart, my talent and my soul into Christ whose love will not let go. I pray these things in the name of the powerful and unchanging Christ. Amen.

Questions

- What thing, person or power can take you out of His hands?

- Will you reread the words of the song and explain them?

- What is wrong with the best type of human love?

Journal

_____

_____

_____

_____

February 6

That is how it will be at the coming of the Son of Man. Two men will be in the field; one will be taken and the other left. Two women will be grinding with a hand mill; one will be taken and the other left. Therefore keep watch, because you do not know on what day your Lord will come.

(Matthew 24:39-42)

Meditation   *Dudley C. Rutherford*

William Biederwolf describes the triumph and tragedy of the siege of Lucknow, India. A small but brave militia of English soldiers was trapped inside a garrison and surrounded by a band of 30,000 ruthless, bloodthirsty savages. Eerie war screams and frantic shrieks filled the night air. But by the grace of God, and through much trickery and gross deception, the English soldiers managed to slip away quietly unnoticed. However, while the English soldiers were escaping, one of their best soldiers was busy elsewhere and didn't notice their escape. In a moment's time, he discovered his ghastly plight; he realized he was all alone, surrounded by 30,000 brutal and violent savages screaming for the sight of a white man's face, and for the taste of a white man's blood.

But miracles happen. Biederwolf relates that this lone soldier escaped and made it back to reunite with his comrades. Fear and terror had taken its toll. His hair had turned white and eyes were forever glazed and frozen. When he tried to recall his own name, he couldn't think of it, for he had lost his mind. You see, he had been left behind. Every page of this old, blessed, tea-stained Book says to prepare. "You also must be ready, because the Son of Man will come at an hour when you do not expect Him" (Luke 12:40).

Prayer

Dear Father, may there be no confusion on my face nor terror in my heart when I approach the great and notable day of the Lord. May there be no shame or fear in my soul, as I will have prepared for this event by a life of steady commitment to the things of God. Make me wise to be ready for that day and that hour, when an unbelieving world will be forced to look upon Him whom they have pierced. I pray this prayer in Jesus' name. Amen.

Questions

- Will Jesus come back to earth a second time?

- When He gathers His own, will some be left behind?

- What do you need to do to best prepare for that critical hour?

Journal

_____

_____

_____

_____

February 7

Surely he took up our infirmities and carried our sorrows, yet we considered him stricken by God, smitten by him, and afflicted. But he was pierced for our transgressions, he was crushed for our iniquities; the punishment that brought us peace was upon him, and by his wounds we are healed.

(Isaiah 53:4-5)

Meditation   H. Dean Rutherford

The Book of Isaiah was written 700 years before Christ was born at Bethlehem. Yet, when Isaiah writes about the matchless suffering of Christ on the cross, he writes in the past tense. This has been a stumbling block to many enemies of the Scripture. These critics ask, "If Isaiah was written 700 years before Christ, why does Isaiah insist that Jesus *was* pierced and *was* crushed and *was* smitten?" The answer is simple. The balance of the Bible teaches, and makes plain, that Jesus was crucified before the world was created. It was decided in the councils of eternity before the world began that Jesus would die upon Calvary's cross. Before there was ever a star, a tree, a mountain or an ocean, there was a cross. Before Adam and Eve, before Moses and Elijah, the plan for Jesus to die spread-eagle on Golgotha was the plan and in the mind of God.

Calvary predates Eden. Jesus was a bleeding Savior long before man became a breathing soul. The Bible is God's inerrant Word. There are no mistakes in the Scriptures. No wonder Paul vibrantly exclaimed to young Timothy, "All Scripture is God-breathed and is useful for teaching, rebuking, correcting and training in righteousness, so that the man of God may be thoroughly equipped for every good word" (II Timothy 3:16-17). God used human flesh to write the Bible, but He put His divine Spirit into each writer. Your Bible is in every way God-breathed.

Prayer

Dear Father in Heaven, I thank You for my Bible, because I know it has withstood the test of time. It has withstood the critics and atheists of the long, lingering centuries. I know men have tried to burn it, trash it, bury it and silence it, but it is more alive and more up-to-date than the newspaper that fell at my front door this morning. Help me to remember that I can trust Your Word and that You will keep every word of every line of every promise. Thank You for loving me enough to provide for me Your perfect Book. In Christ's name, I pray. Amen.

Questions

- Why did Isaiah write about the cross in the past tense?

- What does "God-breathed" mean?

- How often do you take time to read and study God's Word?

Journal

February 8

Meditation   Dudley C. Rutherford

I heard my father once quote this poem:

"One starry midnight, silvery and still, I dreamed that I received this bill:

Ten thousand breathless dawns all new, and ten thousand roses fresh with dew;
Ten thousand sunsets painted gold and a million snowflakes that fell so cold;
For one million romantic dreams, for moon-drenched roads and flowing streams;
For summer's nights and a gentle breeze, for silent stars and browsing bees;
I wondered when I woke that day how in this world I could ever pay!"

Paul asks his Corinthian brothers, "What do you have that you did not receive?" When I am honest, I must confess that everything I have was given to me. Even the name I wear was given to me. I am a debtor first to God and to His mercy, His Church, His world, His patience and His plan. Why, the very parents I have were given to me. He has given me life, friends, the health to live and a mind with which to think. Forgive me, Almighty God, when I start living for myself. Forgive me when my life telegraphs to the lost world the false message that "it's all about me." Paul said in Romans 13:8: "Let no debt remain outstanding, except the continuing debt to love one another." Indeed, we are all trustees. Because Christ died for us, we should be willing to live for Him. We owe Christ and we owe every person on earth a debt of love and service.

Prayer

Dear Lovely Lord Jesus, we've all been showered with abilities, gifts and talents. Most of us have been entrusted with 40, 50, 60 or more years of time. You have endowed us with the gift of speech, sight, civilization, mathematics, science and observation. I pray that my life may agree with Paul's words when he plainly said, "Now it is required that those who have been given a trust must prove faithful" (I Corinthians 4:2). I want to be faithful to use all the gifts I have been given and to the One who made them possible. In Christ's name, I pray. Amen.

Questions

- Where does every perfect gift come from?

- What do you have that was not given to you?

- Can you make a list of those things that have been given to you?

Journal

February 9

Though the fig tree does not bud and there are no grapes on the vines, though the olive crop fails and the fields produce no food, though there are no sheep in the pen and no cattle in the stalls, yet I will rejoice in the Lord, I will be joyful in God my Savior. (Habakkuk 3:17-18)

Meditation   *Dudley C. Rutherford*

Matthew Henry, a wonderful scholar of another century, was robbed of his wallet. A mature Christian in the fullest meaning of the word, he commented on the unfortunate scene, not out of a sense of whining or complaining, but true thanksgiving. Henry said, "I am grateful and thankful for what happened. First, because that was the first time I was ever robbed. It's never happened before. Secondly, even though they took my money, they spared my life. Thirdly, they took everything I had, but that wasn't very much. Fourthly, because it was I who was robbed, not I who robbed."

All four points of his thanksgiving confession should humble us. He who had been robbed was out of his money. Had he been the robber, he would have been without soul and his character. Matthew Henry still retained everything he needed and much more. To have one's material possessions stolen is no fun but a million times worse is to have one's dignity, honesty and character take a leave of absence.

God keep us from Satan's deception, that houses and automobiles, gadgets and fashions contribute to the cause of genuine and lasting joy. The sinner's thanksgiving is based on self-congratulation and pride. The Christian's thanksgiving is built upon the faith that if we possess Christ, we already have everything.

Grateful and Thankful

Prayer

Dear wonderful God, guide and guard, keep me from the world's "bitterness of loss" when the useful things I have are swept away. I'm afraid that if I am greatly saddened by material loss, I will be rendered unfit for Your Kingdom's service. Thank You for Your admonition to seek first the Kingdom of God and Your promise that all other things will be added unto me. I ask these things in Christ's eternal name. Amen

Questions

- If you lost all material possessions could you still rejoice?

- Name some things you cannot afford to lose.

- Does Habakkuk's testimony ring true with you?

Journal

Do not let your hearts be troubled. Trust in God; trust also in me. In my Father's house there are many rooms; if it were not so, I would have told you. I am going there to prepare a place for you. (John 14:1-2)

Meditation   *Alan Ahlgrim*

Years ago, I was struck by the title of a book by Dr. Paul Tournier, a Swiss psychotherapist. The intriguing title was, *A Place To Be*. It was the author's contention that all of us go through life looking for a place; therefore we are all, to one degree or another, pilgrims and wanderers until we reach our eternal home.

Everyone wants and needs something to look forward to – Jesus knew that. That's why He pointed us toward Heaven. All of us ache for something more. No matter how good we have it, we want something greater. No matter how wonderful our place in this world happens to be, we know it won't last forever. We yearn for a permanent place. A beautiful place. A peaceful place. An eternal place.

That's why we will never be fully satisfied in this world. We can't be. That's because we were made for another world. When the beauty fades, when the problems arise, when the place you call "home" is in need of repair or seems somehow inadequate, take heart. Jesus is right now preparing an exceptional and eternal place for you!

Alan Ahlgrim is Senior Pastor at Rocky Mountain Christian Church in Niwot, CO.

Fully Satisfied

Prayer

O Lord, Creator of Heaven and earth and me, I thank You for preparing a special place for me. Thank You for giving me something wonderful to look forward to! As I live this day with You, may everything that is good prompt me to praise You for my eternal home that will be even better; and may everything that is not good remind me that one day, Jesus will make everything perfect. Thank You, Lord, that the best is yet to be! In Jesus' name. Amen.

Questions

- Where is the place that you feel most at home in this world?

- How can disappointment with your "place" prompt you to praise God?

- What do you most look forward to experiencing in Heaven?

Journal

And what more shall I say? I do not have time to tell about Gideon, Barak, Samson, Jephthah, David, Samuel and the prophets, who through faith conquered kingdoms, administered justice, and gained what was promised; who shut the mouths of lions, quenched the fury of the flames, and escaped the edge of the sword; whose weakness was turned to strength; and who became powerful in battle and routed foreign armies. (Hebrews 11:32-34)

Meditation   *Dudley C. Rutherford*

There is someone just like you in the Bible. The Bible is God's masterpiece. It is composed of 66 books by 40 different authors. These inspired writers represented all classes of men, from kings to peasants, priests to laymen, prophets to fishermen, musicians and shepherds, tentmakers and tax collectors, men and women, old and young, rich and poor, educated and illiterate.

The Bible is a record of men in all possible human situations. There is someone exactly like you, in the same situation you are in now. If you can locate that person, you can find extra help for your soul. One of the strong arguments for the divine origin of the Bible is that it does not exaggerate and glamorize its heroes. It paints the picture as it is, with all the reality of raw, stark human passion. With characters of all descriptions – loyal and true, tricky and deceptive, lustful and sensuous, proud and haughty, murderers and martyrs, suicides and saints, seductive and voluptuous, moral and upright, repentant and contrite, arrogant and defiant.

The human personalities playing significant parts in the Biblical drama were not mere pawns of fate nor predetermined creatures of destiny. They were what they were because they chose to be. Every one of them could have been different. One's choice determines one's destiny. There is somebody in the Bible just like you. You, too, have possibilities for great good or terrible evil. What will it be? Have you read about Paul, John, David, Sampson, Lot, Cain, Jacob, Moses and Philip? Find yourself! Get deeper into the Book of the Ages.

Prayer

O Wonderful Savior of mine, thank You for recording the truth about all the human characters in the Scriptures. Thank You for not covering up the weaknesses and sins of my heroes. I know I must be careful and vigilant in my daily life. If these great men of God could so easily fall into sin, then I am especially vulnerable to Satan's temptations. Help me to study and make the right choices and above all, to keep my eyes on Jesus. In Christ's name I pray. Amen.

Questions

- What person in the Bible do you most resemble?

- God records not only the heroes' good deeds but also their what?

- How many books and authors are in the Bible?

Journal

_____

_____

_____

_____

_____

February 12

Out of the most severe trial, their overflowing joy and their extreme poverty welled up in rich generosity. For I testify that they gave as much as they were able, and even beyond their ability, entirely on their own. (II Cor. 8:2-3)

Each man should give what he has decided in his heart to give, not reluctantly or under compulsion, for God loves a cheerful giver. (II Cor. 9:7)

Meditation   *Dudley C. Rutherford*

A few years back, two Christian businessmen were in Korea and saw the strangest, most perplexing sight. They saw a man in a field with huge ropes around his shoulders pulling a plow. A young boy guided the plow some 15 feet behind the man. Later the businessmen were telling one of the local Christians about that peculiar sight, to which he replied, "Oh yes, that man and his son are members of our church. You see, when the Communists bombed our church and we needed to rebuild it, that man had no money to give. But he loved the Lord so much he sold his only ox, and now he pulls the plow and his boy guides it."

The way the Macedonians in our text and the way this Korean gave are worthy of mention. Notice they gave freely, overflowing and beyond their ability. Their hearts welled up in rich generosity! In the next chapter, Paul says, "We are not to give reluctantly or under compulsion, for God loves a cheerful giver." Paul also says in 9:6, "Remember this: whoever sows sparingly will also reap sparingly, and whoever sows generously will also reap generously."

If a person truly wants to know how deeply he believes and where he stands with God, let him check the stubs in his checkbook. So said Halford Luccock! How we spend our money is an accurate barometer of our character and commitment. Jesus said, "For where your treasure is (check your check stubs), there your heart will be also" (Matthew 6:21).

Prayer

Almighty and All Powerful God, I know Your work has suffered because of the poor stewardship of believers. Help me to stop asking, "What must I give?" and "What is my fair share?" Help me to start asking, "What does God want? What would my gift be if I truly believed in the cause of Christ to win a lost world? What amount would reflect my belief in His everlasting Kingdom?" Bless me, dear Lord, as I try to improve on being a good steward. In Jesus' name I pray. Amen.

Questions

- Describe how the Macedonians gave.

- What kind of a giver does God get excited about?

- What is an accurate barometer of your faith?

Journal

_____

_____

_____

_____

■ February 13

What shall we say, then? Shall we go on sinning so that grace may increase? By no means! We died to sin; how can we live in it any longer? For we know that our old self was crucified with him so that the body of sin might be done away with, that we should no longer be slaves to sin.

(Romans 6:1, 2, 6)

Meditation   H. Dean Rutherford

Mankind, with all of his modern cleverness, with his flair for new inventions, new methods, has been unable to invent a new sin. We have today only new sinners committing old sins. The seven deadly sins are "the seven pallbearers of character." They are: Pride, Greed, Envy, Lust, Anger, Gluttony and Sloth. Each sin is a spiritual tumor radiating its cancerous tentacles to the depths of the soul.

1. Pride is the outcome of an overly inflated ego. It thinks more highly of itself than is warranted and demands that others do so also.
2. Greed is defined as a "passion for riches; covetousness. " In essence, avarice is an inordinate love of things.
3. Envy is a sort of passive decomposition of the soul. Envy leads to covetousness. It may result in taking what you want by the use of illegitimate means.
4. Lust is the fourth deadly sin. The three preceding have been sins of the heart, but lust is the sin of fleshly pleasure. It is the prostitution of love, the debasing of the finest flower that grows in the garden of man's heart.
5. Anger is the outburst when the pressure of desire or frustration or repression goes too far. It is dangerous to others but is devastating to one's self.
6. Gluttony is the sixth fatal sin. It is one of the most universal today. Instead of eating to live, one lives to eat.
7. The seventh deadly sin is sloth. It is defined as "disinclination to exertion," "laziness." The sloth is one who has lost the zest for living. His taste for achievement has withered.

Seven Deadly Sins

Prayer

Dear Lord, I know that all sin is deadly unless it is confessed and forsaken. Forgive me for those times I committed not just one of those seven sins but several at once. Help me to remember that it is sin that separates me from Your presence and it is sin that will keep me out of Heaven. Even though sin may seem to bring instant pleasure, help me understand that its pleasure is only temporary and that only the things of God bring permanent pleasure. In the Savior's name I pray. Amen.

Questions

- Name five of the seven deadly sins.

- Which sins are your weak points?

- The curse of pleasurable sin is that it is only what?

Journal

> *"Bring the whole tithe into the storehouse, that there may be food in my house. Test me in this," says the LORD Almighty, "and see if I will not throw open the floodgates of heaven and pour out so much blessing that you will not have room enough for it." (Malachi 3:10)*

Meditation   *Debbie Johnson*

As a new believer, I was excited and on fire for Jesus. I longed for my husband to know the same joy of salvation. To my sorrow, he was not interested. Four long years I prayed God would touch his heart and the Holy Spirit would lead him to Christ. My husband showed no interest in coming to church with me and our two children.

One Sunday, an elder challenged the congregation to commit to one year of tithing. He said that when we give God His 10%, we allow Him to pour forth His blessings on our lives. I was convicted and committed immediately to tithe each week from my own earnings. The second week as I wrote my check for my tithe, my husband asked if he could come to church with us – at this time, the children and I had been going to church without him for four years. Of course I was delighted. He came with us to church and listened, and I continued to tithe and pray.

After five months of my commitment, one Sunday my husband surrendered, went forward, received Jesus as his Savior and Lord, and was baptized. God keeps His promises.

Debbie Johnson is a member of Shepherd of the Hills Church in Porter Ranch, CA.

Prayer

My sweet Heavenly Father, who hears my prayers and knows my heart, Your Word is true and Your promises never fail. When I trust You, You grant my deepest heart's desires. When I am obedient to Your Word, You truly do open the floodgates and pour out Your blessings on me. Nothing is impossible when what I pray is in Your perfect will. You are so faithful; how can I be any less faithful and trusting? Lord, You are a holy God and You alone are so worthy of our praise and worship. I love You, Lord, with all my heart, all my soul, all my mind and all my strength. In Jesus's precious name, I pray. Amen.

Questions

- Will you commit today to pray about giving God ten percent of all He has given you?

- Why does God command our giving Him ten percent of all we have?

- God asks us to test Him in this. Will you?

Journal

February 15

Meditation   Dudley C. Rutherford

Salvation or regeneration contains two aspects. First is the forgiveness of our sins. And the second aspect is receiving the gift of the Holy Spirit. It is imperative that we remember His Spirit inhabits this temple we call the physical body. Would to God that every one of us would realize that there is no problem too complex, no mountain too steep, no ocean too wide, no storm too bleak and no burden too heavy, but that the Holy Spirit is eager and anxious and willing to bear the heavier part of the load.

Many of our church members, and many of our Christian friends are so worldly, so selfish, so carnal and so fruitless that they are simply not giving the Holy Spirit a chance to work in their lives. His Spirit is in you! It's there! That's every Christian's promise. Are you grieving Him with sin and neglect, or are you encouraging Him? The Christian can cut his problems down to size when he gets on his knees and talks things over with God. You may not know just what to say to God, but the Spirit knows precisely what words to give to the Father.

"But pastor, how do I activate this promised power within?" The answer to this is the same answer to nearly every serious question: "Get on your knees and get into the Book. Let the Spirit speak to you through His Word." In your complete surrender to God, His Spirit will fill you, bless you, protect you and save you.

Holy Spirit of God

Prayer

Dear wonderful God, thank You for the presence of Your Spirit in my life. Give me the grace to activate and encourage Him by the closeness of my daily repentance and surrender. Help me to be more of You and less of self. Help me understand that the greatest job I can ever have is to be a simple, child-like servant of Jesus Christ. May I hearten and bless Your Spirit as I move in closer to You. In the saving name of Jesus, I pray. Amen.

Questions

- When you came to Christ, what gift did you receive?

- What if you can't think of the right words in your prayers?

- How do you activate and use this wonderful gift?

Journal

> *Be very careful, then, how you live—not as unwise but as wise, making the most of every opportunity, because the days are evil.*
>
> *(Ephesians 5:15-16)*

Meditation   *Cameron McDonald*

I have a confession. Recently, I have spent a lot of time on my computer involved in something I should not be involved. I just get sucked in. Every time I go near my computer, I hear it calling my name. No, I am not talking about Internet pornography, but I am talking about something that can be just as potentially devastating: solitaire. You may laugh and say, "Come on, Cameron, are you serious? I thought you were talking about a real problem." But I believe that distraction is a clever tool used by Satan.

Let's face it. We live in a society dominated by distractions. If we choose to, we can come home every evening and sit and stare at a box for hours and then get up and go to bed, never having real interaction with our spouses, never asking our children about their day, never taking the time to sit and open our Bibles for a few minutes.

As Christians, we were made for a purpose, and that purpose is the Kingdom of Jesus Christ. I have told my son Mekai since the day he was born, "You know why your mother and I decided to have you? So that you can tell the world about Jesus." Friends, that is our mission in this life. Now I am not saying there isn't time for healthy distractions that give us a break from our daily work, that let us mentally recalibrate and recharge our batteries. We should always be living with an eternal perspective, and we should always be looking for ways to make the name of Christ known. Someone said, "Wherever you are, be all there." I think that is true for us, as Christians.

I Have a Confession

Heavenly Father, You have called us to be single-minded people, You tell us in Your word that even in a chaotic world, we still need to take time out to just be still and know that You are God. Would You help me not to be dragged away and enticed by some meaningless distraction? Would You give me the supernatural strength I need to overcome distraction and focus on my mission with the short time You have given me in this life? I pray this through the strong name of Jesus. Amen.

Questions

- What are some distractions in your life that are keeping you from your mission?

- What are some things you can do to eliminate those distractions?

- How can you be more single-minded in light of the mission to which you have been called?

Journal

_____

_____

_____

_____

February 17

He was despised and rejected by men, a man of sorrows, and familiar with suffering. Like one from whom men hide their faces he was despised, and we esteemed him not. (Isaiah 53:3)

Meditation   Dudley C. Rutherford

This is one of the most chilling, haunting statements in the Bible. It makes the blood run cold to give it serious thought. Notice this prophecy does not say He will be denied or unaccepted. It predicts He will be despised and rejected. Who are the despisers of His great grace? Those who refuse to receive Him, and those who hesitate to step forward and march under the drumbeat of conviction that Jesus is the One true God.

The non-Christian has been surrounded since birth by the tender mercies of Jesus. Christ has been patient with the sinner; He has given His own life on Calvary's tree. How can anyone despise such mercies? How can one steel his heart against such wooings? How can one trample on such holy blood? How can one be deaf to such divine overtures?

One's refusal of grace is no less than insolent contempt of God. Don't continue headlong in your sin while shaking your fist in the face of the Most High. Quit your action of bitter rebellion. Please dear heart, make a serious inquiry into your esteem of Christ and His Church. Do you weep at His sufferings? Do you love Jesus Christ more than you love all others and all things? If you have despised Him, will you give your life, your all to Him? You are somebody's slave now. Don't be Satan's. Be the slave of Jesus. Don't be numbered on that last day with the despisers of Christ.

Despised and Rejected

Prayer

Dear Jesus, I can see You now on the bloody cross, dying for my sins. Thank You, thank You, thank You. While there is still time and while my heart still beats, I am deciding for You today. I am stepping by faith over to Your side. From now on, I will not be numbered with the despisers and Christ rejecters. I know You receive me with open arms and that my decision will lead to my lasting happiness and salvation. I pray this prayer in the blessed name of Jesus. Amen.

Questions

- Is Jesus ignored or is He despised?

- Have you recently measured your esteem of Christ?

- Have you become a slave to Christ or to Satan?

Journal

February 18

I know that nothing good lives in me, that is, in my sinful nature. For I have the desire to do what is good, but I cannot carry it out. For what I do is not the good I want to do; no, the evil I do not want to do—this I keep on doing. (Romans 7:18-19)

Meditation   *Dudley C. Rutherford*

Paul is saying: "Whenever the 'I want' crosses the 'I know,' sin is the result." Some very educated philosophers have asserted, "Knowledge is virtue." Nothing could be further from the truth. America has reached its zenith in available knowledge but sin and crime are on the rampage. Our moral progress falls far behind our scientific progress. We cram our heads with data and empty our souls of faith. We improve our gadgets and appliances but disgrace and disregard our souls. Ask any sinner, "Why do you sin, knowing it's wrong and that there will be consequences to pay?" The honest answer must always be, "Because my heart wants to."

Education has no answers. If a thief is uneducated, he will sneak down at night and steal goods from a stopped train. If the thief is educated, he will go down and steal the entire train. Ask any sinner, "Would more education or information cause you to stop sinning?" "No!" There is only one solution. The heart must be changed.

Jesus told Nicodemus, "You must be born again" (John 3:5). Paul said, "If any man be in Christ, he is a new creature. Old things are passed away" (II Corinthians 5:17). How does this miraculous transformation occur? John gives us most of the answer: "If we confess our sins, He is faithful and just to forgive us our sins, and to cleanse us from all unrighteousness" (I John 1:9). Man doesn't need a change of mind, or a change of clothes, or new scenery or a different job. He needs a change of heart more than he needs his next breath.

Jesus and Nicodemus

Prayer

Dear Almighty God, I am in need of a new heart. I am far too carnal and worldly. I am too easily tempted to be corrupt, dishonest and sinful. Cleanse my heart, O God; make it ever new. I want to walk the road of personal cleansing and inner happiness. I want to be cleansed and forgiven of the past and empowered to start living each future day for You and Your undefeatable Kingdom. I need nothing less than a rebirth from You. In the forgiving, life-changing name of Jesus, I pray. Amen.

Questions

- Will more education help you in your battle with sin?

- What do you need more than your next breath?

- How does this transformation take place?

Journal

_____

_____

_____

_____

_____

"The most important one," answered Jesus, "is this: 'Hear, O Israel, the Lord our God, the Lord is one. Love the Lord your God with all your heart and with all your soul and with all your mind and with all your strength.'" *(Mark 12:29-30)*

Meditation   *Barbra Miner*

Being raised as a Jewish child, I was taught to recite these words as soon as I could speak. This verse is referred to as "The Sh'ma," and it is the most sacred Hebrew prayer. My parents taught me to say these words every evening when I went to bed and every morning when I awoke, just as it says to do in Deuteronomy 6:7.

Jewish children are taught that these words are supposed to be on our lips when we die, and I feel certain they were spoken by many of the Jewish people who perished in the Holocaust, including my great-grandparents. Imagine my surprise when, as a new believer, I read that Jesus also said this was the most important commandment! My Jewish parents had no idea they were teaching me the same words Rabbi Yeshua (Jesus) taught were the most important!

Most Jewish people don't realize that the Hebrew word *echad*, which refers to the word "one" in these verses, is a plural form of "one." There is another Hebrew word that refers to a singular form of "one," but that word was not used in these verses. Just as a cluster of grapes is one cluster but consists of many grapes, this word *echad* refers to the plurality of God's nature.

Barbra Miner is a member of Shepherd of the Hills Church, Porter Ranch, CA.

Prayer

Baruch Atah Adonai, Eloheynu Melech ha Olam. Blessed are You, Lord our God, King of the Universe. I pray that You would open the eyes, hearts and minds of Jewish people, especially my parents, to the truth of Your Son, <u>Yeshua Meshacheinu</u>, Jesus, our Messiah. May Your *Ruach ha Kodesh*, Your Holy Spirit, fill them so that the veil will be removed from their eyes and hearts, and they will experience Your Shalom, Your peace, eternally. Amen.

Questions

- What is "The Sh'ma"?

- What would you pray if you were about to die?

- Do you have any unsaved relatives? What specifically do you pray for them?

Journal

_____

_____

_____

_____

_____

February 20

He who conceals his sins does not prosper, but whoever confesses and renounces them finds mercy. Blessed is the man who always fears the Lord, but he who hardens his heart falls into trouble.

(Proverbs 28:13-14)

Meditation   *Dudley C. Rutherford*

We love to wear masks. If we are middle class, we like to make folks think we are upper class. If we are homely, we try to look pretty. You can get a new mask at a beauty parlor. Some purchase a $25 degree and wear educational masks to pose as doctors or lawyers. Religious masks are in abundance. The mask tries to give the impression of inner humility and piety. All masks do the same: make a person appear to be what he is not. All masks emphasize the outside, the external. We use them to cover up and conceal. The good, honest man needs no mask. The greater sinner a man is, the cleverer his mask must be to hide his defiance. Usually though, after some time, the mask comes off, the true identity is revealed and all are embarrassed.

The Bible warns: "You may be sure your sin will find you out" (Numbers 33:23). Some people can wear a mask and remain unexposed to the very end of life. Some of us are more sinful, more clever and more duplicitous than others. If not here, every person will someday stand before the Lord, naked and unmasked. No mask will be available on that Day of Judgment. Please, dear heart, let our Lord cleanse you internally so there is no need for an external mask. Expose your evil to Him right now and allow him to remove that sin from your heart, so that you will no longer need a mask.

Naked and Unmasked

Prayer

Dear Father, look deep inside me, cleanse me and forgive me that I will no longer have to pretend I am somebody else. Let me not be like the Pharisees, whom Jesus said were like graves "painted white and clean on the outside but full of dead men's bones on the inside." I repent and ask that You clean the interior part of me, so that my exterior will not need a cover-up. Give me the faith to unmask now, so that I will not be forced to later. In Christ's name I pray. Amen.

Questions

- Can you prosper if you conceal your sin?

- Of what does Numbers 33 say you can be sure?

- How can you take off some of your masks?

Journal

> *Enter through the narrow gate. For wide is the gate and broad is the road that leads to destruction, and many enter through it. But small is the gate and narrow the road that leads to life, and only a few find it.*
>
> *(Matthew 7:13-14)*

Meditation   *Dudley C. Rutherford*

When the Titanic sank, it emphasized what God had been trying to tell us: "There is a huge difference between fact and theory." Theory said the ship was unsinkable. In fact, that's about all that ship ever did: sink. Theory said that the ship could cut through an iceberg of 66,000 tons. Fact is, they struck an iceberg that equaled 947,000 tons. Theory said the lookouts on the crow's nest would give ample warning of icebergs. Fact said there was not enough time.

Many a person today is placing his hope of Heaven on theory rather than fact. Theory says, "No one will ever know my sin." But the fact is, "Be sure your sins will find you out" (Numbers 32:23). Theory says, "All roads lead to Heaven." Fact says, "More will be lost than saved" (Matthew 7:13). Theory says, "A loving God would not send a man to hell," but the fact is, "many shall enter through it" (Matthew 7:13). Theory says, "If I do go to Hell, I can surely find a way out." The fact is, "The smoke of their torment rises for ever and ever. There is no rest day or night" (Revelation 14:11).

"But, pastor, that seems so narrow." You are right, but God's Word is narrow and His commandments are plain.

When the White Star office in New York posted the news of the great sinking, there were just two columns: "Saved or Lost." Not "rich saved" or "rich lost." Not "talented lost" or "good-looking lost." At the end of our earthly journey, there will still be only two columns: "Saved" and "Lost." Where will your name be?

Theory Versus Fact

Prayer

My precious God and Father, help me to avoid theorizing about Your demands upon my life and let me go back to the Bible to determine my spiritual lifestyle. I don't want to hear what some friend or neighbor says; I want to know what You have to say on the matter. I keep thinking of that verse in the Bible that says, "Let God be true and every man a liar!" (Romans 3:4). Since You are going to be my final judge (John 5:22), I want to know what You say on all matters. Help me to get back to the study of Your Word. In Jesus' name, I pray. Amen.

Questions

- Is the gate to Heaven wide or narrow? (Matthew 7:13)

- Who is the "narrow gate"?

- How many people find the narrow path?

Journal

_____

_____

_____

_____

■ February 22

If we claim to have fellowship with him yet walk in the darkness, we lie and do not live by the truth. (I John 1:6)

There are different kinds of working, but the same God works all of them in all men. Now to each one the manifestation of the Spirit is given for the common good. (I Corinthians 12:6-7)

Meditation   *Bob Hastings*

My experience as an employer in the broadcast industry has afforded me the opportunity to interview hundreds of likely candidates, such as sales, sales management, sales assistance and those on the technical side of radio. Interviewing is an art – an art few master – and you can count me among the "non-mastered" group. I have learned a few great questions to ask. One such question is, "Is it always important to tell the truth?" It is amazing some of the replies I've received:

"Of course not, this is sales!"
"Well, it depends on the situation…"
"I used to tell the truth all the time, and then I got into radio."
"Maybe. Why? Is that important to you?"

The most difficult part of the interview process, besides the decision, was keeping a calm, straight face when the answers were given. Candidates trying to show their best face to the interviewer, stumped for an answer when a simple, "Yes," was sufficient. Our society tends to downplay the importance of truth. Lying is only a problem if you're caught. Society tells our children that cheating on tests is okay because everyone else does it, and you need to get a 4.3 average (on a scale of 1 to 4) to be accepted to a good college.

As Christians, we are in the spotlight as examples to others. As fallen humans, we strive and fail, repent, and strive again. The hard part is that when we fail and non-Christians see it, they are quick to point and say, "And you call yourself a Christian?" It's difficult enough for us to understand repentance, forgiveness and God's grace. Trying to explain the concept to a doubting non-believer is a daunting task; like putting toothpaste back in the tube.

Bob Hastings is Regional Sales Manager for Salem Communications, in Glendale, CA.

Why Do You Ask?

Heavenly Father, Creator and Lord, thank You for another opportunity to seek Your will. I ask this for today only, sunrise to sunset, living life one day at a time, as You would have me live it. Only You can direct my path to the path of righteousness. Only You can give me strength today to stay on Your right path. Only You can keep me in truth. Lord, hold me gently in Your hands; hold my face upward toward You all day. Let me be Your humble servant today. Keep me from harm. Keep me in Your Word. Lead me through every challenge. Let Your words fill my head with purpose and joy. In Jesus' name. Amen.

Questions

- Who can you reach with the testimony of your actions today?

- If you knew this was your last day on earth, would it matter whether you told the truth all day?

- Can you explain, "Not perfect, but forgiven," to the non-believers and new believers you encounter today?

Journal

Isaac reopened the wells that had been dug in the time of his father Abraham, which the Philistines had stopped up after Abraham died, and he gave them the same names his father had given them. (Genesis 26:18)

Meditation   *Dudley C. Rutherford*

It is the task of every person, every church and every Christian to rebuild those good things by which our forefathers were once blessed. Isaac's daddy, Abraham had come into the enemy stronghold and dug wells so that his people might have water to drink. Years afterward, the Philistines came along and filled them all back up. Enemies are standing by for a chance to stop up the wells of Godliness. It is difficult for us to imagine the laborious job of digging in that desert with primitive tools. It was no cakewalk. It would take months even years to reopen these wells. Cursing the Philistines will remedy nothing. It's seldom easy to reclaim that which has been lost. A daring, pioneering spirit can be far easier than the task of rebuilding and restoring.

Are there some wells, some channels in your life that have been stopped by the enemy that need to be reopened? What about the well of stewardship? Do you need to start allowing that spirit of generosity to flow? What about the channel of Bible reading, Bible study and prayer? Is your love and fervor for the House of God and fellowship with His people what it once used to be? Are those now mere trickling streams that once used to flow through your heart? Get out the shovel, dear heart, and dig! The task is arduous, unglamorous and backbreaking, but bit-by-bit and inch-by-inch you can reopen that clogged river. Pass the Bible please; I need to start digging up some things.

Redigging Old Wells

Prayer

Help me, dear Father, to start reopening some wells that have been too long congested for good use. Even though many may scoff and few will cheer, I need to try to restore again the things that our grandparents once thought essential. I feel that Isaac's heavy burden falls also on my shoulders. Give me the grace and courage today to reach for the shovel and start digging the hardened and fallow ground of my heart. I ask this sincere prayer in the name of my Lord and Savior, Jesus Christ. Amen.

Questions

- Have you read the story in Genesis 26?

- Is it easier to blaze a new trail or reopen an old one?

- What wells in your life are at least partially plugged?

Journal

> *As Jesus started on his way, a man ran up to him and fell on his knees before him. "Good teacher," he asked, "what must I do to inherit eternal life?" Jesus looked at him and loved him. "One thing you lack," he said. "Go, sell everything you have and give to the poor, and you will have treasure in heaven. Then come, follow me." At this the man's face fell. He went away sad, because he had great wealth. (Mark 10:17, 21-22)*

Meditation   *Dudley C. Rutherford*

I promise if you study this passage, your heart will be pierced. This rich, young man came running to Jesus. He believed in Christ! He was handsome, healthy, rich and had many rare charismatic qualities. Jesus saw unlimited possibilities in this millionaire teenager, if only he would relinquish his passion of greed. He confronted Jesus head-on: "What must I do to inherit eternal life?" Christ quickly X-rayed his shriveling soul and saw that he was absorbed with materialism. The Bible says Jesus just looked at the lad and loved him. Jesus then gave him His best, surest and quickest test: "Go, sell everything you own and give it away and come follow me!" There the young man stood where we all must inevitably stand: choosing between Christ and money, Christ and things, while only one can occupy the heart's throne.

Who knows what the young man might have become had he surrendered to Christ? A wise prophet? An author of one of the Gospels? The preacher at Pentecost instead of Peter? Had he only surrendered, we would know his world-famous name. His name would rank with Peter, Paul or John. But he remains an aimless, nameless soul who stared into the face of the tender Christ at the crossroads of decision and greatly failed. He disappeared into oblivion, being mastered by things and not by Christ. He chose cash instead of Christ, gold instead of God, greed instead of grace, money instead of the Master. He turned his back on the only remedy there is for a sin-sick soul: Jesus the Christ.

Prayer

Thank You, Lord, for telling me about this young man with everything in his favor, who was so close to Heaven and salvation, yet turned his back on the gentle, sensitive, suffering Savior. He symbolizes so many who are on the top stair to eternal life, and yet refuse to acquiesce to the one great demand that Jesus makes on us all: complete surrender. May I remember that surrender to You is not failure but total victory for me, both now and forevermore. I ask this prayer in Christ's holy name. Amen.

Questions

- Name some good traits of the man in this text.

- Why do you think he went away?

- When you walk away from Jesus, what does that say about your heart?

Journal

_____

_____

_____

_____

_____

Enter his gates with thanksgiving and his courts with praise; give thanks to him and praise his name. For the LORD is good and his love endures forever; his faithfulness continues through all generations.

(Psalm 100:4-5)

Meditation   *David Macer*

Have you ever felt that you just can't find the closeness and spiritual intimacy you really long to have with God? It may be for just a season of time. Yet it often seems to happen during a serious trial, when you really need to spend time with God, but you just can't seem to connect. I have had so many people ask about this subject and had so little understanding of the "spiritual dryness" in myself – until I focused on Psalm 100.

Let's think about the visual image that verses 4 and 5 bring to mind. The psalmist tells us that we enter His gates with thanksgiving and His courts with praise.

Do you know what I finally realized? If I do not go through the gate or walk through the courtyard, how can I possibly get to the inner sanctuary of God? If my heart is not full of thankfulness, then I will not make it through the gate. If I do not enter into His courts with praise, then I will not even get close to His presence.

He is worthy of every bit of my gratitude and praise and so much more. When I come to Him with the right attitude, I am able to hear His voice so much more clearly. When I am hearing Him clearly, there is no spiritual dryness – ever!

David Macer is the Adult Singles/LIFE! Groups Pastor at Shepherd of the Hills Church, Porter Ranch, CA.

Prayer

Abba Father, I pray that I will stop seeking You on my terms and start seeking You on Your terms… with a heart that is full of thankfulness and with praise on my lips. You alone are worthy of all my praise. You alone are the One that gives life. I pledge to live my life knowing that the joy of the Lord is my strength (Nehemiah 8:10). Your presence is what I will seek all the days of my life. In Jesus' name. Amen.

Questions

- How often do you feel that you experience something along the lines of "spiritual dryness"?

- What specific steps do you take to overcome "spiritual dryness"?

- How effective have you been at overcoming it?

Journal

u

From one man he made every nation of men, that they should inhabit the whole earth; and he determined the times set for them and the exact places where they should live. He did this so that men would seek him and perhaps reach out for him and find him, though he is not far from each one of us. (Acts 17:26-27)

Meditation   *Heather Flaig*

God made us. He determined the times and places for us to live. Why? Why blessing-filled homes for some and heartbreaking experiences for others? Why comfort and convenience or trial and tragedy? So that we will seek Him, reach out for Him, find Him… and realize He is not far from each one of us, regardless of our circumstances. God will allow or orchestrate situations in which we need to seek Him, reach out for Him and find Him. He wants us to identify our need for Him, so that He can satisfy us. God is concerned with changing our attitudes and actions – even when that means using difficulties.

Soon after their birth, newborn lambs have to reach out to and find their mothers (who are certainly not far from them!) to discover the source of milk for their survival. The more they eat, the bigger they grow and the stronger they become. Those who don't may die. They are vulnerable to malnutrition or illness or predator's attack. The same is true for us. Our spiritual life or death is determined by our seeking, reaching out for and finding God. Jeremiah 29:13 says that when we seek God, we will find Him when we seek Him with all our hearts. God is near, waiting to be found so that He can fill us!

Heather Flaig is the wife of Dave Flaig, Emerging Generation Pastor at Shepherd of the Hills Church.

Prayer

Gentle Shepherd, thank You that You made me and determined the time and place for me to live. I want to seek You and reach out for You. I so need to find You and realize that You are not far from me – especially when life is hard. Help me to look for You and listen to You and discover You in Your Word, Your creation, Your family and in Your answers to my prayers. Thank You that though You may sometimes seem silent, You are never absent! Thank You for being my Source for life. In Jesus' name. Amen.

Questions

- What are you learning about God from the times and places in which He determined for you to live?

- How are you going about seeking, reaching and finding God?

- Which attitudes or actions would you like God to change in you?

Journal

February 27

Therefore God exalted him to the highest place and gave him the name that is above every name, that at the name of Jesus every knee should bow, in heaven and on earth and under the earth, and every tongue confess that Jesus Christ is Lord, to the glory of God the Father. (Philippians 2:9-11)

Meditation   *Dudley C. Rutherford*

R.G. Lee, the late, great preacher from Memphis, Tennessee, could write like no one else. I have adopted some of his beautiful words concerning the precious name of Jesus.

"His name blossoms on the pages of history like the flowers of a thousand spring times in one bouquet. His name sounds in the corridors of the centuries like the music of all choirs, visible and invisible, poured forth into one anthem. His influence, like spice gales from Heaven, has perfumed the air of all the continents. His name like a great tidal wave has washed the shores of twenty long centuries.

"And when Mary went down into that mysterious land of motherhood, she came back holding in her arms the only child in this universe not to have a human father. And His every muscle was a pulley divinely swung, His every nerve was divine handwriting, His every bone was divine sculpture, His every heartbeat was divine pulsation, His every breath was a divine whisper."

R.G. Lee

Prayer

Dear lovely Lord Jesus, there never was and never will be another name like Jesus. You have the name that is above every name. The very sight or sound of that name makes me desire to walk with You, to know You and to be Your friend. I'll never tire or grow weary of saying the name of Jesus. At Your name, I confess You once again as Lord and Savior. At Your name and at Your feet, I ask for strength to live the type of life that would honor that wonderful name. In Jesus' name, I pray. Amen.

Questions

- What is the one name in the universe that outshines all others?

- Was it an accidental name or one divinely chosen?

- How can you live your life so you can bring more honor to that name?

Journal

February 28

Meditation   Dudley C. Rutherford

I was at breakfast recently with my father, and he told me of something he had read. There is nothing more dirty and useless than an old, muddy, slimy footprint traipsing out of a coal mine. What does a dirty footprint have to do with my life? A scientist was writing an essay about the sooty, coalminer's footprint. He said such a footprint contains only four basic elements: clay, sand, coal dust and water. Look at clay. Put it under great heat and pressure and it will turn into a breath-taking sapphire. Sand is silica; put silica under great heat and pressure and you will have an iridescent opal. Coal dust? Put some of that under mountains of pressure and heat and you end up with a diamond. What about the element of water? Let the sun shine on it and it will evaporate upward into a cloud and waft across some mountain range; as it hits colder temperatures, it will fall as a scintillating snowflake.

What's the point? The point is that our wondrous God can take the impurities of nature and turn them into something precious. I've talked with so many people who say, "I am such a sham, such a counterfeit, such a hypocrite, God can never use me." I've got thrilling news in the name of Christ! If only you will invite Him into your heart He will, this moment, begin to turn the impurities of your life into something priceless, costly, rare and eternal. You may be so spiritually discouraged that you believe you are as valueless as a muddy footprint, But please know that my God can take all the elements of your past days and transform you into a vision of perfection.

Prayer

Dear Heavenly Father, please, please, please help me in this moment to turn over the doubts, the fears, the sins and the impurities of my life so that You can once again produce something beautiful. I've seen You do it in nature, and now as I surrender anew unto You, I want You to repeat that miracle in my life. Help me to seek holiness and not happiness. Help me to seek Christ instead of covetousness. In Jesus' name I ask these favors. Amen.

Questions

- How does Paul say you are transformed?

- Into whose likeness are you to be transformed?

- Name some examples from nature that prove this is possible.

Journal

■ March 1

Can you make a pet of him like a bird or put him on a leash for your girls? (Job 41:5)

Meditation   *Kerri Rutherford - Age 9*

When my mom asked me to name a Bible verse I like, this verse in Job popped into my head. I like it because I think it sounds silly. Can you imagine your dad giving you a pet crocodile (or leviathan) on a leash? Can you imagine trying to put a collar on a powerful animal? The entire process would be a very scary thing for me.

In this verse, God is pointing out to Job how silly it is to think he could control God. God is very, very powerful, wouldn't you agree? Think about all the mighty things in God's creation, like a huge crocodile, a lion, the sun, the oceans, the mountains, or a bear. God is more powerful than all of these things combined.

When we look at all the mighty things God created, we begin to understand a little more about God's amazing power. He truly is awesome! He truly is powerful! We don't have to be afraid, because He is taking care of us every moment. The thing I like about my dad is that I feel safe around him. I don't like it when he is gone on a trip and not home. In the same way, I feel at ease when I know God is with me every day. I don't have to be scared of anything, because God, my Heavenly Father, is all-powerful.

Kerri Rutherford, age 9, is the youngest daughter of Pastor Dudley Rutherford

God's Amazing Power

Prayer

Dear God, thank You for Your amazing power and for taking care of us. I know that if You made all these powerful things, You can certainly look after me. I admit I get scared sometimes, but only when I forget who You are. Help me, God, to never forget Your power or Your love. I thank You for the awesome creation I am part of. In Jesus' name. Amen.

Questions

- Do you think you can control God?

- How do you know God is so powerful?

- Do you think you should be scared of Him?

Journal

You turned my wailing into dancing; you removed my sackcloth and clothed me with joy, that my heart may sing to you and not be silent. O LORD my God, I will give you thanks forever. (Psalm 30:11-12)

In him was life, and that life was the light of men. The light shines in the darkness, but the darkness has not understood it. (John 1:4-5)

Meditation   *Dudley C. Rutherford*

Helen Keller, hopelessly blind and deaf from birth, relates that wonderful moment in life when she discovered that language existed, that every object had a word. Let her tell you in her own words:

"We walked down to the well-house, attracted by the fragrance of honeysuckle with which it was covered. My teacher, Anne Sullivan, placed one of my hands under the spout. As the cool stream gushed over my hand, she spelled into the other the word w-a-t-e-r. I began to sense some wonderful, cold substance that was flowing over my hand. I knew now for sure that every object in life had a word, and this new knowledge had given light and hope to my soul. There were barriers still, it is true, but barriers that in time could be swept away."

She called that moment "my detonation." By detonation, she is saying that every aspect of life and language virtually exploded in her mind with that one, simple, thrilling discovery. Could I add that the discovery of Jesus Christ should be every person's "detonation"? One's entire universe will explode with music and glory beyond expression, if only they would open the door of their darkened heart and invite Him to enter. The simple word J-e-s-u-s rightly spelled out in one's soul will unlock every mystery and problem that exists. All the dread, the doom and gloom of darkness will begin to disappear. Let Him in, and the most boring, blind, deaf, silent world will explode with vital purpose and power.

Prayer

My dear wonderful Lord Jesus Christ. Thank You for coming into my life and giving me a light that shines the way for me to walk. You have given new meaning and purpose to my existence. I don't want to live on the level of this world's culture, where the main goal is only to make money and live for the things of the flesh. I have been trying to live for You and I want to finish my life's race that same way. Help me to help others to invite this bright light of Christ into their lives. I pray in Your name. Amen.

Questions

- Why did Helen Keller call the word "water" her "detonation"?

- Is it only the life of Christ that can change people's hearts?

- Who alone can turn your mourning into dancing?

Journal

_____

_____

_____

_____

I was appointed from eternity, from the beginning, before the world began. When there were no oceans, I was given birth, when there were no springs abounding with water; before the mountains were settled in place, before the hills, I was given birth, before he made the earth or its fields or any of the dust of the world. (Proverbs 8:23-26)

Meditation   *Dudley C. Rutherford*

This simple, world-famous essay whose author is unknown expresses the uniqueness of Jesus. Jesus did not have many of the qualifications we associate with success, but look what He did!!

"He was born in an obscure village, the child of a peasant woman. He worked in a carpentry shop until he was thirty, and then for three years he was an itinerant preacher. When the tide of popular opinion turned against him, his friends ran away. He was turned over to his enemies. He was tried and convicted. He was nailed upon a cross between two thieves. When he was dead, he was laid in a borrowed grave. He never wrote a book. He never held an office. He never owned a home. He never went to college. He never traveled more than two hundred miles from the place where he was born. He never did any of the things that usually accompany greatness. Yet all the armies that ever marched, and all the governments that ever sat, and all the kings that ever reigned, have not affected life upon this earth as powerfully as that one solitary life."

Dear reader, let Him, who has influenced this planet, affect your personal life. Invite Him into your heart today. Invite Him in to stay. If you have invited Him only halfway in, invite Him all the way in at this moment. His silent, steady power can transform your entire life and destiny.

One Solitary Life

Dear Lord of Lords and King of all Kings, forgive me when I have underestimated and ignored Your power to bless and influence my life. I do understand that if You possess the ability to change governments and move national boundaries, You can certainly change the direction of my life. If You can move mountains and calm the seas, and walk on the waves of the water, I know You maintain enough power to control my life. Help me to know that as I surrender to Your love and Word, that Your great grace will begin to operate in my daily walk. In Jesus' sweet name, I pray. Amen.

Questions

- What inspires you the most about the essay "One Solitary Life"?

- What, if any, are the comparisons between Jesus' life and your life?

- How has Jesus redirected your life?

Journal

_____

_____

_____

_____

_____

But I trust in your unfailing love; my heart rejoices in your salvation.
I will sing to the LORD, for he has been good to me. (Psalm 13:5-6)

Meditation   *Bob Russell*

If you could ask God one question and you knew He would answer, what would you ask? Pollster George Barna surveyed a cross-section of adults with that question, and the number one response was, "I'd ask God why there is so much pain and suffering in the world."

When you're hurting, it's difficult not to get angry with God. It's not that we blame Him for everything bad that happens. We know that some suffering is the result of living in a fallen world and some is the direct attack of Satan. We know that God allows suffering to mature us (Romans 5:3-5), to comfort others (II Corinthians 1:4), to test us (James 1:12), to discipline us (Hebrew 12:5-6), to help us appreciate Jesus' suffering (Philippians 3:10-11), and to keep our focus on Heaven (II Corinthians 4:17).

The key to endurance is not a divine explanation but genuine worship. David didn't report any answers as to why his pain was prolonged. God didn't reveal a three-step formula to eliminate it. But after expressing his frustration, he ends this powerful Psalm by reaffirming his beliefs.

Although he wondered why his suffering was so ongoing, David never lost faith in the end of the story. He believed God's goodness would prevail in the end. God eventually delivered David from his oppression and now has granted him eternal life.

Why, God, Why?

Prayer

Father God, I want to trust You: when times are tough, when I can't see the end of my scary circumstance, when the road seems too long and too dark. Allow me to worship You even when pain is prolonged. When I feel that the darkness is all around, remind me of what You have told me in the light. I praise Your name and pray these things in Your Son Jesus' name. Amen.

Questions

- Why does God allow so much pain and suffering in the world?

- Do you panic at the mere thought of experiencing difficulty?

- Like David, are you willing to worship and trust the Lord when times get tough?

Journal

March 5

Meditation   *Dudley C. Rutherford*

David's heart was bursting with gratitude now that the plague of suffering was over. He was trying to buy a piece of land from a farmer, so he could erect an altar and sacrifice a burnt offering to his God. The farmer said: "David, don't pay me anything for the land. It's for God, so I won't charge you anything."

"Oh, yes you will," replied David, "because I will not offer my God a gift which costs me nothing."

That is the perfect spirit and attitude toward Christian giving. How many times have people cried, "Oh, if I were only rich, or if only I had more time or more talent I would do this or I would give that to God." No, you wouldn't! And if you did give it to God, He wouldn't want it. God doesn't want the leftovers after we have spent the best on ourselves. God doesn't want the smoke of a misspent life blown in His face, after we have burned the candle of our lives for Satan. God doesn't want the crumbs after we have had the steak and lobster. Does God rejoice when we party late Saturday night and then drag ourselves half-conscious into His presence on Sunday morning? David knew that an offering which cost little was in reality no offering at all.

Prayer

Dear precious Lord, I know You gave everything for me. You gave it all. I know You are not only interested in my giving, but You are interested in the giving of my heart. Help me not only to give but also to give with the purest motives and purposes. I never want to give You something which costs me nothing. I know You not only want my treasure but my time, my talent and my very life. Help me to remember that half-surrender is no surrender. This day I renew my heart unto You. In Christ's name, I pray. Amen.

Questions

- Why wouldn't David take the free land?

- Why do we tend to give gifts that cost us nothing?

- When was the last time you gave something that was truly a sacrifice?

Journal

_____

_____

_____

_____

■ March 6

How great is the love the Father has lavished on us, that we should be called children of God! And that is what we are! The reason the world does not know us is that it did not know him. Dear friends, now we are children of God, and what we will be has not yet been made known. But we know that when he appears, we shall be like him, for we shall see him as he is. Everyone who has this hope in him purifies himself, just as he is pure. (I John 3:1-3)

Meditation   *Dudley C. Rutherford*

One morning as Robert Browning, the great poet, sat writing at his desk, his wife, Elizabeth Barrett Browning, a world-class poet in her own right, ambled up behind her husband, and gently and slowly kissed him on the side of his face and simultaneously slipped a poem into his side coat pocket. The words she put into his pocket have been described by one critic as the noblest sequence of love words ever put together in the name of romance. Hidden in the sonnet she gave him were these now famous lines: "The face of all the world has changed since first I heard the footsteps of your soul."

My, my, what a statement and what a truth to consider! That's the way all of us should feel about Christ. For Jesus yearns and begs each of us to have a personal relationship with Him. Can we honestly say, "Dear Lord, the face of all the world has changed since first I heard the footsteps of Your soul"? Or would we be forced to say, "Well, Lord, You are a fascinating force and I believe You exist, but not much has changed since I was first introduced to You"? Ours must be a reciprocal love affair or it has no chance of eternal success. Who will open his heart right now and invite Him in? Who will start anew this love affair with Christ? Will you now bow your head and make this hour a turning point?

Elizabeth Barrett Browning

Prayer

Dear Jesus, lover of my soul, the face of all the world has changed since I first heard of Calvary, the cross and Your undying love for me. I can never be the same person. Please come again into my heart just now. I open my heart's door to You. Come in, come way in, come on in deep and stay long. Never, never leave. Nothing has ever been the same since I first met You and nothing can ever remain the same. You and You alone are the difference-maker in my life. In Jesus' name, I pray. Amen.

Questions

- Since you first met Jesus, has He changed your life?

- Name several changes that have taken place.

- Now that you are lavished by God, what is your title?

Journal

■ March 7

So do not worry, saying, "What shall we eat?" or "What shall we drink?" or "What shall we wear?" For the pagans run after all these things, and your heavenly Father knows that you need them. But seek first his kingdom and his righteousness, and all these things will be given to you as well.

(Matthew 6:31-33)

Meditation   *Dudley C. Rutherford*

I used to scan that passage and think it was just another nifty, neat verse in the Bible. But years of study have taught me that my utmost concern and my primary priority in this earthly life should be the Church for which Christ died. That verse says I must daily bathe my life in Kingdom affairs. Church dare not be a one-hour session or some ancillary side issue. It must be something of such profound significance that I must eat, drink and sleep church matters. I must be so captured and fascinated by its power and mission that I can think of little else. I must be like a vacuum salesman that can talk about nothing else but selling sweepers. It must be my daily program.

The Church is my meat, my music, the very air I breathe. Only then do I have the promise that all the eternal and beautiful things of life will be given to me. Every morning I need to be seeking how I can get more missionaries on foreign fields. How can I enroll more youth in Bible Colleges to prepare for the full-time ministry of the Kingdom's King? Every day I must ask, "Who can I bless today?" "Who can I lead closer to the Kingdom today?" "Who needs love and understanding this very day?" I believe all these questions must be answered every morning if I have truly put Jesus and His Kingdom first in my heart.

Priority of the Church

Prayer

My Dear Father in Heaven, I hear Your voice like a trumpet call when You command me to seek first in my soul, the Church, the Kingdom of God. I don't want to add You to a list of many other things I consider imperative. I want to put You at the top of the list of all that I love. I want to use what time and talent I have left to expand the borders and boundaries of Your undefeatable Kingdom. Help me to ever seek righteousness and holiness and Kingdom matters that Your Church may advance and prosper. In Jesus Christ, I pray. Amen.

Questions

- What are you promised if you seek the Kingdom first in your life?

- How do you describe the Kingdom?

- What things should you consider each and every morning?

Journal

■ March 8

Dogs have surrounded me; a band of evil men has encircled me, they have pierced my hands and my feet. (Psalm 22:16)

Meditation   David Reagan

Psalm 22 was written by King David of Israel about one thousand years before Jesus was born. Yet incredibly, it describes the death of Jesus in detail, including the precise manner in which He would be killed.

Though the method of execution among the Jews was stoning, David prophesied that the Messiah would die by having His hands and feet pierced. Amazingly, this prophecy was made 700 years before the Romans perfected crucifixion as a form of execution. The psalm also prophesied that the Messiah would be deserted by His friends, and His executioners would cast lots for His clothes.

The Old Testament contains 108 separate and distinct prophesies about the Messiah, every one of which was fulfilled in the life of Jesus. These Messianic prophecies are proof positive that the Bible is the Word of God and that Jesus was the promised Messiah.

David Reagan is the Director of Lion & Lamb Ministries in McKinney, TX.

Prayer

Heavenly Father, I thank You for the way Bible prophecy confirms the authenticity of Your Word and Your Son. Help me, Lord, to believe Your Word with child-like faith, and through the power of Your Spirit, may I be obedient to Your Word and transformed by it. In Jesus' name. Amen.

Questions

- Do you believe the fulfillment of prophecy in the life of Jesus could be coincidental?

- Can you name five other specific prophecies that were fulfilled in the life of Jesus?

- Besides fulfilled prophecy, what other evidence can you think of that proves Jesus was the Messiah?

Journal

■ March 9

If you obey my commands, you will remain in my love, just as I have obeyed my Father's commands and remain in his love. I have told you this so that my joy may be in you and that your joy may be complete.

(John 15:10-11)

Meditation   *Dudley C. Rutherford*

Salvation is delightful. When Christ calls us to follow Him, He is not inviting us to a funeral parlor or concentration camp. He isn't asking us to eat a strict diet of cactus. Old Satan has marvelously tricked many into thinking that the Christian walk is dull and drab and utterly void of fun. I know one man in particular, and I swear to you, I have seen happier faces on a bottle of vinegar. A few modern day saints look like they were born in crabapple time and baptized in dill pickle juice. I know one sad lady who has a face longer than a saxophone. I had a church treasurer who walked around with a coffin under one arm and a tombstone under the other.

Oh, dear heart, if Jesus is your Savior, if Jesus has forgiven you and carefully written in crimson red your name in His Lamb's Book of Life, then you should radiate joy every day and every night. Luke writes that the faces of the apostles were of such shining courage and countenance that it was easy to detect that, "They had been with Jesus" (Acts 4:13). We cannot always be happy, but as followers of Christ we can always have joy. We might not always be giddy or giggly, but we can always have peace. Isaiah reminded us that the secret to real joy was obedience: If only you had paid attention to my commands, your peace would have been like a river, your righteousness like the waves of the sea (Isaiah 48:18).

Prayer

Thank You, precious Lord, for the perfect peace that You and You alone can give. Help me to stop chasing all the mirages that appeal so invitingly and would lure me away from true joy and happiness. Let me always know and remember that if I obey and hearken unto Your commandments, peace will flow like a river in my life and my righteousness shall spread out like the pounding waves of the sea. I ask these things in the saving name of Christ. Amen.

Questions

- If you keep Christ's commandments then your joy shall be what?

- Can the Christian always be happy?

- Name five reasons you should always have joy and peace.

Journal

Therefore, there is now no condemnation for those who are in Christ Jesus. (Romans 8:1)

That at the name of Jesus every knee should bow, in heaven and on earth and under the earth, and every tongue confess that Jesus Christ is Lord, to the glory of God the Father. (Philippians 2:9-11)

Meditation   Dudley C. Rutherford

Some day, every human that has ever breathed life on this planet will bow on his knees before Jesus Christ and confess His holy name. No one can escape this. If you don't confess Him here and now, you will some day be forced to do so. All the people who have lived before Jesus, and since Jesus, all the atheists, all the rich, poor, uneducated, heathen and every least, last, and lost soul will confess and confess quickly and convincingly, gladly, succinctly and unerringly that Jesus Christ is Lord. If you fail to confess Him here as Savior, you will some day confess Him as Judge. If you refuse to confess Him in conversion, you will confess Him in condemnation. If you refrain from confessing Him as the Lamb of God, you will confess Him as the Lion of the tribe of Judah.

This dynamic passage in Romans declares that the Christian will never face judgment, for he has settled his case out of court. Do you believe Jesus? He said in John 5:24: "Whoever hears my word and believes Him who sent me has eternal life and will not be condemned: he has crossed over from death to life." O dear friend, why not confess Him today? Remember the very same confession you make today that brings salvation, if postponed, will bring condemnation in that hour of judgment. Settle your case out of court! Jesus is the finest attorney in the world. He has never lost a case. Give Him the power of attorney right now and forever.

Confess Now or Later?

Prayer

Dear Lord Jesus, I know You are not only the Great Physician but also the Great Advocate and Attorney. I come before You today to settle my case out of court. I want to surrender my life, my love, my talent and my obedience to You this very moment. I want to skip and completely circumvent judgment. It comes as a huge relief that my Attorney is also my Savior, my friend and my judge. I confess that there is only one name, and one Lord, and one God and that One is Jesus Christ. In that same holy name I pray this prayer. Amen.

Questions

- How many in this world will confess Jesus as Lord?

- When and where did you confess Jesus as Lord?

- What is the difference between confessing Jesus as Lord and confessing Jesus as Savior?

Journal

_____

_____

_____

_____

_____

■ March 11

The king was shaken. He went up to the room over the gateway and wept.
As he went, he said: "O my son Absalom! My son, my son Absalom!
If only I had died instead of you—O Absalom, my son, my son!"

(II Samuel 18:33)

Meditation   H. Dean Rutherford

I have a son-in-law down in Florida. He is married to my daughter Dreama. They had a four-year-old boy with a brain stem tumor. Day by day, they listened to various physicians tell them there was no hope. No patient had ever recovered from such a tumor. Every doctor said he would die, and die soon. Shortly before his death, I called down there to talk with Curt, and instead Curt's mother answered the phone. I said, "How is Curt?" She said, "He is not having a good day. Just this morning, he walked into the house, screaming at the top of his voice; looking up, he said, 'God, don't ask me to give him up. Ask anything else of me but don't ask me to give him up.'" That's amazingly close to what David said, when he sobbed out, "O my son Absalom! My son, my son Absalom! If only I had died instead of you – O Absalom, my son, my son!"

I believe Jesus is saying the same thing about you today. "I can't give him up. I just can't give her up. Ask me anything but don't ask me that." If you listen with ears of faith, you can hear Christ saying, "O Bill, my son, my son. O Jim, my son, my son. O Mary, my daughter, my daughter. Would God I could take your place at judgment." But that is not just a wish or a prayer. It actually happened. Jesus took your place and He took my place on the cross.

Can't Give Him Up

Prayer

Dear Wonderful Jesus, thank You for never giving up on me. I realize that You died on the cross for my salvation. I was as lost as lost could be, yet You willingly took my place. I will forever be indebted to You, so please allow me to serve You with all my heart. I want to get deeper into Your Word and I want to be as close to You as possible. Thank You and praise You for Your eternal grace. In Your divine name, I pray. Amen.

Questions

- Can any friend or relative take your place at judgment?

- What is one of life's saddest realizations?

- Does God grieve over the thought of having to give you up?

Journal

■ March 12

Or do you think Scripture says without reason that the spirit he caused to live in us envies intensely? But he gives us more grace. That is why Scripture says: "God opposes the proud but gives grace to the humble."

(James 4:5-6)

Meditation   *Dudley C. Rutherford*

It is a scary moment when I'm driving a car and lose control. I step on the brakes but the car doesn't stop. I have my hands on the wheel but the car does not respond. I have lost control. My automobile is now at the mercy of other forces. I am its prisoner and victim. No matter what may be the cause of my lack of control, I am now helpless. What a fatal, frightful feeling! More horrifying is the fact that many persons have lost control of their spiritual lives. They are careening through life, plunging head-on toward destruction. The end – the wreck – is only a matter of time.

Somebody is in control of your life right now. If you are not in control, who is? Temper, drugs, alcohol, lust, pleasure, greed, materialism? Are you a slave to habit? Does your love for money, pleasure, position, power or social approval cause you to be controlled by them? Or do you control them? The cause of all moral and spiritual wrecks is sin. There are no moral accidents. All spiritual tragedies are the result of deliberate, willful choices.

There is only one way to regain control of your life: turn it humbly over to Christ. He can put you on the right lane and on the right road. He alone can snap the chains of sinful habit. He can cleanse you from carnal desires. He will give you a new steering wheel and give you a road map, a new purpose and new course.

Who's Driving?

Prayer

Great and exalted God, thank You for putting me on the right road, the road that leads to Heaven and eternal life. I pray that my life will never be out of control and that I will always make sure that You place Your hands on the wheel and be my guide and my direction. I know there are so many forces and sins that would desire me to get off track and lose control of my future destiny with You. Keep me strong and safe in Your hands. I pray in Jesus' name. Amen.

Questions

- What happens if you try to come near to God?

- Name some things that might control you.

- How can you get the control back in His hands?

Journal

> *He ran to his son, threw his arms around him and kissed him. The son said to him, "Father, I have sinned against heaven and against you. I am no longer worthy to be called your son." But the father said to his servants, "Quick! Bring the best robe and put it on him. Put a ring on his finger and sandals on his feet. Bring the fattened calf and kill it. Let's have a feast and celebrate. For this son of mine was dead and is alive again; he was lost and is found." So they began to celebrate. (Luke 15:17-24)*

Meditation   *Dudley C. Rutherford*

Our God is a genius at turning tragedy into triumph. I thrill to watch Him at work. There is an old, old fable that tells the story of the tree from which Adam and Eve partook in the Garden of Eden. One of the seeds of that tree survived several centuries and grew into another tree, from which they took the lumber to fashion the cross upon which Jesus died. Yes, it is just an old legend, but there is a haunting truth contained therein. The Almighty took the very instrument of our initial sin and transformed it into a device for salvation.

Remember that drama back in Exodus 21 when God sent poisonous snakes into the camp, because the people had complained against Him while He was in the process of attempting to redeem them? Many were dying but God said, "Put a snake of brass on a high pole and everyone who looks at it will live." The very thing that had stricken them now could be their salvation. That's just like my God! Look what He did at Calvary! He turned the scene of execution into an act of redemption. He turned the pain and suffering of the crucifixion into a power source of salvation. That's the way He works. From bad to great! He wants to do that with your life and mine. He wants to take someone that's fallen many times and is sinfully miserable, and turn him or her into something that will be a thing of beauty forever. If you have not fully surrendered to Him yet, will you do so now?

Poisonous Snakes

Prayer

Dear Everlasting Father, I know You hate nothing You have made and that You are quick to forgive the sins of all who are penitent. Spare all those who this day confess and repent of their transgressions. Give me the extra strength and determination to live so close to You that I will become an example of Your marvelous ability to change bad into good, and sin into glory. I want others to look at me and say, "Look what *God* has done." In the eternal name of Jesus, I pray. Amen.

Questions

- Have you read the story of the prodigal son in Luke 15?

- Have you read about the serpent of brass in Exodus 21?

- When is God at His very best?

Journal

_____

_____

_____

_____

_____

He who began a good work in you will carry it on to completion until the day of Christ Jesus. (Philippians 1:6)

Continue to work out your salvation with fear and trembling, for it is God who works in you to will and to act according to his good purpose.
(Philippians 2:12-13)

Meditation David Roadcup

In the above verses, God makes us an amazing promise. If our hearts are open and we are willing to follow His lead, once we come to Christ and accept Him as our Savior, God begins the amazing work of bringing us to maturity. That's exactly what Philippians tells us. Because God loves us, after we come to faith in Christ, He will begin the process of using people, circumstances, His Word and other factors to bring us to a level of spiritual maturity, discernment and sensitivity.

When parents bring their child home from the hospital after birth and you ask them how the child is doing, they will always reply in quantitative terms. "He has grown one inch and put on six ounces!" Things that are alive grow and eventually come to maturity. Our verses today tell us that God makes us this promise: God will continually pursue the process of bringing us to maturity. It is one of His major roles in our lives. He wants us to grow in our walk with Christ, to become spiritually discerning, personally pure and morally solid. He wants us to become as much like Jesus in our daily lives as possible. So know that you are "in process" now and as long as you are willing, will be, until the day Jesus returns or we go to be with the Lord. Enjoy the journey!

David Roadcup is the Executive Director of the Center for Church Advancement and Professor at Cincinnati Christian University in Cincinnati, OH.

Prayer

Holy Father, I thank You that You love me so much that You are willing to continue to motivate, move, discipline and encourage me to grow in my relationship with You. Help me to do all that I can to assist You with that process. Please forgive me when I resist Your teaching or leading. And Father, do everything You can to make me as much like Jesus as possible. In His name. Amen.

Questions

- Who has God been using in your life to mold and direct you in your spiritual pilgrimage?

- Can you think of a circumstance the Lord used in the last month to teach you an important lesson?

- What attitude does the Lord want you to have on a daily basis toward this process He has you in?

Journal

_____

_____

_____

_____

■ March 15

If we claim to be without sin, we deceive ourselves and the truth is not in us. If we confess our sins, he is faithful and just and will forgive us our sins and purify us from all unrighteousness. If we claim we have not sinned, we make him out to be a liar and his word has no place in our lives. (I John 1:8-10)

Meditation   *Dudley C. Rutherford*

God commands us to confess our sins. Church is not a good place for this, because you will need more time and quiet than is usually allowed. Find a good, solitary place, kneel down and ask the Holy Spirit to help you in your confession. I usually begin by reading such penitential psalms as Chapter 51. It is good to take a piece of paper and write down the sins you can remember. Specificity is a must! Spell it out to God. He wants to know that you know. If you can't think of any, go to the Ten Commandments (Exodus 20), and let that list stir your memory. You can also write down sins into two categories: sins of omission (good things we fail to do) and sins of commission (bad things we commit). I know some folks who put down three categories of sin: sins against God; sins against my fellow man; and sins against myself. Of course, some sins seem to be more destructive to your neighbor or yourself. All sin is against God.

No need to write down details – just a word or two to trigger your memory. Then you will need to spend some serious time in prayer while confessing your sins. Maintain the list and go back in a few days to see if you have made spiritual progress. God wants you to confess your sins in the hope that if you actually know what your sin is, by that very knowledge and confession, you might just be willing to forsake and refrain from such transgressions. Rest assured the moment you confess your sins, God is faithful and will forgive you of your sins.

Confession

Prayer

Dear God, I thank You for making a way for me to have my sins expunged from my dismal record. Grant that through Your cross, my sins may be put forever away and placed in the sea of God's forgetfulness. Create in me a clean heart and renew in me a right spirit, so that when I sin, I shall immediately come to Your throne and confess in a specific way the details of my sin and seek Your immediate forgiveness. I take up my cross daily and follow You. In the name of Jesus Christ, I pray. Amen

Questions

- Is church a good place to make a thorough confession?

- If God knows everything, why does he want you to confess?

- What happens to your sins after you confess them? (See text above.)

Journal

■ March 16

To him who overcomes, I will give some of the hidden manna. I will also give him a white stone with a new name written on it, known only to him who receives it. (Revelation 2:17)

The people of Israel called the bread manna. It was white like coriander seed and tasted like wafers made with honey. (Exodus 16:31)

Meditation   Dudley C. Rutherford

The Bible closes with God's promise to give the hidden manna to the redeemed. You remember what manna from Heaven is, don't you? Way back yonder in the Old Testament, when God's people were being freed from slavery and were wandering the wilderness, they had no food, no convenience stores, no 7-11's, no concession stands, no supermarkets or warehouse stores. God sent down from Heaven a miraculous bread called manna. I have always called manna "God's Heavenly honey buns." The manna was a wafer-like bread or pastry that fell each morning. The people of God would wake up, run outside and gather up from the ground this miracle bread called manna. It was manna that sustained them, fed them, kept them and nourished them. Without manna, they would have died. They would have covered the desert sands with their carcasses.

Now in God's last will and testament called Revelation, God promises that some way, somehow, in Heaven, the saved will have a new hidden manna. Scholars have determined that the hidden manna is none other that the matchless Christ. Jesus will be our bread! Not only is He the Bread of Life in this world, but He will also be the Bread of Life in the next. Jesus has not been seen for over 2,000 years; thus He is called the Hidden Manna. I think God is saying: Don't worry or fret about what you are going to eat in Heaven. Don't worry about being sustained in Glory land. We will have the Hidden Manna, Jesus Christ, on which to feed. And all God's people said, "Amen!"

Heavenly Honey Buns

Prayer

Dear Savior of mine, You are the source of life. You are the One who gave me hunger, and You are the One who provides for my food. I know You fed and sustained our forefathers in the wilderness and that You can sustain me in Heaven. Your presence, light and glory will be all I will ever need in that perfect land. I know that if You can feed the little birds here, that You can sustain me in that celestial land You are now preparing. I will always feed on You. In Jesus' name, I pray. Amen.

Questions

- What is manna?

- Have you read the 16th Chapter of Exodus?

- Do you feel that Jesus is the One who is sustaining you today?

Journal

_____

_____

_____

_____

_____

■ March 17

For, "All men are like grass, and all their glory is like the flowers of the field; the grass withers and the flowers fall, but the word of the Lord stands forever." And this is the word that was preached to you.

(I Peter 1:24-25)

Meditation   *Dudley C. Rutherford*

The first steel skyscraper was built in New York back in the 1880's by architect Bradford Gilbert. It was to be a steel frame building, 13 stories high and only 21 feet wide. People said it couldn't be done; that it would never withstand high winds. In 1886, when the building was ten stories high, New York was hit by 80-mile-per-hour winds. Crowds gathered to watch the building blow down. But Gilbert himself went to the top of the building at the height of the storm and let down a plumb line. He proved the structure had not moved and that it was safe and secure.

Architect Gilbert knew he was right all along. His faith was founded on the forces of engineering, gravity and stress built into the universe by the Creator. Our magnificent skyscrapers stand tall and erect today, because man has put to use the materials and laws of God's universe. So it is with human lives that stand up to the blasts and stresses of living. The winds blow at gale force at times. Doubts and fears arise that will not go away. Change, sorrow, ill health and death are the lot of us all who live upon this earth. Evil influences challenge the very foundation of truth and goodness.

We need something more than our own skills and wisdom to deal with these things. The structure of our lives must be grounded on God's Word and Law. Only then can we weather any tempest that blows. In His Word only do we find refuge from wind and decay.

Prayer

Dear God in Heaven, I want to build my life on the right foundation, the word of God that endures forever. I don't want to collapse from storm and adversity. I want to prove to You and to my family, friends and myself that my life is built on the Bible. May You help me to be disciplined to read it, study it, love it and memorize it. Lastly, help me to apply it and share it. In Christ's name, I pray. Amen.

Questions

- How are you like grass and flowers?

- What is not like grass and flowers?

- How much time do you set aside for studying God's word?

Journal

_____

_____

_____

_____

_____

> *Then know this, you and all the people of Israel: It is by the name of Jesus Christ of Nazareth, whom you crucified but whom God raised from the dead, that this man stands before you healed. Salvation is found in no one else, for there is no other name under heaven given to men by which we must be saved. (Acts 4:10, 12)*

Meditation   *Dudley C. Rutherford*

Years ago, a fire burned joy out of hearts and homes in Camden, South Carolina. A wooden schoolhouse caught fire and 70 young souls perished in only minutes of time. Horror-stricken parents raced to the rescue. In fleeting moments, the school had become a deathtrap. During the heroic attempts at rescue, one little boy looked out though the burning inferno and spotting his dad, screamed, "Daddy can't you save me?" The father, suffering an eternity of torture, could not save him. In fact, the dad did not live long. His hair turned white and his health broke, because night and day he could not stop hearing that cry, "Daddy, can't you save me?"

Our old Bible-bankrupt world cries out to Medicine, "Medicine, can't you save me?"

Medicine answers, "With a little luck, I may medicate you and patch you up and help you to live a few years longer, but I cannot save you."

Our pleasure-seeking generation calls out to Science, "Can't you save me?"

"No. I can give you computers, wireless palm pilots, technology, laser beams, gadgets and toys, but I am not in the saving business."

This lost, Christ-less culture cries out to Education, "Can't you save me?"

"I can give you facts and data ad infinitum, but I cannot save you."

Then the world turns to Jesus and cries out, "Jesus, can't you save me?"

Jesus answers, "Him that comes to me I will in no way cast out." He answers, "For the Son of Man came to seek and to save what was lost."

Prayer

Dear loving Father, I know I have only one problem and that is I desperately need my many sins forgiven. I know there is only one person, one source, one power and one name that can forgive to the uttermost and that name is Jesus. Help me to stop trusting in those things that may seem for the moment to make me happy, but in reality cannot save me and in fact cannot forgive a single sin. I put all my trust in You. In Christ's glorious name, I pray. Amen.

Questions

- Who is the only One who can heal and save?

- How will medicine and science eventually fail you?

- How exactly does Jesus save?

Journal

Jesus said to Simon Peter, "Simon son of John, do you truly love me more than these?" "Yes, Lord," he said, "you know that I love you." Jesus said, "Feed my lambs." Again Jesus said, "Simon son of John, do you truly love me?" He answered, "Yes, Lord, you know that I love you." Jesus said, "Take care of my sheep." (John 21:15-16)

Meditation   *Dudley C. Rutherford*

The silver morning mist arises from Galilee, as we see Jesus speaking to His disciples after His resurrection. Jesus looks at Peter and three times asks, "Do you love Me more than these?" This is a vital question. This is recorded in the last chapter of the last Gospel and it is the last question our Lord asked during His earthly ministry. What does this haunting and disturbing question mean? Was Jesus pointing to the boats, the fish, the nets, the sea and all the things that make up our material lives? Was He saying, "Do you love Me more than houses, land, bank accounts, things or clothes?" Or was He pointing to the rest of the disciples? Are you in love with Me Peter, or are you just trying to outdo the other apostles? Have you sought your own advantage rather than My glory?

Whatever the question meant, one thing we know for certain: That feeding lambs is the correct answer and proof that we love Him. No other proof will do! Every other response is bogus. Any other answer is treason. Jesus' last question demands an answer! If my answer is yes, then I have no choice but to busy my life with the feeding of His sheep, the spreading of the Gospel and giving encouragement to the weak and the wayward. Conclusion: Either we give this love away or we lose it. If we are not daily sharing this love, then the answer to our Lord's daunting question is "No."

Three Questions

Prayer

Dear Lord, help me to answer Your outstanding question and answer it correctly. Help me to so love You that I cannot help but share Your glory and victory with others. Forgive me when I selfishly want to keep my salvation a secret. May my heart hold such love that I will not and cannot refrain from sharing it with Your other sheep. May my life be so beautiful that others will want what I possess. May I be eager to distribute my life to others. I ask in the name of Christ. Amen.

Questions

- Do you love Jesus?

- If your answer is "Yes," what must you be busy doing?

- When will you start?

Journal

■ March 20

My heart is not proud, O Lord, my eyes are not haughty; I do not concern myself with great matters or things too wonderful for me. But I have stilled and quieted my soul; like a weaned child with its mother, like a weaned child is my soul within me. O Israel, put your hope in the Lord both now and forevermore.   (Psalm 131:1-3)

Meditation   *Francis Chan*

During Christmas Eve service, I thought about checking myself into the emergency room. My heart was beating irregularly. In 37 years, I had never felt a bit of irregularity. I was scared. When service was over, I prayed. The more I prayed, the more I was convinced my condition was caused by stress. Unlike the Psalmist, who did not concern himself "with great matters or things too wonderful," I was trying too hard to accomplish things that were out of my control. Unlike the Psalmist, who was "not proud," I was arrogant and believed I could make things happen. The Psalmist had a soul that resembled a "weaned child with its mother." My soul was like a two-year-old running about frantically, trying to accomplish as much as he could to please his Father. God doesn't want us worrying about and trying to solve the problems of the world. He wants us to rest in Him. As I learned this truth, my heart problems went away. And I saved myself a trip to the hospital.

Francis Chan is the Senior Pastor of Cornerstone Community Church, Simi Valley, CA.

A Peaceful Heart

Prayer

Father, I surrender my worries to You now. Forgive me for my arrogance in thinking that I had control over these situations. Help me to rest in Your sovereignty. You control all things, and You love me. I have nothing to fear. The God of the Universe is my Dad. Help me to still my soul and just enjoy being in Your arms today. Thank You so much for loving me, protecting me, guiding me and using me.

Questions

- Does your soul look anything like a "weaned child with its mother"?

- Do you spend more time focusing on your problems or on your God?

- Would those around you label you as a person who is at peace?

Journal

Come, all you who are thirsty, come to the waters; and you who have no money, come, buy and eat! Come, buy wine and milk without money and without cost. Why spend money on what is not bread, and your labor on what does not satisfy? Listen, listen to me, and eat what is good, and your soul will delight in the richest of fare. (Isaiah 55:1-2)

Meditation   *Dudley C. Rutherford*

Guy de Maupassant's story, "The Necklace," tells the tragic story of a girl named Mathilde. Invited to an exclusive and elegant dance, she borrowed a most costly necklace from a rich friend. The necklace had its intended effect, as many complimented her beauty that night. Horror of all horrors, she lost the necklace. She was so ashamed to confess it to her friend; she purchased a necklace just like it the next day for 40,000 francs. She gave it to her wealthy friend and did not tell her about the one she lost. She and her husband labored overtime and at many extra jobs trying to pay off the loan for the replaced necklace. Finally paid off, Mathilde spoke to her rich friend and confessed to her that they had slaved for ten years to pay for the replacement. The rich friend replied, "What a shame. The necklace was imitation and almost worthless. It was made of paste."

This story is a perfect picture of us when we spend our time and energy on things of little value. Isaiah asked this pointed question: "Why will you spend money on what is not bread, and why will you labor for things that cannot satisfy?" Many have spent a lifetime trying to buy into the world's system and its pleasure, which always ends up in the "paste" category. The nonbeliever's life is a life of chasing mirages. The treasures of the world always seem so real, but they are phony and fake.

Prayer

My gracious Lord and Savior, thank You that You have allowed me to choose the best, the pure, the real and the lasting. Forgive me when I go chasing those things that can never shed light or dry a tear or fill a heart with truth and joy. Forgive me for wanting those cheap things that, if my heart were right, I would never want in the first place. I want to spend my life's love and energy on those things that satisfy. I want to drink the water of life and eat the bread of life freely. In the Savior's name, I pray. Amen.

Questions

- Name some false things you've chased and labored for.

- Why do these "things" never bring true joy?

- In the long history of mankind, what is the only thing that satisfies?

Journal

_____

_____

_____

_____

■ March 22

On the evening of that first day of the week, when the disciples were together, with the doors locked for fear of the Jews, Jesus came and stood among them and said, "Peace be with you!" (John 20:19)

Meditation   *Fred Rodkey*

Disappointment seems to be a part of everyday life anymore. Bad grades at school, bad reports from the doctor, bad news at work, and the list goes on. The followers of Jesus knew that same feeling. Their King, their Messiah had been executed and laid in the tomb, and they were in fear of what might happen to them next. They had so longed for the King to establish His authority, and now He was dead. Disappointed? Yes. And in that room, they were looking at the walls, the floor, the people in the street below and every one of them was looking inside themselves.

Maybe their disappointment came from how they reacted to the bad news. We've been there. We can't seem to find a way out of the hurt. Despair robs us of hope. Life seems too heavy. Then we turn to the One who took the downward pull of the grave and changed it into the upward call of God for each one of us. "Peace" comes from Jesus, and our trust in His perfect love will cast out our fear.

Fred Rodkey is Senior Pastor at Chapel Rock Christian Church in Indianapolis, IN.

Prayer

Father in Heaven, when things get heavy and I seem to be stuck in the disappointments and despair of this life, help me to look to You, my only true source of peace. Teach me, Lord, to put my trust in You, my hope in Your mighty hands, and my fears in proper perspective. In Jesus' name. Amen.

Questions

- What disappointment is robbing you of joy?

- Have you looked inside yourself to see how you are reacting and why?

- Do you trust God? If not, why not?

Journal

■ March 23

From this time many of his disciples turned back and no longer followed him. "You do not want to leave too, do you?" Jesus asked the Twelve. Simon Peter answered him, "Lord, to whom shall we go? You have the words of eternal life. We believe and know that you are the Holy One of God." (John 6:66-69)

Meditation   *Dudley C. Rutherford*

Jesus had preached a sermon so demanding and so hard that people were evacuating His audience in droves. Jesus knew even His own disciples were contemplating abandoning ship. Jesus pierced their hearts with an arrow when He queried, "Do you want to leave also?" Leave it to Peter! Peter cut to the chase and summarized the entire problem by asking, "Lord, to whom shall we go?" My, my, my, what a question! He could have easily asked, "Lord, *when* shall we go?" Speculation about dates, times and seasons fascinates us. Peter knew that in the company of Jesus all possible endings or eventualities would be divinely and perfectly handled. Peter could have asked, "Lord, *where* shall we go?" Peter also knew that "where" doesn't make any difference if Jesus is there!

I remember my own home when I was just a boy. I can remember many things about the house, but what made the house wasn't the carpet or the rooms; it was the presence of Mom and Dad. I'm humbled when my wife and family infer they would move anywhere, as long as I would be there. Christ is the centerpiece of Heaven. Going to Heaven is not going to a place; it is going to a person. Peter didn't ask, "Lord, when shall we go?" or "Where shall we go?" He asked the Lord, "To *whom* shall we go?" Who else has the words of eternal life? Who else can save us? Who else has power over sin and death?

What A Question!

We know, dear Father, that in this world of sin, decay and death there is only One who has the words of eternal life. That One is You, the Lord Jesus Christ. Help me, dear Lord, to start learning and memorizing the language of that eternal fellowship. That we are going from one place to another, or going today or tomorrow is of little consequence. What matters is that You will be there and we will be with You if we hear and obey Your words for eternal life. In Christ's name, I pray. Amen.

Questions

- Why were people leaving Jesus?

- If you left Jesus, where would you go?

- Who alone can save?

Journal

_____

_____

_____

_____

March 24

Someone in the crowd said to him, "Teacher, tell my brother to divide the inheritance with me." Jesus replied, "Man, who appointed me a judge or an arbiter between you?" (Luke 12:13-14)

Meditation   *Dudley C. Rutherford*

In this scene, our Lord is masterfully teaching, as no one else can, when all of a sudden a raspy voice interrupts, "Lord, tell my brother to divide the inheritance with me."

Our Lord refused to get involved when He said, "Who made me a referee between you and your brother?" Jesus was saying that to get involved over something so useless would be a waste of everyone's time. Then He dropped the hammer: "Watch out! Be aware that greed comes in all forms." Then Jesus made a statement for all the ages, but which no age ever needed more than the one in which we live: "A man's life does not consist in the abundance of his possessions." Did you hear that right? Would you read that again? Do you believe Jesus knew what He was talking about?

Number ten on the list of the Ten Commandments (Exodus 20:17) says, "You shall not covet (be greedy for) your neighbor's house. You shall not covet your neighbor's wife, or his manservant or maidservant, his ox or donkey, or anything that belongs to your neighbor." The Tenth Commandment is another way of saying that greed comes in all forms. Question: If life does not consist of material or fleshly possessions, then what makes life worth living? The Bible does not abandon us at this critical point. Luke 12:21 plainly imparts to us that we are to be rich toward God. Are you ready now for the question of your life: How do you become rich toward God? Are you brave enough to face and answer that life-changing question?

Abundance of Possessions

Dear God, I recognize that I am basically selfish and materialistic. I am now confessing my sin and I seek Your forgiveness. I am coming to You to put my greed in subjection to Your will. I want Your Spirit to touch my heart and renew my selfish mind. I want to be rich only toward You. That is my goal. I do not want to seek materialism or even happiness; I want to seek holiness, knowing that You will then supply all my inner and outer needs. In Jesus' name, I pray. Amen.

Questions

- What is the difference between Christ's teaching and the current teaching of our world?

- Name some forms in which greed may appear.

- What specifically do you need to repent for?

Journal

_____

_____

_____

_____

March 25

To the Jews who had believed him, Jesus said, "If you hold to my teaching, you are really my disciples. Then you will know the truth, and the truth will set you free." (John 8:31-32)

Meditation   *Gary York*

The second of the two verses listed above is one of the most famous statements in all the Scripture. It is quoted all the time, generally by people who take it out of context. Let's put it in context and let it redefine our perspective on spiritual growth. The word "hold" is a key to the meaning and application of what Jesus is saying in verse 31. Jesus is saying, "I know it's tough at times, and the things I teach are certainly outside your upbringing, and may even go against all your parents taught you; but if you hang with Me, I will redefine and realign your life. Don't retreat or run away. Even if what I say is uncomfortable, offensive or seemingly impractical, keep trying it. Over time, a redefinition of your life will begin to emerge."

Then (don't slide past that word in verse 32, because the rest of the verse doesn't make sense without it), after you've absorbed Jesus' teaching, accepted and started practicing His teaching, and submitted yourself to His teaching (that's what it means to "hold" or "abide"), it makes sense. You will begin to understand it, and grasp the reality of it, along with the changes it makes in you. Then you will escape the condemnation of sin and fear of the future; find joy though your kids went haywire; recover from an ugly divorce; find forgiveness following an affair; break free from sinful habits; and discover a meaningful life though your spouse recently died. When you stand in the light of Jesus' teaching long enough, His truth will redefine your life.

Gary York is Senior Pastor of Eastview Christian Church in Normal, IL.

178

Prayer

Heavenly Father, I praise You for this bountiful promise. Only someone with Your power could make it possible. I commit today to soak up and abide in Jesus' teaching, even if I don't understand it. I will set my heart toward obedience and know that my emotions will catch up over time. Please help me succeed. I long for a fresh start and a redefinition of my life for the future. I offer these things in Jesus' name. Amen.

Questions

- Do you find Jesus' teaching too offensive at times? Why?

- Do you really seek to know the God of the Bible… or what you've made Him up to be?

- What's holding you captive?

Journal

March 26

Command those who are rich in this present world not to be arrogant nor to put their hope in wealth, which is so uncertain, but to put their hope in God, who richly provides us with everything for our enjoyment.

(I Timothy 6:17)

Meditation   Dudley C. Rutherford

Jesus had more to say about money than He said about Heaven and hell put together. Money is the second most talked about subject in the Bible. Nearly one half of his 37 parables are about stewardship and money. One out of every six verses in the Gospels is about money so, if God wants us to talk about anything, He wants us to talk about this. Why did He talk about money so often? Not to get money for Himself. He never took up a collection, never passed the plate that we know of. The only possession He owned was a robe that He wore.

Jesus talked about money because He knew money was the heart's biggest competitor. Jesus wanted man to serve Him with the same intensity that He displays everyday when He rises and goes to work and labors all day just to earn some money. He knew that money would make us shortsighted and cause us to think there is nothing else in life that matters. It is very easy and almost natural to make ministering to our physical needs and desires paramount. The long history of mankind proves that when we put money first and make it our god, we will always end up disillusioned and filled with failure and gross disappointment. Here is a truth which no age has ever needed more: When we give our lives to material acquisitions, we eventually discover that the things it buys or life itself is not worth having.

His Only Possession

Prayer

Help me remember, dear God, that my money belongs to You. May I use it for Your glory and Your Kingdom. Keep me from making it the center of my life. Strange, but when I pursue money I always end up spiritually bankrupt. When I pursue holiness, I end up being more spiritual and always having more than enough of the necessary things of life. Dear God, help me to live by faith and not by sight. In Jesus' name, I pray. Amen.

Questions

- Why do you think the Bible talks so much about money and material possessions?

- How does the love of money make you shortsighted?

- Why does one's giving truly reflect what's in a person's heart?

Journal

March 27

But now that you have been set free from sin and have become slaves to God, the benefit you reap leads to holiness, and the result is eternal life. For the wages of sin is death, but the gift of God is eternal life in Christ Jesus our Lord. (Romans 6:22-23)

Meditation   *Dudley C. Rutherford*

We sometimes start believing that because everything else in our culture has changed, maybe God has changed. Maybe the Bible has changed. Truth is: nothing important has changed. The wages of sin is exactly the same today as it was in the Garden of Eden. That is *death*. Sin still pays off in the same wages. No discounts. The cost of a lie will still cost you someone's trust. Unchecked, it will lead you to the same end as Ananias and Sapphira. No radical change in culture can lessen the cost of a lie. The cost of jealousy is still the same. It will gnaw on you like a cancer. Unchecked, it will lead you to the same action when Cain killed his brother Abel. Cheating and lust will still cost you the same. There are no bigger sins.

There may be more sinners but there are no new sins. Death, Heaven, hell, eternity and the Bible are still the same. Sin will make you pay your wage whether you live in the ritzy section of town or the slums. Preachers may change. Creeds may change. The culture in which we live may change. Styles and fashions may change, but Jesus and His Word never change. Sin slaves, but Christ saves. Please, dear heart, don't get to thinking that maybe, just maybe God and Christ have changed since there is so much change everywhere around us. The Old Testament closes with these words of Malachi: "I, the Lord, do not change" (Malachi 3:6).

Prayer

Dear Father, I am so grateful that I serve a God who never changes, a God that will keep His word no matter how many changes take place in my world. I am the one who needs to change – change into Your likeness by the simple, child-like faith in my heart. Help me to remember that no one can ever win the sin game. May I also remember that everyone wins the obedience game. Thank You for never changing and for making it possible for me to have eternal life with You. In Christ's name, I pray. Amen.

Questions

- How would you describe sin?

- What does it mean: the wages of sin is death?

- What is God's great gift to the faithful, obedient believer?

Journal

■ March 28

If I had cherished sin in my heart, the Lord would not have listened; but God has surely listened and heard my voice in prayer. (Psalm 66:18-19)

Meditation   *Jane Kasel*

The key to opening up God's ears, the channel between you and Him, is confession and repentance of sin. When we hold on to "our rights," our issues," "our thoughts," and idolize "our justification," we stifle the line of communication with the Lord.

We must always begin prayer asking Him to "Search me, O God, and know my heart; test me and know my anxious thoughts" (Psalm 139:23). Anxiety is sin, from God's point of view; it says to Him that we do not trust Him in all things. Hanging on to stress says we don't think He is in control.

It's when we massage the issues of our lives over and over in our minds, rather than trusting them to Jesus, that we crowd out any room in our hearts for Him to speak. Instead, we need to turn off all the "noise" (our thoughts, TV, radio, cell phones) to be still and know He is God (Psalm 46:10).

This decision not only opens up the lines of communication with God but also gives us receptive ears that truly "hear." Then we can rejoice and say, "Praise be to God who has not rejected my prayer, not withheld His love from me!"

With a cleansed heart and mind set not on our problems, but rather fixed on His lips, the watching and waiting results in a deep, inner connection where we hear Jesus with pristine clarity.

Jane Kasel is a member of Shepherd of the Hills Church, Porter Ranch, CA.

Open Up the Lines

Prayer

Dear Heavenly Father, thank You that Jesus' shed blood has opened up the way to You and allowed the Holy Spirit to descend, so that we would have two intercessors in Heaven, Jesus and the Holy Spirit. As I come boldly before Your throne of grace, I am grateful that through confession of sin and true repentance, I can know that I am forgiven and free to hear Your voice saying, "This is the way, walk in it" (Isaiah 30:21). Thank You for unstopping my ears. Speak, Father. Your servant is listening.

Questions

- Is there any sin that is un-confessed that might be making your communication with the Lord "fuzzy"?

- In what areas of your life are you keeping secret or separate from the Lordship of Christ?

- What would your family and friends say about whether you "hear" from the Lord?

Journal

■ March 29

"This is my blood of the covenant, which is poured out for many," he said to them. "I tell you the truth, I will not drink again of the fruit of the vine until that day when I drink it anew in the kingdom of God."

(Mark 14:24-25)

Meditation   Dudley C. Rutherford

Jimmy Davis, the former Governor of Louisiana, used to sing an old country western hit, "Come home. Come home. It's supper time." The gist of the song is recalling the days of his youth, when evening would come and the shadows were lengthening fast and his mother would step out on the back steps and call, "Come home, come home, it's supper time." All of us can remember the deep emotions of being called at supper time. There is something quite extraordinary about this simple ceremony: sitting around a table at the end of the day, with those we love and who love us. We know this meal will satisfy and provide all of our needs for the rest of that day. It signals we are gravitating toward the end of the day's journey and that we have been taken good care of. Then the songwriter says as wonderful as that childhood experience was, it will be far greater to come to the end of life's journey to hear Jesus step from the Portals of Glory and call, "Come home. Come home. It's supper time."

Jesus used this same metaphor when describing the Lord's Supper. In Mark 14:25, Jesus promised His disciples that He would share this supper with them in the next world. What a scene! Who can imagine the pathos and splendor of that supper time? The big question is, are you ready? Are you prepared? Are you anticipating this grand reunion? It may be tomorrow but it may be today!

Supper Time

Prayer

Dear Lord, we look forward to being in church and enjoying supper time around Your table of Communion. And we greatly anticipate the great supper time and that special table You have been working on for the past 2,000 years. Someday we will sit with You around the table of eternal salvation and thank You for the victory. I look forward to that day when You shall say, "Come home. Come home. It's supper time." I want to be ready when that hour arrives. I pray this earnest prayer in the name of Jesus. Amen.

Questions

- When will the real suppertime come?

- Where in the Bible did Jesus make this promise?

- What can you do to get ready for that suppertime?

Journal

March 30

We love because he first loved us. (I John 4:19)

This is love: not that we loved God, but that he loved us and sent his Son as an atoning sacrifice for our sins. (I John 4:10)

Meditation   *Dudley C. Rutherford*

One version of an often-told story goes like this: A man named Ed had restored his MG sports car to perfection. He had carefully and, at great expense, restored it to showroom condition. He washed and polished it often and fussed over it like a restless mother hen fusses over her chicks. One day Beth, his wife, had to run an errand and her car wouldn't start for some reason, so she reluctantly took Ed's MG. She knew she had to be extra careful because she knew how much this car meant to him. As fate would have it, she had only driven a few miles from home when the unthinkable happened. Another car ran a stop sign and crashed broadside into her. Beth wasn't seriously hurt, but the entire right side of the MG was crumpled.

When the police arrived and asked for registration papers, she opened the glove box and there she saw a large plain envelope with her name on it. With her shaking hands, she opened the large envelope marked "Beth." She read these words: "Dear Beth: If you are reading this, you have probably been in an accident. Please, please don't worry for a minute about the car. I pray you are all right because, remember, it's you that I love – not the car. All my love, Ed."

Do you know, that is just how Jesus feels about you? No matter how you may think you have wrecked and ruined your life, remember it is *you* that He still loves and has always loved. Will you forget about the past and give your heart to the Lord today?

Prayer

Dear Father, dear loving Father, dear ever and always loving Father, I do thank You that before I was ever born, You knew me and loved me. Even though You knew I would be unlovely, You still overlooked my faults and died for me. I do love You, but I'm afraid my love pales in contrast with Your unfathomable love. I cannot love on Your perfect level, but I can try to live a Christian life of service and devotion to You. Bless me as I pray this prayer in the name of Jesus. Amen.

Questions

- Name some Christ-like qualities that Ed possessed?

- If you were ten times more sinful, yet repented, would God still forgive you?

- How does God express His love for you?

Journal

March 31

I waited patiently for the Lord. (Psalm 40:1a)

...be patient with everyone. (I Thessalonians 5:14b)

Meditation   George Taggart

Throughout Scripture, the word "patience" comes up again and again. Why is the Holy Spirit declaring this message over and over to us? I thought the root of being a patient man was acting in self-controlled ways while grinning and bearing it. Now in part that is true, but that is not what has produced the fruit of patience in my life. The root of being patient is not refraining from acting in an impatient way; rather, it is acting in an understanding way. That's right. *Understanding.*

When I am understanding of people, circumstances and events, I find myself being patient. As with the coming of the Lord... I understand it is His timing, so I am patient. When suffering, I understand God's work in my life, even when it is not revealed; I am patient, knowing He is working. When others are unkind, unfair or just irritating to me, I realize it is about understanding those people and their circumstances, and I find myself patient. To be understanding is to make sense of a matter, to perceive, to be aware, to grasp, to figure out, to sympathize and to take in. Do that, and you will be pleasantly surprised, as the sweet fruit of patience is manifested in greater measure in your life. If patience has been eluding you as a believer, pray.

George Taggart is a member at Discovery Church in Simi Valley, CA.

Prayer

Father in Heaven, I do struggle with being patient. I have tried over and over to grin and bear it, thinking this is what You want, and still I fail to be patient. Now I ask that You give me a spirit of wisdom and understanding, so that I might bear richly the fruit of patience. Open Your word to me, so that in understanding, I will find patience expressed in my life as I never thought possible. Make my life impact others for Your glory, beginning in my home. In Jesus' name, I pray. Amen.

Questions

- Do you know what understanding is?

- Think about the times you have been impatient. Did you find that it was your lack of understanding of the situation?

- I know a number of stories in the Bible in which lack of understanding created impatience and understanding brought forth patience. Can you find at least two?

Journal

For we do not have a high priest who is unable to sympathize with our weaknesses, but we have one who has been tempted in every way, just as we are—yet was without sin. (Hebrews 4:15)

Meditation   *Dudley C. Rutherford*

Jesus, in His final hours of passion leading up to His death, suffered every known kind of pain: physical, mental and spiritual. No other could suffer nor has suffered as He did. In the realm of bodily pain there are five types of suffering:

1. Concussion – caused by being violently hit or beaten by a bloodthirsty mob.
2. Laceration – when the flesh is cut and torn, such as thongs at the end of the scourging whip.
3. Penetration – when the skin and joints are opened by sharp piercings; this describes the thorns that punctured and pierced His sinless brow.
4. Perforation – when holes are opened by the pressure from external objects; great spikes were driven through His holy hands and feet.
5. Incision – when cuts are made into the skin and muscles; the sharp spear not only penetrated His side but also sliced it open until both water and blood flowed out of His body.

Jesus suffered all five of these physical wounds. Strange as it may seem, His bodily suffering was the least painful. It was His mental anguish that shook Jesus to His inner depths. Jesus suffered loneliness, rejection and misunderstanding. As terrible as those physical and mental wounds were, those of the spirit were worst of all. Jesus carried the combined sins of all men. They fell in and crushed Him. His spiritual heart was broken and it affected His physical heart, so that the elastic sac surrounding this organ was broken and out poured blood and water. Yes… "He was pierced for our transgressions, he was crushed for our iniquities" (Isaiah 53:5).

Five Kinds of Wounds

Dear precious Lamb of God, I know that no one ever suffered like You. You have been tempted, punished, tortured and tried in every possible way. You have not only endured it all but You went through the hot fires without sinning. I now know that I have a high priest who has suffered everything I am called upon to experience and that You are the One who can sustain and understand my sufferings. Thank You for suffering and dying for me on Calvary's cross. In Christ's suffering name, I pray. Amen.

Questions

- Review again the five types of wounds.

- Read Romans 5:8.

- What does this meditation teach you about the love of God?

Journal

_____

_____

_____

_____

And the things you have heard me say in the presence of many witnesses entrust to reliable men who will also be qualified to teach others.

(II Timothy 2:2)

Meditation   *Dudley C. Rutherford*

Jesus is the Great Mathematician! He invented multiplication. Here is His simple plan for planet earth: "Somebody told you, now you are to tell somebody else, and that somebody else is supposed to tell others." Jesus wants you and me and everybody to be a personal evangelist. There are three reasons I want to get in on His multiplication plan.

1. <u>My life belongs to God.</u> We call it "my life," but it isn't really. Nothing belongs to us. Even the name you wear was given to you. I am on earth for a short time and that time belongs to God.

2. <u>Life is so brief.</u> The Bible teaches that life doesn't last very long. Life is like a vapor, a plant that withers and dies, a weaver's shuttle, a tale that is told and many other metaphors describing the fleetingness of life. The only way I can make use of this precious gift of life is by inviting others to His matchless love.

3. <u>I want my life to count for something worthwhile.</u> When I come to the end of my life I do not want it said of me what was said of an old couple in Somerset Maugham's *Of Human Bondage*: "It was as if they had never lived at all." I want to live for the Lord with the ever-limited time I have left and help magnify and multiply His undefeatable Kingdom.

Multiplication

Prayer

Dear Lord of Life and all that is, I thank You that someone once told me about You. Now give me the grace, strength, desire, gratitude and courage to tell others about the wonderful Christ and His story of redemption. Help me to realize that sharing this prized possession called Jesus does not lessen my personal reward, but rather enhances it completely. Don't let me forget how terribly lost people are without You and the Gospel of grace and forgiveness. Help me to be a multiplier of Your Kingdom. In the name that is above every name, Jesus Christ, I pray. Amen.

Questions

- Name three reasons you would want to be a multiplier.

- What is God's plan, listed in II Timothy 2?

- Name some common excuses for not sharing Jesus.

Journal

> *"Teacher, this woman was caught in the act of adultery. In the Law Moses commanded us to stone such women. Now what do you say?" ... "If any one of you is without sin, let him be the first to throw a stone at her."* *(John 8:3-7)*

Meditation   *Cal Jernigan*

Of all the Christian virtues, forgiveness should be the easiest to practice. Considering we all have experienced firsthand the joy of being forgiven, forgiving others ought to come as naturally to us as breathing. What has been so freely and lavishly poured out upon us is now ours to give away just as freely and lavishly. How hard can this be?

Yet too often, the tendency to condemn others is what comes most naturally to us. This is part of our human depravity. When we stand in judgment of others, we think ourselves superior and hold them in our debt. Refusing to forgive someone is often about power and control. Christ calls us to release them.

Ephesians 4:32 says, "Be kind and compassionate to one another, forgiving each other, just as in Christ, God forgave you." The two most important words in this verse are "just as." What excuse do we have for not forgiving others? Could Christ have made it any more obvious to us?

Cal Jernigan is Senior Pastor of Central Christian Church of the East Valley in Mesa, AZ.

Two Important Words

Prayer

Father, I want to thank You for Your grace and Your mercy that has been so abundantly poured out upon me. I know there is nothing I have ever done or ever could do that would warrant such kindness and generosity from You. I understand that You have forgiven me because it's an expression of who You are – for You are good. May I learn to become more like You. Teach me to love and to forgive "just as" You do. In Jesus' name. Amen.

Questions

- What is the greatest sin you have committed against God?

- What is the greatest sin that has been committed against you?

- What would it mean if God chose to forgive you in the same way you forgive others?

Journal

April 4

Meditation   *Dudley C. Rutherford*

"I'd go to church and serve the Lord but there are too many hypocrites in the church!" You've never, ever heard that one before? Sure, there are hypocrites in the church and maybe that's exactly where they ought to be. We've said it many times: "The church is not a hotel for saints; it is a hospital for sinners." I know of a church that has a huge sign at its front entrance that reads, "Welcome, sinners only!" If a hypocrite is someone that doesn't live up to the full meaning of the term 'Christian' then we are all hypocrites. And by the way if you're looking for the perfect church and find it, please stay away from it and don't dare join it. You'd ruin it!

And let me hastily add this: Imitation is the sincerest form of flattery. No one has ever gone to prison for counterfeiting pennies, but many have served time for counterfeiting twenty-dollar bills. There is no profit in imitating that which is useless. The hypocrite is the best recommendation genuine Christianity can have. Did you ever see a counterfeit infidel? No, those things aren't worth counterfeiting. And I must add that even if you could live a splendid, perfect, moral life, it wouldn't help you get to Heaven. We are not saved by our works or morality. We are saved because we have, by faith, accepted His simple plan of grace for our lives.

Hospital For Sinners

Prayer

Almighty God and Father of us all, You are the only One who is perfect. The rest of us miss the mark by a million miles. We thank You for Your mercy and patience because with us, You don't have much to work with. But I want my life to ring more true than it has in the past. I don't want anybody to look at me and think, "That's why I'm not a Christian. I don't want to be like him." God, I'll always fall short, I'm sure, but I'll always strive to be more like You. In Jesus' name, I pray. Amen.

Questions

- The church is not a hotel for saints… it is a what?

- What areas of your life could be described as hypocritical?

- Who is the only perfect One?

Journal

May I never boast except in the cross of our Lord Jesus Christ.

(Galatians 6:14)

Meditation   *John Wooden*

I have always tried my best to walk and live by the principles instilled in me during the days of my youth. Those principles still guide my heart today. In the year 1942, while receiving an award at church for faithfully attending 52 consecutive Sundays, my minister and friend, Reverend Frank Davidson came up to several of the young men in the congregation who had enlisted for the honor of defending our country. He handed each one of us a small metal cross which I have carried in my hand or pocket ever since.

Over the years, many people have seen me on the sidelines coaching college basketball, with a rolled-up program in my hand. Although involved in what some may call a highly competitive and immensely stress-filled athletic event, there was always a calm inside my soul, even during the most pressure-packed moments of a game in its waning seconds.

What most people didn't realize was that, in the palm of my hand, beneath the rolled-up paper, was the small metal cross Reverend Davidson had given me so many years ago. That cross has been a constant reminder of the peace and tranquility that can only come from having an understanding of the love of God!

John Wooden is the former Head Men's Basketball Coach at UCLA.

The Small Metal Cross

Dear Father in Heaven, thank You for the power of the cross. It reminds me on a daily basis of how much You truly care. Your peace is a peace that passes all understanding. Your love is a love that has no boundaries. May I take all the worries and burdens of my life and lay them down at the foot of the cross. Thank You for the cross! In Jesus' name. Amen.

Questions

- What does the cross mean to you?

- Where do you look for peace and tranquility?

- What burden can you place at the foot of the cross?

Journal

_____

_____

_____

_____

When Jesus saw her weeping, and the Jews who had come along with her also weeping, he was deeply moved in spirit and troubled. Jesus wept.
(John 11:33, 35)

Meditation   *Dudley C. Rutherford*

When our Master saw Mary and Martha weeping over their dead brother Lazarus, He began to bathe His face in briny tears. His heart was broken because their hearts were broken. Some have suggested that the only reason Jesus cried was that He knew if He called Lazarus back to life, He would be calling a man to leave a perfect Heaven for a valley of tears called earth. Maybe. I think Jesus had His heart broken because He loved these two sisters and their brother. He loved them dearly.

Oh, dear heart, do you know that the day you die and the day we have your funeral, Jesus will cry? I promise you that He, who cried over the death of Lazarus, will cry over you and your sorrowing family. Jesus wept over death. He wept over sin so often. Not His sin; mine. When Jesus saw the sinful city of Jerusalem from the Mount of Olives, He wept over their sin and lostness (Luke 19:41). I have seen politicians and athletes cry on TV when they retired. Every Labor Day, Jerry Lewis sheds tears while singing, "When you walk through a storm keep your head up high."

Do we cry? When was the last time you cried over a lost soul, a struggling church, an unsaved loved one? Jesus wept! Will we?

Prayer

Jesus, thank You for weeping over me. I know You cry over me, because I know You hate my sin and You don't want it to destroy me. You are the only One I know who worries and cares about my sins. Help me to realize the seriousness of being lost and missing out on the great rewards You planned for those who are faithful to You. Help me to cry over things over which I have never cried before. I want to be like You, and it's in Your name I pray. Amen.

Questions

- Name two times Jesus wept.

- Name two subjects over which He wept.

- Name the last time you cried over something spiritual.

Journal

_____

_____

_____

_____

For no one can lay any foundation other than the one already laid, which is Jesus Christ. (1 Corinthians 3:11)

And I tell you that you are Peter, and on this rock I will build my church, and the gates of Hades will not overcome it. (Matthew 16:18)

Meditation   *Dudley C. Rutherford*

Who is the foundation of the Christian Church? Certainly not man. Not rules or traditions. Not even the Holy Spirit or God the Father. Certainly not Mohammed, Buddha, Joseph Smith or any other earthling. We have sung before: "My hope is built on nothing less than Jesus' blood and righteousness; I dare not trust the sweetest frame, but wholly lean on Jesus' name. On Christ the solid rock I stand, all other ground is sinking sand."

When is the last time you heard an entire sermon on Jesus Christ, or have you ever attended a seminar on Jesus Christ? We have a tendency to take the precious Lamb of God, the Lion of the tribe of Judah for granted. Remember when John was marooned on that ghastly prison island of Rome called Patmos? Oh, he had been with Jesus before and after His resurrection, but since His ascension John of course had not seen Him. But on Patmos, God pulled back the curtain and John got a glimpse of Jesus.

Here is what John saw: "His head and hair were white like wool, as white as snow, and His eyes were like blazing fire. His feet were like bronze glowing in a furnace, and His voice was like the sound of rushing waters. His face was like the sun shining in all its brilliance. When I saw Him, I fell at His feet as though dead" (Revelation 1:14-17).

I beg you, friend, to fix your heart upon Jesus Christ. Stay in your Bible and learn who Jesus is. He is the foundation of the Church and of life and all eternity.

Prayer

Even now, as I contemplate Your greatness dear Lord, my dormant faith begins to rise. I realize as I never have before that all other ground is sinking sand. Help me to see not only the lowly Christ of the Gospels, but the majestic Christ of John's vision in Revelation. As I recall, all human history has been written in terms of rulers who have failed, but You are the One who is our blessed, returning Prince and cannot fail. In the strong name of Jesus, I pray. Amen.

Questions

- Who is the foundation of the Church and your faith?

- Is Jesus the cornerstone of your life?

- How would you describe Jesus?

Journal

Be joyful always; pray continually; give thanks in all circumstances, for this is God's will for you in Christ Jesus. (I Thessalonians 5:16-18)

Meditation   H. Dean Rutherford

My sweet mother died in 1994. My sister and two brothers were always faithful to call her by phone at least once a week. But she loved to receive letters. She lived by herself, along with her cat. Some of those phone calls would go something like this: "Well, Mom, what have you been doing today?" "Oh, I just went out to the mailbox and I got a letter from your brother. It just made my day. I must have read it four or five times over." Or she would say, "I went to the mailbox and got nothing but some old advertising." We got the hint. She not only wanted a weekly phone call but also a deliberately written letter.

I suppose it is human nature to want to hear from someone you love, and from someone who loves you. I know somebody wants to hear from you. His name is Jesus! I think every day Jesus walks out to the mailbox and anticipates hearing from you. He loves you so much. Wouldn't you like to hear from your child more often? I'm certain that's one of the reasons our Lord devised prayer. Would you speak your love to Him just now?

Prayer

Dear Lord, I want to commune with You. Communicate with You. I know You want to hear from me. Perhaps like an aging mother, separated by miles from her children, You yearn to hear something personal from me. Help me today to begin a closer walk and quiet time with You. I pray that You'll hear from me every moment of every day. In Jesus' name, I ask. Amen.

Questions

- Why would Jesus want to hear from you?

- What does He want you to talk about?

- In what ways can you make more time for prayer in your life?

Journal

_____

_____

_____

_____

So you also must be ready, because the Son of Man will come at an hour when you do not expect him. Who then is the faithful and wise servant, whom the master has put in charge of the servants in his household to give them their food at the proper time? (Matthew 24:44-45)

Meditation   *Dudley C. Rutherford*

Once upon a time, a man shipwrecked on a desolate island. As he staggered ashore, he was met by a group of natives. Expecting to be killed, he was shocked when the natives expressed to him that he was a very lucky man. They had a rule on this particular island that if any one landed on this shore on this one day of the year, he would be king of the island for one full year. He would be king and the island's entire population would be his servants. They also made it clear to him that at the end of the year, he would be put out to sea on a makeshift raft and set adrift.

The man thought and thought. He could spend the year living a life of comfort and ease. He could have his every whim granted. Or he could use the year as a time of preparation for the time of departure. He wisely chose the latter. He had the men of the island cut trees and fashion a large boat. He had the natives gather fruit and foods and store them on his new vessel. He worked diligently for the entire year. Exactly one year to the day after his arrival, he went to the water's edge unafraid and well prepared. He had not frittered away his year of opportunity. He had absolutely no regrets. You and I have a certain but unknown time on this planet. We can waste our lives living for ourselves, or we can live for Christ and for others and thus be prepared when the day of our departure arrives.

Maybe Today

Prayer

Dear Father God, I know You are coming back some day. I have no idea what day You have chosen. Since I don't know what day, I want to be ready every day, so that when You return I won't be caught off guard, afraid and lost. Help me to arise each morning and pray, "This could be the day that my Lord comes back for His own." Help me to spend this day doing those things that count the most. In the name of my returning Christ, I pray. Amen.

Questions

- When do you think Jesus will return to earth?

- Are you prepared for His return?

- Name some things you would do today if you knew He was coming tonight.

Journal

If your hand or your foot causes you to sin, cut it off and throw it away. It is better for you to enter life maimed or crippled than to have two hands or two feet and be thrown into eternal fire. And if your eye causes you to sin, gouge it out and throw it away. It is better for you to enter life with one eye than to have two eyes and be thrown into the fire of hell.
(Matthew 18:8-9)

Meditation   *Dudley C. Rutherford*

I remember a preacher telling this story. He said a famous evangelist was preaching at a large western university. He preached a moving, evangelistic message about surrendering to Christ. The preacher extended the invitation hymn and an altar call for any in that collegiate audience to surrender and dedicate his life to Jesus. As the audience sang, a harsh, grating and raspy noise was heard above the singing. Down the aisle came half of a man. He had no body from his waist downward. With twisted arms and hands he scooted himself forward on a homemade skateboard until he reached the front of the massive auditorium. He motioned for the preacher to bend over where he could whisper something to him.

When the audience had finished singing and sat down, the evangelist relayed to the crowd: "This man just pushed himself forward on a skateboard and asked me a most unusual question. He asked me if I thought God could use only half a man?" I told him and I am telling you now, the answer is "Yes." "God can use a half of a man, if that half of a man is truly and totally dedicated to Christ. However, he cannot use a full man or a full person if that person is not altogether sold out to Christ."

Prayer

Dear God, wholly and fully I want to dedicate my body to the service of my Lord and Savior Jesus Christ. To the full extent, I want to use my energy and gifts to promote the Church for which Jesus died. I do not wish to be a complete, whole person and be only halfway dedicated to the cause of Christ. I know I need to delve into Your Bible and log more prayer time in serving You. When I meet You on that appointed day, I want to hear You say, "Well done, good and faithful servant." I pray in Christ's name. Amen.

Questions

- What were your thoughts as you read through this devotion?

- Do you believe God has the ability to measure your commitment to Him?

- How would God describe your level of devotion to Him?

Journal

April 11

We do not want you to be uninformed, brothers, about the hardships we suffered in the province of Asia. We were under great pressure, far beyond our ability to endure, so that we despaired even of life. Indeed, in our hearts we felt the sentence of death. But this happened that we might not rely on ourselves but on God, who raises the dead.

(II Corinthians 1:8-9)

Meditation   Chris Seidman

Have you ever been under great pressure, far beyond your ability to endure? Has your heart felt like it was on Death Row? As Paul gazed into the rearview mirror of his life, he reflected on the reason he suffered adversity in the province of Asia. "But this happened that we might not rely on ourselves but on God, who raises the dead."

I've been privileged to watch the birth of all three of our sons. One of the amazing wonders of the labor and delivery process is that, in some cases, a baby's frame is of such size that his collarbone naturally compresses to the point of breaking as he passes through the birth canal. His birth into the new world is preceded by brokenness.

This is quite a parallel to our spiritual lives. The truth is that every one of us must first be broken in order to be birthed. Adversity, regardless of whether it's brought upon us by Satan, other individuals or even ourselves can actually become an opportunity for us to be birthed to a new level of dependence upon God. Adversity so often ushers us to the end of ourselves. And it's at the end of ourselves that we meet God and a whole new world of intimacy with Him and empowerment by Him.

Chris Seidman is the Senior Minister of Farmer's Branch Church of Christ in Farmer's Branch, TX.

Prayer

Father, I receive You this day as One who allows me to become weak enough in my knees that I might more easily fall to my knees. It's in the falling to my knees before You that I believe I'll find the strength to ultimately stand. I ask for grace to see my challenges as Paul saw his. On this day and at this moment, I come to the end of myself and to a new beginning through You and in You. In the name of Jesus. Amen.

Questions

- Who's been a modern-day example to you of what Paul wrote in II Corinthians 1:8-9?

- What is a difficulty you've faced in the past that, looking back on it now, God used to shape you into the person you are today?

- What are you facing right now?

Journal

_____

_____

_____

_____

_____

> *The god of this age has blinded the minds of unbelievers, so that they cannot see the light of the gospel of the glory of Christ, who is the image of God. (II Corinthians 4:4)*

Meditation   *Dudley C. Rutherford*

Today's modern person is suffering from an identity crisis. Housewives are weighing whether to work out of the home and be a breadwinner or stay home and be a mom, or both. Businessmen are torn between the busy demands of the office or company and the needs of their families. Teenagers don't know whether to follow the world or the church, or both. People at work have been wondering about you: is he a Christian or not? Which of those hats he is wearing is real? Does she believe or doesn't she? One minute she invites me to church and she later tells an off-color story. Who is this person, anyway?

We need not be confused about how we should live or who we should be. We should be conformed to the image of Christ. We are to walk and talk and act and look like Jesus Christ. An aerospace engineer with NASA, Bob Slocum, said, "I became convinced that Jesus Christ is the God behind the physical universe. The important question then became not whether I thought God was real, but whether God thought I was real. The idea took hold that in Christ, God does love me and takes me seriously; and I began the experiment of placing my life in His hands and setting out to discover what it means to live for him." There are three views: the person you think you are, the person others think you are, and the person God knows you are and can be through Jesus. Will the real you please stand up and identify yourself?

Prayer

Dear God, we know why You sent Jesus into this world: so that we could visualize how we are supposed to act and react and live our daily lives. My heart's desire is to be conformed to the image of Your dear Son. When others are around me, may they think, "That is just what Jesus would say," or, "That is just what Jesus would do." I know I can't be conformed to Your image overnight, but help me to consistently work on it. In the name of Jesus Christ, I ask these things. Amen.

Questions

- Who is the image of God in II Corinthians 4:4?

- Do you consider yourself to be consistent or inconsistent in your walk with the Lord?

- Reread the quote from Bob Slocum.

Journal

Is not God in the heights of heaven? And see how lofty are the highest stars! (Job 22:12)

Meditation   *Dudley C. Rutherford*

Our great God has shrunk in the minds of modern Christians. He has become a dwarf rather than a giant. We get to thinking that He is too blind to see our stark misery, too deaf to hear our painful entreaties; His arms are too short and too weak to save us. I want to ask you: How big, how tall is your God? Have you squeezed Him into some tiny corner of your soul, or does He rule and reign on the throne of your life? That's the question. How tall is your God? I'm telling you He is taller than we know! No storm, no wave is bigger than the Man of Galilee who calmly sits in the back of the boat. He is waiting now to speak peace to the ocean and to your soul. No road or path is so long or rugged that He cannot suddenly appear beside you and walk you to your safe destination.

God is bigger than our needs. He is taller than our dreams, taller than the hunger of my soul, taller than the homesickness I have for Heaven and to live eternally. He is taller than all our heartaches, than our most regrettable setbacks, than our briny tears of grief. He is bigger than all my failures. I can trust Him. Now, I know I have gigantic needs. But I also know I have a God bigger than all my needs. How tall is your God? Is He big enough to trust? Is He big enough to save you? Is He big enough to bring you home safely?

Prayer

O great God, bigger than I will ever know: I want to tell You that You not only can preside over a funeral but over my evening meal, as I bow and ask Your blessings. You are not only big enough to create and sustain this universe, but You are big enough to heal my personal hurts, forgive my sins and guide my daily conduct. You are big enough to trust, and to save, and to eternally bless. I rededicate my life to Jesus Christ today, and I pray this prayer in His wonderful name. Amen.

Questions

- How tall and how big is God in your life?

- Can you name ways that you have treated Him as if He were short?

- Spend some time reading Job 21 and 22.

Journal

_____

_____

_____

_____

_____

April 14

But do not forget this one thing, dear friends: With the Lord a day is like a thousand years, and a thousand years are like a day. The Lord is not slow in keeping his promise, as some understand slowness. He is patient with you, not wanting anyone to perish, but everyone to come to repentance.

(II Peter 3:8-9)

Meditation   *Dudley C. Rutherford*

On April 14, 1912 at 11:40 PM, in the deep end of God's ocean, the greatest maritime disaster the world has ever known took place. The Titanic, the pride of the White Star Fleet struck, on its maiden voyage, an iceberg off the coast of Newfoundland.

The ship was billed as the world's only unsinkable ship. The tragic truth is that it not only sank but that was about all it ever did: sink. Twenty three hundred persons were on board and only 711 people were saved in 20 lifeboats. Twelve hundred could have been saved if only they would have boarded a lifeboat. The Titanic movies picture men writing million-dollar checks for a seat on a lifeboat, or men dressing up like women so they could get a safe seat. But the truth is, almost no one wanted to get on the lifeboats. The lifeboats could hold 65 persons on each boat. The average number of persons on each boat was 17. Most boats had only 20 or 30 passengers. People simply refused to believe the Titanic could sink. It is true that the officers and stewards had to actually beat down the doors of the staterooms to beg people to board the lifeboats. It was unthinkable that such a huge ship could sink.

The second coming of Jesus Christ is similar, in that most of us just simply do not believe that some day, all time and life will be interrupted by the second coming of our Lord. Yet over 100 times in the New Testament alone, the Bible says Jesus is coming again.

Prayer

Dear saving Lord of Life, help me to remember that You are going to keep Your Word and come back to earth again to claim Your own. I know You are going to come back and shock millions of people, but I want to be ready and looking forward to my first day of eternity with You. Help me to live a life so that I won't have to be scared and afraid of the future. Thank You God for making Your plan so simple that even I can understand it. In Christ's name, I pray. Amen.

Questions

- One thousand years is like what to the Lord?

- Will the Lord keep every promise He has made?

- Would you be ready if Jesus returned today?

Journal

April 15

For God did not give us a spirit of timidity, but a spirit of power, of love and of self-discipline. (II Timothy 1:7)

Meditation   *Yvonne Vollert*

In the midst of personal pain and worldly troubles, is it realistic for God to call me to feel and think above my circumstances? I have found that it is not only realistic, but also essential! And God goes so far as to command it, because He knows I will not choose it on my own – it goes against my human nature. He is calling me to His nature and to His way. I resist this, because I stubbornly want my way, even if it is unhealthy or self-defeating. I protest that I do not have enough faith or that I feel helpless to change. Like a little child, I hear myself saying, "I can't. It's too hard."

Yet God gently tells me in this verse that living in fear and timidity is the harder way – much like crawling is ultimately harder than walking, walking is harder than riding a bike, biking is harder than driving, and driving is harder than flying. Choosing to live in His power, love and perspective is, of course, the better way; but the better way takes hard work and discipline. It also requires an act of the will – in a surrendered and unwavering belief that God's ways are better than my ways.

God wants me to be a faithful thinker, so that my troubles drive me into His presence and fill me with His peace. This will translate my faith into action that is both Biblical and productive. The "fearful" alternative is to be driven to hopelessness and despair. Jesus told us, "Come to Me all who are weary and heavy burdened, and I will give you rest. My yoke is easy and My burden is light." The Apostle Paul demonstrated in his life that God's way is ultimately the easier way, even when it is hard. With daily persistence and practice, it becomes as easy as riding a bike… with no hands.

Yvonne Vollert is Women's Ministries Teacher at Calvary Community Church, Westlake, CA.

Prayer

Heavenly Father, thank You that You have given me everything I need for victorious living today. Help me to resist fear and timidity; to take up, instead, my position in Christ, with all its benefits, including the power of Godliness, the love of Christ and the peace of a sound and settled mind. Daily penetrate my mind with Your Word, so I can be "mature and complete, lacking no good thing." Empower me to turn from negative reactions; to turn, instead, toward Biblical and positive responses that build up my life and the lives of those around me. Teach me to trust You more and more with my past, present and future. "You are God, there is none like You!"

Questions

- What fears or worries – realistic or unrealistic – do you need to surrender to God today?

- What true and Biblical thoughts do you need to replace your fearful thinking?

- When fear or a sense of powerlessness troubles you, how can you invite God to transform your thinking?

Journal

_____

_____

_____

_____

Do your best to come to me quickly, for Demas, because he loved this world, has deserted me and has gone to Thessalonica. Crescens has gone to Galatia, and Titus to Dalmatia. (II Timothy 4:9-10)

We all, like sheep, have gone astray, each of us has turned to his own way; and the LORD has laid on him the iniquity of us all. (Isaiah 53:6)

Meditation   *Dudley C. Rutherford*

Take an ordinary coffee cup and simply turn it over. When you do, you accomplish three definite, different tasks: One, you make it empty of its contents. Two, you make it awfully dark inside. Three, you make it incapable of any future blessings. The same is true when you turn your back to the Lord. When you turn away from Jesus you do three things: One, you make your life empty. Two, you make it very dark on the inside. And three, you make your life incapable of receiving any future blessings. "Come near to God and He will come near to you" (James 4:8).

In the above text, Demas was helping Paul evangelize, but the devil gave Demas a glimpse of the bright, dazzling lights of Thessalonica and he turned his back on Paul, on Christ and His Kingdom. I don't know if Demas was cognizant of the fact that at the moment he deserted Paul, he was emptying himself of all good things. I wonder if he also knew that by turning away, he was making his soul dreadfully dark and rendering his life utterly incapable of any future, meaningful blessings. Oh the futility, the darkness, the vainness, the senselessness of turning away from Christ.

Bright Lights of Thessalonica

Prayer

Dear God, I recall that song that goes, "My heart is night, my soul is steel, I cannot see, I cannot feel, in simple faith I must appeal, to Him whose name is Jesus." Jesus, that's just how I am when I turn away from You. Today, I want to come back home to You. I want to turn my cup back over and open myself to Your blessings and Your proven promises. I don't want to be a deserter like Demas. I pray this prayer of help in Jesus' name. Amen.

Questions

- What three things happen to a cup when it's turned over?

- When will God come near to you? (James 4:8)

- Have you ever seen someone desert the cause of Christ?

Journal

> *Religion that God our Father accepts as pure and faultless is this: to look after orphans and widows in their distress and to keep oneself from being polluted by the world. (James 1:27)*

Meditation   *Clark Tanner*

One sunny morning on the southern coast of Australia, a little boy discovered hundreds of starfish had washed up on the beach and were dying in the sun. Frantically, he began to grab the starfish and fling them back out to sea. A man stopped to observe the boy in this seemingly futile exercise. There were far too many starfish to be saved. "I understand what you're doing, son," the man said, "But do you really think it will make a difference?" The boy looked up at the man, then down at the starfish in his own hand. "I don't know, mister," he said. "But I think it will for this one."

How many in the Christian community have this attitude when it comes to meeting human needs? Do we know the value of what we might call the insignificant acts? At Christmas, I was asked to accompany several people from our church to serve an evening meal to the homeless and give out gifts under Burnside Bridge in downtown Portland, Oregon.

My experience with those 75 homeless people was the most inspirational and convicting thing I did that Christmas. My task was to share a devotion and offer Communion to anyone wanting to be saved. As I stood before a table holding cups of grape juice and a loaf of bread, I listened to prayers that humbled me. I have never heard more thoughtful and heartfelt prayers.

It's my prayer that I made a difference for some homeless person on that cold winter night. I would hope a "hot cup of coffee" was given in His name. May our acts of kindness always be an outgrowth of a heart that really loves God. Let's pray for Burnside Bridge experiences, because meeting human needs can be the purest form of religion. (James 1:27)

Clark Tanner is Senior Pastor of Beaverton Christian Church in Beaverton, OR.

Prayer

Father, thank You for teaching me to make a difference in someone's life. I may not be able to help the whole world but I can help someone. May I look for ways to serve, to care, to love and to minister. Help me to keep my eyes open and my heart tuned in to You. Point me in the right direction to the person in need and I will be faithful to help them on Your behalf. In Jesus' name. Amen.

Questions

- What are you doing to meet human needs?

- How would a short-term mission trip impact your life?

- How can you adjust your schedule to care for people in need?

Journal

_____

_____

_____

_____

_____

■ April 18

Then the master called the servant in. "You wicked servant," he said, "I canceled all that debt of yours because you begged me to. Shouldn't you have had mercy on your fellow servant just as I had on you?" In anger his master turned him over to the jailers to be tortured, until he should pay back all he owed. (Matthew 18:32-34)

Meditation   Dudley C. Rutherford

Jesus said there was once a very rich king, and there was a man who owed the rich king the sum of one million dollars. As the law carefully stipulated, it was time for the king to put the man into a debtor's prison. The king, by law, was supposed to sell the man's wife and children and all the man's assets to help pay the debt. But the man who owed the money begged and pleaded. The king had great compassion and said, "You don't need years. You don't need days or even seconds. I forgive the debt."

Now the plot thickens. The newly forgiven man is dancing along, counting his good fortune when he meets a man who owes him only 23 cents. This newly forgiven man screams, "Pay me my 23 cents now!"

"Look, I don't have it but give me just a few days and I'm sure I can repay you." This newly forgiven man says, "No! I'm having you cast into prison until every penny is paid off." The news of this gets back to the rich king and the king is wroth. The king's blood is boiling.

He has the man summoned before him and asks, "Why is it that after I forgave you a debt of one million dollars, you couldn't forgive a debt of 23 cents?"

The king not only has the man cast into prison but also insists that the man be tormented until every penny of that debt is paid.

Twenty-Three Cents

Dear loving God, thank You for forgiving me for all my sins. I know they must number in the millions. And dear Lord, if You can forgive me of every last one of my countless sins, it seems that I should be able to find in my heart the quick willingness to forgive others for the wrongs they sometimes commit against me. I pray this sincere and earnest prayer in the name of my forgiving Savior, even Jesus. Amen.

Questions

- Name some things for which Jesus has already forgiven you.

- Are you harboring ill will against anyone?

- What does this story teach you personally about the issue of forgiveness?

Journal

_____

_____

_____

_____

_____

When the Sabbath came, he began to teach in the synagogue, and many who heard him were amazed. "Where did this man get these things?" they asked. "What's this wisdom that has been given him, that he even does miracles! Isn't this the carpenter? Isn't this Mary's son and the brother of James, Joseph, Judas and Simon? Aren't his sisters here with us?" And they took offense at him. (Mark 6:2-3)

Meditation   *Dudley C. Rutherford*

There was a day when Jesus was known and referred to as the Carpenter. He was a master at making chairs, tables and cabinets. Children brought their broken toys to Him and others brought broken furniture. This Nazarene Carpenter is still on the job and still available. He's open for business! The tools with which He miraculously works are love, mercy, grace and forgiveness. My Carpenter can mend broken hearts. I've seen Him do it countless times. What He's done for others, He can do for you. I know He can mend broken vows. Maybe someone reading this once made a sacred pledge to be faithful but that promise has long since been scuttled. He can fix even that!

Jesus never did some basic things you and I do every day: talk on the phone, work at the computer, ride in a car or airplane. But oh, He can do things that you and I could never do in a million years. He can heal broken homes, broken hearts, broken hopes and broken commandments. He can turn the drunkard sober and set the addict free. Watch the Carpenter as He skillfully delivers and unchains the gambler, the adulterer or the liar. *Only Jesus can mend the broken things of life*. Oh friend, let this Carpenter from Nazareth touch your life. Bring to Him all your broken things. He who built strong tables and chairs so long ago can build strong men, women and families today.

The Carpenter

Prayer

Dear Carpenter from Nazareth, I hand over to You in this moment all the broken things of my life. I know You need no apprenticeship, for You are the Master of all masters. Take my life as I so surrender it to You and help me build this body and soul into a temple that would bring honor and glory to the great Carpenter of Heaven. I'm weary of trying to fix things on my own; I want my life to be in the hands of the world's greatest repairman. And I pray these things in Jesus' name. Amen.

Questions

- Jesus grew up in what town and what was His vocation?

- What are some things in your life that need to be repaired?

- What's your part in this "Extreme Makeover"?

Journal

_____

_____

_____

_____

_____

For whoever wants to save his life will lose it, but whoever loses his life for me and for the gospel will save it. What good is it for a man to gain the whole world, yet forfeit his soul? (Mark 8:35-36)

Meditation   *Dudley C. Rutherford*

I've heard the story told that when Charlemagne (Charles the Great) died in 814 AD, the world seemed to stand still. Europe as you see it today remains the scattered fragments of his once invincible empire. When this proud monarch died, they carried him into his regal sepulcher and placed him on a priceless throne of ivory, gold and precious stones. On his head scintillated a diadem of jewels. In his propped-up right hand, a royal scepter. On his finger was his signet ring. On his lap, a scroll that chronicled his larger-than-life deeds. About his magnificent body was a purple robe of royalty. Then they sealed forever the tomb of Charlemagne.

Centuries later, they decided to break the seal of the tomb and view one of history's most illustrious figures. To their shock, time had eaten the flesh until on the throne sat only a skeleton. The purple robe lay in a heap of debris at his skeletal feet. The crown had slipped over his skull and was resting awkwardly on his shoulder. The signet ring had slipped from his finger to the floor. Time, like a rat, had gnawed the prop that raised the arm that held the scepter, and the scroll that was once on his lap had unrolled. Strange as it may seem, when Charlemagne's right hand dropped to the floor, it fell on the open scroll and his index finger was pointing to the words of Scripture that read, "What good is it for a man to gain the whole world, yet forfeit his soul?" (Mark 8:36)

Ripley's Believe It or Not

Prayer

Dear God in Heaven, I full well know the answer to Your haunting question and the answer is "Nothing." If I had the whole world and everything in it and didn't have You in my heart, I would have "Nothing." I also admit that if some day I have nothing but penury, poverty and woe, but have You deep in my heart, I would have everything and be absolutely rich beyond measure. Help me to put this knowledge into practice, and in the name of my wonderful Jesus, I pray. Amen.

Questions

- If you own it all and have not Him, what do you have?

- Charlemagne's index finger fell on what words?

- If you have nothing of this world but have Him, what do you have?

Journal

_____

_____

_____

_____

_____

Now listen, you who say, "Today or tomorrow we will go to this or that city, spend a year there, carry on business and make money." Why, you do not even know what will happen tomorrow. What is your life? You are a mist that appears for a little while and then vanishes. (James 4:13-14)

Meditation   Cameron McDonald

I was on the Internet the other day, and I came across a rather odd website called "Death-Clock.com." On this site, you were asked to answer a few questions about yourself, to type in your date of birth, height and body mass index. After you clicked a button, it calculated for you the date you were going to die and how much time you had left, and it began a countdown.

According to this website, I am set to expire June 11, 2068. By just clicking, you could download a clock; your desktop could now have this mortal reminder, counting down your seconds left to live.

In a sense, don't you wish that were true? Don't you wish you could magically type in a few answers and Voila! There would be your date of death. We wish we were like a gallon of milk in the grocery store, all having an expiration stamped on us. But we all know it doesn't work that way. God never intended it to.

I think we don't know when this will happen because God wants us to live every day as if it were our last, living with an eternal mindset and not an earthly one, because the things of this earth are so frail, so temporary and so uncertain.

Prayer

Heavenly Father, for most of us, even as Christians, death scares us, and rightfully so, as it is the most powerful weapon in Satan's arsenal. Father, help me to remember that if I have made a commitment to Jesus Christ, my future is secure in Him. Give me the courage when that time comes to say with the Psalmists, "That even though I walk through the valley of the shadow of death, I will fear no evil because You are with me." Father, thank You for that promise, and thank You that because of Jesus Christ, I have nothing to fear. In Jesus' name. Amen.

Questions

- You are going to die someday. Are you ready?

- Look up I Corinthians 2:9 and read it. Now, write down how this verse makes you feel in light of your own mortality.

- God wants us to live our lives with an eternal mindset. How would you live today if this were your last day on earth? Who namely would you tell about Jesus?

Journal

_____

_____

_____

_____

April 22

In a flash, in the twinkling of an eye, at the last trumpet. For the trumpet will sound, the dead will be raised imperishable, and we will be changed. For the perishable must clothe itself with the imperishable, and the mortal with immortality. When the perishable has been clothed with the imperishable, and the mortal with immortality, then the saying that is written will come true: "Death has been swallowed up in victory." (1 Corinthians 15:52-54)

Meditation   *Dudley C. Rutherford*

The foundation of the Church and of life itself is the Resurrection of Jesus Christ. We are so familiar with it that we tend to overlook its power and meaning. The Resurrection of Jesus is the very picture-promise of what will happen to us. Romans 6:5 tells us, "If we have been united with Him in His death, we will certainly also be united with Him in His resurrection." That means if we die to sin as Jesus died on the cross, then just as Jesus rose from the grave, so will we rise from the dead.

The Resurrection of Jesus was the rallying cry of the early Church. It became the favorite message of the apostles. They were sure of this fact. It gave them authority over all other religions. They knew the Resurrection was forever. They knew that in Heaven there not only would be no death, there would be no effects from death. They would not just be alive, but alive without wrinkles, stooped shoulders, gray hair and painfulness. We are dying while we are living and we are living while we are dying. They knew even in that primitive day that while man was alive on earth, the body was actually in the process of dying and decaying. They also knew that in Christ they would be living while they were dying. Not only will there be the removal of death but also the removal of all traces of death. And all God's people said, "Amen!"

Death and Victory

Prayer

Dear Lord, I'm so glad I have a Savior that cannot be held by the grave. I'm glad You gave us the perfect illustration that when we die, we actually begin to live. If You conquered the grave for Yourself, You can easily do so for me. Since I met You and fell in love with You and obeyed You, I no longer fear death the way I once did. My greatest need and desire is to serve You and look forward to that day when my perishable body becomes imperishable. In the ever-powerful name of Jesus, I pray. Amen.

Questions

- What besides death will be abolished in Heaven?

- What was the main, central message of the early Church?

- What is your greatest motivation to get you through the trials of life?

Journal

And he said: "I tell you the truth, unless you change and become like little children, you will never enter the kingdom of heaven." (Matthew 18:3)

Repent, then, and turn to God, so that your sins may be wiped out, that times of refreshing may come from the Lord. (Acts 3:19)

Meditation   *Dudley C. Rutherford*

Conversion, repentance and turning are not politically correct terms anymore, except in God's Holy Book. Conversion means to turn your life, as it drifts away from God, back toward God. Conversion and repentance are turning to a person. Doctrines will not save you. Programs will not save you. You are not a Christian because you attend church and Bible school regularly. You are not a Christian just because you hold a hymn book or place an offering in the plate. Your relationship depends upon a very personal experience and relationship with Christ. It means to turn from self to God. It means giving up your self-authority and self-sufficiency and admitting your utter dependence upon Christ.

Conversion is not gradual reform. It is not cosmetic surgery. It is radical surgery. It means a sudden decision, a sudden change of heart. It is unconditional surrender. It has never been and never will be easy to say, "I'm a sinner and I'm no good like I am. I hand over to Jesus all the plans, loves and purposes of my life." A Christ-centered life will always mean new desires and new affections. If you have never repented, never been converted, do so today. It is life's most marvelous experience to be headed in the right and proper direction. There is nothing like feeling clean and wholesome again. There's nothing like being loved and wanted like God's little children.

Prayer

Dear Lord of lords and King of all kings, thank You for reminding me once again that I must become converted like a little child or I cannot go to Heaven. Help me to stop placing so much prideful confidence in myself and to rely upon Your power to save and forgive. I'm tired of taking the same old detours away from Your love and care. I want to get back on the road again, the road that leads to joy, peace and eternal salvation. In Christ's wonderful name, I pray. Amen.

Questions

- By turning to God, what kind of times (Acts 3:19) can you expect?

- You can't enter Heaven unless you become as a what? (Matthew 18:3)

- What are some things that, by themselves, cannot save you?

Journal

But Mary stood outside the tomb crying. As she wept, she bent over to look into the tomb and saw two angels in white, seated where Jesus' body had been, one at the head and the other at the foot. (John 20:11-12)

Meditation   *David Reagan*

These two verses seem like a simple historical statement, but they are far more than that.

Remember the Ark of the Covenant? It was a sacred box that sat in the Holy of Holies in the Jewish temple. It contained Aaron's rod that budded, a pot of manna and the tablets of Moses on which were engraved the Ten Commandments. It was covered by a lid called the Mercy Seat. On the top of the seat, at each end, were two angels whose wings stretched forth and touched each other.

Once a year, the High Priest sprinkled blood on the Mercy Seat, indicating prophetically that one day the blood of the Messiah would make it possible for the grace of God to cover the law of God.

When Mary looked into the tomb, she saw where the body of Jesus had lain – where His blood had been spilled. At each end, overlooking this sacred spot, was an angel.

What Mary saw was the fulfillment of the Ark of the Covenant! The blood of Jesus made it possible for the grace of God to cover our violations of His law.

Prayer

Dear Lord, give me an overwhelming hunger for Your Word, and give me the spiritual eyes to see and understand Your deepest truths. In Jesus' name. Amen.

Questions

- Do you think Mary recognized the significance of what she saw?

- Does this example illustrate how prophecy can help you to better understand the Bible?

- Are you encouraged to read the Bible more carefully and meditatively?

Journal

Peace I leave with you; my peace I give you. I do not give to you as the world gives. Do not let your hearts be troubled and do not be afraid.
(John 14:27)

"I have had enough, LORD," he said. "Take my life; I am no better than my ancestors." (I Kings 19:4)

Meditation   *Dudley C. Rutherford*

Once a man said, "Discouragement is having faith in the devil." That may be true. Discouragement means we don't think Christ has the answers. Here are four causes of discouragement:

1. Taking your eyes off the Lord Jesus.
2. Yielding to self-pity and false pride. Self is always your biggest enemy.
3. Expecting God to quickly and miraculously solve your problems. God seldom uses the dramatic explosion or the proverbial earthquakes to solve dilemmas.
4. Counting what you don't have instead of counting what you do have.

Now here are four Biblical cures for discouragement:

1. Get busy! There are always others that need your help and blessing. Helping others will do wonders for you.
2. Realize that God is in complete control. His knowledge is perfect and He never sleeps.
3. Admit that this world is not all about you. God's will and work is always bigger and more urgent than your personal plans.
4. Become aware that you are never alone. There are always others of "like precious faith." I so love that remarkable passage in Hebrews 13:5-6: "... God has said, 'Never will I leave you; never will I forsake you.'" So we say with confidence, "The Lord is my helper; I will not be afraid. What can man do to me?"

Prayer

Dear God, I want to be encouraged and not discouraged. My faith is in You and not in Satan and his kingdom. If King David could say, "You restore my soul," then I know You can restore my soul as well. I promise You that from now on, I will try to "Lift up mine eyes unto the hills." I pray this and ask this in the saving and encouraging name of Jesus Christ. Amen.

Questions

- When was the last time you were discouraged?

- Name some causes of discouragement.

- Name some cures of discouragement.

Journal

■ April 26

Again he said, "What shall we say the kingdom of God is like, or what parable shall we use to describe it? It is like a mustard seed, which is the smallest seed you plant in the ground. Yet when planted, it grows and becomes the largest of all garden plants, with such big branches that the birds of the air can perch in its shade." (Mark 4:30-32)

Meditation   Dudley C. Rutherford

Two old farmers were talking one evening in Hardin County, Kentucky in the year 1809. One asked the other, "Anything important happenin' around these parts today?"

"Nah, not around here," replied the other. "Nothin' ever happens around these parts that's important. Well, I guess I did hear that Tom and Nancy Lincoln had a baby boy this morning, but guess nothin' important happenin' around here."

Talk about blindness! My dad used to tell about his dad reminiscing about those days when the first tin lizzy hit the streets. As soon as the new-fangled contraptions broke down, the whole neighborhood would yell sarcastically, "Get a horse!" The old jalopies were laughed at, sure enough. True, there were still a lot more horses than cars, and there were more paths than streets; but the truth is, when that first automobile appeared, it sounded the death knell of the horse-drawn carriage. However ridiculous looking, it was the start of a new age.

If someone would take Jesus into their heart right now, it might not seem like much is happenin' around here; worse, it might seem like some kind of decision to make acquaintances laugh; but it could well sound the death knell of sin and the beginning of salvation. If you will let that tiny seed called Jesus fall into your heart today, and if you will invest in its nurturing, the results will be earth-shattering and life-changing.

Prayer

Dear Heavenly Father, I know that little can turn out to be much, if that "little" is Jesus. I want this day and this moment to be the first day and the first moment of the rest of my life. I want to plant You into my heart, and I intend to nurture that seed with prayer and Bible study and determined faithfulness. I want to grow into Your likeness by blessing You, myself and others. In the strong name of Christ, I pray. Amen.

Questions

- What is unusual about the mustard seed?

- What is the beginning of the end of the sinful life?

- How do you nurture the good seed in your heart?

Journal

April 27

Obey them not only to win their favor when their eye is on you, but like slaves of Christ, doing the will of God from your heart. Serve wholeheartedly, as if you were serving the Lord, not men. (Ephesians 6:6-7)

Meditation   Dean Bradshaw

Can you be trusted to do your best, even when your boss is not around? You should work hard and with enthusiasm! Make the people around you feel your enthusiasm and excitement. Spread the love and importance you're giving, and watch the results you get in return.

Christian employees should do their job as if Jesus Christ were their immediate supervisor. No matter whom you work for, and no matter who works for you, the one you should want to please is God. Whatever place God has drawn up for you to fill in life, ask Him to allow you to do it with pleasure, confidence and determination. Christians should treat those we work for fairly and with a great deal of respect.

The great John Wooden said, "A leader's most powerful ally is his or her own example. Leaders don't just talk about something; they do it!" Do your very best – even when your boss is not around! It's a great feeling. If you truly mean it, it will show.

Dean Bradshaw is a Teacher at Simi Valley High School and a coach at Hillcrest Christian School in Granada Hills, CA.

Enthusiasm

Prayer

Dear Lord, I get so wrapped up in my own little world that I forget You are watching and I allow negative thoughts and negative actions to creep in. Father, help me to remember that I should be motivated every day to do my best because of You. May I set a good example by working hard and by honoring You. In Jesus' name. Amen.

Questions

- Do you work hard and with enthusiasm?

- What do you want people to admire most about you?

- How do you react when given an impossible task?

Journal

_____

_____

_____

_____

> *But there is a friend who sticks closer than a brother. (Proverbs 18:24)*
>
> *May our Lord Jesus Christ himself and God our Father, who loved us and by his grace gave us eternal encouragement and good hope, encourage your hearts and strengthen you in every good deed and word.*
> *(II Thessalonians 2:16-17)*

Meditation   Dudley C. Rutherford

Perhaps you've forgotten, but you have the best friend in the world: Jesus! There is nothing like a close friend that sticks closer than a brother. Jesus is the perfect description and fulfillment of His own definition of friendship: "Greater love has no one than this, that one lay down his life for his friends. You are My friends if you do what I command" (John 15:13). He proved His friendship, allowing His blood to seep crimson-red on the floor of Calvary. He loves you. Have you ever had a friend like Him? He died on the cross — not for His own sins, for He had none. He died for you, dear lonely, searching soul.

Now I know you might be thinking, "No, no; Christ could not be my friend. I'm far too evil and wicked. My past is too jaded. I've crossed that invisible line beyond His ability to redeem." Not true! "He is a friend of sinners." Have you forgotten that verse: "But God demonstrates His own love for us in this: While we were still sinners, Christ died for us" (Romans 5:8). This Christ of the centuries is calling your name again just now. You may feel you are on your spiritual death row, or beyond His reach and love, but you are wrong. He has a gift just for you. What He longs to give you, you could never earn in a billion lifetimes. That gift is salvation, forgiveness of sins and His eternal friendship. You'll never have a better friend!

Prayer

Dear Lord Jesus, thank You for being my friend. I know You stick closer to me than any member of my own family. The only flaw in our friendship has been my lack of devotion, not Yours. I know if I just do my best at obeying Your commands and following You in simple faith, that You will be my best friend not only in this world, but also in that world which is to come. I look forward to seeing my best friend's face on that notable day of reunion. In Christ's name, I pray. Amen.

Questions

- According to II Thessalonians 2:16-17, who is your loving friend?

- According to John 15:13, how do you show your friendship?

- According to Romans 5:8, does Christ actually love sinners?

Journal

> *Do not be anxious about anything, but in everything, by prayer and petition, with thanksgiving, present your requests to God. And the peace of God, which transcends all understanding, will guard your hearts and your minds in Christ Jesus. (Philippians 4:6-7)*

Meditation   *Julie Gariss*

I'm sick and tired of worrying! I have concluded (after much wringing of the hands) that while I possess within myself a paltry amount of personal power to change most circumstances, I do possess a natural (carnal) ability to mull and stew over those same situations until I am literally "sick" and "tired." What about you? Are you finding that your natural instincts... well... stink? Take heart, my fearful friend, because in the verse above, Paul gives a no-fail formula for frettin'. He begins with the reminder that God is near. Now, that certainly casts a different shadow on the problem – *His* shadow, which is rather significant. You stand in the shadow of Him whose ear is inclined toward you, so go ahead and tell Him everything. You've got His attention, and that's reason enough for thanksgiving (verse 6).

Look what happens then, my anxious friend. Paul says the Lord will send to you *peace*. What a present is the presence of Jesus. His peaceful presence will act as a shield, guarding your most vulnerable areas: your heart (steadying your emotions) and your mind (sharpening your logic). It's a tried and true principle, weighed and found "working." It won't sink – Paul suffered three shipwrecks. It takes a beating – Paul endured five floggings. It handles pressure – the churches concerned Paul.

Now... what do you have to worry about?

Julie Gariss is the wife of Randy Gariss, Senior Pastor of College Heights Christian Church in Joplin, MO.

Tired of Worrying

Prayer

Father, I ask forgiveness for refusing to let You handle my problems. In doing so, I am aware that I question Your ability to work in my best interest, and to be honest, I show that I doubt Your willingness to do so. I want the peace of Christ to act as my shield. That is why You and I need to have a long conversation. Even though You know everything, I'll give You my version. And as I wait for You to act, I will rest in the shadow of Your wing. In Jesus' name. Amen.

Questions

- What good thing has ever been brought about by worrying?

- What evidence do you have that shows He is a capable God?

- What evidence do you have that shows He cares for you?

Journal

_____

_____

_____

_____

_____

> *Therefore everyone who hears these words of mine and puts them into practice is like a wise man who built his house on the rock. The rain came down, the streams rose, and the winds blew and beat against that house; yet it did not fall, because it had its foundation on the rock. But everyone who hears these words of mine and does not put them into practice is like a foolish man who built his house on sand. (Matthew 7:24-26)*

Meditation   *Dudley C. Rutherford*

I heard the story about a trusted employee of a very rich man. This employee was an outstanding carpenter and builder. After years of faithful service, the rich man called the carpenter aside and told him that he would be gone for a year; while he was away, he wanted the carpenter to build him a new home. "I'm leaving you $200,000 with which to build the home," he said. After the owner left town, the carpenter, far from the scrutiny of his boss, proceeded to cut all the corners. He used inferior materials, fewer nails and studs, and cheaper hardware and appliances, thinking he could save that money for himself.

The owner came back and looked at the new home. It looked beautiful. The rich man said, "You have done well, and I present this house to you to own and live in." Oh, the chagrin and remorse of that carpenter. He now had to live in the cheap, tawdry and faulty house he had carelessly constructed. The carpenter was such a good builder that he knew the house he had built would not long endure, and that he had made the colossal mistake of his life.

Jesus is saying in this parable that a person who does not go to church, does not read the Bible, does not pray, serve or love is like the builder who cut corners, by building his spiritual house on the sand and not upon the rock, Jesus Christ.

$200,000 Home

Prayer

Dear Lord, I'm sorry, and I owe You and myself both an apology for all the times I've cut corners while trying to build my life's house. I want to start over again and build my house on the rock of Jesus Christ. I know if I put You first in my time, my thoughts and my actions, that I shall not only live in a secure home here but will end up in the Father's fair mansions. I ask these many things in the rich and strong name of Jesus. Amen.

Questions

- What's wrong with a cheap foundation?

- When you cheat on Christ, whom else are you cheating?

- What kind of material are you sending ahead for your eternal home?

Journal

May 1

> *Now all has been heard; here is the conclusion of the matter: Fear God and keep his commandments, for this is the whole duty of man. For God will bring every deed into judgment, including every hidden thing, whether it is good or evil. (Ecclesiastes 12:13-14)*

Meditation   *Dudley C. Rutherford*

These sentences are jam-packed with God's moral absolutes. Five of them to be exact. Here they are.

1. This truth is God's conclusion of the whole matter of life.
2. Fear God.
3. Keep His commandments.
4. This is the whole, entire duty of mankind.
5. God Himself will judge us for everything we ever do, whether good or bad.

Wow! That hits us with devastating impact. This small book of Ecclesiastes is Solomon's dramatic autobiography. He was a brilliant billionaire and he had the means and the desire to look for life's meaning. He had the wealth and the resources to discover what could secure lasting happiness to his soul and body. He tried higher education. He gave himself to pleasure. He was the original Hugh Hefner (700 wives). He tried drinking, laughter and building great monuments to himself. He tried the acquisition of material goods, jaded music and the pursuit of heathen, godless cults.

After a lifetime of searching for life's real joys, only to find them stale and bitter to the taste, he said, "I have reached a conclusion: Every human being must fear God by keeping His commandments and will be judged for certain." The entire purpose of man is to have a personal relationship with God. That is every person's number one imperative. Oh my friend, your relationship with Christ is what life is all about. Salvation and eternity are everything. Don't throw it all away.

A Brilliant Billionaire

Prayer

Dear Heavenly Father of mine, I thank You that You let me peer into the life of this rich king who searched Heaven and earth for life's meaning and finally came to the only true conclusion: that my life belongs to You. I have known it myself that the only payoff in life comes when I surrender my whole heart and life to the Christ of Calvary and the empty tomb. May I always fear You and keep Your commandments. In Your Son's name, I pray. Amen.

Questions

- Does God know everything, hidden or otherwise, about you?

- What is life's final conclusion?

- There will not be peace and fulfillment until you are at peace with what?

Journal

_____

_____

_____

_____

_____

■ May 2

As Jesus approached Jericho, a blind man was sitting by the roadside begging. When he heard the crowd going by, he asked what was happening. They told him, "Jesus of Nazareth is passing by." He called out, "Jesus, Son of David, have mercy on me!" (Luke 18:35-38)

Meditation   *Dudley C. Rutherford*

One of the great scenes in the Bible is this blind beggar at Jericho. He was the most unlikely man ever in line for a miracle. As the day broke, old bent-up, beat-up, bruised, broken and blind Bartimeus was at his usual spot begging for a few pennies. Parade sounds and crowd noises he had never before heard were now falling on his ears. "What's the excitement about?" he cried. Back came the reply: "Jesus of Nazareth is passing this way." When he heard that it was Christ who was passing, Bartimeus began to scream with a shrill voice, "Jesus, Son of David, have mercy on me. Give me back my eyesight" (Mark 10:46 & Matthew 20:29). Jesus healed him then and there, right on the spot. Let me ask, do you think Jesus would have healed him had he not cried out in faith?

You see, once Bartimeus knew Jesus was passing by, he acted. His action was not some nebulous, wistful dream. He acted on faith. He had heard of the miraculous reputation of the lowly Galilean. He had heard of others who had been divinely healed. Jesus was this close to him now, and he would no longer be denied. Are you willing to cry out for help? When Jesus passes by, things begin to happen. He's passing by you right now. Will you call out to Him? From the recesses of your soul and of your deepest need, will you say, "Blessed Jesus, Son of David, help me!" Act now; He may not pass this way again.

Prayer

Dear Lord, as I close my eyes, I can see You passing by me in this very moment of decision. I want to reach out and touch You just now with hands of faith. I want to cry out with the voice of faith and say, "Jesus, Son of David, have mercy on me, and help me, and hear me, and deliver me." I know now that no matter how hopeless and desperate life may seem, Jesus is passing by. Lord, I believe. In Jesus' name, I pray. Amen.

Questions

- Is Jesus passing by you right now?

- Will He always be passing by?

- When was the last time you cried out to the Lord?

Journal

> *"I tell you the truth," Jesus answered, "before Abraham was born, I am!" At this, they picked up stones to stone him, but Jesus hid himself, slipping away from the temple grounds. (John 8:58)*

Meditation   *Lloyd Ogilvie*

Struggles are the stuff of life for most of us. Anxiety is no stranger to us. Fears and frustrations track us like angry dogs. We've all had periods of discouragement, disappointment and feeling depressed. Every one of us has memories that haunt, and unfulfilled dreams that hurt.

Listen to Christ as He speaks about who He is and what He can do to help us with our struggles. Twenty-two times in the Gospel of John, we hear Jesus declare His divine authority over our sin, sickness and suffering. In His bold "I Am" assertions, He claims to be none other than Yahweh, the "I Am" of Moses' burning bush, Immanuel, God with us. Each of Jesus' "I Am" statements – I Am the bread of life; I Am the light of the world; I Am the way, the truth and the life – is His answer to our aching needs. Christ is the reigning Lord. He comes to you and me to save us from our sins and to free us from our burdens, so that we can live the abundant life.

That is what we need to know in our struggles. The Lord, the "I Am" – "who defeated the demons of despair that deplete us and who vanquished death and all its power" – is alive! Here and now. With you and me at this moment! He has the power to help us turn our struggles into stepping stones.

Lloyd Ogilvie is former Chaplain of the US Senate and former Pastor of First Presbyterian Church of Hollywood

Stepping Stones

Prayer

Lord, I begin this day with praise for Your blessings. I thank You for all of life's struggles, in which You reveal Your supernatural power and personal guidance. I dedicate this day to confront the perplexities that force me to seek You and Your limitless grace. You are the Lord of my life and the indwelling power for its challenges and opportunities. Lord, go with me: before me to show the way, beside me to befriend me, behind me to encourage me, above me to watch over me and within me to give me power to turn my struggles into stepping stones. In Your powerful name. Amen.

Questions

- If you knew you could not fail and were sure of the Lord's strength and guidance, what would you attempt today?

- In the past, what ways has Christ turned your struggles into stepping stones?

- Who in your life is struggling and needs the Lord to intervene today?

Journal

_____

_____

_____

_____

_____

■ May 4

The heavens declare the glory of God; the skies proclaim the work of his hands. Day after day they pour forth speech; night after night they display knowledge. There is no speech or language where their voice is not heard. Their voice goes out into all the earth, their words to the ends of the world. In the heavens he has pitched a tent for the sun. (Psalm 19:1-4)

Meditation   *Dudley C. Rutherford*

This short poem came to me over the Internet. It is entitled "Touch Me." I hope it will bless you as it did me.

The man whispered, "God, speak to me" and a meadowlark sang.
But the man heard nothing. So the man yelled, "God, speak to me"
and the thunder rolled across the sky. But the man did not listen.
The man looked around and said, "God, let me see you,"
and a star shone brightly. But the man did not see.
And, the man shouted, "God, show me a miracle,"
and a life was born. But the man did not notice.
So the man cried out in despair, "Touch me God,
and let me know you are here."
Whereupon, God reached down and touched the man.
But the man brushed the butterfly away and walked on.

Author Unknown

This should be a great reminder that God is always around us, in the little and simple things we take for granted. We should understand that God, through the Holy Spirit, walks with us every day and every hour. His presence is always far closer than we can ever know.

The Butterfly

Prayer

Dear Lord, I know that the greatest thing You can do for me is to love me, and the greatest thing I can do for You is to love You. I know Your love is far better than my love could ever be, but I do love You and intend to walk with You every day and notice You in nature and in the lives of others. Your love is far too much for my capacity to understand, but I accept it and thank You for it. In Christ's name, I pray. Amen.

Questions

- How did God show His greatest love for you?

- How can you show your greatest love for Him?

- Name some different ways the Lord expresses His love and friendship to you.

Journal

_____

_____

_____

_____

_____

■ May 5

Therefore I endure everything for the sake of the elect, that they too may obtain the salvation that is in Christ Jesus, with eternal glory. Here is a trustworthy saying: If we died with him, we will also live with him; if we endure, we will also reign with him. (II Timothy 2:10-12)

Meditation   *Dudley C. Rutherford*

Will everyone eventually go to Heaven? There is a common belief that everyone will somehow make it through the pearly gates. I've heard people say, "God is such a God of love, so none of us needs to worry." I must admit there is much in the future I do not know, but I am sure and certain of the following facts:

1. God will be there.
2. Jesus Christ will be there.
3. The Holy Spirit will be there.
4. God's angels will be there.
5. The redeemed will be there.

God says, "Blessed are they that do His commandments, that they may have rights to the tree of life, and may enter in" (Revelation 22:14). I've had people ask, "Will God finally overlook everyone's sins?" Or "Will God place a sinner in purgatory and perfect him until he is fit for Heaven?" The answer is "No!" We must fully accept the Lord, and accepting the Lord includes our submission and obedience to His commandments. I love that promise in I John 2:17: "The world and its desires pass away, but the man who does the will of God lives forever." Nowhere does the Bible teach that all people will go to Heaven. Heaven has been prepared for those who love God. Can I leave you with one more verse? "Blessed is the man who perseveres under trial, because when he has stood the test, he will receive the crown of life that God has promised to those who love Him" (James 1:12).

Prayer

Thank You, dear God, that I need not be confused about life after death. Your Bible teaches me plainly and makes it everlastingly clear that Heaven is a prepared place for a prepared people. Please help those who think that merely believing in a higher power and existence of a Creator will suffice. May I live the kind of gentle, Christian life so that others will want the same God which I possess. In Christ's name, I pray. Amen.

Questions

- Who will make it into Heaven?

- Name some people that will be there.

- Will you be there?

Journal

_____

_____

_____

_____

And I will do whatever you ask in my name, so that the Son may bring glory to the Father. You may ask me for anything in my name, and I will do it. If you love me, you will obey what I command. (John 14:13-15)

Meditation   *Dudley C. Rutherford*

I have been asked many times, "Why doesn't God answer all my prayers?" Some have asked, "Does prayer really work or is it just good therapy?" Prayer does work. It's real. God answers prayer, but many times His answer is "No!" The prayer that pleases God is prayer according to God's will, prayed in faith, in Jesus' name; prayer that is backed by simple faith and purity of heart. Maybe God didn't answer because there was sin in your life. David said, "If I had cherished sin in my heart, the Lord would not have listened" (Psalm 66:18).

Neighbor, if you think you have hidden some sin in the backyard of your life and that you have covered it up and fooled God, think again! Neither you nor I can make a fool of God. Isaiah 59:1-2 reminds us that it is sin that plugs up God's ears and separates His answers from our prayers. An unforgiving spirit will hinder the best prayer ever prayed. Please read Matthew 5:23-24 and you'll see for yourself what turns off the ears of God. God says in I Peter 3:7 that man and wife arguing will turn His ear away. God says that a stingy spirit or a tightwad attitude will block the channel of prayers. Read about this in Proverbs 21:13.

Does prayer really work? The Lord's brother said in James 5:16 that the prayer of a righteous man is powerful and effective.

Prayer

Dear Lord Jesus, I've had too many answered prayers to start doubting You now. I know You hear and answer all my prayers but I also know that my prayers have to meet some simple and honest conditions. I also know that when most of my prayers concern the needs of others my prayer life is on the right track. I do love You Lord and thank You for answering my prayers. This prayer is prayed in Jesus' name. Amen.

Questions

- Does God answer every prayer?

- What are some reasons He refuses to listen?

- When can you tell your prayer life is on the right track?

Journal

_____

_____

_____

_____

_____

■ May 7

Consider it pure joy, my brothers, whenever you face trials of many kinds, because you know that the testing of your faith develops perseverance. Perseverance must finish its work so that you may be mature and complete, not lacking anything. If any of you lacks wisdom, he should ask God, who gives generously to all without finding fault, and it will be given to him.

(James 1:2-5)

Meditation   *Dana Potter*

Finding joy in our trials is an idea that is totally foreign to most men and women today. When we encounter trouble today, we often ask, "Why did God let this happen?"

God uses trials for many reasons – some to get us back on the path of true discipleship. Some trials help mold us into the type of people God wants us to be. Other trials and suffering are to bring God glory, as in the case of the Book of Job.

So, how should we react to trials? God wants us to persevere. "For God did not give us a spirit of timidity" (II Timothy 1:7). We must put on the full armor of God as described in Ephesians 6:10-20. No soldier ever goes into battle without equipment designed to defeat the opponent. We must ask God for His wisdom.

We should be greatly encouraged that these troubles force us to stop relying on our own strength and draw us closer to God. This is a blessing, which we should consider pure joy. Trials are a means by which we are sanctified – another blessing to consider it joy. We often see evidence of God's faithfulness during our times of trouble; consider it joy. It's during these trials that God desires to form in us the character of Christ. Consider it joy.

Dana Potter is an elder at Shepherd of the Hills Church.

Prayer

Dear God, we praise You as our great comforter and a Father of compassion. We thank You for comforting us in all of our troubles and giving us the strength to endure and persevere. Thank You that You never give us more than we can handle. I pray that You help me fight the good fight, to finish the race strong and that I do it with joy in my heart. I pray that through my troubles that others will see Christ in me. Help me to put on the armor of God before I start my day. I pray this in the precious name of Jesus Christ. Amen.

Questions

- How can others see a reflection of Christ in you as you endure a difficult circumstance?

- Are you choosing to live a life comforted by God, or a comfortable life?

- How will you approach your next trial? With perseverance through spiritual maturity, or an earthly desire to get it over with at all cost?

Journal

Therefore everyone who hears these words of mine and puts them into practice is like a wise man who built his house on the rock. The rain came down, the streams rose, and the winds blew and beat against that house; yet it did not fall, because it had its foundation on the rock.

(Matthew 7:24-25)

Meditation   *Dudley C. Rutherford*

God not only has a plan for your life and mine but also for everything in nature. The tiny, fragile Monarch butterflies fly hundreds of miles to spend the winter in warmer climates. These flocks of butterflies span the North American continent each year and arrive in late October at Pacific Grove, California. Two million Monarchs spend the winter year after year on the same trees in a six-acre area. Here's the mystery! Their lifespan is so short that no butterfly could possibly make the round trip twice. How do these gossamer winged, fragile wayfarers find their way home over such a vast distance? Only one answer will fit! God gives them compass and direction.

But pastor, how do I know the will of God, the plan of God for my life? Human error is possible in seeking God's will, but start with the first step, and then, through prayer, trust the Holy Spirit to indicate the course you are to follow. Rest quietly before Him in prayer. There is no limit to what the soul can learn by unselfishly talking to God and allowing Him to talk with you. All decisions should be reached after searching your heart to eliminate wrong motives and prejudices. Decisions made on our knees have a way of turning out to be the right ones. The same God who guides the butterflies, the birds and the fish of the seas will not permit you to lose your way, if you will allow Him into your heart through serious prayer.

Prayer

Dear God, I thank You for guiding the tiny, frail butterflies to find their way home. I know that if I surrender my life to You through prayer and supplication, You will not permit me to wander through life confused and lost. From this new day forward, I want to dedicate my life, my loves and my purposes to You. I earnestly make this solemn commitment to You. Since everything else in nature obeys Your will, I want to follow the path You have given for me. In Jesus' name, I pray. Amen.

Questions

- What's the wisest thing you can do, according to Matthew 7:24-25?

- Does God who guides the butterflies, the birds and the fish of the seas plan for everything and everyone?

- How do you go about discerning what His plan is for you?

Journal

_____

_____

_____

_____

And if I go and prepare a place for you, I will come back and take you to be with me that you also may be where I am. You know the way to the place where I am going. (John 14:3-4)

Meditation   H. Dean Rutherford

Bob Jones, Sr. was the founder of the college that bears his name in South Carolina. He preached for 70 years. When he was just a young preacher at about age 25, his mother died. He was so close to his momma and loved her so much that he got desperate and went to a spiritualist. Someone assured him that a spiritualist could help him contact his dead mother. Here was this young shouting Methodist evangelist sitting there in a séance trying to talk to his dead mother.

Sitting there in the dark, he cried out, "Mother, can you hear me?" Dr. Bob Jones said, "So help me, a voice came out of the dark that was identical to my mother's voice. I was thrilled to hear her voice once again." He said, "Mother, tell me about Heaven. What's it like?" "It's wonderful here. I saw your Aunt Mary, and your Uncle Jim. I even saw one of your cousins yesterday."

Dr. Bob Jones, even as a young preacher, jumped up from his chair in that séance and screamed at the top of his voice, "Let me out of here, it is a fake! It's a fake!" They heard him scream and asked, "What do you mean it's a fake? That was your mother!" "No, that wasn't my mother. I know my mother. All my mother ever talked about was Jesus. All she ever thought about, sang about was Jesus. I know if I had asked my mother what is Heaven like, she would have said, 'O Bobby, I've just seen Jesus.'"

Prayer

Dear Lord in Heaven above, I thank You that You have gone to Heaven to prepare a place for me, and that You will be there to welcome me. May I never forget that the most thrilling part of Heaven will be to see the face of the One who paid my sin's full penalty. Help me to be faithful to that wonderful day and hour when we shall meet face to face. In the name of Christ Jesus, I pray.

Questions

- Do you think it's possible to talk with the dead?

- Who will be the main attraction of Heaven?

- How do you get into Heaven?

Journal

_____

_____

_____

_____

_____

The Lord will guide you always; he will satisfy your needs in a sun-scorched land and will strengthen your frame. You will be like a well-watered garden, like a spring whose waters never fail. (Isaiah 58:11)

Meditation   *Judy Russell*

I love scrapbooking. I realized when I started putting pictures on pages that my photos were sometimes unworthy for the "whole world" to see. I began searching how to take better photos of family, friends, children, flowers and scenery. I read everything I could find on the subject. Soon, my photos were much better – not perfect, but better. I am still reading and learning. I never dreamed I would enjoy photography so much and could share it with so many.

That is the way it is with the Christian life. We are excited but we soon discover we aren't cutting it. We aren't living like the pastor in the pulpit or the teacher in the classroom or the leader in the pew. Why? Why can't I be a good teacher? Why can't I sing a solo? What can I do that would let my light shine for Christ?

God created each of us with special gifts. Perhaps it is surfing, photography, writing, teaching, volunteering or singing. Often we stumble, failing to find our gift. Sometimes it takes years before we realize what we love doing.

Remember, God has a plan for your life. He wants to be by your side, even in those mundane tasks we all plod through. Take some time to read, pray and ask those around you for suggestions. Pray and study God's Word. Ask for His guidance as you search for what you think He wants you to do, so you too can shine for Him.

Judy Russell is the wife of Bob Russell, Senior Pastor of Southeast Christian Church in Louisville, KY.

My Gift to Shine for Him

Prayer

Dear Lord, I thank You for giving me the desire to shine for You. Yet it is difficult to do. I seem to compare myself to others too often. There are too many distractions, too many choices. I don't know what is best for me. So please Lord, I want to be open to Your leading in my search for the best place to use my gifts and shine for You. In Jesus' name. Amen.

Questions

- Do you compare yourself to others who are gifted in ways you wish you were?

- Do you let that comparison beat you down and mope around feeling useless?

- Instead, think about what you love to do best and how you can use your gifts to serve the Lord.

Journal

■ May 11

All inhabitants of the earth will worship the beast—all whose names have not been written in the book of life belonging to the Lamb that was slain from the creation of the world. (Revelation 13:8)

Meditation   *Dudley C. Rutherford*

It has been said that God is no respecter of persons. That is, that God loves all people the same and that He has no favorites. That is Biblically correct. The Good Book says so again and again. Some well-intentioned folks also say that God is no respecter of places; that He loves all places the very same. I think in this they could be wrong. For there is one spot on the earth that exceeds all others in its nearness to the heart of our mighty God. There is one spot of ground, one small piece of real estate that God must love more than any other. It is God's little acre near the eastern wall of Jerusalem, chief city of Judea, where rises a small hill called Calvary.

Do you believe it? Here on this tiny piece of ground, all the hate and also all the love in the universe met head-on. Was ever crime so wrong and was ever love so strong? All of the furies and forces of hell run headlong into the full, infinite love and compassion of God. At the same moment in time and place, where men are trying to commit the most awful and vicious hate crime of the centuries, God is busy on that same spot erecting an altar of love and sacrifice on which the Lamb of God will be slain for sinners. While Satan is busy trying to fill earth's cup of wrath to the brim, by killing the only perfect person who ever lived, God gets busy in turning the place of execution into a scene of supreme sacrifice, where the entire world can find eternal salvation.

Prayer

I recognize, dear Lord, that Your love for me is completely beyond my comprehension. I am aware that no matter where I go, Your love goes with me. For reasons I do not now understand, You love me and gave Your life and blood for me. You defeated all the forces of death and hell at Calvary. How am I to ever properly thank You? I pray that by the way I live my life, in total and complete obedience, that You are able to see my devotion and my appreciation. In Jesus' name, I pray. Amen.

Questions

- What two forces met head-on at Calvary?

- Jesus turned the scene of execution into a scene of what?

- Over what two forces did our Lord prove His power and victory?

Journal

_____

_____

_____

_____

_____

He was despised and rejected by men, a man of sorrows, and familiar with suffering. Like one from whom men hide their faces he was despised, and we esteemed him not. Surely he took up our infirmities and carried our sorrows, yet we considered him stricken by God, smitten by him, and afflicted. (Isaiah 53:3-4)

Meditation   *Dudley C. Rutherford*

One can understand the gist of a chapter by looking at just the pronouns. It was Dr. Carlyle Marney who offered the idea that we do this as a study on the 53rd chapter of Isaiah. This is one of the prophetic chapters that so graphically depicts the suffering of our Lord on the cross. Marney said the dominant pronoun in this chapter is "*He*." "*He*" was despised and rejected by men. "*He*" has borne our griefs, and carried our sorrows. "*He*" was bruised for our iniquities. "*He*" was oppressed, and "*He*" was afflicted.

Who was the "He?" That can be only one person, the Lord Jesus Christ. Christ alone fulfills all these prophecies. But who did these awful things to Him? "We" did. "We" esteemed Him not. All "we" like sheep have gone astray. "We" have turned everyone to his own way. You and I are the people who crucified Him. We share in their sins.

The eternal question is why? Why would Jesus do this and why did He allow it happen? He did it for "our" sakes. He has borne "our" griefs, and carried "our" sorrows. He was wounded for "our" transgressions. I have read this chapter many times and it gets a little sweeter each time I read it; for it sheds great light on just how much the Savior cared for me and how great a price He paid for my sins.

Prayer

O, dear Sacrificial Lamb of God, how much You have loved me and how much You care! I don't understand everything I should, but this one thing I know: You died spread-eagle on the cross to pay the penalty I should have paid. Thank You, thank You and thank You for paying for every last sin I have committed. May I live a life that is worthy of Your supreme act of redemption. May my life reflect my appreciation for Your love. In Christ's name, I pray. Amen.

Questions

- Read the entire chapter of Isaiah 53.

- Name three things the pronouns tell you in verses 3 and 4.

- What should your response be after studying this chapter?

Journal

_____

_____

_____

_____

_____

■ May 13

You were running a good race. Who cut in on you and kept you from obeying the truth? (Galatians 5:7)

Meditation   *Greg Laurie*

Imagine for a moment that we are competing in a race. When the starter pistol is fired, we take off, and I leave you in my dust. I'm running really well. Let's say we are going for ten laps, and we are coming to the last lap. I say to myself, "I am creaming the competition." Then suddenly I decide, "I'm going to leave and get a Krispy Kreme doughnut now." So I wander off the track. Let's say that you cross the finish line ten minutes later. It is clear that I beat you, but if I didn't run the tenth lap and cross the finish line, I have lost the race. It doesn't matter if I led for nine out of ten laps. I had to finish the race I began.

In the same way, there are people who started off with a great burst of energy and followed the Lord. Maybe you were one of those people. Maybe you came to Christ during the days of the Jesus Movement. Or perhaps you came to Him more recently. That is great. But listen: that was then and this is now. How you were running a year ago or even a month ago is no longer significant. How you are running right now is. Are you keeping up the pace? Are you going to make it across the finish line? You can make it if you want to.

There will be times when living the Christian life will be hard. You will have to hold on to God's Word and the promise that He will complete the work He has begun in your life (Philippians 1:6), but will you make the effort to cross the finish line?

Greg Laurie is the Senior Pastor of Harvest Christian Fellowship in Riverside, CA.

Finishing Strong

Prayer

Dear Father in Heaven, help me to run the race that is marked out before me. I need Your strength to run each and every lap to the fullest. Shortcuts won't get the job done. May I keep my eyes on You every day. When I start to get tired, I pray that I'll be disciplined enough to say, "No" to any and every temptation that comes my way. Lord, may I grow closer to You in every area of my life. In Jesus' name. Amen.

Questions

- Why is it difficult to live each day to its fullest?

- Name some distractions that keep us from "running the race."

- What is your plan to finish strong?

Journal

_____

_____

_____

_____

_____

■ May 14

> *This is the message we have heard from him and declare to you: God is light; in him there is no darkness at all. If we claim to have fellowship with him yet walk in the darkness, we lie and do not live by the truth. But if we walk in the light, as he is in the light, we have fellowship with one another, and the blood of Jesus, his Son, purifies us from all sin.*
>
> *(I John 1:5-7)*

Meditation   *Dudley C. Rutherford*

Are you a Christian? Boy, oh, boy, now that's a ridiculous question to ask a person like me. I might even consider that to be a stupid question for a Christian pastor to ask a Christian person from a Christian pulpit: "Are you a Christian?" But I'm not so sure that is an unnecessary question. The Bible says to test ourselves, to see whether or not we are Christians. There is a way that a person can tell whether or not he or she is a Christian. If a person who is not a member of your family asks you to produce evidence of your family membership, what would you offer as proof?

For God's family proof test, here is the question: Do you walk in the light as God is in the light? The answer to this is most important, because if we walk in the darkness, we cannot claim to be a member of God's family. What is it to walk in the light? It means that we speak, act and react the same way Jesus would in any situation. Are we, as Luke says, "The children of light"? And do we wear, as Paul puts it, "The armor of light"? Walking in the light is more than just thinking, Somebody up there loves me and died for me. Walking in the light requires rigorous honesty, confession of sins and daily meditation with God and His Son Jesus Christ.

Prayer

Dear Father of Light, I want to walk as You would have me walk. I want to walk in the light as You are in the light. I know that You do not simply create or produce light, for You are light. You are the only real light this world has ever known. Help me to keep my heart and mind in Your word so that I shall be so surrounded by Your light, I would not feel comfortable walking anywhere near the darkness. In the name of Jesus, the Light of the World, I pray. Amen.

Questions

- Can you know for sure if you are a Christian?

- What is the big test question?

- What does it mean to walk in the light?

Journal

_____

_____

_____

_____

_____

The LORD gives strength to his people; the LORD blesses his people with peace. (Psalm 29:11)

Now may the Lord of peace himself give you peace at all times and in every way. The Lord be with all of you. (II Thessalonians 3:16)

Meditation   *Dudley C. Rutherford*

I read about a farmer who got too old to farm. He moved into town and prepared to hire someone to tend the farm. During an interview, the applicant was asked to write down what he could do best. He wrote down, "I know how to sleep on a stormy night." It was a weird answer but he was hired anyway. One midnight, a bad storm swept over the area. Remembering what the farmhand had written, the farmer jumped into his truck and raced to the farm. He imagined when he got to the farm, the man would be sleeping and the livestock scattered and the hay blown away. He found the man asleep all right, but everything was undercover and all the animals were in their stalls. Now he knew why the man could sleep on a stormy night. He had done his best to prepare before the storm had hit. He had left no chore undone; he could sleep well.

The best time to prepare for a storm is before it happens. The Bible teaches us that same truth in many ways. The Scriptures teach that the only real peace in this world comes from knowing God and serving Him honestly, sincerely and faithfully. There are many mirages of peace, but the only true peace comes from above. Many things seem to promise peace but cannot deliver.

Before The Storm

Prayer

Dear Lord, I know I will never have any lasting peace or satisfaction until I am at peace with You. When I have tried to do my best, then I know I can face any situation or sleep through any stormy night. I want to spend more time in Your Word and spend more time in prayer, that I may be preparing for any stormy night I cannot possibly now see. Bless me in my prayer, and I pray this in Christ's name. Amen.

Questions

- Who is the only author of peace?

- What is the difference between happiness and peace?

- What is the best way to prepare for future storms?

Journal

May 16

We have different gifts, according to the grace given us. If a man's gift is prophesying, let him use it in proportion to his faith. (Romans 12:6)

Meditation   *John Caldwell*

My wife and I enjoy going to the symphony, where we thrill to the music produced by nearly one hundred outstanding musicians performing under the leadership of the conductor. At a recent concert, while enjoying the music of Tchaikovsky and Verdi, I was struck by how a great orchestra so beautifully pictures what the Church is intended to be. All the members played together, harmoniously and compatibly under the direction of the maestro. There was a concertmaster who got the orchestra in tune. There were principal players in each grouping of instruments. Some instrumentalists were more prominent than others, but all played what the one score demanded of their particular instrument. There were soloists, but their playing was greatly enhanced by the music of the remainder of the orchestra.

For those who have trouble with allegory, let me suggest that the orchestra, known as the Church, has only one conductor, the Lord Jesus Christ. The pastor serves as concertmaster while staff and elders serve as section leaders. We are all to play from the same score, the word of God, whose composer is the Holy Spirit. The idea is for all of us who are members of this orchestra to work together, harmoniously and compatibly under the direction of our conductor, as indicated by the score. We have different abilities and gifts, and we have those in varying measure; but when all of us work together, the result is a thing of beauty that glorifies God and accomplishes His purposes.

John Caldwell is Senior Pastor of Kingsway Christian Church in Indianapolis, IN.

Tchaikovsky and Verdi

Prayer

Lord, thank You for making me special and for giving me spiritual gifts. Help me to use those gifts under the direction of the Conductor; and whether or not my part is prominent, help me to do my best, so that in concert with the other members of our Church, that which is accomplished will be all that You intended for it to be. Lord, may You be pleased, honored and even delighted. In Jesus' name. Amen!

Questions

- What are your spiritual gifts?

- How are you using them?

- Do you really care if someone else has a more prominent part to play?

Journal

_____

_____

_____

_____

_____

May 17

Are not two sparrows sold for a penny? Yet not one of them will fall to the ground apart from the will of your Father. And even the very hairs of your head are all numbered. So don't be afraid; you are worth more than many sparrows. (Matthew 10:29-31)

Meditation   *Dudley C. Rutherford*

I hold in my hands a crisp one hundred dollar bill. Is there anyone who would be willing to take this if I gave it away? (No doubt many hands will go up.) Now watch carefully as I wad it up and crease it and wrinkle it. Well, here it is. Would anybody still be willing to take this wadded up one hundred dollar bill now? (Many hands are extended.) I'm not through yet. Now watch me as I throw this wad of money on the floor. I'm going to step on it and stomp it several times. Now look at it. It's been wadded up, creased, wrinkled and walked on. Is there anyone that would still take this one hundred dollar bill? (Many hands are raised.) Why would you still want it? I know why you want it. Because it has not lost any of its worth. Oh, for sure, it's been stepped on and soiled. It's been kicked around and trashed. But it hasn't lost one penny of its value.

We are like that as God's children. We get beaten up and kicked around in life. We make many mistakes and we sin greatly and often. Our hearts get broken and our lives get soiled. But we haven't lost any of our worth. Not any! Listen carefully. If Christ died on the cross for you, then you are worth the entire world to Him. Maybe you feel worthless but you are worth more than ever right now. Don't sell yourself short. Start over this moment.

Prayer

Dear Lord in Heaven, and in my heart, thank You for loving me. Thank You for loving me when I forget to love You. I sometimes get to thinking that because of my sins, my worth is of little value. But in my heart, I know if You loved me enough to die for me, I must really be of intrinsic value. Even though I am a sinner, You make me feel like the pearl of great price, the returning prodigal son, the apple of Your eye. I thank You in Your name and pray this in Your name. Amen.

Questions

- Who's more important, you or a sparrow?

- When you greatly sin, is your intrinsic worth affected?

- What did Jesus do to prove your importance?

Journal

_____

_____

_____

_____

_____

■ May 18

Just as there were many who were appalled at him—his appearance was so disfigured beyond that of any man and his form marred beyond human likeness. (Isaiah 52:14)

Meditation   *Dudley C. Rutherford*

Pictures are powerful. Can you still see the picture of the World Trade Center towers collapsing? Do you remember the pictures of JFK's assassination in Dallas? What pictures! Jesus knew pictures were powerful and wanted us to see a picture of Him on the cross. Mel Gibson's depiction of Jesus suffering on the cross was considered too violent for some, but the truth is the Bible paints a far more drastic photograph of the Suffering Savior. In our text, we find that no human has ever been so disfigured as the beaten and crucified Christ.

In review, take one more look at this Scriptural photo. When He arrives at Calvary, He already wears the diadem of thorns on His broken brow. His lacerated back has already been torn to ribbons by their whips. A crisscross of bloody furrows covers most of His body. His hands and feet are now driven through with spikes. And His distorted face reveals the deeper agony of soul, as all the sins of all the world are piled mountain-high on Him in this moment. As the fever mounts to staggering proportions, the spear is thrust through His chest that spews forth His saving blood. Forgive me, I know it's not politically correct, but I think this is the picture Jesus wants us to see. When we pray, when we think of our salvation's cost, and when we take the Lord's Supper, Jesus wants us to see what He endured for us.

Prayer

Dear Lamb of God, we marvel again at this haunting scene of Calvary, when and where You shed Your sinless blood for our awful sins. Bless us as we try to envision this again. And since it was for our sins that You died, we cannot see this picture without profusely thanking You for Your sacrifice. We've seen this picture before, but we want to look at it again and again and again, for in this picture we have eternal life. I pray this prayer in the name of my eternal redeemer, Jesus Christ. Amen.

Questions

- Describe what Jesus looked like on the cross.

- Has any person ever suffered as much as Jesus?

- Why? Why would Jesus suffer so?

Journal

Elijah went before the people and said, "How long will you waver between two opinions? If the Lord is God, follow him; but if Baal is God, follow him." But the people said nothing. (I Kings 18:21)

Meditation   *John Derry*

Some questions make people uncomfortable. Inquiries about one's personal life, age, weight, family problems, etc. may go unanswered, because we don't think they are appropriate. The context of this question placed before the Israelites by Elijah came during a period of rampant idolatry and immorality, under one of the most wicked kings in the nation's history. Ahab's wife, Jezebel, was systematically killing the Lord's prophets, as the people of Israel stood by and watched.

Elijah called upon the Israelites to take a stand, but they responded to his questions with silence. Was it fear that prohibited them from speaking up? Or was it because they were trying to walk both sides of the line? Maybe in their minds, they wanted to play it safe and maintain a cordial relationship with the Lord, while also indulging in the sinful practices associated with the worship of Baal. This situation led to an event that demonstrated the power of God and the futility of worshipping idols. The people witnessed fire from Heaven consume a sacrifice prepared by Elijah, and their hearts were turned back to God.

Christians who try to maintain ties to the world and engage in activities that are unacceptable to God, while also playing it safe with just enough "religion" to stay on His good side, are wavering. Silence is not an option. God has demonstrated His power and victory over sin through the resurrection of Jesus Christ. We, like the Israelites, must fall before Him and proclaim, "He is Lord."

John Derry is President of Hope International University in Fullerton, CA.

Take A Stand

Prayer

Almighty God, I praise You for the demonstration of Your power that is recorded in Your word, and for the many times I have witnessed Your work in my life and in our Church. Help me to courageously proclaim You as Lord, and forgive me for those moments I have wavered. You know my heart and my motives. Make them pure, and guide me to walk in paths of righteousness all the days of my life. I pray this in the name of Jesus. Amen.

Questions

- Have you ever remained silent when faced with a choice between right and wrong? Why?

- When have you witnessed the power of God?

- How can you be prepared to make difficult decisions?

Journal

_____

_____

_____

_____

■ May 20

For the life of a creature is in the blood, and I have given it to you to make atonement for yourselves on the altar; it is the blood that makes atonement for one's life. (Leviticus 17:11)

Meditation   *Dudley C. Rutherford*

The Bible you hold and believe has much to say about the benefits of the blood of Jesus, which He shed on Calvary's cross. Let me list a few things for us to consider:

First, it redeems: "For you know that it was not with perishable things such as silver or gold that you were redeemed from the empty way of life handed down to you from your forefathers, but with the precious blood of Christ, a lamb without blemish or defect." (I Peter 1:18-19).

Second, the blood brings us near to Christ: "But now in Christ Jesus you who once were far away have been brought near through the blood of Christ." (Ephesians 2:13).

Third, the blood justifies: "Since we have now been justified by his blood, how much more shall we be saved from God's wrath through him!" (Romans 5:9). Justification means that our standing with God is changed from sinfulness to perfection.

Fourth, the blood of Christ makes peace: "...and through him to reconcile to himself all things, whether things on earth or things in heaven, by making peace through his blood, shed on the cross." (Colossians 1:20)

Fifth, the blood of Christ purifies: "But if we walk in the light, as he is in the light, we have fellowship with one another, and the blood of Jesus, his Son, purifies us from all sin." (I John 1:7). Let us not take lightly the Lord's love, death and sinless blood and its marvelous benefits.

Prayer

Thank You, dear God, for dying on Calvary's cross for me. Your precious, sinless blood is the only saving fluid that can wash away my sin and lift me from the miry clay and plant my feet forever on the rock of ages, the rock of eternal salvation. Help me to be faithful, respectful and attentive to the special powers and results of Your wonderful blood. I now know more about the importance of Your shed blood. Thank You. I pray these things in Christ's name. Amen.

Questions

- Name some benefits of Christ's blood.

- Describe justification in a sentence or two.

- Can you name two ordinances or sacraments where we symbolize the death of Christ?

Journal

_____

_____

_____

_____

_____

■ May 21

Better is one day in your courts than a thousand elsewhere; I would rather be a doorkeeper in the house of my God than dwell in the tents of the wicked. For the LORD God is a sun and shield; the LORD bestows favor and honor; no good thing does he withhold from those whose walk is blameless. (Psalm 84:10-11) (Also See Psalm 63:1)

Meditation   *Dudley C. Rutherford*

In the first passage, David is saying that all good things will be his if he puts the Lord first in his heart. In the second passage, David is saying, "My heart longs for God, like a man without water in a dry and arid desert longs for a drink of cool water." That leads us to this conclusion: Only Jesus can satisfy the human heart. Sports and athletics cannot satisfy. Music cannot satisfy; lust cannot satisfy. Try it. It's so temporary that it leaves no satisfaction. Pleasure and money cannot satisfy your heart. Jesus said, "Blessed are they, which do hunger and thirst after righteousness for they shall be *filled*" (Matthew 5:6). The only thing that fills and satisfies is Jesus.

Take your heart, for example. It's only so big. For the sake of illustration, let's pretend your heart is the size of a one-gallon container. You can put anything into it. What will you put into it? It will only hold so much. If you cram it with worldliness, it will only force Christ out. Put Christ in and worldliness will start flying out. Your heart is only so big. You can't put in a whole lot of Jesus and a whole lot of the world at the same time. Put liquor in there and you're still going to be unfulfilled. Try lust, education, narcotics, pleasure, fame, family, good health, travel or culture, and you will not be happy or satisfied. Only Jesus fulfills.

Heart-Shaped Void

Prayer

Forgive me, Lord, for I am always chasing mirages. I've tried to put so many false pleasures into my heart, hoping that in these cheap things I could find the satisfaction so many others have found in You. I know now that I need to go back to the basics and start putting into my heart chiefly those things You say can put a true song and melody in my heart. I want to make up for lost time and fill my heart will Your good things. In Jesus' name, I pray. Amen.

Questions

- What kinds of things have you been chasing?

- What can you put into your heart that will result in great satisfaction?

- Can you fill your heart with travel, education and pleasure, and still have joy? Explain.

Journal

_____

_____

_____

_____

May 22

Therefore go and make disciples of all nations, baptizing them in the name of the Father and of the Son and of the Holy Spirit, and teaching them to obey everything I have commanded you. And surely I am with you always, to the very end of the age. (Matthew 28:19, 20)

Meditation

She seemed a bit confused as she wandered down the grocery store aisle. When I stopped to ask if I could help, she became more interested in just having a conversation than finding dairy products or fresh produce to put in her grocery cart. I remained with her until she went through the checkout line. When the cashier commented on my kindness in helping this stranger, I simply replied, "That's what Christians do." He smugly responded, "Do you think Christians are the only ones who do good things?" His words cut deep.

At that moment, the Holy Spirit convicted and challenged me to move beyond this "do-gooder" description of my actions. Having received the woman's address during our conversation, I went to her home and began to develop a relationship with her over the following weeks and months. I introduced her to the family of God who lived in her community. She was lovingly embraced by many, and came to know Jesus Christ as her personal Lord and Savior. It was in the fulfillment of Jesus' Great Commission that I sensed what truly sets Christians apart from other benevolent people. You see, it is only Christians who have the unique privilege of changing the face of eternity one person at a time! "Therefore, as we have opportunity, let us do good to all people…"

Divine Commission

Prayer

Father in Heaven, thank You for selecting every Christian to be on Your personal ministry team. We thank You for setting us apart with Your divine commission to change the world… one person at a time! Your Son died a gruesome death, because You do not want "any to perish, but for all to come to repentance." Convict each of us to move beyond mere humanistic efforts to do good, so that our benevolence is with this motive: "That all may come to the saving knowledge of our Lord and Savior, Jesus Christ." We pray in His name. Amen.

Questions

- What is God's main purpose in allowing this present world to continue? (II Peter 3:9)

- What are Paul's comments regarding whatever you say and do? (Colossians 3:17)

- If you have no conviction regarding the Great Commission, are you really under the authority of Jesus Christ at all? (Matthew 28:18)

Journal

I have told you these things, so that in me you may have peace. In this world you will have trouble. But take heart! I have overcome the world.
(John 16:33)

Let the peace of Christ rule in your hearts, since as members of one body you were called to peace. And be thankful. (Colossians 3:15)

Meditation   Dudley C. Rutherford

The whole world could use a little cheer. If Paul the apostle could stand on board a storm-tossed ship (Acts 27:25) and say, "Cheer up," it seems that you and I could be a little more hopeful. I like the Apostle John's advice while marooned on a prison island: "Be of good cheer, for I have overcome the world." Let me suggest a few ways to help you cheer up.

1. Count what you have, not what you don't have. Remember to do that every day for the rest of your life. If you start counting what you don't have, you'll go crazy.

2. Find something in your life right now that's going well. It can't all be bad.

3. Try to remember the worst thing that ever happened to you. You did live through that, didn't you?

4. Think of one person, just one, who is glad you're alive. Everybody has somebody.

5. Read some of the Psalms every day. There are 365 "fear nots" in the Good Book. One for every day of the year.

6. Remember Jesus Christ loved you enough to die for you. You are worth plenty to Him, since He gave His life for you.

Prayer

Dear God, You know how easily I fall into worrying. Teach me to learn from some of the saints in the Bible, that we not only get through difficult trials but we also are made far better people because of the experience. If my life is lived with great faith in Your powerful and protective hands, then I know I have nothing to fear. Teach me, Lord, that through You I have "overcome the world." I pray all these things in the name of Jesus. Amen!

Questions

- Name two Bible men who could rejoice in great conflict.

- Are you promised to have much trouble in life?

- What are some of the listed methods of overcoming?

Journal

_____

_____

_____

_____

■ May 24

For I received from the Lord what I also passed on to you: The Lord Jesus, on the night he was betrayed, took bread, and when he had given thanks, he broke it and said, "This is my body, which is for you; do this in remembrance of me." (I Corinthians 11:23-24ff)

Meditation   *Dudley C. Rutherford*

Someone new might be asking, "Just what is the breaking of bread? What is this Communion?" Let me quickly explain. On the night Judas betrayed his master, Jesus was seated around a table with the Twelve partaking of a Passover meal. The purpose of the Passover meal (Exodus 12) was to celebrate the occasion on which the death angel (Jesus) passed over the Hebrew family, sparing its firstborn while killing the firstborn of the Egyptians.

After Jesus and His men had finished the Passover meal, they were still seated around the table with some of the foods from the Passover menu left on the table in front of them. Jesus took some of the unleavened bread and said, "Fellows, I'm instituting a new meal; this bread without yeast will represent My body and this pure, unfermented grape juice will represent My blood. I want you to gather each week and partake of these two emblems. Yes, I am going to be killed in a few hours, but I will rise again. Each week, you are to gather together and partake of this meal in remembrance of Me." For 2,000 years, the Church has been gathering around this mystical table, celebrating our deliverance and that special hour that Christ passed over our sins by dying on the cross. Will you be faithful to this meal?

Prayer

Dear Lord, thank You again and again for dying for my sins on Calvary's cross. Thank You for sacrificing Your body and allowing Your blood to be poured out for me. Thank You for making it possible for me to be faithful to You and Your meal by gathering around this spiritual table with people of like faith and remembering all the benefits I have in Christ. It is in the name of Jesus Christ, I pray. Amen.

Questions

- Where did Paul get his information about Communion?

- What does the cup and the bread represent?

- Have you read about the Passover in Exodus 12?

Journal

> *"Therefore go and make disciples of all nations, baptizing them in the name of the Father and of the Son and of the Holy Spirit, and teaching them to obey everything I have commanded you. And surely I am with you always, to the very end of the age." (Matthew 28:19, 20)*

Meditation   *Milton Jones*

If you actually analyze the Great Commission, there is only one commandment, and it is *not* "Go!" No, the only command in the Great Commission is to "make disciples." There are three participles (those tricky "ing" words) connected to making disciples. Two of the participles are pretty easy to discern: baptizing and teaching. However, the third is a bit harder to find. It is "go." Where is the "ing"? That's a good question, but it is still one of those participles.

As a result, the Great Commission really doesn't say, "Go." Instead, it says, "Going," or maybe you could best say, "As you are going." This changes the perception quite a bit, doesn't it? To make disciples as I am going is very different from going someplace to make disciples.

I don't have to go someplace to make disciples. It is simply a matter of what I do as I am going. As you are going, make disciples. You are going places all the time. You go to school. You go to work. You go to the mall. You go to church. You go home. All of us are going. Our generation is the most "going" group of all time. We hardly ever stop going.

Francis of Assisi summarized it well. He said, "Unless you preach everywhere you go, there's no use going anywhere to preach."

Milton Jones is the Senior Minister of Northwest Church of Christ in Seattle, WA.

Prayer

Lord, please open my eyes that I might see the people You put in my life. Help me to see them as people You created, loved and, most of all, died for. Let me realize that my purpose on this earth is to reach as many people as possible before You return. I pray that every place I go, no matter where I'm traveling, I will be quick to share the message of salvation. Lord, give me some "giddy-up" in my "going." In Jesus' name. Amen.

Questions

- Where are you "going"?

- Who are your friends, relatives, co-workers and neighbors who need Jesus?

- How can you better put in a good word for Jesus where you are?

Journal

_____

_____

_____

_____

_____

But made himself nothing, taking the very nature of a servant, being made in human likeness. And being found in appearance as a man, he humbled himself and became obedient to death—even death on a cross! (Phil. 2:7-8)

Unlike the other high priests, he does not need to offer sacrifices day after day, first for his own sins, and then for the sins of the people. He sacrificed for their sins once for all when he offered himself. (Hebrews 7:27)

Meditation   *Dudley C. Rutherford*

Put on your imagination cap. Picture this. Imagine, if you can, a wealthy young prince of a man, handsome and rich beyond measure. And across town in a lowly tenement district, in a hovel of a shanty, an older unsightly woman lives in poverty. She is ragged, dirty and unkempt. And the four filthy walls that stare at her from morning until night are bare. She is poor, penniless and sick.

Imagine, if you can, the handsome young prince leaves the splendor of his palatial estate and moves into that ghetto only a few houses away from her, and begins to court and woo this unsightly girl, on her level of squalor and dinginess… until the day comes when he can honestly and sincerely say, "I love you. Please marry me and let us go and live in my palace, in splendor and luxury."

If you picture that scene, then you have some faint idea of what Jesus did for us. We were so lost, so unlovely, so steeped in our sins. The Bible says our righteousness is like filthy rags. But still the handsome Prince Jesus came to our world, to our level, and with His Church He is trying to win us, to woo us and take us to be forever with Him in Heaven. Jesus wants to spend an eternal honeymoon with you.

Eternal Honeymoon

Prayer

Dear Father, Your spectacular love is beyond our understanding or explanation. We cannot fathom why You love us so, because we know we are so unlovely. But we thank You and ask for strength to so live our lives that we will never forget Your supreme sacrifice on our behalf. Thank You for coming to our level and wooing us. In the name of Jesus Christ, I pray. Amen.

Questions

- How did Jesus take on the form of a servant?

- How many times must He die for you?

- Should His humiliation challenge or discourage you? How?

Journal

May 27

But he gives us more grace. That is why Scripture says: "God opposes the proud but gives grace to the humble." Submit yourselves, then, to God. Resist the devil, and he will flee from you. Come near to God and he will come near to you. Wash your hands, you sinners, and purify your hearts, you double-minded. (James 4:6-8)

Meditation   H. Dean Rutherford

There are only three times in the entire Bible that Satan speaks. His footsteps and evil deeds are recorded throughout the Scriptures but his verbal words are recorded only thrice. He speaks first in the Garden of Eden while seducing Adam and Eve (Genesis 3). The second time Satan's speech is recorded is found all through the book of Job, where he tries his best to get godly Job to renounce his God. The third and final speech by Satan is when he tries to tempt Jesus in the wilderness (Luke 4). He failed two out of these three different attempts, as you can see.

Satan is speaking today to you and me. He has not given up. The divine remedy to defeat the devil is found in our above text in James 4:7, "Resist the devil and he will flee from you." And notice that you cannot do the one without the other. You cannot resist the devil without submitting unto God, and you cannot submit unto God without resisting the devil. Let me add this: Resisting the devil halfheartedly will not get the job done. Satan must know for sure that he can no longer make good use of his time trying to tempt you. Then, and only then, he will flee.

Satan Speaks

Prayer

Dear Father above, I want to so resist Satan that he will become discouraged and leave my soul alone. I want to live so close to You that he will know once and for all that I belong to You and that I can't be bribed or tempted anymore by his deceptive ways. I know I can't serve You both at the same time. I've tried that and it doesn't work. I submit myself to You today to be Yours and Yours alone. In the name of Jesus, I pray. Amen.

Questions

- What is the best way to resist Satan?

- Can you resist Satan without submitting to God?

- What would your life look like if you truly had victory over Satan?

Journal

_____

_____

_____

_____

_____

> *Moses said to God, "Suppose I go to the Israelites and say to them, 'The God of your fathers has sent me to you,' and they ask me, 'What is his name?' Then what shall I tell them?" God said to Moses, "I am who I am. This is what you are to say to the Israelites: 'I AM has sent me to you.'" (Exodus 3:13, 14)*

Meditation   *David N. Rutherford*

Although numerous names for God were given in the book of Genesis, when it was time to lead His people in a massive migration, God instructed Moses to use His forever name. From within the burning bush, He further specified that this particular name was to be handed like a torch from generation to generation. While the Israelites relished the familiar stories of God's directives for Abraham, Isaac and Jacob, both God and Moses knew they would soon question His personal guidance of their own generation. Tragically, the 40-year mass exodus turned into a massive graveside. Only two individuals from that entire generation actually trusted in "I AM" to chart their course.

Hundreds of years later, the unbelief became even more severe. This time, instead of sending someone else to deliver His people, the Great "I AM" actually arrived in flesh and blood. Brazenly, that first-century generation "picked up stones to stone Him" and later had Him hung on a cross to die. But even that tragedy did not halt God's faithfulness, for He has sent His "I AM" Spirit directly into the hearts of our generation. "Today, if you hear His voice, do not harden your hearts!" He is not only the God of history and Heaven, but He longs to be known as the God of your here and now!

David N. Rutherford is the Senior Pastor of Northside Christian Church in Clovis, CA. and the brother of Dudley C. Rutherford.

Prayer

Dear Heavenly Father, it astounds us to know that You, the Creator and Sustainer of the entire universe, want to be involved in our everyday affairs. But why else would You delight in such a name as "I AM?" As we live from day to day, continue to remind us of Your forever name. We thank You and praise You for Your faithfulness to us each and every moment. Fill us now, so that we will have the power to be faithful to You in the moments we have left on this earth! In Jesus' name I pray. Amen.

Questions

- When does God want you to listen to His voice? (Hebrews 4:7)

- How long does God want to be known as "I AM?" (Exodus 3:15b)

- What did Jesus say in reference to Abraham that made the people want to stone Him? (John 8:56-59)

Journal

_____

_____

_____

_____

_____

> *"Come," he said. Then Peter got down out of the boat, walked on the water and came toward Jesus. But when he saw the wind, he was afraid and, beginning to sink, cried out, "Lord, save me!"*
>
> *(Matthew 14:29, 30)*

Meditation   Mike Maiolo

The Coast Guard Marine Safety Office requires all commercial fishing vessels to carry distress signals. The type and number of distress signals required depends on how far offshore they go. Many Christians miss an opportunity to realize the need to equip themselves with distress signals. We begin our faith life as new creations. Oftentimes, we are so excited about the adventure of living in God's grace that, we don't realize the need to take emergency precautions. In the course of learning how to sail and navigate along the Way, we may not learn how to ask for help. If we find ourselves adrift or off-course, there can be deadly consequences.

What if there was a Christian Safety Office that required all healthy vessels of God to be equipped with distress signals? Sunday mornings would come and the usual greeting exchange would begin, "Hi, how are you today?" The person in distress would start to say, "Fine, thank you," but the distress signal would send forth a loud, *"Beep. Beep.* Believer in distress! Mayday!" At the sound, all mature believers would run to assist: offering prayer, physical help and encouragement. God desires us to be a grace-based community of believers that cares for each other. We were created to be interdependent. We need to learn how to ask for help, as well as how to offer it.

Mike Maiolo is Senior Pastor at Mission Viejo Christian Church in Mission Viejo, CA.

Beep Beep

Prayer

Heavenly Father, I praise Your name because You are Perfect. In Your divine wisdom, You created me to need others. Give me the humility to ask for help when I am caught off-course. Help me to respond with an immediate prayer response. Help me to stay genuine enough to cry, "Mayday!" Guide me to wise counsel from other believers. Help me to receive such counsel with wisdom and grace. Remind me, Lord, to be aware of the needs of others. In Jesus' name. Amen.

Questions

- How far offshore do you usually find yourself before you realize you need to send a distress signal?

- Who are three people in your life from whom you can ask for spiritual help?

- How prepared are you to notice and respond to distress signals in other Christians?

Journal

■ May 30

And you, my son Solomon, acknowledge the God of your father, and serve him with wholehearted devotion and with a willing mind, for the LORD searches every heart and understands every motive behind the thoughts. If you seek him, he will be found by you; but if you forsake him, he will reject you forever. (I Chronicles 28:9)

Meditation   H. Dean Rutherford

Here are some old-time words I borrowed from a Bible expositor and illuminator:

The knowledge of Christ is a purse full of gold; it will pay your way in all the strange places of life. The knowledge of Christ is a flower that never fades; carry it in your bosom and it will fill your life with fragrance. It is a light that cheers the darkest night; the longer it burns the brighter it grows, and fierce winds only make it shine more clearly; it turns a hovel into a palace, makes a rough road smooth, is easily carried and costs nothing.

It is a well, whose crystal stream makes all around beautiful and pure, refreshes the weary passerby, never knows the drought of summer, and from life's morning to its latest evening flows steadily carrying joy and song throughout its course.

It is a sunbeam from paradise, a smile from the face of God, the songbook of saints, the harp of angels, the key to Heaven's treasury, and the passport into the presence of the King. It makes rainbows on storm clouds, transforms tears into pearls, and thorns into apple trees, and causes the desert to blossom as a rose. It makes the heart larger than a kingdom, richer than a bank, brighter than a palace, and happier than a grove in which a thousand birds are singing. Get this knowledge above all things. Increase it, teach it, live and prize it above rubies, for it is your happiness, your glory, and your life.

Prayer

Sometimes God, You are not very easy to see. Maybe that's because I'm so half-hearted in my seeking You. Help me to seek You with my whole heart and know that when that happens, You will be near to me. May I spend the best part of my life energies and action in finding the knowledge of Your dear Son, Jesus. I need Him now, and I will always need Him. I need Him more than I need my latest breath, and in His name, I pray. Amen.

Questions

- Name the ways God seeks you.

- In what two ways should you serve Him, according to this passage?

- What happens if you forsake Him for all time?

Journal

May 31

Ask and it will be given to you; seek and you will find; knock and the door will be opened to you. For everyone who asks receives; he who seeks finds; and to him who knocks, the door will be opened. (Matthew 7:7-8)

Meditation   *Dudley C. Rutherford*

Here are six ideas and suggestions for improving one's prayer life. They are all taken from the Bible as well as from years of experience:

1. Depend totally upon the merits and powers of the Lord Jesus Christ as the only ground of any claim for requested blessings. (John 14:13,14 & John 15:16)

2. Separate yourself from all known sin. If we regard iniquity in our hearts, the Lord will not hear us, for it would be sanctioning sin. (Psalm 66:18)

3. Have faith in God's Word and reputation that He will keep His promises. Not to believe Him is to make Him both a liar and a perjurer. (Hebrews 11:6 & Hebrews 6:13-20)

4. Always ask in accordance with His divine will. We must not seek any gift of God merely to consume it upon our lusts. (I John 5:14 & James 4:3)

5. Have great patience. There must be waiting on God, and waiting for God, as the farmer has long patience to wait for the harvest. (James 5:7 & Luke 18:1-8)

6. Read the Bible in conjunction with prayer, believing that God and His Holy Spirit will instruct you and help you with study and understanding.

Prayer

Dear wonderful Father, thank You that I can communicate with You. You are my intimate friend. I want prayer to become more and more a part of my daily life, so each and every thing I do will be a prayer that brings me and ties me closer to You. I intend to start living a prayerful and prayer-filled life. Help me to make this my top priority in life. In Christ's precious name, I pray. Amen.

Questions

- What are some prerequisites to prayer?

- Why read the Bible when you pray?

- Why does God want you to separate from sin?

Journal

■ June 1

However, to the man who does not work but trusts God who justifies the wicked, his faith is credited as righteousness. David says the same thing when he speaks of the blessedness of the man to whom God credits righteousness apart from works. (Romans 4:5-6)

Meditation   *Dudley C. Rutherford*

Jesus took all my punishment. Oh, come on now Dudley, you're not such a bad person, and you don't deserve to be punished. Wrong! If you think that, then it's because you simply don't know me very well. If you knew me like Jesus knows me, you would probably not be reading this. I have sinned. I continue to sin. I deserve God's punishment. But reflect on this: Jesus, on the cross, took all your punishment. He paid the full price. He took our stain and our blame at Calvary.

You think that's good? I have something even better than that. Jesus imputes His righteousness to your record. That means all the miracles Jesus performed, the good deeds He did, dying selflessly on the cross, I get the credit for. I'm excited. Someday when they open up the Dudley Rutherford book, all the sin and the filth will be blotted out and all the good that Jesus did will be written under my name. I can hardly wait. God our Heavenly Father will say, "Hey Dudley, did you do all this stuff that's under your name?" I'll say, "Father, it's not me, it's Jesus!" The Bible puts it another way. It says we will be clothed in His garments, garments of righteousness.

Prayer

Dear Lord, it's so thrilling and exciting to think that all Your good deeds are now on my record and that all my dirty sins and betrayals are on Your record. I don't deserve anything even remotely close to that but I accept Your grace. The realization of those truths makes me want to live a better and closer life with You and for You. Help me in this, for I pray these things in the name of my Savior, Jesus Christ. Amen.

Questions

- How would you explain grace and mercy?

- Whose record book now holds the good deeds of Jesus?

- In which spiritual direction should this knowledge lead you?

Journal

_____

_____

_____

_____

_____

I have come that they may have life, and have it to the full. (John 10:10)

But the widow who lives for pleasure is dead even while she lives. (I Timothy 5:6)

Meditation   *Dudley C. Rutherford*

Have you ever seen Thornton Wilder's play entitled *Our Town*? It's a famous stage play and movie, and most high schools and colleges present it in their drama department. *Our Town* is a story about a family of which Emily is the daughter and the star of the play. As Emily grows older and gets married, she dies giving birth to her baby. In the afterlife, she is treated very kindly and is given permission to go back and visit for just one day. She chooses the day of her 12th birthday. She walks into the room and no one can see or hear her, but there she is looking at herself and her family as they celebrate her 12th birthday.

She is shocked by what she sees: the carelessness and casualness with which they live life. Her family does not enter into these experiences with appreciation or awareness of the preciousness of life. She yells at the family, even though they can't hear her. "Don't you care? Don't you understand you won't have this moment forever?" Then she turns and looks at the audience and screams, "Do any of you really ever live life when you're alive?" I think Emily is saying what the Bible would say to us all. Live life to its fullest, and that means to reflect and determine the important things as you go along.

Prayer

Dear Lord of my life, help me to live each day one at a time. Help me to see life's brevity and that I should be using a part of each day to follow Your will and plan for my life and to serve You and Your Kingdom. I have always known it is easy to spend hours on unimportant things that glorify no one and bless no one. Help me live my life as one who truly cares. In Christ's perfect name, I pray. Amen.

Questions

- Name ways in which God desires for you to live life to the fullest.

- If you spend most of your life in pleasure, what are you?

- What are some things you do that prove you really care?

Journal

> *I tell you the truth, anyone who has faith in me will do what I have been doing. He will do even greater things than these, because I am going to the Father. (John 14:12)*

Meditation   *Tony Campolo*

Many of us can give testimonies of miracles that have been wrought by prayer, and we have heard testimonies of what God has done that defy scientific explanation. Nevertheless, we have never heard of miracles performed in the name of Christ that have exceeded those performed by Jesus. Yet Jesus tells us in this verse that we will be able to do "greater works" than He did, because He goes to His Father. Obviously He is not referring to miracles, but rather He is referring to the love that lay behind the miracles. Every one of the miracles Jesus performed was motivated by love, and He makes it quite clear in His teachings that love is more important than the miracles. It's love that is of prime importance in His ministry.

When Christ was here in the flesh, He could only personally connect in love with one person at a time. If He was looking into the face of Mary, He was not looking into the face of Martha. If He was connecting with Andrew, He was not connecting with Peter. But if the Christ that was incarnated in Jesus is alive in every one of us in the Church, then at any given moment, Christ could be loving – through the members of His Church – millions of people around the world. Obviously, those millions of people exceed the number one. It's as though Jesus were saying, "I can only love one person at a time right now, but after I ascend to the Father and then enter into you through the power of the Holy Spirit, I will be able to be even more loving, because I will be incarnated in millions of people around the globe." That's why He could say, "The work that I do (loving people), ye shall do because I go unto the Father; and because there will be so many of you, you will be able to love even more people at any given moment than I was able to do when I was incarnated into the flesh."

Tony Campolo is Professor of Sociology at Eastern University in St. Davids, PA.

Greater Miracles

Prayer

Dear Father, I pray that You will send the Holy Spirit to fill me, so that Christ might be every bit as alive in me as He was in Jesus 2,000 years ago. I want to be an instrument of Your love, even as Your Son was an instrument of Your love 2,000 years ago. I know it was not through the power of miracles, but rather through the love of humble people that the world has changed, and I want to be an instrument of change in the name of Jesus. Cleanse me, fill me with Christ, and let me be a conduit of love for Christ's love to the world. Amen.

Questions

- Do you spend time each day surrendering to Christ, and asking for His presence to become increasingly manifest in you?

- Do you consciously communicate love to the people around you in your everyday life?

- To what extent have you seen the love of Christ that flows through you reap fruit in other people, for the Kingdom of God?

Journal

■ June 4

Do not be afraid of what you are about to suffer. I tell you, the devil will put some of you in prison to test you, and you will suffer persecution for ten days. Be faithful, even to the point of death, and I will give you the crown of life. He who has an ear, let him hear what the Spirit says to the churches. He who overcomes will not be hurt at all by the second death.

(Revelation 2:10-11)

Meditation — Dudley C. Rutherford

One of the most thrilling things in all secular literature was a man by the name of Tigernese. He and his wife were captured by the King of Cyprus and put in prison, and their fate was certain death.

Of course, they were separated in cells, and the King of Cyprus went first to Tigernese and said, "What would you give me if I were to let your wife go free out of this prison?"

"I do not need to take time to think about that. I would gladly, in an instant, without any regret at all, die if you would just let her go free."

The king was rather impressed with that statement of loyalty.

He made his way down the hall and went into her cell and said, "You know, I just talked to your husband, and do you know what he said? He said he would gladly die if I would just let you go free."

And she said this – it's a part of recorded history. She said, "The love of that man makes me forget all others."

Will you be faithful to Him who gladly died for you? When you think of how much Jesus has proven His love for you, does the very thought of Him make you forget all others?

Prayer

Dear sweet Lover and Savior of mine, Your love for me overwhelms me and makes me more determined than ever to love You and to be more faithful to You. When I reflect on Your love and some of the great things You have done for me, it makes me forget all others. I pledge again my first love and loyalty to my Lord and Savior Jesus Christ. And in that divine name, I pray. Amen.

Questions

- What should your attitude be when called upon to suffer?

- How can you escape the second death?

- Christ's love is so great it should cause you to forget what?

Journal

> *Do not love the world or anything in the world. If anyone loves the world, the love of the Father is not in him. For everything in the world—the cravings of sinful man, the lust of his eyes and the boasting of what he has and does—comes not from the Father but from the world. The world and its desires pass away, but the man who does the will of God lives forever.*
>
> *(I John 2:15-17)*

Meditation — *Dudley C. Rutherford*

Once upon a time, you met Jesus Christ. Admit it! You fell in love with Him and promised to be faithful to Him. For some of you, it was at church camp, or during a revival, or on an Easter Sunday. But you met Jesus. You promised Him you would be true. You said, "I love You, Jesus. Whatever it takes, I'll be yours." But the world is always whispering into your ear, "Hey, you can have fun. You can be popular, rich and famous." Satan says, "I can give you pleasure, ease, happiness, money. I'll put you on the map. I can take you to Hollywood." Jesus is saying, "Be faithful until death and I will give you the crown of life." Jesus is saying, "Satan is not what he's cracked up to be. He promises things he cannot deliver. Following Satan is a life of chasing mirages."

Do you know that 16 times in the Bible, Jesus says, "Meditate on Me" or "Think on Me"? The world is saying to you today, "Give me your attention." "Hey," Satan says, "We're having a reunion next Sunday. You haven't seen your brother in two months. Why not come over to the coast and visit?" As Christians, we are always being tempted not between good and evil, but rather between good and better. To whom are you listening?

Prayer

Dear ever faithful Jesus. You are always faithful to me. I am not always faithful to You. But I want to be. I want to stop listening to Satan and his false promises and I want to heed the still small voice of my Master, Jesus Christ. You always keep Your Word. Your promises are always true. I am going to stay so close to You that I won't hear the roaring lion Satan trying to tempt me away from the things of Your Kingdom. In Jesus' name, I pray. Amen.

Questions

- Which voice speaks to you the most?

- Why is Satan called a liar?

- Can you think of some of Satan's lies you have believed?

Journal

June 6

And one thing more: Prepare a guest room for me, because I hope to be restored to you in answer to your prayers. (Philemon 22)

Meditation   *Victor Knowles*

Does prayer matter? Can my prayers have any possible effect on those I am praying for? Is it really worthwhile to take time to pray? This text shouts, "Yes!" to these questions. The great Apostle Paul was in prison, chained to a Roman soldier. Yet he instructs his friend Philemon to prepare a guest room for him. How amazing is that? But then Paul says, "For I trust that *through your prayers* I shall be granted to you."

Through your prayers, great things can happen today. Through your prayers, someone unjustly imprisoned may be released. Through your prayers, a discouraged missionary may suddenly be filled with hope and stay on the field. Through your prayers, a rocky marriage may experience calmer waters. Through your prayers, someone who is weak may feel power returning to their body. Through your prayers, the hungry may be filled, the naked may be clothed, the lonely may be visited.

But faith in the power of prayer must be matched by deeds of love and mercy. "Prepare a guest room for me." Faith without works is dead. Let us pray in faith. Let us act in mercy.

Victor Knowles is the Director of Peace On Earth Ministries in Joplin, MO.

Does Prayer Matter?

Prayer

Loving Father, there are so many people who depend upon the prayers of others. Some of them are too tired, too discouraged, too weary to pray. We confess to You that we have been where they are before. Hear our prayers for them today. We lay these petitions at the foot of Your throne, always grateful that it is a Throne of Grace. Give them grace today, we pray. And help us to remember to "prepare a guest room" for someone today, whatever form that "guest room" may take. Receive this prayer of faith, in the name of Your Son Jesus Christ. Amen.

Questions

- Does this verse motivate you to be more earnest in prayer for others?

- Who might be depending on your prayers right now?

- In anticipation of answered prayer, what kind of "guest room" should you be preparing?

Journal

_____

_____

_____

_____

_____

> *Remember your Creator in the days of your youth, before the days of trouble come and the years approach when you will say, "I find no pleasure in them." (Ecclesiastes 12:1)*

Meditation   *Dudley C. Rutherford*

As you read this chapter, I want you to know that Solomon is saying everyone should start serving Christ in the days of youth, because old age finds it much more difficult to do so. I've added a few parentheses to help with the understanding. The above passage continues in verse two: before the sun and the light and the moon and the stars grow dark (difficult to discern things), and the clouds return after (things don't seem to improve), the rain when the keepers of the house (bodily nerves) tremble, and the strong men (shoulders) stoop, when the grinders (teeth) cease because they are few, and those looking through the windows (eyes) grow dim; when the doors to the street are closed and the sound of grinding (eating) fades; when men rise up at the sound (light sleepers) of birds, when men are (two feet too high) afraid of heights, when the almond tree (pure white hair) blossoms, and desire (sexual) no longer is stirred. Then man goes to his eternal home. He makes it clear that one can serve Christ in old age but it becomes more burdensome. Solomon closes out this wonderful chapter with this dramatic declaration: "Now all has been heard; here is the conclusion of the matter: Fear God and keep his commandments, for this is the whole duty of man. For God will bring every deed into judgment, including every hidden thing, whether it is good or evil" (Ecclesiastes 12:13-14).

Conclusion

Prayer

Dear God of wisdom, thank You for reminding me that youth is the best time to start serving the Lord. I have always sensed that, but it's good to read it for sure in Your record book. I want to serve You in the days of my youth and I want to remain faithful during my middle years and be found faithful in old age toward the end of the journey. I pray these things in Jesus' wonderful name. Amen.

Questions

- Why is it best to serve Christ in the days of youth?

- What are some of Solomon's descriptions of old age that you can relate to?

- What is the conclusion of the matter?

Journal

> *And the devil, who deceived them, was thrown into the lake of burning sulfur, where the beast and the false prophet had been thrown. They will be tormented day and night for ever and ever. (Revelation 20:10)*

Meditation   *Dudley C. Rutherford*

The Bible says that even though Judas was in the inner circle, he went to hell. And he went to hell for all of eternity. I am prone to forget that last part sometimes. It's such an awful scene, but in hell Judas begs for someone to come and dip their finger in water and cool his tongue, for he is in flames and torment. When Augustus was emperor of Rome and ruled the world, Judas was in hell. When Martin Luther shouted defiance and corruption against his Church, Judas was still in hell. When Christopher Columbus discovered America, Judas was in hell. When George Washington walked amid the snowstorms of Valley Forge, it was no concern to Judas, for he was in flames. When Abraham Lincoln stood at Gettysburg and cried out, "Fourscore and seven years ago our fathers…" Judas was still in hell. When the Wright brothers lifted that heavier-than-air machine into the air at Kitty Hawk, N.C., it was of no consequence to Judas. When President Kennedy was assassinated in Dealey Plaza in Dallas, Texas, it caused no concern to Judas; he didn't even blink, for he was in hell. On January 29, 1986, when the space shuttle Challenger exploded over the coastal waters of Florida, Judas wasn't interested. When the Berlin Wall came crashing down and democracy flourished, Judas paid no attention. And today while you and I are eating lunch, Judas is still in hell. I know this isn't proper or politically correct, but my Bible demands that we not ignore this terrible truth.

Prayer

Dear Father in Heaven, You live where I want to live. I don't ever want to be lost beyond Your love and Your presence. Give me the strength to give up those things that would hinder my journey to You, and to forsake those sins that would put me in eternal company with Judas. Lord, thank You for saving me through the shed blood of Jesus Christ. I fervently pray in the name of Jesus. Amen.

Questions

- Name some reasons Judas went to hell.

- How would you describe the length of eternity?

- What will Heaven be like?

Journal

June 9

> *Trust in the Lord and do good; dwell in the land and enjoy safe pasture. Delight yourself in the Lord and he will give you the desires of your heart. Commit your way to the Lord; trust in him and he will do this: He will make your righteousness shine like the dawn, the justice of your cause like the noonday sun. Be still before the Lord and wait patiently for him; do not fret when men succeed in their ways, when they carry out their wicked schemes. (Psalm 37:3-7)*

Meditation   *Don Wilson*

Everything in life begins with commitments. Think of commitments you have made in life: accepting Christ, getting married, buying a house, etc. Commitment always builds character. Commitment is keeping your word no matter what happens.

After we commit our way to the Lord, we then must learn how to trust Him. Trust means we put our faith in the Lord to do what is best. So often we say we trust the Lord, but when the Lord does not answer our prayers, we quickly put ourselves in charge and take control of the situation.

The third key to balance in life is to delight in the Lord. Delight gives energy and momentum to life. Laughing actually extends your life. Joy helps you get through the tough times of life. One reason Christians have difficulty finding balance is that we tend to take ourselves too seriously and God not seriously enough. We need to reverse that.

The fourth key to balance is learning how to rest and be patient. Most of us in our fast-paced culture would like to go directly from commitment to rest, but rest is hard-earned. It comes after we make commitments, trust God to work in each situation, and then delight as we see God work.

What do you do after you rest? You get up the next morning and repeat the cycle. You grow in your relationship with the Lord as you commit more, trust more, delight more and rest more.

Don Wilson is the Senior Pastor of Christ's Church of the Valley in Peoria, AZ.

Finding Balance in Life

Prayer

Father I come to You right now admitting that my life is out of balance. In this world it is so hard to submit completely to You. I feel if I am going to compete in this culture I need to take the reins. Would you allow me to not take myself so seriously, and give me the mind and heart to begin to take You more seriously? Father on a planet of chaos, would You be my equilibrium? Please give me the strength I need to find balance and just be still for a while and know You are God. In Jesus' name. Amen.

Questions

- Why do so many people today seem to lack balance in their lives?

- What are some things that are difficult for you to turn over to the Lord?

- Which of the four keys do you need to work on to find balance?

Journal

_____

_____

_____

_____

_____

Some men came, bringing to him a paralytic, carried by four of them. Since they could not get him to Jesus because of the crowd, they made an opening in the roof above Jesus and, after digging through it, lowered the mat the paralyzed man was lying on. When Jesus saw their faith, he said to the paralytic, "Son, your sins are forgiven." (Mark 2:3-5)

Meditation   *Dudley C. Rutherford*

Can't you picture this scene? Four people doing everything within their power to get their friend in front of Jesus, even if it meant to destroy the roof of a house. I wonder if we have that same burden, that same desire to see people saved. So often we get sidetracked and easily become disengaged with what should be the priority of our life. Evangelism and winning people to Jesus should be at the core of everything we do.

I've always imagined these four friends being different. One was tall, one was short, one was fast and one was slow. Yet they worked in unison for the salvation of their unsaved colleague. It is a portrait of the Church! We, who make up the Body of Christ, are uniquely different in our makeup, yet we are to be extremely compatible when it comes to reaching people for Christ. Looking beyond our differences and our preferences and simply working shoulder to shoulder to lead people to Jesus.

The above text tells us that when our Lord saw the faith of the four, He turned and forgave the paralytic of his sins. This forces me to ask what kind of faith the Lord sees in me.

Will you join me, in faith, to literally and figuratively carry people to our Savior?

What A Scene

Prayer

Dear Father in Heaven, cleanse me from my indifference and give me a burden to lead people to Christ. I have lost my focus and neglected my responsibility to make a difference in the world around me. People would be saved if I were willing to actually lead them to You. You alone have the power to save, but Father, may You grant me compassion to see lost people saved. Give me faith, Lord, to fight through crowds, to dig through roofs, to lower mats and to usher people into Your presence. Help me, Lord, to remember what's important. In Jesus' name. Amen.

Questions

- When was the last time you shared your faith?

- When was the last time you brought a visitor to church?

- Who do you need to call right now?

Journal

June 11

Meditation   *Dudley C. Rutherford*

King David sinned. His heinous offense was primarily against the God that he loved so dearly. One can almost hear that agonizing, plaintive cry of repentance in Psalm 51, when David screamed, "Against You, You only, have I sinned…" Well, that was only partially true. As a matter of fact, David had sinned against Bathsheba, against Bathsheba's husband, against his own family, against the law of his land, against his kingly office and against all society and everything that was decent and righteous. But when David considered the enormity of his sin against his holy God, that overshadowed everything else.

You see, after all is said and done, God is the heart of the universe. God's character is the moral law of the entire planet. Every little sin and every big sin is a sin against a holy God. When I lie, I am really lying to God. When I betray a friend, or an enemy for that matter, in reality I am betraying Christ. Indeed we do, in our recklessness, sin against our own families, our own children and against society. However, we should remember that our greatest offense is also a major slap in the face of God, who desires us to live in righteousness and obedience.

Prayer

Dear Father, I get so lost and confused in my own little world that I forget that when I sin, I sin against my best friend and lover, Jesus Christ. Help me to remember that my omissions of right and commissions of wrong are in reality aimed at You. The carelessness of my sin dulls my senses and causes me to insult and neglect the only One who ever truly and purely loved me. I ask this prayer of repentance in the name of Jesus. Amen.

Questions

- When you sin, whom do you sin against?

- Why does it seem that David did not acknowledge his sin against Bathsheba?

- Read I John 1:9 and explain how sin can be forgiven.

Journal

> *...will make the Valley of Achor a door of hope. (Hosea 2:15)*
>
> *The LORD is slow to anger and great in power; the LORD will not leave the guilty unpunished. His way is in the whirlwind and the storm, and clouds are the dust of his feet. (Nahum 1:3)*

Meditation   *Dennis Bratton*

What moves you? How do you change anything in your life? Thoughts and ideas fascinate us, but do they have the power to change us? People influence us, but is friendship a motive to change? There seems to be a common denominator when it comes to real change in our lives, when we actually move from saying we believe something to really believing it. When Nahum wrote the "...clouds are the dust of God's feet..." (Nahum 1:3) he was talking about God's change agent. The "clouds," sorrow and suffering, are a precursor to a different future. Hosea referred to it as "...the valley of Achor (trouble)" that becomes "...a door of hope." He said it's on the other side of trouble that we celebrate a changed relationship with God.

It seems change occurs most effectively within us when we experience a personal crisis in which our equilibrium is disturbed. The plague of modern Christianity is that we're so interested in ourselves, we fall prey to one arrogant attempt after another to satisfy ourselves apart from dependence on God. It's the first snare of Satan to get us to refuse to sacrifice or surrender our wills to God; it's a sin that seems emminently reasonable to most of us. But in His relentless pursuit of our souls, God sends the clouds. He shepherds us through the valley of trouble to teach us to surrender to Him.

We don't tremble when we have everything under control. God wants us to tremble. He wants us to live our lives before an Audience of One, with nothing to prove, nothing to gain, nothing to lose. Living a fulfilling Christian life is not the purpose of our redemption. Getting what we want isn't guaranteed to believers. Christianity is a call to surrender our will, to become lost in God's purpose and glory. If it takes a "dust storm" to get us there, God loves us enough, desires us enough to take us through "...a valley of trouble" which can become our "...door of hope."

Dennis Bratton is Senior Pastor of Mandarin Christian Church in Jacksonville, FL.

Door of Hope

Prayer

Father God, teach me to trust You even when it is not safe. Teach me to come to the deepest, darkest place and still trust You. Forgive my selfish desires that have tried to turn You into the key that unlocks the treasure. Teach me to love You as the Treasure. And, Father, do to me whatever it takes to bring me to the place that pleases You. Amen.

Questions

- Identify a "valley of trouble" God took you through.

- What was the "dust of His feet" supposed to change in you?

- Did it become your "door of hope"?

Journal

Search me, O God, and know my heart; test me and know my anxious thoughts. (Psalm 139:23)

I the Lord search the heart and examine the mind. (Jeremiah 17:10)

Meditation   Dudley C. Rutherford

What is the heart? It's that inward man. Envy is a sin of the heart. Jealousy is a sin of the heart. Hatred is a sin of the heart. Grudges are sins of the heart. Stinginess and covetousness are sins of the heart. God searches our hearts. I want you to imagine a metal detector here. Here is a door you must walk through. If this door were a gossip door, would the alarm go off? Faithful church attendance door? Stingy door? Would it sound the alarm? Door of jealousy? Door of adultery? Door of lust or laziness?

David walked though the door of adultery and it went off. He then walked through the door of murder and it screamed. Yes, David committed adultery and murder, but he repented. He cried out, "Lord, cleanse thou me. Create in me a clean heart. Renew in me a right spirit." But notice all the Psalms David wrote after he repented. David knew precisely where his trouble began, in his heart. David knew he had failed to start the day off in prayer. He knew he had neglected his Bible reading, his quiet time, his time alone with God, his worship time. He knew his heart had grown cold and he allowed the devil to take over his heart. David knew that if way back yonder, he had started each day with, "Lord, search me," he wouldn't have gotten in all the trouble he was now in.

Lord, Search Me

Dear lovely Lord Jesus, I think the wisest thing I could ever do would be to start each day off by saying, "Search me, O God, and look into my heart." God, I want to walk all day, each day with You. Look deep inside, Lord, and help me take out everything that is sinful and harmful to my spiritual walk. Help me to keep You so close in my heart that I think about Your presence living in me. Like David in the Old Testament, help me to be honest and transparent before You. And I ask all this in the name of Christ. Amen.

Questions

- Who is the world's greatest heart doctor?

- Name some things in your heart that should not be there?

- Be honest: Do you really want God looking at your heart?

Journal

_____

_____

_____

_____

June 14

Search me, O God, and know my heart; test me and know my anxious thoughts. See if there is any offensive way in me, and lead me in the way everlasting. (Psalm 139:23,24)

Meditation   *Dudley C. Rutherford*

King David wrote the Psalms. Years ago, when I first started studying the life of David, I would wonder, "Lord, why didn't You let David die young? It seems to me, God, that You would have been wise to have taken David out of this world before he committed his awful sins. You know… when David was young, after he killed the mighty giant, Goliath, and after he became king and led his people to many great military victories… that would have been the perfect time to let him die." Instead, he lived long enough and fell into deep sin. It didn't seem right.

Then one day it dawned on me. If David had never sinned, we would never have had Psalm 51 or Psalm 139. We would never have had this model prayer of deep repentance. I'll tell you something else about David. I used to wonder why God kept insisting that David was a man after His own heart. I mean, David committed the scarlet sin of adultery and then he committed murder to cover it up, and God said years later, "David is a man after my own heart." Then I figured it out. David genuinely repented. David had to have his God back. These later Psalms were written after David had repented. David loved the things of the world. But he loved his God more. David was saying, "I don't have to be carnal. All I have to have is God. Search my heart, O God; You know it's true; all I really need is You. I can get by with some things. But I can't get by without You."

Authentic Repentance

Prayer

Dear God, like David, I want You to search deep into my heart. I want You to see if I have any offensive ways in me. Like David, I must have my God back. I don't have to have anything but You, dear Lord. If I have You and nothing else, I still have everything. If I have everything else and don't have You, I have nothing. Thank You for the real-life example of David repenting and asking for another chance to begin anew. I pray this petition in Your saving name. Amen.

Questions

- How does God test our hearts?

- Read Psalm 51.

- Why was David considered a man after God's own heart?

Journal

_____

_____

_____

_____

_____

■ June 15

From him the whole body, joined and held together by every supporting ligament, grows and builds itself up in love, as each part does its work.

(Ephesians 4:16)

Meditation   *Curt Ayers*

Several months ago, I had to take a trip to the emergency room because of a knee injury I received while jogging. I am a pastor of a church, so when my church friends found out I had gone to the emergency room, the news spread quickly. While I was being treated by the doctor, several people came into the reception area asking the receptionist about my condition, if I was all right, etc.…

So many people inquired about my condition that the receptionist asked me as I checked out of the clinic, "Who are you?"

Who am I?

First of all, I am a child of King Jesus. Second, I am a grateful Christian who belongs to the loving, compassionate body of Christ. Thank God for my Christian friends and family who ministered to me in a time of need.

The question is, are you an active, committed part of a local church? Are you intimately connected to a group of faithful Christians in a church family? Have you allowed other faithful believers into your life? If you're not in a church right now, find one and join it. If you are in a church, get more involved, give to it and serve other believers. "Who are you?"

Curt Ayers is Senior Pastor at Capri Christian Church in Naples, FL.

Who Are You?

Prayer

Dear Jesus, I want to thank you for the church of Jesus Christ. When this body of believers works together the members' needs are met. I want to thank you for the faithful members of my church who have constantly encouraged me, prayed for me, loved me and cared for me. Help me to give myself to my church. I want to be connected to a group of faithful believers and take up my role in ministering to others. Lead me to my new Christian friends. Thank You, Lord, for opening my eyes. In Jesus' name I pray. Amen.

Questions

- Name some occasions when you were ministered to by others.

- Why does God want you to connect with others?

- What steps can you take today toward connecting?

Journal

_____

_____

_____

_____

June 16

Meditation   *Dudley C. Rutherford*

I can't die for you. My blood is sinful. But I'll tell you what I can do. I can give my love to you and to others. I may not be able to be the best preacher. I may not be able to be the best teacher or singer. But I can love with the best of them. If Jesus lived here, I'm sure He would put an ad in the classifieds section: "Help wanted. Good pay. Eternal life." Job Description: "Wanted. Help to encourage the sick and the poor and the homeless and the blind." Do you know there are widows who are lonely and hurting? Some of them need yards mowed or wood cut, or a way to get to the grocery store. Do you know there are young mothers who are working two jobs just to pay rent? Do you know there are many kids who have no dad around who would love to go hiking or fishing?

I think if Jesus were here today, He would be knocking on your door saying, "What can I do for you? Can I wash your car? Can I buy you some groceries? Can I clean out your garage or mow your lawn? Do you have a relative who is sick and hurt that I could go visit and pray for?" Now since Jesus isn't here in the flesh any longer, you and I are to take His place. The next time you have an extra evening off, try the hospitals or the convalescent centers or the nursing homes. The world will never care what we know until it knows how much we care.

Your Hands and Feet

Prayer

Dear Father above, I know the world needs Your touch and it will only receive it through my life. I forget that You have no hands or feet except mine. Help me to be Your nurse on earth. Help me to be Your helper, Your lawyer, Your minister and Your doctor. Help me to heal broken lives by the love I have for You. May I spend the rest of my life loving others the way You have loved me. In Jesus' name, I pray. Amen.

Questions

- What keeps a person from living effectively for others?

- Did Jesus come to be served or to serve?

- When was the last time you remember helping a widow or an orphan?

Journal

June 17

Meditation   Dudley C. Rutherford

What are these verses saying? Simply this: if we are going to be like Jesus, we are going to make seeking and saving the lost among our top priorities in life. I can never forget that haunting woman at the well in John 4. She was a vile woman who met Jesus at the well outside the little town of Sychar. Jesus, being far more than psychic, said, "I see you have had five husbands and that you are now living illicitly with a another man." Her heart was touched. Her soul was strangely warmed. Now watch her as she goes back into town. She does about the bravest thing any person has ever done in the history of our planet. She starts going from door to door saying, "Come out to the well and meet a man who told me all the secret things of my life." She kept saying, "Let me introduce you to Jesus." I imagine she knew people were saying, "Lady, you're the last person on earth to be talking about God." I think she went to some of her past husbands and even the man with whom she was now sleeping and begged him to come meet Jesus. It just seems to me if the woman at the well could walk up and down the street, in the face of great humiliation, inviting people to Christ, it makes sense that we could go to our next-door neighbors and our associates at work, and ask them to come meet Jesus.

Woman at the Well

Prayer

Dear Heavenly Father, I want to imitate You and do exactly what You did when You were here on earth. I know that I need to spend more time in my life inviting others to Your Throne of Grace. Help me to stop wasting valuable time and make out a list today of those folks I need to invite to Your saving table. I thank You that someone once invited me. Help me to repay this debt often. Pour out boldness upon me, O Lord. In Jesus' name, I pray. Amen.

Questions

- Who are you supposed to be imitating with your life?

- For what reason did Jesus come to earth? (Luke 19:10)

- Will you make a list of people you need to invite to Jesus?

Journal

June 18

Meditation   Dane Johnson

As a freshman wrestler, my oldest son Matt was brought up to varsity one night to take on "the beast," a 215-pounder from a rival school. Matt's coach said his sole job was to avoid being pinned or injured. When I saw his opponent, I understood why there was no mention of winning! This guy pounded my chubby little freshman for two-and-a-half periods. I sat in the top bleachers the entire time, shouting encouragement and praying that he wouldn't be permanently damaged.

With 30 seconds to go, Matt caught the guy in a head and arm hold and nearly pinned him. As his dad, I went nuts! I came up out of my seat, bounded down the aisle, out onto the edge of the mat and began screaming, "Stick him! Stick him!" After the match was over, someone in the stands yelled, "Whose kid is that?" I shouted back, "That's *my* boy!"

You know, your Heavenly Father feels the same about you. He's cheering for you, desiring the very best for you. He groans when you struggle and He shouts with joy when you are victorious. To anyone who will listen, He says, "That's *my* child!" As you go about your day, remember who you are and who you belong to, then live like it. By the way, Matt won that match 10-9 and went on to win a CIF heavyweight championship his senior year. And yes, I'm still his dad and proud of it!

Dane Johnson is the Pastor of Sports & Men's Ministry at Christ's Church of the Valley in San Dimas, CA.

That's My Boy!

Father, thank You for being my Father. So often I forget that I am joint heir with You. You have provided for me and taken care of my every need. I know You love me and are cheering for me. Help me to live today in a way that will honor Your name and will allow You to be proud of me. In Jesus' name I pray. Amen.

Questions

- How does it make you feel to be a child of God?

- Can people readily see that you are a child of God?

- What one thing can you do today to bring honor to your Father?

Journal

_____

_____

_____

_____

June 19

In this way, love is made complete among us so that we will have confidence on the day of judgment, because in this world we are like him.

(I John 4:17)

Your attitude should be the same as that of Christ Jesus.

(Philippians 2:5)

Meditation   *Dudley C. Rutherford*

When Jesus went to Heaven, He left us in charge to show the world what He looks like. Did you know we are not here to make money or rear a family? We are not here to accumulate material goods. We are not put here on earth to be happy, or to be healthy. One of the greatest books ever written is *In His Steps* by Charles Sheldon. The theme of the book is this: What would Jesus do if He lived in modern America? How would He act on an elevator, a plane, in an office complex? What kind of a driver would He be?

One of the most challenging verses in the New Testament for me is this: Your attitude should be the same as that of Christ Jesus" (Philippians 2:5). That verse tells me I am to live so close to Christ, I soon take on His mind and His attitude. We are to act and react like Jesus. We are to walk like Jesus. We are to talk like Jesus and even look like Jesus. We are to say to all who see us and know us, "Look here, look at me. Jesus isn't here anymore, but here is the way He acts. Here is the way Jesus forgives. Here is the way He gives, and here is the way He loves." W.W.J.D.

Attitude of Christ

Prayer

Dear Lord, it humbles me to say this, but I want Your mind and intellect to be in me and I want to have Your attitude toward life and all that it presents. I know this cannot happen unless I invest quality time in Your Word. Help me to spend more time on these two knees that You gave me. Help me to start living a life of faith and stop living for my own pleasures. In Christ Jesus' name, I pray. Amen.

Questions

- Read Philippians Chapter 2.

- Which of these attributes are most difficult for you to live out?

- When people look at your life, who do they see?

Journal

Surely the arm of the LORD is not too short to save, nor his ear too dull to hear. But your iniquities have separated you from your God; your sins have hidden his face from you, so that he will not hear. (Isaiah 59:1-2)

Meditation   *Dudley C. Rutherford*

Sin always places a distance between man and God. Adam and Eve ran from the Creator in the hour of their disobedience. When they rebelled against the Lord, they should have run up to God and cried, "O, God we are so sorry. Is there any way we can restore this broken fellowship?" Instead, they ran and hid themselves. Sin is the sponsor of every trip away from God. Sin makes us break our appointments with Him.

The main reason we don't read the Bible is that we know if we read it very much, we will have to give up our sins. We would rather be separated from God than be separated from our sins. That is why we don't go to church. We are afraid it might lead us to confront and abandon our sins.

I hope none of you is running from God. I hope if you are in the far country of sin today, you are not foolish enough to think you can get away with it, even though all others have failed in the attempt. Please, please don't try to hide. The mills of God grind slowly, but they grind to powder. The legs of God's judgment are of iron and walk ever so slowly, but ever so surely.

The Gap

Prayer

Dear loving Savior of mine, I don't want to be separated from You. And I know that the only way I can stay with You is to have my sins forgiven. Help me from this hour forward to confront my sins, to confess my sins and to forsake my sins. Help me day by day to close this gap that my own sins have created by turning to You. Thank You for Your grace and mercy that You lavishly pour out upon me. I do not deserve Your goodness. In Jesus' forgiving name, I pray. Amen.

Questions

- What separates you from God?

- Whose fault is that?

- How does Jesus close this gap?

Journal

_____

_____

_____

_____

_____

> *But God demonstrates his own love for us in this: While we were still sinners, Christ died for us. (Romans 5:8)*

Meditation   Dave Hamlin

I spend a lot of time at the golf course now. The golf ball is the only ball I can hit because it isn't moving. It has been an incredible place to meet men who are far from having a personal relationship with Christ. I simply play in their golf leagues and try to build relationships.

It is amazing how many times a golf cart or the deck behind the clubhouse turns into a confessional. Imagine a sin and I have had it confessed to me at the golf course. Many of the men will thank me for being a friend and for not "preaching" to them. Most will end the conversation by saying something to the effect of "whenever I get *this* (whatever their personal sin issue is) under control, then I am going to start coming to your church and become a Christian."

At that moment, I struggle to find a polite way to tell them that if they are going to solve all of their problems and quit sinning before they come, then they will never come. If we could solve our sin problems without Jesus, we wouldn't need Jesus. The beauty of this verse is the reminder that while we were still in the midst of sinning, God loved us enough to give us Jesus, the ultimate answer to our sin!

Dave Hamlin is Senior Pastor of Shelby Christian Church in Shelbyville, KY.

Golf Confessional

Prayer

O, God, I love You so much! Thank You for being such a caring Father. Thank You for loving me before I knew to love You. Thank You for promising to help me conquer all of my "THISes." Please help me to turn all of my sin over to You and not to take things back and try to fix them myself. Thank You for giving me Jesus. Please help me to boldly share Him with people stuck in their "THISes."

Questions

- What specific "THISes" has God helped you to conquer?

- What "THISes" are you still trying to fix on your own?

- Who do you know that needs to turn their "THISes" over to Jesus? Pray for them right now.

Journal

_____

_____

_____

_____

_____

I eagerly expect and hope that I will in no way be ashamed, but will have sufficient courage so that now as always Christ will be exalted in my body, whether by life or by death. For to me, to live is Christ and to die is gain. (Philippians 1:20-21)

Meditation   *Dudley C. Rutherford*

Take any letter of the alphabet, and you'll find a title word the divine writers used in trying to describe Jesus:

A. He is the Adam, Advocate, Anointed, Apostle, Author, Amen, Alpha and Ancient of Days.

B. He is the Beginning, the Begotten, Beloved, Branch, Bread, Bridegroom, Bright and Morning Star, Brightness of His Father's glory.

C. He is the Christ, the Cluster of Campfires, Captain, Consolation, Cornerstone, Counselor, Covenant and Chosen of God.

D. He is the Daysman, Deliverer, Dayspring, Daystar, Door and Desire of all nations.

E. He is the Elect, Ensign, Everlasting Father, Emmanuel.

F. He is the Finisher of our faith, Forerunner, Friend, First Fruits, Faithful Witness and Fountain of Life.

G. He is God, Gift of God, Governor, Guide and Glorious Lord.

H. He is our Help, Hope, Husband, Horn of Salvation, Hearer, Head of the Church, Heir of all things, High Priest, Hell's dread and Heaven's wonder.

I. He is the I Am, Inheritance, Image of God's person, Immortal and Invisible.

J. He is Judah, Judge, Just, Jesus.

K. He is King of kings, King of glory, King everlasting.

L. He is the Life, the Light, Love, Lily, Lion, Lamb, Lawgiver, Living Stone, The Lord of glory.

M. He is the Messenger, Mediator, Master, Messiah, Mighty God and Mercy.

Only time and space keep me from finishing the alphabet. He is all things through all ages; He is the lovely and mighty Christ, beyond all comprehension of the infinite mind. His is the "sweetest name on mortal tongue, sweetest carol ever sung."

Prayer

Dear Wonderful Christ, thank You for being my Lord and Savior. Thank You for being greater than anything, any person or any power. Thank You for being beyond my capacity to describe or express. Help me to thank You each and every day. I pray all these things in the matchless, eternal name of Jesus. Amen.

Questions

- What is this meditation trying to tell you?

- Can you think of some names for Jesus that start with other letters, such as R, S, T?

- Why do you think there are so many names to describe Him?

Journal

> *The twenty-four elders fall down before him who sits on the throne, and worship him who lives for ever and ever. They lay their crowns before the throne and say: "You are worthy, our Lord and God, to receive glory and honor and power, for you created all things, and by your will they were created and have their being." (Revelation 4:10-11)*

Meditation   *Dudley C. Rutherford*

No human vocabulary can express the greatness and uniqueness of Christ Jesus our Lord. This whole world put together has not enough talent or originality to adequately describe Him. Others have tried. I've read these statements and countless others. Architects, striving to build cathedrals worthy of Him, fall short of their objectives. Painters with brush and palette and blazing colors cannot do Him justice. Sculptors in all of the earth's quarries nowhere can find enough marble or granite to express Him. Singers have not enough melody or range, beauty or power to declare His perfection in song. Musicians, striving to build palaces of music sweet enough for His praise, fall woefully short. Orators whose words are flights of golden arrows express only a meager measure of honor due Him. Writers, whose words dropping from their pens like golden pollen from stems of shaken lilies, fail miserably in trying to describe His beauty. If I had ten thousand tongues and each tongue could speak ten thousand languages, and could speak uninterrupted for ten thousand years, there would not be enough time or words to approach the greatness of Christ.

Inadequate Words

Prayer

Dear Lord Jesus Christ, I don't have enough words to praise You. You are completely beyond my ability to understand, describe or express in any measure. But I can worship You in my deepest heart by daily lifting up my life to You. I look to You and to Your majesty to lead me into Your presence. Lord, I am humbled by Your love and greatness. In the name of Christ, the name above every name, I pray. Amen.

Questions

- Who created all things?

- Is it possible to accurately define and express Him?

- What is it about Jesus that humbles you?

Journal

I have been crucified with Christ and I no longer live, but Christ lives in me. The life I live in the body, I live by faith in the Son of God, who loved me and gave himself for me. (Galatians 2:20)

Meditation   *Dave Stone*

Satan wants us to be concerned about what others think. We all love to keep a good reputation. We have all worked very hard to build an image. It comes out when we embellish our resume to make it look better than it really is. Or when, in a job interview, we exaggerate our achievements to make us look like we are a real catch. The truth is that's all image; it's not authenticity.

A ministry friend recently sent me some personal ads from his community. One lady described herself by writing, "Senior goddess. Fifties. Active. With youthful look and viewpoint. Slim, attractive. Loves creativity, culture, beauty, loyalty, integrity and Pink Floyd."

One man wrote, "Stray cat seeks kitten. Tall, nice looking professional. 33. Blond hair and green eyes seeks attractive professional kitten to keep me out of the alley."

Truth be known, we don't want to be authentic. We prefer to be airbrushed. We need to forget about the image and concentrate on who we really are. You see, in the grand scheme of things, we're really not much. We might look attractive but that will soon fade. We might be in shape but soon arthritis will set in. Instead of focusing on image and exterior, we need to focus on Jesus Christ. He is the One who brings us true worth; we need to find our identity in Him, because of who He is and what He has done for us.

Dave Stone is the Senior Pastor at Southeast Christian Church in Louisville, KY.

Prayer

Heavenly Father, thanks so much that I do not have to walk through this life in constant insecurity, always fretting and wondering what other people are thinking of me. Father, when I go into situations where I am tempted to try to impress others, help me to remember that my true worth comes from You. Help me to remember that I am who the GREAT I AM says I am. In Jesus' name. Amen.

Questions

- Think back and try to remember a time when you intentionally said or did something to make yourself look better than you really were.

- What does Paul mean when he writes that he has been crucified with Christ?

- How has it changed you to understand that you no longer have to try to be valuable, but that you are valuable because God loves you?

Journal

> *John answered them all, "I baptize you with water. But one more powerful than I will come, the thongs of whose sandals I am not worthy to untie. He will baptize you with the Holy Spirit and with fire. His winnowing fork is in his hand to clear his threshing floor and to gather the wheat into his barn, but he will burn up the chaff with unquenchable fire."*
>
> *(Luke 3:16b-17)*

Meditation   *Susan Wilson*

John the Baptist delivered a bold and life-changing message as he waited for the Messiah to make Himself known. Aren't Christians today playing a role similar to John's, as we await Christ's second coming? We have the same basic message to deliver: "When Jesus comes again, He's going to clean house. He'll place everything true in its proper place before God; everything false He'll put out with the trash to be burned." Personally, I don't want to be in that garbage bag, nor do I want the people I care about to be in it!

But what about all the people I have no earthly reason to care about? Shouldn't I have some feelings about what happens to them, if for no other reason than the fact that God does? My love has to extend beyond the boundaries of human confines and be the kind of love Jesus had for those who pounded the nails in His hands. If I'm not willing to be a little bit offensive and "in your face" with people about their eternal destiny, then maybe I don't really care about them as much as I think I do.

Susan Wilson is the wife of Don Wilson, Senior Pastor of Christ's Church of the Valley in Peoria, AZ.

Being Bold

Prayer

Lord, I don't want to offend anyone, but You seem to be telling me that if I never speak out with love against sin in the lives of those around me, no matter how hard it is to do, then I have failed my duty as Your child. Help me find the words; help me find the courage; help me find the love. I pray that I can learn from John how to take a bold stand in the face of opposition – not because I want to put anyone down, but because I care about their eternal destiny. In Jesus' name. Amen.

Questions

- What are the things that keep you from boldly confronting sin in your world?

- What is the worst thing that could happen to you if you shared your faith with someone?

- What are some ways you can show the love of Jesus to the people you meet each day?

Journal

_____

_____

_____

_____

June 26

As was the earthly man, so are those who are of the earth; and as is the man from heaven, so also are those who are of heaven.

(I Corinthians 15:48)

Conformed to the likeness of his Son. (Romans 8:29)

Meditation   H. Dean Rutherford

Bob Stamps was, at one time, on the faculty at Oral Roberts University. Bob has a good sense of humor. He is also bald. I mean *bald*. Bald like a cue ball. Bald as an eagle. He is more bald than Michael Jordan. One night, after Bob and his wife had returned from an evening out, they returned home to find the babysitter engrossed in a television program. While she wasn't paying attention, their little boy, Peter Andrew, got into his father's electric shaver and shaved a big landing strip right down the middle of his head. Bob was furious. He said, "Peter Andrew, I told you never to play with my electric razor. Now you are going to get the whipping of your life."

He was just about to administer the punishment when Peter Andrew said, "Just wait till you see my little sister." About that time, she came out without a hair on her head. She looked like a skinned rabbit. Maybe more like a peeled onion. He grabbed up Peter Andrew in his arms and said, "Now you are really going to get it." Just as Bob was about to start disciplining his son, Peter Andrew looked at his dad and, with big tears in his eyes, said, "But Daddy, we were just trying to look like you!" Bob Stamps said, "I'm in no condition to discipline anyone." Do you realize the whole Bible can be summed up in this picture? We are supposed to spend our entire lives trying to look like Jesus.

Prayer

Dear Lord, make me like You. I want to be conformed to the image of Your Son. As I live my life from day to day, may others look at my life and say, "I see Jesus, his Father, in him." It's not always easy, because of all the distractions that come my way; but I pray that I would conform to the likeness of Your Son. Let me start today by casting off everything that hinders this process, and may Your Holy Spirit transform me into Your image. In the name of Christ, I pray. Amen.

Questions

- Name three things you can do to improve your likeness of Him.

- What happens to your witness if you're not like Jesus?

- Who do you know that reminds you of Jesus?

Journal

_____

_____

_____

_____

_____

Train a child in the way he should go, and when he is old he will not turn from it. Folly is bound up in the heart of a child, but the rod of discipline will drive it far from him. (Proverbs 22:6, 15)

Meditation   *Dudley C. Rutherford*

A few years ago at one of our state fairs, a crowd was gathered about a prize hog. That hog was about all that a hog ought to be. His hair was slickly parted in the middle and neatly combed. His hoofs were manicured in such a fashion that any manicurist would envy them. Everybody who saw this hog realized the wise man that raised him knew his business.

Now, the boy who was set to look after this prize hog seemed to have been chosen as a foil to further emphasize the hog's perfection. He was a little weasel-faced, hollow-chested fellow, who seemed bent on smoking all the world's remaining cigarettes as quickly as possible. He could not have walked a mile for a camel, or even a block, for he was not strong enough. The boy was frail and sickly. But the most startling fact about the whole situation was this: The father of the boy and the owner of the hog were the same man. In the hog business, this father was a huge success. In the boy business, he was a complete washout. I have a feeling that if the man had spent the same amount of time and care on the boy, the picture would have been much different. This story would be funny if it weren't so true. How many times have we seen people who put other insignificant things above their children?

Prayer

Dear Heavenly Father, I thank You for children. I thank You that You have placed them in my life. Help me to work on their spiritual condition more than their clothes, education and vocational choices. I know we only go around once, so I pray that I might do it right. I need Your help to keep me in the picture. I tend to get busy with insignificant things, and I want to be sure that my family and children are never short-changed. In Jesus' sweet name, I pray. Amen.

Questions

- If you train your child right, what can you expect?

- Have you ever been guilty of putting other things above your family?

- What do you need to change to keep God first in your life, and your family second?

Journal

No one can serve two masters. Either he will hate the one and love the other, or he will be devoted to the one and despise the other. You cannot serve both God and Money. (Matthew 6:24)

Meditation   *Dudley C. Rutherford*

I saw in the news this week that a woman who lived with her husband in a house, kept a second, secret husband in the same house... under the same roof! She kept him hidden from her real husband. At night, her secret husband slept under the beds and in the closets. Just when you thought you've heard of everything. That gives new meaning to words like "insanity" and "stupidity."

I hate to confess this, but sometimes I am spiritually like that woman. Oh sure, as a Christian I'm married to Jesus. Jesus is my rightful lover. I'm committed to Him. I once said it in public: "Now I belong to Jesus." But in my weaker, dumber moments I get to thinking I can entertain old Satan too, and keep my worldly friend hidden from Christ. There is surely room for Jesus and Satan in my heart at the same time. I'm pretty clever. I can juggle this small problem. After all, there are only three of us.

As I approach this time of prayer, this would be a wonderful time to take a spiritual-house inventory and make sure we have only one husband (Christ) in our hearts. This is an ideal time to boot old Satan out of the house, out of our hearts and come clean with our forgiving Savior, who wants us for Himself. We are the bride and Jesus is the Groom.

Prayer

Dear God, thank You so much for Your Holy Word. Thanks for reminding me that I can only truly serve one master at a time, and if I am wise, that Master will be You, the Lord Jesus Christ! Come on in, Lord Jesus. You are the only One I want in my heart and life. Forgive me when I fail You; but today, I pray that as You look into my heart, You will see that You are my Lord and perfect Savior. And it is in Your wonderful name, I pray this prayer. Amen.

Questions

- How many masters can you serve and love at the same time?

- Is that answer true for some days or every day?

- Do you know what it means to be the bride of Christ?

Journal

_____

_____

_____

_____

_____

> *Who is he that condemns? Christ Jesus, who died—more than that, who was raised to life—is at the right hand of God and is also interceding for us. (Romans 8:34)*

Meditation   *Rick Atchley*

Steve Winger from Lubbock, Texas tells about his last college test – a final in a logic class known for its difficult exams:

"To help us on our test, the professor told us we could bring as much information to the exam as we could fit on a piece of notebook paper. Most students crammed as many facts as possible on their sheet. But one student walked into the class with a blank sheet of paper. He put it on the floor and had an advanced logic student stand on the paper. The advanced logic student told him everything he needed to know. He was the only one to receive an 'A.' "

The Bible says our enemy, the devil, is an accuser of the burden. He attempts to fill our hearts with doubt by reminding us of all our faults and flaws. But we have an advocate, the Lord Jesus Christ, who is ready to speak for us, and to defend us to the Father. Do not allow Satan to rob you of the joy of your salvation this day. Let Jesus be your answer. He knows what to say when you don't. When He speaks on your behalf, there is nothing more the Deceiver can say!

Rick Atchley is Senior Minister of Richland Hills Church of Christ in Richland Hills, TX.

Prayer

O God, we thank You in Jesus' name for the assurance of our salvation – for the blood that continually cleanses us of all sin, for the Holy Spirit who fills us with joy and hope, and for the knowledge that even now, Your Son is pleading for us! May we run to Him and never away from Him. I pray that Jesus will be the answer to all of life's questions. In Jesus' name. Amen.

Questions

• When are you most vulnerable to doubt your salvation?

• How can you display the joy of salvation today?

• In what ways can you encourage other believers to have confidence in Christ?

Journal

■ June 30

Jesus turned and said to Peter, "Get behind me, Satan! You are a stumbling block to me; you do not have in mind the things of God, but the things of men." (Matthew 16:23)

Meditation   *Dudley C. Rutherford*

Of all the people in the Bible, Simon Peter is the easiest for me to relate to. Why? Because we all make mistakes – that makes it easy to relate to Peter. Solomon was wealthy and smart. I can't relate to that. He also had 700 wives. That's just difficult to relate to. I can't relate to Abraham either. He became a daddy at age 100. Besides that, he was willing to kill his own son. I can't relate to that. I can't relate to Noah. He was asked to build an ark. I couldn't build a fan with fudgesicle sticks. Neither can I relate to Jonah. He spent three days in the belly of the whale. That's too fishy for me.

But I'll tell you who we can all relate to and that's Peter. His level of commitment was up and down like a yo-yo. One day he was red hot for Jesus. The next day you couldn't find him. Poor Pete would take three steps forward and two backward. Like the average one of us preachers or Christians, he was always talking without thinking. I'm glad one of the Bible's heroes often had his foot in his mouth. I'm encouraged to do better and try harder. We should never justify our mistakes, but we can learn from our failures and try, try again.

Prayer

Dear caring Father, I'm so thankful You can use imperfect people. That gives me a great incentive, not to coast spiritually but, to be more determined to serve a God who is laden with such grace, mercy and love. Thank You, Lord, for allowing me to start over. Without such kindness, I would be lost. I pray that from this day forward, I'll learn to be more faithful and more consistent. In Jesus' name, I pray. Amen.

Questions

- What Bible character do you relate to the most?

- What was Peter's greatest problem?

- Which Bible story about Peter is your favorite?

Journal

_____

_____

_____

_____

July 1

> *"Come," he said. Then Peter got down out of the boat, walked on the water and came toward Jesus. But when he saw the wind, he was afraid and, beginning to sink, cried out, "Lord, save me!" Immediately Jesus reached out his hand and caught him. "You of little faith," he said, "why did you doubt?" (Matthew 14:29-31)*

Meditation — *Dudley C. Rutherford*

I think Jesus has many times pondered over my doubts and fears. In all honesty, I believe the Lord looks at my life and says, "Dudley, you of little faith! Why do you doubt?" Jesus looks at my ministry and says, "You of little faith!" Why do I think this? If He felt that way about Peter, who did at least walk a few steps on the rolling waves, how do you suppose He feels about those of us who haven't yet left the boat?

I'm sure Jesus said something like this to Peter many times: "Peter, remember I'm the same Lord who put a rainbow in the sky and painted the rose, and gave the songbird its melody. I'm the One who delivered the Israelites, divided the Red Sea, tore down the walls of Jericho and caused the sun to stand still. O, you of little faith."

"But God," we say, "These mountains are too high, and these debts are too burdensome." I can almost hear Him say, "You of little faith." "But God, these roads are too rough, and my problems are so real, and others are so wicked." Again, I hear the echo: "You of little faith. Why did you doubt?"

You of Little Faith

Prayer

I know, dear Lord, that You have marveled at my squeamishness and timidity. I ask forgiveness for those many times I have, with cold feet, failed to step out in faith. Give me a new holy boldness, that I may not doubt again. I pray that Your strong love and powerful protection will guide me. Help me during my times of trial and testing to see only Your faithfulness. May I one day hear You say the words, "O, you of great faith!" In the strong name of Christ, I pray. Amen.

Questions

- Can you name a specific time when you have lacked faith?

- Where does lack of faith come from?

- Has God proven faithful to meet all of your needs?

Journal

Let both grow together until the harvest. At that time I will tell the harvesters: First collect the weeds and tie them in bundles to be burned; then gather the wheat and bring it into my barn. (Matthew 13:30)

Meditation   *Dudley C. Rutherford*

This entire chapter is one of the more haunting and disturbing passages in the Bible, and I don't enjoy studying it. How is it that two people can walk the aisles, and one is saved while the other is not? How is it that two people can be baptized, and one is saved while the other is not? You say, "Preacher, I don't know how that happens." So I'll ask you to go back to the time of your conversion. Try to determine whether or not your decisions were genuine. Did you repent? Did you turn your life over to Jesus? Do you now have a personal walk, a personal relationship with Jesus?

You might answer, "Now, see here, preacher, my daddy was a pastor, my mom was a great Christian lady. I grew up in church." That's not what I asked. I asked, "Are you personally saved?"

"Now, just a minute, preacher. I'm a tither, and I've been a member of this church for seventeen years." That's not the question. The question is this: "Do you have a personal relationship with Jesus?" Please study this parable in Matthew 13 and ask yourself some serious questions.

Wheat and Tares

Prayer

Dear wonderful Christ and Lord, thank You for reminding me that while I cannot live a perfect life, I must have a working, living, growing walk with You. I don't want to come to the end of the way and be cast aside. I want to be gathered into Your great storehouse of salvation. Help me to look deeply into my own heart, and to earnestly determine whether or not I have surrendered completely to the Lord Jesus Christ. He alone is my Rock and my Salvation. In Jesus' name, I pray. Amen.

Questions

- In this text, what do the wheat and the tares represent?

- In this text, what does the fire and the barn represent?

- How do you know for sure that you are saved?

Journal

_____

_____

_____

_____

_____

July 3

Meditation   *Larry Jones*

Many miracles that Jesus performed took place when He was interrupted. Such is true of an event in my life.

Twenty-six years ago while speaking in Haiti, I was interrupted late one night by a little boy. Jerry hadn't eaten all day and asked if I could spare a nickel for a roll. I readily gave Jerry the money, but I couldn't really dismiss the image that haunted my mind. Upon returning to the States, I contrasted the surplus in American grain elevators to the empty storehouses of a neighboring country. "Why should children starve," I urged those who would listen, "when we can give them bread to eat?" My pleas fell on caring ears, for within weeks, over two million pounds of wheat had been donated. From a single roll for a single child, Feed the Children was born.

I often wonder what would have happened had I not responded that night to someone in need. The priest and the Levite in the Samaritan story were too busy to stop and help. Had they done so, they would have found, just as I did, that God does His best work when people are willing to let Him interrupt their lives.

Larry Jones is the founder of Feed the Children, Oklahoma City, OK.

Prayer

Dear Lord, in my busy life, I don't know how many miracles I've missed because I've maintained my schedule instead of stopping for Yours. Please help me be willing to feed the hungry, tend the sick and comfort the dying. Give me a listening ear for those who cry, a tender heart for those who hurt, and a gentle touch for those who are lonely. Help me acknowledge the necessity, appreciate the opportunity and accept the responsibility to do Your work in our world. Please, God, just as Jesus lived His life, let me be willing to be interrupted. Amen.

Questions

- Has God ever burdened your heart to make a difference in other people's lives?

- Read Matthew 9:35-38.

- What did Jesus say to pray for?

Journal

■ July 4

Submit yourselves, then, to God. Resist the devil, and he will flee from you. Come near to God and he will come near to you. Wash your hands, you sinners, and purify your hearts, you double-minded. (James 4:7-8)

Meditation   *Dudley C. Rutherford*

In 1776, our 13 colonies got together and called their meeting the Continental Congress. With great caution and much debate, of one heart they decided to send a Declaration of Independence to England. Essentially, in everyday language, this is what the declaration said:

"Dear King George and to all the parliament and all armies and navies. We realize we came over here from England and that our small and newly formed colonies are not much compared to you. We realize we owe a lot to England, but we just want you to know that we no longer want to be a part of the British Empire. We are declaring our total independence. We know you have vast armies and navies, and you surely can bring them over here and wipe us off the earth. But we want you to know, King George, that we are through with you. Come on over and kill us. You have all the power. We will fight and probably die, but we are more than willing."

That was in July 1776. By October 4, the English had not only sent over their best army, but they had tragically defeated Washington at Germantown, Pennsylvania. Washington retreated to Valley Forge where they wintered for the rest of the year. The bloody war would continue for five more years until 1781, when Cornwallis was defeated by George Washington at Yorktown.

Prayer

Dear God, just now I am declaring my independence from Satan and the world. I no longer want anything to do with them. I am born again. My Savior's blood has purchased my freedom. I know Satan is powerful and I will face some serious battles, but I believe that right shall triumph and wrong shall fail. Bless me as I declare total dependence on You and declare total independence from Satan and his unholy cause. In Jesus' name. Amen.

Questions

- To whom do you owe your declaration of independence?

- How does a person "cleanse his hands and purify his heart"?

- How would you describe Satan's power?

Journal

_____

_____

_____

_____

_____

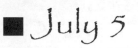

July 5

> *Jesus Christ is the same yesterday and today and forever.*
>
> *(Hebrews 13:8)*

Meditation   *Dudley C. Rutherford*

I heard about a Fourth of July event several years ago, where the people had enjoyed a great time all day long; now they were just waiting for darkness, so the fireworks display could begin. One young father was holding his five-year-old son, and they watched intently as the fireworks lit up the night sky. As a finale to the celebration, a star with colors of red, white and blue burst across the sky and spelled out the name of Abraham Lincoln. It seemed to just hang there for the longest time. The small boy said, "What is that, Daddy?" "Oh," the father said, "That's a man's name." After several more minutes, the restless and sleepy child asked, "Daddy, won't that man's name ever go out?"

Two thousand years ago at Bethlehem's manger, a star burst over the Judean sky. It announced to the waiting world that a child was born in a stable and wrapped in swaddling cloths, and that His name would be Jesus. For 2,000 years, this cold, Godless old world has been asking that question: "Won't that man's name ever go out?" The answer comes reverberating across the centuries of time: "No, no. A million times no. His name will never go out. Jesus Christ is the same yesterday, today and forever."

Prayer

Dear Lord Jesus, I thank You that You are the same yesterday, today and forever. I am fickle; I change my mind and intentions from day to day. But You remain the same. I know the One who saved others so long ago can still save today. I place again my life, my faith and my trust in the saving name of Jesus Christ, in whose blessed name, I pray. Amen.

Questions

- What is the one name that is the same yesterday, today and forever?

- Can you be as steady and faithful to Him as He is to you?

- How is Jesus faithful to you?

Journal

July 6

Meditation   Dudley C. Rutherford

Years ago, America started singing a prayer: "God bless America, land that I love." God has smiled upon this proud land and answered that prayer in many ways. We have great abundance of crops in our fields, wondrous natural beauty, minerals in our mines. We have been successful materially and victorious in our necessary wars. But how long will God continue to bless America? There is a "statute of limitations" that God stipulates in His Book. We have forgotten the Book of the Ages. We have forgotten the things that caused God to bless this land. We need a return to the Good Book.

Let me remind us of some Scripture: "Righteousness exalts a nation, but sin is a disgrace to any people" (Proverbs 14:34). "'But if any nation does not listen, I will completely uproot and destroy it,' declares the Lord" (Jeremiah 12:17). "The wicked shall be turned into hell and all nations that forget God" (Psalm 9:17). If you love America, then become a Christian. If you are already a Christian then turn back to the Bible, to the Church and to the Lord's Day. Be an active servant of the Almighty and give Him a reason for blessing this land – a land He has blessed so many times before. If God continues to bless America, will it be because of me or in spite of me?

Prayer

Heavenly Father, we thank You for Your magnificent blessings on our homeland. You have surely had Your hand on our shoulder for over two hundred years. We must acknowledge that whenever we have followed the Bible, You have prospered us. We also sadly observe that in times when we have forgotten You, that You have allowed us to lose our way. Help me to so live that You once more delight in leading us and blessing us. Amen.

Questions

- In what obvious ways has God blessed America?

- Why will He not continue to do so?

- How can you live that will cause Him to continue?

Journal

_____

_____

_____

_____

■ July 7

For as he thinks within himself, so he is. (Proverbs 23:7)

Meditation   *Jim Garlow*

How we think matters – lots. I am embarrassed to admit it, but I have been overweight much of my adult life. In fact, very overweight. I finally addressed the situation: I lost 80 lbs. Now I eat fruits and vegetables when I used to eat sweets. After no exercise for nearly 20 years, I now exercise almost every day. What changed? Succinctly stated, my thinking. I knew that I must learn to "think like a loser" – a loser of weight. I began to memorize key concepts that have helped me not merely lose weight and keep it off, but also change my lifestyle:

1. Desperation – Capacity to change is in direct proportion to the amount of felt desperation.
2. Acknowledgement – Three words will change your life: "I need help."
3. Ownership – I didn't create my body, and it doesn't belong to me; thus I am a steward of it.
4. Excuses – I can have excuses or I can have results, but I cannot have both.
5. Decisions – Seemingly inconsequential decisions add up to have cumulative impact.
6. Exercise – I might not like exercise, but I love having exercised.
7. Pleasure – It is "pleasure now and pain later," or it is "discipline now and pleasure later."
8. Learning – I choose to learn, daily.
9. Spirit-Mind-Body – My spirit, filled with God's Spirit, rules over my mind, which is being renewed, which rules over my body.
10. Focus – I chose to fill my mind with wholesome thoughts that take me to healthy results.

Jim Garlow is the Senior Pastor of Skyline Wesleyan Church in La Mesa, CA.

The New Me

Prayer

Dear Father, I pray that You will fill my mind with Your thoughts. I have been guilty many times of not living to the full potential that You planned for my life. But Lord, I truly desire to live above my "circumstances" and to please You in every way. Instead of thinking negatively, I ask that You renew my mind and give me the ability to live my life the way Jesus lived His. In Jesus' name. Amen.

Questions

- How does your thinking affect your actions?

- What areas of your mind need to be renewed with the mind of Christ, so that you live under the Lordship of Christ?

- When will you begin thinking differently? Today?

Journal

But each one is tempted when, by his own evil desire, he is dragged away and enticed. Then, after desire has conceived, it gives birth to sin; and sin, when it is full-grown, gives birth to death. (James 1:14-15)

Meditation   *Dudley C. Rutherford*

I read an amazing story about a snake trainer demonstrating his gigantic snake act before a huge circus crowd. As the lights dimmed and the blue spotlight focused on the center ring, the trainer entered. The atmosphere was electric. When the trainer gave the signal, the snake obeyed and came down the tree to slowly wrap itself around the trainer. The trainer then gave another signal; because of the premature applause, the snake refused to release its grip. The giant serpent began to kill the trainer. All anyone could see and hear was the spurting of blood and the crunching of broken bones. In no time, it was over. Men came in and shot the huge snake and rescued the trainer's dead body.

Later that night, newspaper reporters were asking questions of this fellow's friends. One man said, "I told him. I told him one day that thing would turn on him." Another man said, "I just never thought that would happen." A reporter sat down beside a man crying and asked, "Did you know him?" "Yes, in fact I remember the day he ordered that snake from a catalog. It came in the mail, in a package no bigger than a small box. I remember when he held it in the palm of his hand. It was so tiny he could have crushed it with his hand. But he kept it, and it grew and grew, and now it has crushed him."

Sin is like that. Maybe some of us have a sin today that seems so tiny, harmless and under control. But if it's allowed to grow, it will kill us.

Prayer

Dear God, I know I'm no match for sin. Help me to get rid of the small sins in my life, because I know the nature of sin is to grow and destroy. I have been fooled into thinking sin is not going to hurt me, and that I will always be able to control it. But Lord, help me to repent and rid myself of any and all sin. I need Your strength and help, and I pray this in the name of Jesus. Amen.

Questions

- Can sin be tamed?

- Why is the nature of sin so destructive?

- How can you keep sin from crushing you?

Journal

_____

_____

_____

_____

_____

July 9

Make every effort to live in peace with all men and to be holy; without holiness no one will see the Lord. (Hebrews 12:14)

Meditation   *David Bycroft*

Most of us have watched the TV series, "Extreme Makeover." I especially am overwhelmed by some of the people whose faces and bodies go through almost miraculous transformations. None of us would be drawn to that show if all they did was change a few areas of outward appearance but left some glaring unsightliness. We want the whole body to glow with newness.

That is exactly what God is calling for when He asks us to pursue holiness. He wants a whole life and character transformation into the image of Christ. However, we often seem content to change two or three sinful actions while allowing other unholy characteristics to remain unchanged.

What would you think about loaning the church's piano to be used in a bar room on Saturday nights? Most of us would throw a fit if our church allowed such actions. We would declare, "That instrument was dedicated for God's use and not for such unholy purposes." Think with me, dear Christian. That piano does not have a soul. It will never stand before God in judgment. We will. Why do we allow our souls to be used in unholy purposes and give it little thought?

Today, choose to never again be used by the sinful world. Dedicate your heart again to God's Extreme Makeover – Holiness Edition.

David Bycroft is the Senior Pastor at Tyro Christian Church in Tyro, KS.

Extreme Makeover

Prayer

Holy Father, I know I cannot be holy by my own effort. I need Your grace and forgiveness. I also need the sustaining power of Your Holy Spirit to help me continue to fight temptation and have victory over sinful habits, attitudes, and actions. Help me to stay in the battle and never give up. I give You permission to continue the extreme makeover of my mind and heart. Thanks for not giving up on me! In Jesus' precious and holy name. Amen.

Questions

- Do you allow yourself to be used in any area that God would classify as unholy?

- Do unholy people take up most or all of your time outside of church activities?

- Is there a habit in your life that needs to be surrendered to the Lord?

Journal

July 10

Meditation   *H. Dean Rutherford*

An artist of lightening technique drew a picture of the highlands: blue hills, azure skies and green foreground, a cottage with smoke curling from the chimney, and a shepherd as he watches his sheep – a lovely pastoral idyll. He drew it as rapidly as I described it, and his audience cheered him to the echo. Then he dipped his brush into a pot of black paint and made six murky smears across the canvas. It seemed as if he had surely ruined this beautiful picture, and when he bowed again, no one cheered. But he knew his art. He took the canvas from the frame and placed it upside down, and then we saw a new picture – one far more beautiful than the former. To make it beautiful, every stroke of the black brush had been necessary.

Here is another picture: A young father and mother and two happy children. Everyone is healthy, happy and loving, and the house is filled with song. But then the black brush is dipped into the ink-black pot of suffering. As the years pass, the children leave home; the mother dies, her song forever hushed; the home is lost; and a stricken man lives on alone. Oh preacher, that picture is ruined. Yes, it is to the world. But to the Christian comes the day when God takes that poor picture from its earthly setting, places it in the perspective of eternity, and there in His eternal Heaven, we see a lovelier picture by far. To make it so, every stroke of that brush was needed.

392

Prayer

O God, help me not to be shortsighted but to always be looking at Your "big picture." Help me to remember that all my pains and poverties are but temporary and will bring about my ultimate sanctification, as I remain faithful in Your wonderful Kingdom. Ultimately, I know trials sharpen and strengthen me, yet when I'm in the middle of the storm, my vision is weak and untrusting. I pray that I will trust in Your sovereignty all the days of my life. I ask these things in Your strong name. Amen.

Questions

- What can your troubles achieve for you?

- What things can be seen and what things are unseen?

- How would you explain the sovereignty of God?

Journal

July 11

Three times I pleaded with the Lord to take it away from me. But he said to me, "My grace is sufficient for you, for my power is made perfect in weakness." (II Corinthians 12:8-9)

Meditation   *Dudley C. Rutherford*

There is an ancient Norse proverb that says, "The north wind made the Vikings." What does that mean? If Scandinavia had been as sunny as the Mediterranean countries, the Viking Corsairs would never have left their shores. But the savage winds and bleak winters drove them forth. The north wind made the Vikings. And many a rugged man admired by the world today has faced the north wind too. Some years ago, my friend Andrae Crouch wrote a song entitled, "Through It All." One of the lines of that song says it so well: "If I never had a problem, I wouldn't know that He could solve them." Think about that. If we never had problems, never had heartache, we could never testify to His power to bless and to heal and to make us well.

Here in the New Testament, the Apostle Paul was seized by an infirmity; he was handicapped in some way. "Three times I pleaded with the Lord to take it away from me. But He said to me, 'My grace is sufficient for you, for My power is made perfect in weakness.' Therefore I will boast all the more gladly about my weaknesses, so that Christ's power may rest on me. That is why, for Christ's sake, I delight in weaknesses, in insults, in hardships, in persecutions, in difficulties. For when I am weak, then I am strong" (II Corinthians 12:8-10). Jesus was saying to Paul what He sometimes says to us: "No, I'll not remove the sickness, but I'll give more grace to cope with the problem."

The North Wind

Prayer

Lord Jesus, I thank You for every trial and heartache that's come my way. Please don't stop allowing me to face trials, for it is through trials that I am made strong. It may hurt me and I may not understand why, but in the depths of my soul I must believe that You have everything under control. If and when I'm weak, may Your grace and mercy be sufficient. I want to be strong for You. In Jesus' name, I pray. Amen.

Questions

- What do you think Paul was suffering from?

- What did God give to Paul instead of healing?

- How often do you, like Paul, thank God for trials?

Journal

_____

_____

_____

_____

July 12

Consider it pure joy, my brothers, whenever you face trials of many kinds, because you know that the testing of your faith develops perseverance. Perseverance must finish its work so that you may be mature and complete, not lacking anything. (James 1:2-4)

Meditation   David Cruz

Recently, a friend of mine was telling me of an experience that turned a terrible day into a great day. It was one of those days when anything that could go wrong was indeed going wrong. There was not even a glimpse of relief on the horizon. The day was full of life's pressures, business pressures and family pressures.

My friend had a business meeting with a client, a minister, who asked my friend, "How is your day?"

To which my friend responded, "Don't ask. It's one of those days when everything is upside down."

Without hesitating, the client exclaimed, "Well, that's good!"

Confused by such a response, my friend asked, "What do you mean that is good?"

The client, in a very affirmative voice said, "When you are having a terrible day, it means that you must be doing something right, otherwise Satan would leave you alone."

My friend quickly responded, "Say no more."

If that is what is taking place, then I thank God for trials.

David Cruz is an elder at Shepherd of the Hills Church.

How Is Your Day?

Prayer

Dear Precious Heavenly Father, there are times full of trials in life that I just can't resolve on my own. I know that when I pass through life's valleys, Your hand is at work in me, so that I may grow in wisdom, courage and spiritual strength. Help me to recognize such times, so I may count them pure joy and have a deeper and more meaningful relationship with You. In Jesus' name I pray. Amen.

Questions

- Had a bad day lately?

- Where do you seek help in times of trouble?

- Can others see Christ at work in your life during tough times?

Journal

_____

_____

_____

_____

_____

> *"My son, do not make light of the Lord's discipline, and do not lose heart when he rebukes you, because the Lord disciplines those he loves, and he punishes everyone he accepts as a son." (Hebrews 12:5-6)*

Meditation   *Dudley C. Rutherford*

Remember, not all suffering is the result of sin. We often hear good people cry, "For what sin am I suffering now?" Probably no sin at all! Remember, Jesus said in the Sermon on the Mount, "He causes His sun to shine on the evil and the good, and sends rain on the righteous and the unrighteous" (Matthew 5:45). Christians and non-Christians have about the same number of car wrecks, cancers and family deaths. Why? Because God lets the sun shine on the good and the evil. He sends His rain on the just and the unjust (Matthew 5:45).

Remember Job back there in the Old Testament? Some of his so-called friends said, "Man, what sins have you been committing?" God answered back, "None. He hasn't committed any sins; he's just being tested." It is so good for man to be tested, because testing makes us stronger, not weaker. Douglas Malloch caught this theme in the poem called "Good Timber":

Good timber does not grow in ease
  The stronger the wind the tougher the trees
    The farther sky, the greater length
      The more the storm the more the strength.
        By sun and cold, by rain and snows, in tree or man,
          good timber grows.

Good Timber

Prayer

Dear Lord, thank You for all the times You have allowed me to be tested. You have allowed events to come into my life that I never would have chosen, but now that I've gone through those experiences, I wouldn't take any amount of money for it, because I know I am a better person. Keep me on track. I pray this in the name of Christ Jesus, my Lord. Amen.

Questions

- Why do bad things happen to good people?

- What kind of person would you be if you had never been through trials?

- Of all the promises in the Word of God, which is your favorite?

Journal

■ July 14

Meditation   *Dudley C. Rutherford*

I was asked if I had only one sermon to preach, what would it be? I said, "I'm not sure. But here is what my last sermon would be to the world."

1. Become a Christian. "He said to them, 'Go into all the world and preach the good news to all creation. Whoever believes and is baptized will be saved.'" (Mark 16:15-16)

2. Build your life around the Church. "Husbands love your wives just as Christ loved the Church and gave Himself up for her." (Ephesians 5:25)

3. Win other people to Christ. "He that wins souls is wise." (Proverbs 11:30)

4. Spend your life in service to others. "I tell you the truth, whatever you did for one of the least of these brothers of mine, you did for me." (Matthew 25:40)

5. Find some quiet time for God in your life. "Be still and know that I am God." (Psalm 46:10)

6. Whatever you are going to do for Christ, do it today. "Why, you do not even know what will happen tomorrow." (James 4:14)

My Last Sermon

Prayer

Dear Heavenly Father, help me to get a grasp on the very basics of life. Help me to realize that the most important treasure I can accumulate is my obedience to the things of God. May I remember that happiness and success in their purest forms come from a total surrender of my spirit to You. I know that my time here on earth is limited, so please help me to use every spare moment for the purpose of serving You and leading others to the cross. In Your blessed name, I pray. Amen.

Questions

- If you only had one day to live, how would you spend that last day?

- If you could encapsulate the most important message to the world, what would it be?

- If you surrender everything to God, would you experience more or less enjoyment?

Journal

_____

_____

_____

_____

Never be lacking in zeal, but keep your spiritual fervor, serving the Lord. (Romans 12:11)

Meditation   *David Faust*

When coaches see it in their players, they call it "drive," or "the will to win." When bosses see it in their employees, they call it "motivation," or "the desire to succeed." When teachers see it in their students, they call it "determination." When the Lord sees it in His followers, He calls it "zeal." Zeal is the ardent pursuit of a goal, a passionate devotion to a person or a cause. It's the fuel that keeps your spiritual motor running.

What are you zealous about? Jesus was consumed by zeal for His Father's house (John 2:17), and He wants us to be "zealous for good deeds" (Titus 2:14). Unfortunately, instead of being zealous, many today are zeal-less and cynical. Their motors may be running, but their lives are in neutral.

How sad when Christians lack passion for Christ and His work! Spiritual dullness sets in, like the way you feel when you eat too much Thanksgiving dinner – drowsy and overstuffed. At the opposite extreme is misguided zeal, when we care deeply about the *wrong* things or about things that are relatively unimportant.

We need to be zealous for the right things! We must care deeply about what Jesus said matters most: "Love the Lord your God with all your heart and with all your soul and with all your mind and with all your strength," and "Love your neighbor as yourself" (Mark 12:30, 31). Loving the Lord has to be our top priority. Then we must pour ourselves into the noble cause of neighbor love, serving those in need. What else can compare with these great goals?

David Faust is the President of Cincinnati Christian University in Cincinnati, OH.

Zealous or Zeal-less

Prayer

God, keep me zealous for the things that really matter. I get sidetracked too easily. Show me what's truly important in Your eyes. Move me to care deeply about those things. And let me refuse to worry about everything else. In Jesus' name. Amen.

Questions

- What are you really "zealous" about? What is your passion?

- Are you passionate about the things that matter most in the eyes of God?

- What can you do today to renew and rekindle your zeal for the Lord?

Journal

I am not ashamed of the gospel, because it is the power of God for the salvation of everyone who believes: first for the Jew, then for the Gentile. (Romans 1:16)

Meditation   Dudley C. Rutherford

Let me give you the greatest facts in the entire universe: Jesus died on a small hill outside Jerusalem. He was buried. Three days later, He rose from the grave. He walked here and there for 40 days, showing His scars from the horrible crucifixion. Then He ascended into Heaven. Just before He went to Heaven, He said this to the people standing there with Him, His disciples: "All authority in Heaven and on earth has been given to Me. Therefore go and make disciples of all nations, baptizing them in the name of the Father and of the Son and of the Holy Spirit, and teaching them to obey everything I have commanded you." (Matthew 28:18-20)

Those are the facts of the Gospel. There are five terrific, indisputable truths in these final marching orders:

1. Jesus is sending us. He has all the authority in Heaven and earth to do so.

2. We Christians, not angels, are to go make disciples for Jesus.

3. We are to make disciples of all nations.

4. We are to baptize these disciples from all nations.

5. We are to teach these newly baptized disciples all the commands of Jesus.

Prayer

Dear loving, precious Lord, thank You a million times over for bringing Your message to our world. Help me to scour this world, looking for people I might influence to come into Your Heavenly Kingdom. Forgive me for letting so many golden opportunities pass me by, with little concern or effort on my part. Imprint Your Great Commission upon my heart. Give me boldness and help me to share my faith on a daily basis. In Jesus' name. Amen.

Questions

- According to Matthew 28:18-20, who are you supposed to baptize?

- Where are you supposed to go?

- Does this passage (Matthew 28:18-29) command you to teach first or baptize first?

Journal

Therefore, if anyone is in Christ, he is a new creation; the old has gone, the new has come! All this is from God, who reconciled us to himself through Christ and gave us the ministry of reconciliation: that God was reconciling the world to himself in Christ, not counting men's sins against them... We are therefore Christ's ambassadors, as though God were making his appeal through us. We implore you on Christ's behalf: Be reconciled to God. (II Corinthians 5:17-20)

Meditation   *Dudley C. Rutherford*

One thing these verses scream is that God will not and does not use angels in spreading the Gospel of Christ. He leaves all of that to you and me. No one else! "But preacher, isn't preaching foolish?" Yes, it is. Paul said in I Corinthians 1:18: "For the message of the cross is foolishness to those who are perishing." You ought to try a little preaching sometime. We preachers are mimicked and made fun of, but in that foolish-looking preaching, our God wins people to Christ. A person may say that when he starts to talk to someone about Christ, he feels that he looks and sounds foolish. You do, my friend, but in that foolishness God works His miracles. You'll soon get over it. The job is not for angels. It is for us.

Paul was writing the Church at Rome and said in Chapter 10:14: "How then can they call on the One they have not believed in? And how can they believe in the One of whom they have not heard? And how can they hear without someone preaching to them? And how can they preach unless they are sent? As it is written, 'How beautiful are the feet of those who bring good news!'" (Isaiah 52:7). How can someone be saved without preaching? They can't, and since angels can't do it, God in His wisdom has left the entire matter up to us.

Prayer

Dear saving God, I know now You've left this business of evangelism up to me. Give me the boldness to start witnessing every day. I may look and sound foolish, but I know You can work miracles through me. I know I'm not miraculous, but Your Word is. Help me to take this responsibility seriously, and to build friendships and relationships that will enable me to share Christ. In Your wondrous name, I pray. Amen.

Questions

- Who is exclusively given the message of reconciliation?

- Why are angels not given this responsibility?

- What does it mean that you are Christ's ambassador?

Journal

> *Therefore, I urge you, brothers, in view of God's mercy, to offer your bodies as living sacrifices, holy and pleasing to God—this is your spiritual act of worship. (Romans 12:1)*

Meditation   *Renee Rutherford*

A living sacrifice… what does that mean? How are we meant to sacrifice ourselves to the Lord? To be a living sacrifice means we are to give ourselves completely to God every day. To turn our lives over utterly, sacrificially to Him. All of our thoughts and plans. Our hearts, our eyes and ears and mouths. Every part of ourselves and our lives belongs to Him. This sacrificial living is not easy. The sobering reality is that every day, our fleshly, sinful nature battles for our attention. It's easy to make each day all about us – our personal desires and goals – rather than all about God. We want to give ourselves completely to God, but too often it seems we don't know where to begin. We feel too inadequate for sacrificial living.

In my days teaching stress management, we talked often about a concept called "reframing." Reframing is putting a new "frame" around a situation to see it differently. Imagine looking at a scene through a camera lens – what would happen if you changed to a completely different lens, one that altered the image? You would see the same picture quite differently. It's the same when we look at our lives. If we reframe the way we see ourselves, we will find a way to begin truly offering ourselves as a living sacrifice. Paul offers a huge clue to this in Romans 12:1. He urges us to view our lives through the "frame" of God's mercy. When we begin to see ourselves as part of God's eternal plan, we have a different perspective. Suddenly we have a very powerful impetus to live righteous lives that are holy and pleasing to God.

Renee Rutherford is the wife of Dudley Rutherford, Senior Pastor of Shepherd of the Hills Church, Porter Ranch, CA.

A Sacrificed Life - Reframed

Prayer

O merciful Father! Help me this day to have spiritual eyes to see and appreciate Your infinite mercy. Thank You for the many ways You demonstrate Your love and mercy in my life. Help me to grow in my understanding of You, and to seek You in such a way that my only impulse is to offer my life, wholly and completely, to You. Take my life and let it be consecrated to You, Lord. Amen.

Questions

- View God's mercy – At this moment, what evidence is there of God's wonderful and amazing mercy?

- Make the offer – Have you actually offered God every part of your life?

- Examination – What areas of your life are not holy and pleasing to God?

Journal

July 19

Meditation   *Dudley C. Rutherford*

All the way through His ministry, Jesus asked His disciples to major in love. When it was time for Jesus to go to the cross and return to Heaven, He gathered His Twelve Apostles around Him for a Last Supper. To be quite honest, I think they overlooked the message of love Jesus was trying to teach them. I say this because even at that Last Supper, they were quarreling about who would be the greatest in the new Kingdom, who would get to be this and who would get credit for that.

Jesus would summarize His entire purpose and ministry in the next few minutes. He slowly got a basin of water and a large towel, knelt and began to wash the dirty feet of His chosen disciples. Jesus knew the dramatic events of the next few days would be so traumatic, His disciples might forget some things; but He knew they would never forget this example of love and humility. The Bible says that when Jesus finished washing their feet, He got back up off His knees and took His place at the table again. Then He said these unforgettable words: "I have set you an example that you should do as I have done for you. I tell you the truth, no servant is greater than his master."

Prayer

Dear God of infinite love, I know that I am never so much like You as when I am in the act of serving others. Let this be my daily goal. I want to wake up each morning asking, "Whom can I bless and help today?" The world is filled with people who do not know You, Lord. It is my prayer that they would see Jesus in me, by the way I live my life. I ask this huge favor in the name of Jesus. Amen.

Questions

- Why did Jesus wash the disciples' feet?

- What should one of your first thoughts be each morning?

- Do people see Jesus in you?

Journal

_____

_____

_____

_____

Our hope is that, as your faith continues to grow, our area of activity among you will greatly expand, so that we can preach the gospel in the regions beyond you. For we do not want to boast about work already done in another man's territory. (II Corinthians 10:15-16)

Meditation   *Dudley C. Rutherford*

Do I have faith? Do I need faith? If Satan himself can persuade us not to believe, he has won an awesome victory, because it is simply impossible for one to grow and mature in Christ without faith. There is simply no mystery about the way we are to obtain faith. It is to expose oneself to God and His word in obedience. Open your heart's door to the Bible and faith will come right on in. Then your faith becomes contagious. It inevitably spreads as we share it with others. Friends and neighbors will draw faith and inspiration from us.

The Bible says by faith we live: "The life I live in the body, I live by faith" (Galatians 2:20). By faith we walk: "We walk by faith and not by sight" (II Corinthians 5:7). By faith we stand: "And you stand by faith" (Romans 11:20). By faith we fight: "Take up the shield of faith, with which you can extinguish all the flaming arrows of the evil one" (Ephesians 6:16). By faith we become bold: "You of little faith, why are you so afraid?" (Matthew 8:26). By faith we are shielded: "Through faith we are shielded" (I Peter 1:5). It is by faith we are healed: "The prayer offered in faith will make the sick person well" (James 5:15). To be truthful, it is by faith that our faith grows and increases. It is by faith that we mature in our Christian walk on the way to Heaven.

Prayer

Almighty and wonderful God, thank You for making faith possible. I know You are the One who thought it all up and You are the One who knows how I can obtain faith. I want to surrender to Your will. I want to vow to spend more time each day in Your word because I know that every moment, every tick of the clock that I am in Your word, faith is pouring into my thirsty soul. Bless me in my continued search for faith. In Christ's name, I pray. Amen.

Questions

- Name at least two powers faith gives you.

- How does your faith help others to have faith?

- How does a person obtain faith?

Journal

> But as for me, my feet had almost slipped; I had nearly lost my foothold.
> For I envied the arrogant when I saw the prosperity of the wicked.
>
> (Psalm 73:2-3)

Meditation   David Flaig

Have you ever caught yourself from falling? Your body reacts, fear kicks in and you do whatever you can to save yourself from getting hurt. The Psalmist in this passage understands how close to danger he had come, because he envied others. You and I can relate, can't we? We envy prosperity: big houses, fancy cars, arrogant lifestyles and freedoms without apparent consequences. While the media celebrates people's prosperity, they can't show how people's hearts are trapped by it. While they show the arrogance of those who live as they please, they don't show the long-term consequences of hate, selfishness, promiscuity, pride and violence.

We all run the risk of falling into the envy trap. All day long, there is plenty to envy, plenty to long for, plenty to cause our feet to slip. Words you would like to say, things you would like to buy, pleasures you would like to enjoy, speeds you would like to drive… you get the idea. A woman once said, "It is when I realize *who* I am focusing on, that my jealousy comes into perspective." The key to keeping our balance is allowing God's Word to ground us on a regular basis. We need it every day! Today, as you study the Word of God, allow it to catch you where you are in danger of slipping.

David Flaig is the Emerging Generation Pastor at Shepherd of the Hills Church, Porter Ranch, CA.

Fear of Falling

Prayer

Sweet Jesus, I admit that I have begun to envy the arrogance of others: their prosperity, their power and their pride. Guide me by Your word right now to regain balance. Keep me from falling and from experiencing the consequences that lead to destruction. May what is important to You become all I desire in this life. In Jesus' name. Amen.

Questions

- Where have you been feeling that your lot in life is unfair?

- Are you content with who you are… or are you always needing something more?

- What sin is captivating your heart and leading you where you do not want to go?

Journal

■ July 22

If you love those who love you, what reward will you get? Are not even the tax collectors doing that? And if you greet only your brothers, what are you doing more than others? Do not even pagans do that? Be perfect, therefore, as your heavenly Father is perfect. (Matthew 5:46-48)

Meditation   *Dudley C. Rutherford*

Here is a prayer I should pray more often: "Heavenly Father, help me remember that the person who cut me off in traffic last night is a single mother who worked nine hours that day, is rushing home to cook dinner, help with homework, do the laundry and spend a few precious moments with her children.

"Help me to remember that the pierced, tattooed, disinterested young man who can't make change correctly is a worried 19-year-old college student, balancing his apprehension over final exams with his fear of not getting his student loans for next semester.

"Remind me, Lord, that the scary-looking guy begging for money in the same spot every day is a slave to addictions I can only imagine in my worst nightmares.

"Help me to remember that the old couple walking annoyingly slow through the store aisles, blocking my shopping progress, are savoring this moment, knowing that, based on the biopsy report she got back last week, this may be the last year they go shopping together."

Loving the Unlovable

Prayer

Heavenly Father, remind us each day that, of all the gifts You give us, Your greatest gift is love. It is not enough to share that love with only those we hold dear. Open our hearts, not just to those who are close to us, but also to all humanity. Let us be slow to judge and quick to forgive, to show patience, sympathy and love. In Christ's name, I pray. Amen.

Questions

- What is your reward if you only love your friends?

- Why is it difficult to love the unlovable?

- What does the word "perfect" mean in the verse above?

Journal

_____

_____

_____

_____

> *Live in harmony with one another. Do not be proud, but be willing to associate with people of low position. Do not be conceited.*
>
> *(Romans 12:16)*

Meditation   *David Patrick*

I love the story Bob Shannon tells in his book, *Christ Above All*, when the Duke of Wellington visited an Anglican Church. Everyone in the area was geared up for this visit from such an important dignitary. At the designated time for Communion, the people went forward row by row to receive the elements. When the Duke of Wellington and his entourage went forward and knelt before the altar, every eye was on him.

To the horror of the congregation, the back doors suddenly swung open and the town drunk staggered in. He came straight down the aisle and knelt beside the monarch. A quick-thinking usher responded to the scene. He tapped the man on the shoulder and whispered, "Sir, you're going to have to leave. This is the Duke of Wellington."

But the Duke placed his hand on the drunk's shoulder and said, "Stay where you are. There are no Dukes here."

David Patrick is the Senior Pastor of Tri Lakes Christian Church, Branson, MO.

Duke of Wellington

Prayer

Loving Father, help me to rid myself of all conceit, pride and unloving attitude toward any human being. Please allow me the opportunity today to associate with those who are different than me, so that I may love them the way You love them. Who knows, but perhaps then they would not just see and experience the love of Jesus but they would want to commit in their hearts to follow Jesus. May I realize that the ground at the foot of the cross is level! In His name. Amen.

Questions

• Is your heart full of pride and conceit?

• Are you willing to associate with other people to the point that when they walk away from you, they understand that you love them?

• Does your attitude bring harmony or division in your church, community and home?

Journal

I tell you the truth, unless a kernel of wheat falls to the ground and dies, it remains only a single seed. But if it dies, it produces many seeds.

(John 12:24)

Meditation   *Rebecca Hayford Bauer*

Years ago, I read a story about a lady who, due to disappointment and hurt, had isolated herself and made her home on a tiny island. She was self-sufficient on her island. She never had to see anyone. She lived alone, and eventually died alone.

How like this woman we are! How often we find ourselves hurt or disillusioned; and rather than seeking restoration, we separate ourselves from those around us. We all understand hurt and the desire to isolate ourselves. But the Lord calls us to live differently. He calls us to die to ourselves – to our "rights," to our hurts, to the things that "eat us up inside." Look again at what Jesus says in John 12:24.

Life in Jesus is about dying… not dying so that we can be alone, but dying so that we can live in the joy of fruitfulness. Much of that fruitfulness flows out of our relationships to one another. And He calls us to sow something bigger than our own hurts; He calls us to sow forgiveness, restoration and unity. Why?

Because He has so much that He wants to work through us *together*! Because He is building us *together* to be a spiritual house – a body – unto Him! Because the fields are ripe for harvest and He has called us to labor *together* for Him! The Lord has an incredible future for us *together* – in ministry, in relationship, in forgiveness, in growth, in restoration. We only have to die.

Rebecca Hayford Bauer is an Associate Pastor at Church on the Way in Van Nuys, CA.

Joy of Faithfulness

Prayer

Lord, today I hold before You the things of which I cannot let go, and ask that You would intersect each situation. I repent for any way that I have sowed my own hurts, rather than the restoration of relationship. I repent for allowing myself license to separate myself from others and live in self-protectiveness. Father, I ask that You would help me let go of hurt. Help me to advance healing and forgiveness. And help me to sow beyond myself. Bring in the harvest, Lord! As we labor together, as we love one another, let us lift You up for the whole world to see. In Jesus' name. Amen.

Questions

- Are there places in your life where you have allowed yourself to isolate from others?

- Is there a point where the Lord is calling you to die to your "rights"?

- How does your unity with others in the Body of Christ help to bring in the harvest?

Journal

_____

_____

_____

_____

■ July 25

So, as the Holy Spirit says: "Today, if you hear his voice, do not harden your hearts." But encourage one another daily, as long as it is called Today, so that none of you may be hardened by sin's deceitfulness.

(Hebrews 3:7-8, 13)

Meditation   H. Dean Rutherford

The hardening of the heart is the most terrible calamity and catastrophe that can come upon a human being made in the image of God. If I asked how many of you came to Christ as a youth, most of you would raise your hands. The reason most people are saved as children is because their heart is still tender and has not become calloused. "Preacher, I don't want a hardened heart. How do people get a hardened heart?" Just one way, and one way only! By resisting the Spirit of God and continuing on in willful sin. You know how it works: one gets busy living, and days and weeks fly by. Time goes unknown and unnoticed by the sinner. Meanwhile, the conscience is being dulled every day. Perceptions of right and wrong become faded, skewed and inaccurate. Delay in personal salvation always leads to a hardened heart.

Every blatant serial killer was once an innocent child. Saddam Hussein was once a tenderhearted child who trembled at the thought of sin and disobedience. The Ted Bundys and Charles Mansons were, at one time, beloved of their parents and full of hope for the future. Every painted harlot was once a sweet-faced little girl, precious and gentle, innocent with holy possibilities. But sin accepted, un-confessed and un-rebuked, with the passing of days and time dulls the pangs of conscience. Listen, this is not my word; this is the Word of the Holy Spirit. If you reject Christ again today, your heart will be a little harder tomorrow.

Hardened Hearts

Prayer

Almighty God, I don't ever want to develop a hardened heart. I want to keep it tender. I don't want to dull my spiritual senses. Help me to get into Your precious word and start filling my mind and spirit with righteousness. I am going to turn over a new leaf today, and put You on the throne of my heart where You belong. Help me to always be sensitive to the leading of the Holy Spirit in my life. I pray in Christ's strong name. Amen.

Questions

- Is it possible to have a hardened heart and not know it?

- How does a heart become calloused?

- How can you start renewing your heart today?

Journal

> *Though your sins are like scarlet, they shall be as white as snow; though they are red as crimson, they shall be like wool. (Isaiah 1:18)*

Meditation   *Greg Allen*

There is a part of God's chemistry I just don't understand. How can red be turned to white? Isaiah 1:18 tells us that our scarlet red sin can be turned to white, even as wool. Scripture goes on to teach that it's the blood of Jesus that covers our dark sin and makes us white as snow. How is it that the darkness of sin can be covered with the red blood of Jesus and we are washed white?

Though I don't understand the chemistry, I trust the teaching. Hebrews 9:22 teaches about the blood of Christ and states that "…without the shedding of blood there is no forgiveness." We understand what is being taught. For centuries God provided forgiveness by the sacrificing of lambs and the shedding of blood. Sacrificial lambs offered temporary forgiveness. The sacrifice of the Lamb of God was once for all – from darkness to light, stained to white. His blood was shed and forgiveness of sin became a permanent reality, an eternal opportunity. Now our darkest stains are made clean as we place our trust in Him.

If you put your trust in Christ, would you be encouraged today that the blood of Jesus covers you? As God looks at you, He does not see pride, ego, lust and selfishness; God sees the blood of Jesus, and you are as white as snow.

Greg Allen is Worship Pastor at Southeast Christian Church in Louisville, KY.

Prayer

Father, I don't understand it fully, but I praise You for the Biblical chemistry that takes place when the blood of Your Son covers our sin and makes us white as snow. And thank You, Father, that You don't hold our sin against us when we trust in Christ for the forgiveness of our greed, lust and selfishness. May my life honor You today for the gracious chemistry You've extended to me. In Jesus' name. Amen.

Questions

- When considering the magnitude of God's chemistry, what sin are you most thankful God made white as snow?

- While reconsidering that one sin and knowing that God no longer sees it because of Jesus, how does that make you feel?

- Why is the sacrifice of Jesus enough to be "once for all"?

Journal

_____

_____

_____

_____

_____

■ July 27

And why do you worry about clothes? See how the lilies of the field grow. They do not labor or spin. Yet I tell you that not even Solomon in all his splendor was dressed like one of these. (Matthew 6:28-29)

Meditation   *Dudley C. Rutherford*

Some lilies are never seen. There are millions of lilies blooming, but many are not beside a road, on a secretary's desk, in a hospital room or in a bride's hand. Some lilies will blossom where no human feet have trod, where no human eyes have looked, in a lonesome, uninhabited location where only the wild wind sweeps. The poet Thomas Gray said, "Full many a flower is born to blush unseen and waste its sweetness on the desert air." Some lilies will live, bloom and die just for God, just for His smile and His approval.

Do you understand that lesson? You might never preach a sermon, but there is a corner you can brighten. You might never sing a solo, but there is a widow living in an apartment you can help and bless. You might never teach a Sunday School class, but there is a lonely place where you can serve. Your name might never be on a book cover; you might never be in the spotlight; you might never hear the sound of applause; but there is a place of service for us all.

Prayer

Dear Heavenly Father, I know some flowers will live, bloom and die, and never will be seen by human eyes. They will simply bloom for You, for Your approval. I also know that if I live for Your approval, somebody will see and somebody will know. Please help me to remember that You have a purpose for my life. In the saving name of Christ, I pray. Amen.

Questions

- Why should you not worry about food and clothes?

- Does every flower serve some purpose?

- Is there a place of service for you? Where?

Journal

_____

_____

_____

_____

> *What shall we say the kingdom of God is like, or what parable shall we use to describe it? It is like a mustard seed, which is the smallest seed you plant in the ground. Yet when planted, it grows and becomes the largest of all garden plants, with such big branches that the birds of the air can perch in its shade. (Mark 4:30-32)*

Meditation   *Hongju Choi*

The uniqueness of a mustard seed is its size. The mustard seed is the smallest of seeds. However, do not relate size to significance, because a mustard seed will grow. It will take a while, but it will grow to be a grand mustard tree.

All things begin small, but will eventually grow. The process of growth entails enduring through all circumstances. Although challenging trials and sufferings can make us feel helpless, they are a process of growth to a grand future. Therefore, let's not be ashamed of what we are today. Rather, let's have confidence in hope for the future, because our Lord Jesus Christ is with us.

Small things don't grow only when they don't have life. A grain of sand is something tiny, but it will never grow because it is lifeless. The Gospel is life. Jesus Christ is life. Perhaps, in our inadequacy, we may feel that our life is suffocated by complete darkness. But remember that a mustard seed is also in complete darkness when it is planted in the ground. It will grow, however, because there is life in it. Christ in us is a miracle, and through Christ, we can all become grand people of God.

As the birds of the air can perch in the shade of a mustard tree, our community will find rest in us. As we grow, we will become a place of blessing to our neighbors and the community.

Hongju Choi is the Senior Pastor of Everyday Church in Granada Hills, CA.

Prayer

Dear Father, please help us to know there is a new beginning in Christ, even when we are in trouble. Give us the heart to thank You for all circumstances, and help us to grow faithfully. Show us a vision of a grand future in Christ. I pray in Jesus' name. Amen.

Questions

- Do you struggle with a sense of inadequacy because of the realities before you?

- Do you envision how God will transform you into a grand person of Christ?

- God dreams of using you to bless your neighbors and your country. Do you dream with Him?

Journal

_____

_____

_____

_____

_____

I will praise the Lord all my life; I will sing praise to my God as long as I live. (Psalm 146:2)

Meditation   *Opal McLaughlin*

One way to praise God is through music and singing. Music has been in existence since the creation of the world. Job 38:4-7 speaks of the stars singing and the angels shouting as God created the world. How beautiful and awesome that must have been! The Psalms are full of admonitions to praise God for everything He has done and is still doing. In the Old Testament, we are given many illustrations of praise, such as when the foundation of the Second Temple was laid, Israel sang praise and thanksgiving to the Lord. In the New Testament, the angels sang, "Glory to God in the highest!" when God gave us His only Son, our Savior.

Have we lost the ability to really praise Him with our hearts and minds? Do we praise God when life is difficult? Remember that God is close to you during those times. Sunday is a special day for the followers of Christ, for so many reasons, not the least of which is that on the Lord's Day, Christ arose. Contemplate with me how in every time zone of the world that God created, God is being praised by His people. When worship services are completed in one time zone, the next time zone takes up the praise, and on it goes around the world. Remember to praise God!

Opal McLaughlin is a friend of Dudley Rutherford.

Prayer

Dear Father, You are so very worthy of our praise. If every word I spoke or sang was in praise to You, it would not be enough to express my thankfulness for Your mighty power, Your love, Your justice, Your peace, Your presence and Your forgiveness. Help me to really praise You, no matter what distractions I face. Help me to continually center my life on You and Your saving grace, and to always praise You from my heart. In Jesus' name, I pray. Amen.

Questions

- Have you really considered why God is to be praised?

- Do you really praise Him in word and song, or do you just mouth the words?

- When you praise God, do you feel a definite connection to Him, and are you rewarded with a sense of peace?

Journal

"Father, if you are willing, take this cup from me; yet not my will, but yours be done." An angel from heaven appeared to him and strengthened him. And being in anguish, he prayed more earnestly, and his sweat was like drops of blood falling to the ground. (Luke 22:42-44)

Meditation   H. Dean Rutherford

Jesus drinks the cup. Then He prays the strangest prayer: "Oh Father, if there is any way possible, let this cup pass from Me." I used to wonder what was in that cup that our Lord did not want to drink. I think I know now what was in that cup: Your sins and mine, and all the sins of the world. An insane man and his hot-blooded lust settles in the cup. David's adultery settles in the cup. Noah's drunkenness! A man curses and utters the name of the Living God in vain, and profanity enters the cup. A mother kills her own babies, and depravity falls into the cup. All the sins of all the people who have ever lived, and the total number of sins ever committed fill the cup. Every deed of nameless shame, spawned in the pit of hell itself, every breach of law, every taint of sin, every smear of corruption and the stench of all debauchery, now mingles its odious contents in the cup.

Jesus is saying, "Can't I just die and suffer on the cross? I am so willing to die for the sins of the world, but must I drink this awful cup?" And God must have answered, "Yes, Jesus, drink the cup. Drink all of it. Drink the cup of sin. Drink it for poor, perishing souls. Drink damnation dry. Drink it that sinners might have a Savior. Drink it that whosoever will may drink of the foundation of eternal life."

The Cup

Prayer

Dear sweet Savior, thank You a million times over for drinking that awful cup of sin on my behalf. I can't even imagine how terrible that experience was for You, but I know You were willing to drink it all because of Your love for me. Thank You for drinking the entire cup, because much of that cup had in it my sins. Lord, Your grace and forgiveness covers all of my transgressions. Help me to live a more surrendered life. In Christ's name. Amen.

Questions

- What do you think was in the cup?

- Who assisted Jesus when He had lost much of His strength?

- Do you fully understand what it means to be forgiven?

Journal

_____

_____

_____

_____

_____

> *So do not worry, saying, "What shall we eat?" or "What shall we drink?" or "What shall we wear?" For the pagans run after all these things, and your heavenly Father knows that you need them. Seek first his kingdom and his righteousness, and all these things will be given to you as well.*
> *(Matthew 6:31-33)*

Meditation   *Dudley C. Rutherford*

How many of you believe the Bible? Raise your hand! How many believe the entire Bible, I mean every little, last word of The Book? How many think God just might know what He's talking about? Are you sure about that? All right then; this is your first test. The Bible plainly says, "And my God will meet all your needs according to His glorious riches in Christ Jesus" (Philippians 4:19). Do you believe that verse? Most frustration, fear and doubts are caused by carnal desires unfulfilled. If we believed from the depths of our hearts that God, from His abundant storehouse of riches, would supply our every need, we couldn't possibly worry or fret. Tell me one more time, are you sure you believe that verse? Just checking!

Why does God say that worry is such a great sin? Because worry is the opposite of faith. Worry is a lack of faith in God. We start to believe God is unable or unwilling to solve our problems or supply our needs. I actually insult God when I act as if He isn't big enough, and doesn't know or care enough to handle my problems. Every time I worry, I'm calling God a weakling. I'm saying, "God the reason I'm worrying about this is that I am confident You can help some things but certainly not all things. God, You just aren't going to show up for me. I'd rather worry than fully trust in You."

Prayer

Dear strong Redeemer, forgive me when I underestimate Your presence and power. Forgive me when I worry about things You have promised to provide. I have every reason to rely upon You, and many times I do not. It must be my carnal fleshly nature that keeps me from believing You are an omniscient God, more than able to meet any and all of my needs. I want to start my spiritual life over again now. In Jesus' name, I pray. Amen.

Questions

- Why is worry such a great sin?

- According to Matthew 6:31-33, who are you like if you worry about life's necessities?

- Is God powerful enough to meet your needs…and do you have enough faith to trust in Him?

Journal

_____

_____

_____

_____

■ August 1

> *I do not understand what I do. For what I want to do I do not do, but what I hate I do. I know that nothing good lives in me, that is, in my sinful nature. For I have the desire to do what is good, but I cannot carry it out. For what I do is not the good I want to do; no, the evil I do not want to do—this I keep on doing. (Romans 7:15, 18-19)*

Meditation   Dudley C. Rutherford

There is an old Indian legend that has two Indian warriors talking to each other. One of them begins to describe the inward battle that goes on in any man's soul. The Indian says, "I have two dogs living in my heart. I have a white dog and a black dog, and these two dogs are constantly fighting. They are at war all the time." The other Indian asks, "Which dog usually wins?" "The one I feed the most," comes the pointed reply.

In the above text, Paul the Apostle expresses that same civil war that goes on in every man, woman and child. He agonizes over the battle between good and evil in his own life. Jesus wants your life, your soul and your all. But so does Satan. Who will win? The one you feed the most. How do you feed the good part of your nature? By prayer, Bible study and the practice of a disciplined life for the Lord. How would one feed the baser part of his soul? Through neglect, laziness and staying away from the Bible, church and other spiritual issues. Physically speaking, we say, "We are what we eat." The same is truer in a spiritual sense. We are what we put into our souls and hearts. Which do you feed the most?

Two Dogs

Prayer

Dear Lord of my life, I realize that if the Apostle Paul had this battle raging within, I should expect no less. Help me to start force-feeding the best part of me: my God-created soul. Remind me that the only good in my heart must be placed there, accompanied by some part of my effort. With Your help, I want to feed the best part of me, and I want the best part of me to win this spiritual war. In Jesus' name, I ask. Amen.

Questions

- What do the two dogs represent?

- Describe Paul's dilemma.

- How can you feed the dog that should be fed?

Journal

_____

_____

_____

_____

_____

■ August 2

Let us fix our eyes on Jesus, the author and perfecter of our faith, who for the joy set before him endured the cross, scorning its shame, and sat down at the right hand of the throne of God. (Hebrews 12:2)

Meditation   H. Dean Rutherford

There will never be another Jesus. Never! Some day there may be another Lincoln, Napoleon, Washington or Alexander the Great, another Columbus, Babe Ruth, Michael Jordan, Tiger Woods, Van Gogh, DaVinci or Michelangelo. But there will never be another Savior. There may come another Brahms, another Schubert, Beethoven or Mozart, but there will never be another Jesus. He is the great "forever unlike." He is truly the "One and only." He has no peers. He has no equals. He stands alone, august, unique and supreme.

You cannot exhaust my Jesus. Pile on Him all your sins, and He still has pardon left. Stack on Him all your sorrows and all your tears, and He can still carry and bear ten million more. For who, like Jesus, can welcome the prodigal home? Who, like Jesus, can dry off a tear at the foot of a newly made grave? Who, like Jesus, can give us hope in the valley of the shadow of death? Who, like Jesus, can lift us up from the miry clay and put an eternal song in our hearts?

Prayer

Dear Lord in Heaven, forgive me if I have ever doubted Your divinity. Forgive the times I have tried to add You to my life, as if You were just some ordinary person. Help me to remember that You have all power, all love, and that You have my best interest and happiness at heart. There will never be another Jesus, in whose name, I pray. Amen.

Questions

- What did Jesus endure for you?

- Is there anyone even close to being like Jesus?

- What does Jesus mean to you?

Journal

_____

_____

_____

_____

■ August 3

A record of the genealogy of Jesus Christ the son of David, the son of Abraham... whose mother was Tamar... whose mother was Rahab... whose mother was Ruth... whose mother had been Uriah's wife... and Jacob the father of Joseph, the husband of Mary, of whom was born Jesus, who is called Christ. (Matthew 1:1-16)

Meditation   *James Price*

Ancient genealogies tend to bore modern readers. This one is different. It has blazing flares-in-the-night type entries. In the midst of the long list of acceptable and standard (and somewhat boring) male names are inserted several unusual and totally unnecessary female names. No first-century Jewish reader could miss these insertions; they would jar like emergency sirens on a serene summer afternoon. The female side of the family was not necessary to establish Davidic lineage. Matthew is clearly signaling us – to wake us up – to mark an aspect of the character and action of God.

Each of these females is a standout. Tamar was Jewish, but played the part of a prostitute. Rahab was a full-time prostitute and a Canaanite. Ruth was a wonderful, loyal woman but she was a Moabite. Uriah's wife was Bathsheba – her husband Uriah had been murdered by David in a contract killing after David had an adulterous affair with her. She was also a Hittite. One of the messages Matthew hopes we pick up from these volcanic insertions is that God is radically inclusive. Jesus' ancestry included non-Jews and blatant sinners. This genealogy not only documents Jesus as the promised Jewish Messiah, but also as Lord and Savior available for all humankind. And Matthew, himself a formerly corrupt tax collector, means *all*. "Everyone who calls on the name of the Lord will be saved" (Romans 10:13).

James Price is the Senior Pastor of Diamond Canyon Christian Church in Diamond Bar, CA.

Prayer

O Lord, our Lord, how majestic is Your name in *all* the earth! Thank You for having a place for me in Your family! Thank You for sending Jesus and giving Him as a sacrifice in my place. I needed Him, and I need Him still. Thank You for Your inclusive generosity to sinners like me! Thank You for inviting me to participate in the fellowship and ministry of Jesus Christ in sharing the good news and making disciples of all nations. In His gracious name. Amen.

Questions

- When in your life have you been excluded from a social group, and how did it feel?

- When in your life have you been welcomed, loved and graciously included in a social group, and how did it feel?

- For what in your life are you most thankful to God for giving you?

Journal

■ August 4

Meditation   *Dudley C. Rutherford*

Once after playing golf with some of our church men, one of them came over to me and said, "Do you remember one time a few months back, when you preached on giving and tithing? Remember you asked everyone who believed in God to raise their hands? I raised mine high. Then you asked how many of you who believe in God, believe in God enough to give one tenth of your income as the Bible says?" He said, "Preacher, you need to say that more often." I asked why. He replied, "Up until the time you asked that, I had never given much. Oh, maybe five dollars a Sunday, but I never came close to tithing. I thought ten percent was ridiculous. I always dreaded the offering time. But when you put it like you did, and I added up those two questions of yours, I couldn't stop thinking about it. My wife and I talked it over and we decided to tithe. It has turned our lives completely around in a wonderful way. God has blessed us beyond our wildest dreams. Now, we not only say we believe in God but we actually do, and we know we do because we completely trust Him. We even trust Him with our money."

Truly And Clearly

Oh wonderful Savior, help me to be a giver. I realize I am never quite so much like You, as when I am giving a portion of that money You have given to me in the first place. Help me to remember that if I can't trust You with a dime out of every dollar, then it's very likely that I really don't believe in You. In Christ's eternal name, I pray. Amen.

Questions

- Why does God say He will curse these people?

- Can you say you truly believe in God and yet not trust Him?

- Does the amount you give truly and clearly reflect your best faith and belief in Him?

Journal

■ August 5

I will give them an undivided heart and put a new spirit in them; I will remove from them their heart of stone and give them a heart of flesh. Then they will follow my decrees and be careful to keep my laws. They will be my people, and I will be their God. (Ezekiel 11:19-20)

Meditation   *Dudley C. Rutherford*

The Wall Street Journal recently carried the touching story of a 16-year-old girl who received a heart transplant. She had waited for years. Then came the startling news that someone had died, and she could have this person's heart. Months after the successful surgery, the girl wanted to thank whoever gave her the heart. But all the hospital records were kept strictly confidential. The hospital said, "We can't give you the name, but if you will write the letter, we will see that it gets to the donor's family." So the girl sat down and wrote a letter that touched my heart:

Dear Family,

I am the recipient of the heart you were generous enough to donate in the midst of your own personal, family tragedy. I cannot imagine how difficult it must have been for you to suffer the loss, and then to offer the organs so that someone you don't even know might live. I feel a great responsibility to live my life so that your sacrifice will be worthwhile. I don't have the vocabulary to thank you for saving my life. I just want you to know that I will always feel responsible to bring honor to your family. Sincerely yours.

Even back in the Old Testament, God knew His people would need a heart transplant. Only when we become Christians and all that it means will the surgery be considered successful.

Sincerely Yours

Prayer

Oh Heavenly Father, I want to thank You for my new heart. Your Son Jesus gave me His heart. If I were to compose a letter to Jesus right now, it might say something like this: "Lord, I can't thank You enough for what You have done for me. I want to so live all the rest of my life, that it might bring honor to You and Your family, the Church." I pray these things in the name of the Great Physician, Jesus Christ. Amen.

Questions

- Who, only, can give a new heart?

- If you have a new heart, should it lead to obedience?

- Compose your own thank you letter to God.

Journal

_____

_____

_____

_____

_____

August 6

The sacrifices of God are a broken spirit; a broken and contrite heart, O God, you will not despise. (Psalm 51:17)

Meditation — *Ricky Woods*

Several years ago, the entire country paused and prayed for a little girl in Texas that had fallen into an abandoned oil well. Rescue teams worked for days to save little Jessica, but time was running out. Finally, an idea came to drill a hole parallel to the well Jessica was trapped in and then pull her through to safety. Everything about the plan worked perfectly, with one exception: Baby Jessica could not fit through the new hole to reach safety, because of the way her body was trapped in the well. Rescue teams refused to give up on this obstacle. A member of the team said, "I can save her, but I will have to break her arms to get her through the hole."

Often in a believer's life, we are saved only after being broken. The Psalmist says the sacrifices acceptable to God are a broken spirit. God will not despise a broken and contrite heart. In our brokenness, we discover a need that accepts human capacity, and a gracious God meets that need with mercy. We may be broken, but praise God, we are saved.

Ricky Woods is the Senior Pastor of First Baptist Church-West in Charlotte, NC.

Prayer

Thank You, Lord, for never giving up on us, no matter what condition we find ourselves in. The rescuing power of Your Spirit will not be swayed, whether we are stuck in a well or stuck in sin. The reality of life is that we sometimes find ourselves in a situation or circumstances from which we cannot deliver ourselves. How glad we are in those moments that we have a Savior. Your saving power is so great that even if it requires us to be broken to be saved, You break us in ways that cause healing to be possible and greater strength to be obtained. In Jesus' name. Amen.

Questions

- Can you recall ways in which you may have experienced brokenness that led to deliverance?

- Have you ever experienced frustration in your attempt to aid someone?

- How do you respond to feelings of helplessness?

Journal

■ August 7

If we confess our sins, he is faithful and just and will forgive us our sins and purify us from all unrighteousness. (I John 1:9)

Meditation

Last Wednesday night, I talked about a young woman so heavily in debt that her life was a living nightmare. She owed so much money that it would be years before she could pay it off. But one day, she met a young man. He fell in love with her and she with him. He proposed marriage, but before she could accept the proposal, she said, "I can't marry you without telling you that I am deeply in debt." He said that after they were married, he would pay off all her bills. She had great hope in her heart. They got married, and soon thereafter he kept his word. As he paid off her last bill, you can only imagine what joy was in her heart. Hope had turned to joy and assurance, as he not only paid off her indebtedness but also revealed to her that he was wealthy beyond belief – and that she was on a joint checking account with him. You say, "Preacher, that doesn't happen." Yes, it does. In fact, it happened already… when Jesus paid off all our sins.

Wealthy Beyond Belief

Prayer

God, I thank You that You have forgiven us our trespasses, our debts and our sins. It's so wonderful to be married to a billionaire. When we put our full trust in You, we really don't have any worries or problems. Forgive me when I have doubted Your ability and desire to forgive all my sins. Bless me, in Christ's forgiving name, I pray. Amen.

Questions

- Would you be more at peace if you knew all your debts were paid?

- Who paid your debts and how did He pay for them?

- Should the assurance of your debt-free status make you careless, or lead you to be more spiritual?

Journal

■ August 8

Then the man and his wife heard the sound of the Lord God as he was walking in the garden in the cool of the day, and they hid from the Lord God among the trees of the garden. But the Lord God called to the man, "Where are you?" (Genesis 3:8-9)

Meditation   *Dudley C. Rutherford*

I read recently of a little three-year-old boy by the name of Jaryd Atadero, who had been missing for six days. I looked into some of the faces of those involved with the search. There was a look of absolute desolation no human words can describe. So many had helped: the police, the sheriff's patrol, ordinary citizens, dogs, helicopters and TV reporters. What a mad, desperate search.

Did you know God loves us that much, and God is searching for us many times with that same intensity? Did you know the very first question ever asked in the Bible was when God was searching for Adam and Eve in the Garden of Eden? They had sinned and hid themselves when God came looking for them. The first question asked on the planet was God asking, "Adam, where are you?"

Sin makes us hide from God. Sin makes us break our appointments with God. God always keeps His appointments. Did you know Christianity is the only religion in the world where God is searching for man? All other religions have man searching for God. God is the great searcher! He is now searching for your heart. Will you, right now, open your heart and invite God into your life? Let Him search for you no longer.

God Is Searching

Prayer

Dear gentle Savior, I'm so sorry You have had to search for me so many times. I must confess that I, like Adam and Eve, have tried to hide from You. I want to open my heart to You and invite You to come in today, right now. In fact, I want to help You search for others. Let me be Your voice and Your heart, and let me have Your compassion as I try to assist You in reaching others. In Jesus' name. Amen.

Questions

- Why is God searching for you?

- What is unique about Christianity in connection with searching?

- How can you help God in searching for others?

Journal

_____

_____

_____

_____

_____

■August 9

The Lord bless you and keep you; the Lord make his face shine upon you and be gracious to you; the Lord turn his face toward you and give you peace. (Numbers 6:24-26)

Meditation   *Jim Reeve*

When I was growing up in church, I loved to hear these words. Not so much because of what was being said, but rather because this was the typical benediction spoken at the end of most worship services. As a kid, this meant one thing to me: church was finally over and we could get on with our day. Free at last!

Now I see these same words in a much different light, and with much more meaning. Though largely a forgotten practice today, it was common during biblical days for leaders and parents to stretch forth their hands and speak words of blessing over their people and children. For people of faith, this was not simply the recitation of some nice thoughts; rather, it was an actual transference or impartation of favor from God through the priest, father or leader.

Jim Reeve is the Senior Pastor of Faith Community Church in West Covina, CA.

An Imparted Blessing

Prayer

As a mature adult and pastor, it is a joy and privilege to speak these powerful words over you today: May God bless you and protect you. May He keep you secure. May God smile on you (which is what the Hebrew for "shine" really means) all day long and may He be gracious to you – bestowing blessings you do not deserve. May He turn His face toward you, meaning may He give you His full and undivided attention, not looking through you as if He has more important things to do and people to meet. You are the most important thing in the world to God right now. Finally, may He grant you peace in the midst of a world all too often torn by conflict and stress. It is the peace that the New Testament says surpasses understanding. I speak this over your life, in the name of the Father, Son and Holy Spirit. Amen and Amen.

Questions

- Do you feel blessed by God?

- Do you deserve these blessings?

- If not, then why do you think God keeps shining His goodness on you?

Journal

August 10

And my God will meet all your needs according to his glorious riches in Christ Jesus. (Philippians 4:19)

Cast all your anxiety on him because he cares for you. (I Peter 5:7)

Meditation   Dudley C. Rutherford

I want to ask you today – you who may be feeling left out, or feeling hopeless – will you lean anew upon Jesus? Have you forgotten that Jesus will take care of you? He will provide for you. Life is not always fair but Jesus always cares.

I talked recently with a teenager. He said, "I want to feel loved. Nobody loves me. Nobody wanted me. Nobody planned for me. I'm just always in the way." Could I say to you what I said to him: "Jesus loves you, and my Jesus planned for you. You are not alone in this thing."

I say to the sorrowing widow that Jesus cares. I say to the college student who can't seem to get through: Jesus cares. I say to the heartbroken and lonely that Jesus cares. I say to the sick and dying: oh, how He cares for you. Men who work and work, for whom there is seldom enough money to pay the bills, who are tired and discouraged: my God in Heaven loves you and cares for you. If the one you love has walked out on you, and you don't think you can go on another day, please go on. The God who cares for the plants and the flowers and feeds the birds will take care of you. Do you still believe the Bible? Do you still believe Philippians 4:19 and I Peter 5:7?

He Cares For You

Forgive me, Lord, for those weak moments in my spiritual walk when I have forgotten that You care for me. Sometimes I mistake the negative events of my life to be a sign of Your absence. I know this isn't true. I know now that You always care. I know Your great heart is broken when mine is. I want to reaffirm my complete faith and trust in You. And it's in Your perfect name, the name of Jesus, I pray. Amen.

Questions

- God shall supply your needs according to what?

- When things go wrong, does God still care about you?

- What should you do when you can't feel His presence?

Journal

_____

_____

_____

_____

_____

■ August 11

Meditation   *Dudley C. Rutherford*

No couple, no lovers, no husband and wife can forever live in that wonderful infatuation, the euphoria of the first weeks and months of romance and marriage. Love is not only blind; it is also deceptive. It makes us think the excitement can last forever. It hasn't happened yet. Marriage is not supposed to work that way. And it doesn't. Sometimes we Christians may feel guilty when we fail to keep alive the first joys of our salvation. There is indeed a wonderful euphoria and intoxication in initial grace and salvation! Nothing is more thrilling and contagious than a newborn in Jesus. But we are not called upon to sustain that elation throughout every day of our relationship with Christ. Far more important than any "highs or lows" is our faithfulness to Christ.

All fervor and emotion waxes and wanes. That's where prayer and Bible study come into play. That's why God wants us to be faithful to His Church and His table of Communion. All these things, the Lord has designed that we might not stray too far, but instead renew our faithfulness. Being on the mountaintop is wonderful, but we don't live our lives on the mountaintop; we live in the valleys of life. Many times we do not feel as close to Christ as we have in the past. That is why we need to renew ourselves – and renew our vows.

Prayer

Dear Father, we do not ask to experience every day the exhilaration of "mountaintop" living. But we do ask for a steady measure of faithfulness. At the end of each day, at the end of life's day, the end of our day, may we be found faithful. May we hear Your promised words: "Well done, good and faithful servant." (Matthew 25:23)

Questions

- Is it possible for you to feel close to Christ every hour of your life?

- Amid any feelings of guilt, what should you do?

- God promises salvation to those who are what?

Journal

_____

_____

_____

_____

■ August 12

Submit to one another out of reverence for Christ. (Ephesians 5:21)

Meditation   *Jim Wozniak*

Submitting to another person, especially your spouse, is to be thought of as freely giving up the demand of having your own way in order to help them grow in Christ. Since so often we see this as a difficult task, Paul goes on to tell us the reason our hearts should be thus motivated. It is because our hearts and attitudes are to be influenced by our love for Jesus Christ. As we put Christ in awe, humbly bowing before God as Creator of all, and seeing His children as He sees them, we cannot help but put each one before ourselves.

Jesus gave us a wonderful example of this in John 13. After washing His disciples' feet, He commanded them to go and do for each other as He had done for them. Jesus, out of His great love for the Father, and knowing the spiritual needs of His disciples, illustrated in a physical way how they were to submit to each other, thereby helping one another reach their full potential in Christ. This was a foreign concept to them then, just as it may be to us today. Just remember, this is a precept given to us by God. Every time we give of ourselves in submission to one another, we demonstrate that we love God more.

Jim Wozniak is an elder at Shepherd of the Hills Church, Porter Ranch, CA.

Prayer

Dear Lord God, I confess that many times I have put my own needs and desires ahead of others, especially those I love most. Help me not to demand my own way all the time, but instead to put the needs of others before my own. Thank You that Your Son, Jesus, because of His great love for us, was willing to die to meet my need of salvation from my sin and death. Help me to realize that when I submit to others, I am loving You more. I pray these things in Jesus' name. Amen.

Questions

- When was the last time you submitted to another person in order to help them grow in Christ?

- Have you discovered that submitting to your spouse or family member is a way to worship God?

- Have you experienced the freedom that comes from not demanding your own way?

Journal

_____

_____

_____

_____

■ August 13

Now we know that if the earthly tent we live in is destroyed, we have a building from God, an eternal house in heaven, not built by human hands. Meanwhile we groan, longing to be clothed with our heavenly dwelling.
(II Corinthians 5:1-2)

Meditation   H. Dean Rutherford

Years ago, my brothers and sisters and I all went back home to Tulsa for a reunion. My folks had set the table, and it was the only complete reunion of my family that I can remember. Mom and dad, kids and grandkids… everybody!

During the beautiful meal, my mother disappeared. I excused myself a few minutes later from the table and went searching for her. I found her staring out the large front window. I said, "Mom, what's wrong?" "Oh, everything is right; too right! To tell you the truth, I was just wishing this day would never end." I knew what she meant. I knew what she was thinking, and she was so right. That would be the last time we would all be together again in this life.

Oh, my dear brother and my dear sister. This old Book of the ages, if it teaches us anything, it teaches us that God has prepared and promised a day that will never end. Never! A day in which we will be together forever with those we have loved and lost for a while. One day, known only to God, a day only on God's calendar, we will gather around God's great table of feast. Not only will we gather with our loved ones but also with our great Savior and Redeemer, Jesus Christ. Amen.

Prayer

Almighty God, I look forward to that glorious hour of reunion, that hour of homecoming, when we shall be reunited with family and friends and most of all, our wonderful salvation captain, Jesus. Help me in these next few minutes to picture that indescribable scene of rejoicing. In this solemn hour, I recommit my life to You. In Jesus' name. Amen.

Questions

- What do you think Heaven will be like?

- Who will be there?

- If you died today, how do you know for sure you'll be going to Heaven?

Journal

■ August 14

The one who calls you is faithful and he will do it. (I Thessalonians 5:24)

The Spirit and the bride say, "Come!" And let him who hears say, "Come!" Whoever is thirsty, let him come; and whoever wishes, let him take the free gift of the water of life. (Revelation 22:17)

Meditation   *Dudley C. Rutherford*

The entire Bible, from cover to cover, is a picture of God calling you. He wants to call you to Himself. He wants to call you from sin, from temptation, from lost-ness. He is calling you to church, to salvation and to the only freedom and happiness that exists. Do you think He would call the lower forms of His creation and leave us to find our own way? We know He guides the birds in their uncharted flight, and we know He guides the fish in their pathless seas. If my God put the magnetic North Pole in place, so that every compass in the world points unerringly to it, then we can be sure He will not let me lose my way.

I love the way the Bible ends. In the last book, in the last Testament, in nearly the last verse on the last page, God woos us one last time, to remind us of what He and His Bible are all about. Read that passage again. "The Spirit [that's His Holy Spirit] says, 'Come,' and anyone who has ever heard about Jesus says, 'Come,' and whoever is thirsty or longing can *come*." And finally He says, "And whoever wishes may *come* and drink of the water of life." If God had said, "Dudley Rutherford may *come*," I would have thought He surely meant someone else with my same name. But when He said, "And whoever wishes," I know He included me. If you haven't come to Him yet, would you do so today? Faithful is He that calls you!

Prayer

Dear Father in Heaven, we have never doubted or questioned Your faithfulness to call us; we only marvel at our sluggishness to respond. Help me to listen more carefully to Your "still small voice," and once again to hear and heed Your haunting invitation to come back to You. May I be quick to listen and quick to respond. In Christ's name, I pray. Amen.

Questions

- Why is God so faithful to call you to Him?

- What is nature's proof that God calls you?

- Have you ever experienced or sensed this calling?

Journal

_____

_____

_____

_____

■ August 15

Then the angel showed me the river of the water of life, as clear as crystal, flowing from the throne of God and of the Lamb down the middle of the great street of the city. On each side of the river stood the tree of life, bearing twelve crops of fruit, yielding its fruit every month. And the leaves of the tree are for the healing of the nations. (Revelation 22:1-2)

Meditation   *Dudley C. Rutherford*

You can't study this wonderful book called the Bible without discovering that trees hold a prominent place. The first time God ever talked to man or man ever talked to God was in a garden of trees in Eden. Our first parents stumbled over a tree in paradise and ushered sin into the world. The furniture in the tabernacle was made from trees. The cedars of Lebanon were used to construct the temple. The first night God ever spent on earth was in a wooden manger, in a wooden shed.

Much of our Lord's ministry took place around trees. Didn't Zacchaeus climb up a sycamore tree? Did not Jesus, in His time of passion, pray in a grove of olive trees? Jesus was always talking about the fig trees. And the verse of our text says that when we get to Heaven, we shall be able to see the Tree of Life. That tree is a representation of eternal life and eternal good health. But of all the trees in the Bible, the one that speaks the loudest, clearest, and the most precious is the tree on which our Savior died. We call it the old rugged cross, but we could say it was an old rugged tree. Thank God for trees! If Jesus did not die upon that rugged tree, where would we be?

Old Rugged Cross

Prayer

Thank You, Lord, for trees. Thank You for all the trees. You made them all, so many kinds, and You obviously love them. The one I think of the most is the tree on which You poured out Your sinless blood to pay for our awful and careless sins. Help me to think often of Your love, every time I see a tree. I breathe this prayer in the name of Christ, who died on a tree for me. In Jesus' name. Amen.

Questions

- Why did Jesus have to die?

- Does the cross remind you of the love of God?

- What is the difference between the cross and the empty grave?

Journal

■ August 16

> *Finally, brothers, whatever is true, whatever is noble, whatever is right, whatever is pure, whatever is lovely, whatever is admirable—if anything is excellent or praiseworthy—think about such things. (Philippians 4:8)*

Meditation   *Pat Merold*

I recently received an anonymous letter. The writer expressed the misery of an unhappy marriage, out-of-control kids and dissatisfaction with the job. The writer went on to share that his only joy was to go to bed, pull the covers up over his head and go to sleep. I wanted to give a hug, words of encouragement and share this verse. It's a verse that, when applied, changes one's thought world.

Years ago, when our son was having serious problems and we were drowning in feelings of hopelessness, I was tempted to do just what the letter's author said was his only joy. Instead, I decided to make this verse my "life verse" for that period of my life. That choice enabled me to focus on our son from a different perspective. I had discovered the secret to a much higher happiness quotient.

Imagine what a difference it would make in your marriage if you allowed only the finer qualities of your spouse to occupy your thoughts. Imagine what a difference it would make in your attitude toward life if you applied this verse. Apply this verse to your church and your job. To look for what is true doesn't allow one to deny reality, but let's us deal with a person or circumstance wisely. To look for the admirable, lovely, pure and praiseworthy in people and situations creates a healthy state of mind.

Pat Merold is the wife of Ben Merold, Senior Pastor of Harvester Christian Church in St. Charles, MO.

Prayer

Father, help me to see people from Your perspective. Help me to be charitable in my assessment of others, to see their value to Your Kingdom. Help me to be true in my inner self, to be all You want me to be. I want to be pure in heart; I want to be effective and productive in my knowledge of Your Son, Jesus. I am thankful for Your promise to renew my mind. In the name of Jesus. Amen.

Questions

- What relationship would be strengthened if you applied this verse?

- Take a few minutes and list the three finest qualities of your spouse, children, church and community.

- What qualities of your life would your family and friends find to be praiseworthy?

Journal

Then the word of the Lord came to me: "O house of Israel, can I not do with you as this potter does?" declares the Lord. "Like clay in the hand of the potter, so are you in my hand, O house of Israel." (Jeremiah 18:5-6)

Meditation   *Dudley C. Rutherford*

Our God uses broken things. Did you know that? Did you ever stop to realize that God uses broken ground to produce the crops? Our God uses broken clouds to produce the rain. It takes thousands of blossoms to make one bottle of perfume. Before gold can be beautiful, it has to go through the refiner's fire. In this passage, God told Jeremiah to go down to the potter's house and watch him as he works at the potter's wheel; to study how he carefully picks up the broken pieces when something he is working on breaks, and he starts all over again to make something beautiful. Then lovingly, God says to Jeremiah, "Say to Israel that even though they have failed me and are now broken in pieces, like the potter I can start over with them, and I can still make them a thing of usefulness and beauty."

This is a perfect picture of your life and mine. We are a group of people with broken plans, broken hearts, broken dreams, perhaps broken health. We are all broken. But Jesus, the Great Potter, can pick up the broken fragments of your life and make of it something more beautiful than it was before.

The Great Potter

Prayer

O great God, I come to You today, knowing that I am broken in many ways. But I also know that You are the magnificent Master Potter. You can still take the brokenness of my life and produce something so beautiful that it can last through all eternity. Thank You for all the times You picked up the broken pieces and started over with me. Thank You for being in the remnant business, for if You were not, I would be without hope. I pray in Christ's blessed name. Amen.

Questions

- Where did God send Jeremiah first, and what was he to do?

- What did he see as he gazed at the potter?

- Can you name a specific example of God shaping you?

Journal

■ August 18

Let them give thanks to the Lord for his unfailing love and his wonderful deeds for men. For great is your love, higher than the heavens; your faithfulness reaches to the skies. (Psalm 107:31, 108:4)

Meditation   *Dudley C. Rutherford*

The infamous outlaw "Two-Gun Cowley" had barricaded himself in a house and was shooting it out with the New York police. After many shots were exchanged, Cowley threw his two empty guns out the window. He yelled, "Okay, okay, come and get me! Come and kill me. That's what you've always wanted to do. Come on in. I'm out of bullets. Shoot me; kill me. But I just want you to know, not one person ever, ever said to me, 'I love you.' Not my mother, not my family, not anyone ever took the time to say 'I love you.'"

My friend, he was wrong. God has told Two-Gun Cowley that many times. And He has told you and me also. Not one person on this planet will ever be able to stand on Judgment Day and say, "No one ever said to me, 'I love you.'" I think that as you study this Scripture and this devotional that Jesus is saying, "I love you." Don't sell yourself short. You are of inestimable value to the Lord. A T-shirt read, "God don't make no junk." That's true! He made you, and He thought you were so important and valuable that He went to the cross for you.

Two-Gun Cowley

Prayer

Dear gentle and tender Savior, thank You for every star and every flower, and every day, for they tell me what I so often forget: that You truly do love me. Help me, Lord Jesus, to respond to Your love, by increasing my faith and my service to my fellow man, and my deeper involvement in the things of Your Kingdom. I pray these things in my Great Lover's name, even Jesus Christ. Amen.

Questions

- Can you name one time when God's love has failed?

- Will you ever, one time, be able to say, "Nobody loves me"?

- How can you best respond to matchless, undying love?

Journal

> *Therefore, since we have been justified through faith, we have peace with God through our Lord Jesus Christ, through whom we have gained access by faith into this grace in which we now stand. And we rejoice in the hope of the glory of God. (Romans 5:1-2)*

Meditation   *John Hampton*

Paul explains here that the result of experiencing the grace of God is that we rejoice in hope. So a primary reason I can be joyful is because *I have a hope that is higher than my circumstances*!

It's been said that a person can live 40 days without food, three days without water, four minutes without air, but not one second without hope. We must have hope in the future if we are going to experience joy in the present. Some researchers at Cornell University studied 25,000 prisoners of war from World War II. They concluded that a person could handle almost anything if he has hope. Hope helps you endure. Hope gives you strength to go on. Hope gives you something to look forward to. Hope helps you overcome. Hope never allows you to give up.

An elderly but spry lady lived in a retirement home. She spotted an older and distinguished gentleman who was a new resident seated in the dining hall. She promptly sat down in front of him and attempted to get his attention with warm smiles. Growing uncomfortable, he asked, "May I help you?" She replied, "You look just like my third husband; the wave of your hair, your warm smile, the look of your hands." Now, feeling very uncomfortable, he said, "And how many times have you been married, Madam?" She smiled and said, "Twice."

Hope keeps you going and gets you started again and again and again!

John Hampton is Senior Pastor of First Christian Church in Canton, OH.

Prayer

Thank You, Father, that Christ in me is the hope of glory. Thank You that the Resurrection of Jesus from the grave gives me a living hope that will not perish, spoil or fade away. Make me a model and a messenger of Your hope to the people I will meet today. Remind me to always build my hope on You alone. In Jesus' name. Amen.

Questions

- On what do people place their hopes, other than God?

- How can living with eternity in mind increase your hope?

- Write down a time when your hope in Christ kept you steady.

Journal

_____

_____

_____

_____

_____

■ August 20

Meditation   *Dudley C. Rutherford*

I read a fable one time, about a spider that saw a massive lion go into a cave. The spider was intensely envious of the great king of the jungle and therefore said to himself, "I will imprison that lion, that beast, in this very cave." So while the lion went back into the bowels of the cave and fell asleep, the spider began to spin a web across the mouth of the cave. Carefully but determinedly, he spun back and forth, back and forth, up and down until his spinner was empty. Then the tiny spider sat in a dark spot by the side of the cave and bragged, "Now the mighty beast is my prisoner. Never again will he bask in the golden sunlight. Now I have taken him captive."

But the old lion awoke from his nap, shook the dust from his shaggy mane, gave a yawn and stretched himself. He let out a roar that echoed through the valley and over the hills. And then he walked straight out of that cave and never even knew the spider's web was there.

Likewise, Satan saw Jesus taken off the cross and placed in a cave. Satan said to himself, "A-ha! I will weave this web of death across the mouth of the tomb and He will remain forever my prisoner." But Jesus, the Lion of the Tribe of Judah, came out of His grave and walked straight out of the tomb. He never even knew the devil's flimsy web of death had been placed there.

The Spider and the Lion

Prayer

Thank You, dear Jesus, that You rose from the grave and broke the bonds of death. Now I know for sure that You can conquer death for me also. My hope is placed in Your power and Your strength. I have nothing to fear from this day forward. I will forever praise You for the victory You assure me. I put all my trust in You. In Your name, I pray. Amen.

Questions

- Which is most powerful: death or Christ?

- How do you know this?

- How does His victory relate to your final triumph?

Journal

■ August 21

Therefore put on the full armor of God, so that when the day of evil comes, you may be able to stand your ground, and after you have done everything, to stand. (Ephesians 6:13ff)

Meditation   *Ed Kriz*

We are told to put on the "whole armor of God" – not just a part of it, but the whole of it, and daily. It is something like going out to take honey out of a honeycomb, with thousands of bees circling around, and thinking you can dash in and grab the honey (without a beekeeper's suit) and then dash right out without any bees stinging you. No, you will get stung, because you have not taken the time to protect yourself first. You have to put on the correct suit for battling the bees, to keep safe.

In the same way, we must put on the "whole armor of God" to keep ourselves safe from the Adversary. After we say hello each morning to our Heavenly Father, we need to put on the armor as our very next step, before beginning each day. Jesus said that in this world you will have troubles (John 16:33). And just like the stings of a bee, we all share a common enemy who is out to shoot its stinging arrows at us, but when we don the full armor of God we are promised that his fiery arrows will not penetrate our armor and pierce our souls, because we have One who has, in our place, been pierced for us. Isaiah tells us that, "He was pierced for our transgressions, he was crushed for our iniquities and the punishment that brought us peace was upon him, and by his wounds we are healed." (Isaiah 53:5). The One who endured the piercing for us, is the One who promised that He had overcome the world, and through Him, with our armor intact, we too can overcome the world!

Ed Kriz is former Pastoral Care Pastor at Shepherd of the Hills Church in Porter Ranch, CA.

Honeycombs

Prayer

I want to thank You, Lord, for the helmet of salvation that protects my thinking and for the breastplate of righteousness that helps me to do right. Help me to put on the truth, speaking it at all times. Thank You for the shield of faith that helps me to put away all doubts of the Adversary. I am so grateful for the Word of God (the sword of the Spirit) that defends me from the Adversary. Then help my feet to be shod with the preparation of the Gospel of peace, sharing the Gospel with the lost.

Questions

- Are you completely dressed for the day?

- Will you be looking for opportunities to witness today?

- Will you be meditating on the Word of God during the day?

Journal

> *Now listen, you who say, "Today or tomorrow we will go to this or that city, spend a year there, carry on business and make money." Why, you do not even know what will happen tomorrow. What is your life? You are a mist that appears for a little while and then vanishes. (James 4:13-14)*

Meditation   *Dudley C. Rutherford*

My dad is a great preacher. When I was young, I loved to hear him preach. Now that I am older, I recall many of the things he said. My dad is always at his best during the altar call or the invitation time, trying to persuade folks to step forward and make a decision for Christ. One of his most memorable lines was, "It's your move; it's your turn. It's not God's turn. The ball is in your court."

Could I say to you now, "It's not God's turn – it's yours"? If you are wanting to live a closer life with Christ, if you are wanting to become a Christian, don't wait for God to do more. He's done it all. It's your move. What is your quest? What are your goals? What do you want to be for Him? Do you want to be a Christian? A soul winner, a student of the Word, a great tither, a person of faith and prayer? Then stop waiting for something big or dramatic to come from God. It's your turn. God is not going to some day suddenly ask you to climb some steep mountain; rather, He is calling you today, right now to begin your quest. It's up to you, not God.

Prayer

Dear Father, You have done it all. You have done it already. It's our time to be thankful, and it's our time to repent anew, and to set some serious goals. We know You will help once we start, but it's up to us to begin and take that first step. Forgive us for waiting on You while You've been waiting on us. In Jesus' name, I pray. Amen.

Questions

- Name one honest thing that prevents you from being a better Christian.

- Will God some day break down your door and come storming into your life? Why not?

- What two things can you improve in your daily walk?

Journal

■ August 23

When I consider your heavens, the work of your fingers, the moon and the stars, which you have set in place, what is man that you are mindful of him, the son of man that you care for him? You made him a little lower than the heavenly beings and crowned him with glory and honor.

(Psalm 8:3-5)

Meditation   *Jud Wilhite*

Millions of Americans tune in regularly to the PBS TV series, *Antiques Roadshow*. They watch in amazement as appraisers announce "junk" to be worth huge sums of money. The show reminds us to not judge value by appearance alone. Our junk may be old and beat up, but worth thousands of dollars.

In Psalm 8, the writer looks out at the expanse of God's creation and wonders what possible value one small individual can have before this immense creation. Rather than feel insignificant, he acknowledges God crowned people with glory and honor.

The New Testament quotes Psalm 8 and notes that Jesus "suffered death, so that by the grace of God" we might experience life (Hebrews 2:9). God values you so much that He paid the price of His very Son for you. Value is determined by what someone is willing to pay for it. Even at the *Antiques Roadshow*, a piece isn't worth $20,000 unless someone pays for it. Jesus tasted death so that you could experience life. Your worth is more than an appraisal; the price has already been paid! No matter how you feel about yourself, God has already declared you to be priceless. So let the *Antiques Roadshow* change not only how you look around in your attic; let it change how you look in the mirror!

Jud Wilhite is the Senior Pastor of Central Christian Church in Henderson, NV.

Prayer

Heavenly Father, it amazes me that You would value me so much You would send Your Son Jesus to suffer for me. Forgive me for those times I don't value myself or others the way You do. Thank You for reminding me that I will never lock eyes with a single person who doesn't matter deeply to You. Fill me with Your patience and kindness. Thank You for all You have done for me. You are truly the One who is invaluable!

Questions

- When you look in the mirror, do you see yourself as God's special creation?

- If you will never lock eyes with someone who doesn't matter deeply to God, what are the implications for your life?

- What can you do today to remind someone they matter to God?

Journal

_____

_____

_____

_____

_____

■ August 24

Humble yourselves therefore, under God's mighty hand that he may lift you up in due time. Cast all your anxiety on him because he cares for you. (I Peter 5:6-7)

Meditation   *Dudley C. Rutherford*

Have you ever driven by a Veterans' Hospital and asked yourself why we have such institutions? The answer is simple. Our government made the decision years ago: if any young man or woman will leave the comforts of home, put on our country's uniform and risk death or injury, in order to serve and defend this nation, this same nation will take care of that soldier for the remaining years of his life. As long as a veteran lives, he or she has access to free medical treatment. Also our government, for that same soldier, will provide discount VA loans and help pay for a college education.

Now, if the federal government will try to provide for those who have served, do you think God will do less? If you enlist in His army and serve Him with your life, you can be assured that He will take care of you, not only in this world but also in the world to come. Go ahead! Enlist in His army. Get on the winning side. He will not be defeated. He is far better than our government in taking care of His own.

Better than the Government

Dear Lord Jesus, forgive me when I have not trusted You, and for those many times when I have depended upon my own strength to care for myself. May I never forget that by being a member of Your army, Your special Kingdom, Your Church, I have privileges and rights that others do not have. Help me to have more faith and to realize that because You love me, I shall be lifted up in due time. In the name of Christ, I pray. Amen.

Questions

- Why should you walk humbly, even in days of adversity?

- Name some ways our government tries to take care of us.

- What promise do you have that non-Christians do not have?

Journal

_____

_____

_____

_____

■ August 25

For where two or three come together in my name, there am I with them.
(Matthew 18:20)

Meditation   *Dudley C. Rutherford*

Charles Lamb, the great writer, once said, "Put all the great celebrities and personalities of the world into one circle and have them seated. If William Shakespeare should enter that illustrious circle, every man present would stand in honor to the Bard of Avon." Lamb then said, "If Jesus then entered that same circle, every person present would fall on their faces in homage to the Christ." What would you do if you met Jesus? What if He came into your circle, your house?

What if I said, "Jesus wants to meet with you in the city park at two o'clock this afternoon?" What would you do and what would you say? I'm sure you would be nervous and scared, but you would probably tell Him about three different things. First, you would profusely thank Him. Then you would confess your deepest sins. Finally, you would tell Him how you intend to live for Him this coming week. I've got great news. He is here, and that's exactly and precisely what you can tell Him right now. Talk to Him. He's here now. He is right beside you. He wants to be one-on-one with you. He is only a prayer away!

Jesus at the Park

Prayer

Dear Father, thank You for Your promised presence in my life. Even though my life is so sinful compared to Your life, I thank You that I can talk with You and pour out my heart to You, knowing You are listening and that You care. Help me to talk with You more often. May I become a person who desires to spend every waking moment in Your presence. In Your holy name, I pray. Amen.

Questions

- Should you let the greatness of Christ discourage you from praying?

- How often does Jesus desire to hear from you?

- How would you describe your prayer life?

Journal

■ August 26

"Martha, Martha," the Lord answered, "you are worried and upset about many things, but only one thing is needed. Mary has chosen what is better, and it will not be taken away from her." (Luke 10:41-42)

Meditation   *Ken Long*

In the movie, *City Slickers*, Billy Crystal's character, Mitch, is exhorted by Curly, a crusty old cowboy, to find the "one thing" that all life hinges on. It was something he would have to do on his own.

In this story in Luke about two sisters, Mary and Martha, we come closest to Jesus' "one thing" than anywhere else. Martha, who is busy and bothered by the accumulation of activity in her life (sound familiar?), presumes Jesus is going to side with her complaint that her sister Mary is just wasting time. Not only does Jesus refuse to advocate Martha's position, but He also elevates what Mary is doing. In fact, He makes an amazing statement that Mary is doing the "one thing" that is needed.

What is that "one thing"? Verse 39 gives us the answer: "…she sat at the Lord's feet listening to what He said." How often we struggle to rationalize our busy-ness, many times at the expense of doing the "one thing" the Lord really wants from us: to sit at His feet and soak up all He wants to say to us. What does Jesus want to say to you now? Are you listening?

Ken Long is Senior Pastor of Northshore Christian Church in Everett, WA.

Prayer

Dear Lord Jesus, forgive me for filling my life so full of activity that I fail to value our quiet time together. Cleanse my heart from the things that would become obstacles in our walk together. Help me to realize that nothing is more important to You than a deeper, more intimate relationship with me. I open my heart up to Your Word and Your voice. I want to be obedient to the faintest promptings of Your Spirit. I yield myself to You. In Jesus' name. Amen.

Questions

- How can you reduce busy-ness in your life?

- What are you willing to give up to hear His voice?

- How do you recognize Jesus' voice?

Journal

■ August 27

"I am the Alpha and the Omega," says the Lord God, "who is, and who was, and who is to come, the Almighty." (Revelation 1:8)

I am the Alpha and the Omega, the Beginning and the End.
(Revelation 21:6)

Meditation   H. Dean Rutherford

The alphabet not only makes up every word ever written or spoken, but it also has in it the germ of all the books that are yet to be. When another thousand years have passed, and many more millions of books have been written, the alphabet will be as fresh, as new, as fertile and inexhaustible as ever. So do you see what Jesus is saying about Himself? "I am like the alphabet. Everything else may come and go, change, mutate or become passé. But I remain as new and as fresh as your latest heartbeat."

You cannot exhaust Jesus. Everything else may end up on the scrap heap of history, but not Jesus. Cast a billion burdens at His feet, and there is room for more. Let a trillion souls step forward today and fall at His feet; there is still forgiveness, salvation and pardon for a trillion more tomorrow. Like the alphabet, He is fresh and new and totally inexhaustible. His grace knows no limits, His love and forgiveness have no boundaries.

Do you remember that old chorus we used to sing? "There's room at the cross for you. Though millions have come there's still room for one, yes, there's room at the cross for you." If you have not yet come to His table of grace, do so today. He is bigger than your deepest needs and taller than your greatest wants.

Alpha and Omega

Prayer

Dear God, I know I have a Redeemer who is able to save to the uttermost. Millions have drawn from Your well of salvation, but there is still a fountain of grace for me. I'm so glad I serve a God that is absolutely everything from A to Z. I have no needs that cannot be met. I place again today my total trust in You. Amen.

Questions

- What does that mean, the "Alpha and Omega"?

- Is there any need in your life that God is unable to meet?

- Does He have enough supply of grace to forgive you also?

Journal

Come, all you who are thirsty...Why spend money on what is not bread, and your labor on what does not satisfy? Seek the Lord while he may be found; call on him while he is near. (Isaiah 55:1-2,6)

Meditation   Dudley C. Rutherford

An Eastern Airlines plane, flight 401, was approaching the Miami airport for landing, and the light that indicates proper deployment of the landing gear failed to come on. The plane flew in a large, looping circle over the swamps of the Everglades, while the cockpit crew checked to see if the gear actually had not deployed, or if the signal light was simply defective. When the flight engineer tried to remove the tiny light bulb, it just wouldn't budge, and the other members of the crew frantically tried to assist him. As they struggled with the bulb, no one noticed the aircraft was losing altitude, and the plane flew right into the swamp. Many dozens of people lost their lives. One aviation journalist wrote in the *Miami Herald*, "While an experienced crew of high-priced pilots fiddled with a seventy five cent light bulb, the entire plane and its passengers flew right into the ground."

Many of us are like that. We spend our lives majoring in the minors. We emphasize things of little worth and ignore the vital issues of life. We spend most of our time, our labor and our effort on things that, at the end of the day, will be fruitless and of little value.

Little Light Bulb

Prayer

Dear God and Father of us all, I want to make my life count for something after this world is over. I don't want to spend my life and energy on the mundane things of this world. I want to live a life of faith and obedience. I want to leave a legacy of faithfulness to my children, on behalf of the Christ who gave His life on Calvary's cross for me. Help me to no longer spend money and labor on those things that can never satisfy. I pray in the strong name of Christ. Amen.

Questions

- What are some things people spend their energy on?

- Do you tend to focus more on the minor or major things in life?

- How committed are you to Christ?

Journal

August 29

I have considered my ways and have turned my steps to your statutes. I will hasten and not delay to obey your commands. At midnight I rise to give you thanks for your righteous laws. I am a friend to all who fear you, to all who follow your precepts. (Psalm 119:59, 60, 62, 63)

Meditation   *Ken Idleman*

As you meditate on this text from the wisdom literature of the Old Testament, notice the repetition of the first personal pronoun in this passage: "I have considered... I have turned... I will hasten... I will not delay... I will not forget... I am..." In the presence of God, the Psalmist is making a series of devotional commitments that are foundational for anyone who wants to live a life that honors the Father and blesses others. Of course, to live in such a way also *elevates us* to experience our best life now.

Inherent in these commitments is the power to shape your life and destiny, as you also influence the nearest and dearest on earth to you. There are five components of this "formula for faithfulness" that might structure either a half-day retreat or your daily devotions:

INTROSPECTION. It is so important to consider your ways. Do not live thoughtlessly and aimlessly.

DIRECTION. Have you made changes to reflect the fact that you are moving in God's direction with your life? Your steps tell the story of where you are going.

REJECTION OF PROCRASTINATION. It is so easy to put off doing the right things. But it is so deadly to spiritual growth to postpone doing what we know God wants us to do.

MEDITATION. Remember God's law by calling it to mind faithfully every day. Get under a good light with an open Bible and let Him speak to you and lead you.

RELATION. Connect with people who know and love God. Let them replenish you from the inside out.

Ken Idleman is Chancellor of Ozark Christian College in Joplin, MO.

Commitments

Prayer

My Father, Your word is a lamp to my feet and a light to my path. Help me to walk in Your ways today and every day, in the big areas and the little areas of my life. I want to please You above all others. In doing so, I know I will be the person I want to be in my best moments. In Jesus' name. Amen.

Questions

- What are your strengths and weaknesses as a Christian?

- What verses from God's word can you remember right now?

- Who are the replenishers in your life?

Journal

_____

_____

_____

_____

■ August 30

How great is the love the Father has lavished on us, that we should be called children of God! And that is what we are! The reason the world does not know us is that it did not know him. (I John 3:1)

Meditation   *Dudley C. Rutherford*

If God punished every time we did wrong, not one of us would be alive. It reminds me of a scene that's been reenacted time and again. Daddy comes home from work and Mama says, "Hurry and get the video camera, we want to show you something." And she takes the little baby and holds him under his arms and allows him to put all of his weight on the floor. "Take the picture Daddy, watch our baby walk." And he does walk. He staggers only a step or two and falls to the floor. Now, do these parents rush over to him and bawl him out or whip him? No, no, no. They praise him with shining eyes, and they tell him how good he his and that soon he will be taking many steps.

When we falter or stumble, our God does not strike us down. Instead, He encourages us to get up and try again. More than any human father ever loved a child and desired for that child to grow and thrive, our wonderful God loves us and yearns for our spiritual progress.

Prayer

Dear Father above, thank You for loving us more than we love ourselves, and more than we love our own children, our own flesh and blood. Thank You for not kicking us out of the family every time we fail and fall short of Your will. May the knowledge of Your matchless, deep love and patience encourage me to walk more closely with our wonderful Father. In Jesus' name, I pray. Amen.

Questions

- Does God punish you every time you commit a wrong?

- What are some of the privileges of being a child of God?

- Should the knowledge of His deep love encourage you to sin more or sin less?

Journal

You adulterous people, don't you know that friendship with the world is hatred toward God? Anyone who chooses to be a friend of the world becomes an enemy of God. (James 4:4)

Meditation   *Dudley C. Rutherford*

What an indictment by the Holy Spirit! James is saying in this verse that half-committed Christians are like unfaithful housewives flirting with the world. James adds to this that flirting with the world causes us and leads us to become enemies of God. The root sin and result of adultery is unfaithfulness, whether spiritual or physical. That's the main problem with physical adultery: it reveals not only a lustful nature but also an unfaithful heart. When a spouse steps out and has an affair with another person, he or she screams, "I'm not a faithful person. I am willing to betray my dearest friend. I might not do this if I knew I was going to get caught, but with my unfaithful heart, I am willing to take a chance."

When we as Christians involve ourselves in the world and its tempting trinkets, we are telling God that, while there is still some love for Him perhaps in our souls, deep down we are saturated with unfaithfulness. I don't know about you, but I don't want to become God's enemy. Imagine! On God's enemy list! It seems that several times in my life, for one reason or another, someone has "had it out" for me. I didn't like that one bit. I know I couldn't handle it if God "had it out" for me. I want to be a friend of God – His true friend.

Prayer

O marvelous Savior, help me to always have a faithful heart so that I might be Your friend. I don't want to be in Your enemy column. Forgive me for any amount of unfaithfulness on my part in the past. I want to get into Your word, walk in Your will and fortify my innermost soul. I know You are so beautiful that I don't need to look anywhere else. Help me to stay in Your word and never take my eyes off my True Lover. And in His name, the name of Christ, I pray. Amen.

Questions

- What is the main symptom of physical or spiritual adultery?

- What does your adultery lead you to become?

- What things should you incorporate into your life to help keep you faithful?

Journal

September 1

On the last and greatest day of the Feast, Jesus stood and said in a loud voice, "If anyone is thirsty, let him come to me and drink. Whoever believes in me, as the Scripture has said, streams of living water will flow from within him." (John 7:37-38)

Meditation   *Dudley C. Rutherford*

Three million Jews came to the city for a week to celebrate the Feast of Tabernacles. Everyone lived for a week in tents, to remind them that their forefathers once lived in tents for 40 years in the desert wilderness. Since their forebearers had spent 40 years in the searing desert with no rivers and no lakes, this feast highlighted water as the main celebration. Each of the seven mornings, the white-robed priest filled a golden pitcher with the living, sparkling water of the spring, as the people cried out from Isaiah with one united voice, "With joy you will draw water from the wells of salvation."

On the last day of the Feast, Jesus stood and cried with a loud voice, "If anyone is thirsty…" Jesus would touch a nerve in inviting that generation, whose grandparents had some idea what it was to spend 40 years in a blistering, scorching hot wind with little water. What an unforgettable snapshot of our Lord yelling above the crowd. Jesus spoke that to me and He still speaks to us all, reminding us that the only satisfaction in this world is Jesus. He alone can quench the thirst and can satisfy that God-shaped vacuum that is in every soul.

Golden Pitcher

Prayer

Dear Jesus, I can almost picture You on that last day of the feast. I can hear You crying with a loud voice, "If a man is thirsty let him come to Me and drink." I don't ever want to forget that truth. Thank You for being the only thing that can quench my thirst for truth, happiness and salvation. I humbly confess, "Lord, I thirst." And I gladly proclaim, "Lord, You are the only true water of life." I pray this in the Master's name. Amen.

Questions

- What did this Feast commemorate?

- Why was water the main celebration?

- Was Jesus speaking to that crowd only, or to you as well?

Journal

> *How great is the love the Father has lavished on us that we should be called children of God! And that is what we are! The reason the world does not know us is that it did not know him. And so we know and rely on the love God has for us. God is love. Whoever lives in love lives in God, and God in him. In this way, love is made complete among us so that we will have confidence on the day of judgment because in this world we are like him. (I John 3:1, 4:16-17)*

Meditation   *Dudley C. Rutherford*

The songwriter said, "I can never tell how much I love Him, I can never tell His love for me. For it passes human measure like a deep unfathomed sea."

Oh my dear friend. How much He loves you! Jesus doesn't just like you, He loves you, He adores you, He's in love with you. He is obsessed with you. He is wild about you. We can't explain it, but for some reason God says we are the apple of His eye and the pearl of great treasure. It doesn't make any difference what you may have done this past week. His love for you is not predicated on your morality or your faithfulness. He loves you because He made you and died for you, and He desperately wants to live with you throughout eternity.

"But preacher, I don't understand it. How could God love someone like me?" We don't need to understand it. Just accept it. Receive it. Just bask in His love. Bathe in it and let it soak in. Step onto the track and run the race. You are loved!

Prayer

Dear Father, we all know we are weak and undeserving of such divine affection. But humbly today, we rest upon Your absolute promise that each one of us is the apple of Your eye. You have told us we are the objects of Your desire. Bless us as we try to re-think and re-evaluate Your love for us. May we be so overcome and overwhelmed by Your love that we shall be compelled to live for You. Amen.

Questions

- Why does God love you?

- As a parent, how do you love your children when they do wrong?

- Does such lavish love demand a response? What should it be?

Journal

September 3

Anyone who listens to the word but does not do what it says is like a man who looks at his face in a mirror and, after looking at himself, goes away and immediately forgets what he looks like. (James 1:23-24)

Meditation   *Dudley C. Rutherford*

Have you ever done that? I have many times. I've dressed, put on my best clothes, combed my hair (that was when I had hair), tied my necktie and took a last second glance in the mirror. I then get out to the car, focus on where I'm headed and without even thinking, I'll sometimes take a last look in the car mirror. I guess I'm a little slow, because I forget what I look like.

What would we do without mirrors? Heavens! I know another mirror. This chapter in James calls the Bible a mirror. It warns us that we need to read it and reread it and never stop reading, because it's so easy to forget what the Bible says we look like. It's natural to forget our assignments, our duties, our opportunities and our purpose for living. I read the Bible some this morning, but I better read it some more, because I'm prone to forget.

Prayer

Dear Lord in Heaven above, I forget so quickly what I look like spiritually. I know in my deepest heart that I will get far away from Your plan and from Your will for my life, unless I begin to spend more quality time looking in the mirror we call the Bible. If I gaze at the world and not at Your holy word, I will be self-satisfied with a more worldly life, and I will soon forget what I am supposed to be for You. Please help me to focus on You. I ask this prayer in Christ's name. Amen.

Questions

- How is the Bible like a mirror?

- Why should you keep looking often in the mirror of the Word?

- What does the Word of God reveal?

Journal

■ September 4

Meditation   *Kyle Idleman*

When I was in high school, I went to watch the Kansas City Chiefs play the Oakland Raiders at Arrowhead stadium in Kansas City. Joe Montana was the quarterback that night for the Chiefs. The game came down to a fourth-quarter comeback drive by the Chiefs. Montana pushed the team down the field. When he connected with the receiver in the end zone for a game-winning touchdown, the crowd erupted.

There was this woman sitting next to me and she did the most annoying thing. I'm not kidding you: in the midst of the excitement and celebration, she was sleeping! She didn't know or care who Joe Montana was. She was totally oblivious to the great comeback that had taken place. I just wanted to grab this woman by the shoulders and shake her and say, "*Mom, Mom*, wake up – you don't know what you're missing!"

Right now, we are sleeping through some of the greatest opportunities ever. I imagine Paul would want to shake us and say, "You don't know what you're missing!" Paul could never have imagined the opportunities we have to share the Gospel. In his entire ministry, Paul traveled a total of around 5,000 miles. We can fly 5,000 miles in a single day. Paul spent countless hours writing; correspondence and written communication were an unreliable, timely process. Today, we have the ability to send the entire contents of the Encyclopedia Britannica around the world and receive it back in two seconds. Whether it's the Internet or video, with satellites it's possible to communicate with every human being on the planet at the same time. Paul would drool over the outrageous opportunities available today.

Kyle Idleman is Teaching Pastor at Southeast Christian Church in Louisville, KY.

Prayer

Father, it is so easy today to look at the world in which we live and throw our hands up in the air and say, "We give up!" But God, I ask that You will re-ignite a fire inside us so that we, like Paul, will view obstacles as opportunities; so that we will begin to see people who aren't Christians not as the enemy, but as victims of the enemy. When we start to see people this way, help us to be so consumed with love and compassion for them that we just cannot give up. In Jesus' name. Amen.

Questions

- How can you, like Paul, begin to seize the outrageous opportunities that surround you?

- What allowed Paul to have this kind of spirit, faith and confidence?

- Honestly, have there been times in life when you have looked at the world you are living in and thought it was so bad, that you were tempted to give up and say, "I can't make any difference"?

Journal

_____

_____

_____

_____

_____

September 5

In the past God overlooked such ignorance, but now he commands all people everywhere to repent. For he has set a day when he will judge the world with justice by the man he has appointed. He has given proof of this to all men by raising him from the dead. (Acts 17:30-31)

Meditation   *H. Dean Rutherford*

I got a few goose bumps when Bill Clinton was on trial for his political life. It was an almost sacred, scary moment during that impeachment trial when the Chief Justice said to each juror, to each senator, "How say ye? Guilty or not guilty?"

Magnify and multiply that scene 1,000 times, and you might have a faint idea of what Judgment Day will be like. What will it be like when the Judge of all judges demands, "What say ye? Guilty or not guilty?" I've got good news for every Christian. My Bible tells me that when I stand before His throne and the Eternal Judge asks, "What say ye? Guilty or not guilty," I won't even have to answer. My attorney, Jesus Christ, will answer for me and say, "Not Guilty." No wonder Paul exclaimed, "There is therefore now no condemnation to them which are in Christ Jesus" (Romans 8:1). Talk about a rigged jury! Jesus is our attorney and Jesus is also our judge. And when our attorney, Jesus, says to our judge, Jesus, "Not guilty," that settles it. Case dismissed! Settled! Paid in full! When Christians lead Christians lives, there is simply no condemnation on our record.

What Say Ye?

Prayer

Dear Lord in Heaven above, we have so many things for which we can be thankful, but nothing more than the fact that You paid for our sins and placed them in Your sea of forgetfulness. Thank You for being not only my best friend, but also my lawyer and judge. I am eternally indebted to You, O Lord. I pray in the Savior's name. Amen.

Questions

- Will there be a day of judgment?

- Will you have to defend yourself?

- How can Jesus be your attorney and your judge?

Journal

_____

_____

_____

_____

_____

September 6

Meditation   *Larry Kerr*

Joshua's faithful obedience to God has been an encouragement to me, as I face some of the fears and discouraging times in my job as a college football coach. Controlling my anger when I can't control circumstances in a game has been one of those challenges for me. This is an area of my life that I desired to change, because I wanted to honor God in my coaching.

God put me on that path of change many years ago. It started after the first game with my new staff. After the game, one of the coaches expressed both to me and my wife how shocked he was when my anger and frustration were vented during the game. We had worked together for six months, and he saw a different side of me that surprised him. This struck a nerve with me and I allowed God to provide a simple solution. I asked that coach to say the name "Joshua" to me during those outbursts.

God had provided me with a reminder of how to stand strong during times of turmoil. The Holy Spirit took control and I was able to gain a great sense of peace, and God's presence and control. God began in me a healing process that still goes on today. While the "Joshua" moments are not much less frequent, my desire to be strong and courageous in my obedience to Him has increased.

Larry Kerr is Defensive Coordinator of the UCLA Bruins Football Team.

Prayer

Dear Heavenly Father, how great Thou art! In the midst of all that goes on in this world You created, You know my name. You know all there is to know about me, yet You still love me and desire my love in return. I do love You, Lord. I desire to please You, Lord, and I want to stand strong for You in all that I do. I thank You for Your constant presence, the love, the mercy, the grace that You shower on me. I want to stand before You one day, my Lord, and hear, "Well done, good and faithful servant."

Questions

- Is there something that hinders your ability to honor God at work or home?

- What specific actions can you take to make changes in your life?

- Do you have somebody to keep you accountable for your actions?

Journal

> *Christ redeemed us from the curse of the law by becoming a curse for us, for it is written: "Cursed is everyone who is hung on a tree." He redeemed us in order that the blessing given to Abraham might come to the Gentiles through Christ Jesus, so that by faith we might receive the promise of the Spirit. (Galatians 3:13-14)*

Meditation   *Dudley C. Rutherford*

The terrorists have suddenly resorted to an old, old method: kidnapping. Taking hostages. Whether in Baghdad or Chechnya, kidnapping is now frequently occurring. It always works the same way. One gets kidnapped, and then someone else that loves the victim has to pay a price to the kidnapper to get the victim set free and safely returned.

That's what happened to all of us. In the Garden of Eden, we all belonged to God. Satan came along and tempted us to sin, and we sinned and were taken hostage. We were bound and fettered. But God said, "I'll pay the ransom price." He then let His only Son, Jesus die on the cross. And you and I were set free.

If someone were to take you hostage and put you into strict solitary confinement, can you imagine how terrible that would be? Can you imagine if someone were to come and pay the ransom for you, how wonderful and thankful you would be?

As a boy, I used to hear my parents sing, "There's a sweet and blessed story of the Christ who came from glory just to rescue me, from sin and misery. He in loving-kindness sought me and from sin and shame has brought me, what a Savior, Jesus ransomed me. Hallelujah, what a Savior, who can take a poor lost sinner, lift him from the miry clay and set him free. I will ever sing the story, shouting glory, glory, glory, what a Savior, Jesus ransomed me."

Prayer

Dear God, it's no wonder the Bible calls You Redeemer so many times. We were in hock and You redeemed us. We were imprisoned and You freed us. We were held hostage by Satan and You paid the full ransom. What a Savior, what a Redeemer! Help me, Lord, to know I have been redeemed and that my love and allegiance and gratitude belong to You. And I ask these things in His strong name. Amen.

Questions

- What does a redeemer usually do?

- When you sin, does that make you a hostage?

- You don't owe your captor anything. What do you owe your Redeemer?

Journal

_____

_____

_____

_____

■ September 8

Be patient, then, brothers, until the Lord's coming. See how the farmer waits for the land to yield its valuable crop and how patient he is for the autumn and spring rains. (James 5:7)

Meditation   *Dudley C. Rutherford*

Now I must admit that I've been a city boy most of my life. I never spent much time on a farm. But I have visited with a lot of farmers and I do enjoy talking with them. They exhibit more patience than anyone else I know. I might say to a farmer, "Well John, we haven't had any rain now for two months, and your crops aren't looking all that good. Are you worried?" "No, Dudley, I've been here before. This is nothing new. We'll get a little shower here before too long, and it's liable to be just what we need."

It seems that being a farmer would be most difficult. But God wants me to be like that farmer and to have patience toward His return, and the final victory of His Kingdom. Sure, things look bad much of the time. Sure, it looks like the devil is successful and sin is conquering all. But one of these days, one of God's days, He will make everything right. I should never let His apparent distance keep me from being faithful. I love that verse, "Let us not become weary in doing good, for at the proper time we will reap a harvest if we do not give up" (Galatians 6:9).

Prayer

Dear wonderful Lord and Savior, forgive me for those times I've grown discouraged and felt that no one cared, and that my work for You was all in vain. Help me to have the patience of a farmer whose crops are under the siege of drought. Your goodness and final victory must come sometime soon, and if I remain faithful, I know I shall see the ultimate triumph of Your Kingdom. In Christ's blessed name, I pray. Amen.

Questions

- What word helps describe a veteran farmer?

- What's going to take place, whether you give up on it or not?

- How should this certainty influence your daily conduct?

Journal

■ September 9

Look, he is coming with the clouds, and every eye will see him, even those who pierced him; and all the peoples of the earth will mourn because of him. So shall it be! Amen. (Revelation 1:7)

They will see the Son of Man coming on the clouds of the sky, with power and great glory. (Matthew 24:30)

Meditation

Three hundred eighteen times in the 261 chapters of the New Testament, the Second Coming of Christ is promised. Tennyson called it, "That one far off divine event, to which the whole creation moves." The world is waiting for the sunrise! Paul the Apostle says that all of creation groans for that returning of Christ. Jesus came once to bear a cross; He's coming back to wear a crown. He came once to be our Savior; He's coming back to be our Judge. He came once to convert; He's coming back to control. He came once to be a resident; He's coming back to be the President. When He came once, few beheld Him. When He returns, every eye shall see Him. Every passing moment of every passing day brings us that much closer to this event, for which the "whole creation groans and travails in pain until now."

One great evangelist says, "America is not godless: it has too many gods." America and many modern day Christians have not ruled God out. Rather, they have a plethora of the inbred gods of pleasure, travel, leisure, lust and ambition. Are you trying to cram God into some small corner of your cluttered heart, or are you determined to put Him on the throne of your soul? Please don't delay until some late, crowded, wild, hectic moment to enthrone Him. Right now, in the depths and silence of your groaning soul, ask Him in. He will enter and He will bless, He will rule and He will save!

Prayer

Dear saving Father, I know You once died on an old, rugged, bloody, splintered cross, an instrument of shame. But some day, on one of Your chosen days, I will see You and behold You in all Your splendor and glory. What a day that will be when we shall be reunited – not only with those we have loved and lost for a while, but also we shall forever gaze into the sinless face of our victorious Captian of salvation. In that precious, redeeming name of Jesus Christ, I pray. Amen.

Questions

- How many times is the Lord's return mentioned in the New Testament?

- How many eyes in this entire world will see Him when He comes back?

- How can you best get ready and be prepared for His return?

Journal

September 10

"I will be a Father to you, and you will be my sons and daughters," says the Lord Almighty. (II Corinthians 6:18)

Meditation   H. Dean Rutherford

A few years back, I received a card on Dad's Day. My youngest son, David, tried to express his love for me with these words on the card:

"To My Dad. This is a small effort to say thanks, for all the times you have surely cried inside for what I was doing or how I was doing something. Thanks for the times you showed restraint to let me err and learn, and thanks, especially thanks, for the times you stepped in and bailed me out, or the times when I just couldn't reach my goal and you were there to raise me a little higher, and push me a little farther, or somehow you made the goal move. I wonder how. Thanks Dad, for the times you put your big hand on my head, prayed a blessing and I never even knew you were praying. If God hadn't taken the special care and concern to make you my dad, I would have picked you anyway. David."

Not many sayings are older than "Father knows best." Some of us dads aren't the best in the world, and we are never deserving of such praise. But there is One who holds that title: His name is Jesus. What a Dad! What a Father! Every attribute you would expect a great dad to possess, Jesus does. He is the best parent, guardian, protector and provider the world has ever known.

Dad Knows Best

Prayer

Dear Father of mine. Thanks for being my dad. Nobody ever had a better Daddy than You. You have been there for me every moment of every day. I know I'm not the best kid You ever had, but I so rejoice that I am part of the family of God. Discipline me if You must. Do anything, but don't let me stray from Your family. In my Father's name I pray. Amen.

Questions

- Who is your real Father?

- What are some attributes of a great dad?

- What are some attributes of a good child?

Journal

September 11

Christ Jesus, who died—more than that, who was raised to life—is at the right hand of God and is also interceding for us. (Romans 8:34)

Therefore he is able to save completely those who come to God through him, because he always lives to intercede for them. (Hebrews 7:25)

Meditation   *Dudley C. Rutherford*

The Bible plainly says that Jesus is our intercessor. He is standing at the right hand of God on your behalf. Do you have any idea how important and vital that is? Do you understand the overwhelming power of divine intercession? Listen. Shhhhh! Do you hear that? What is Jesus speaking to the Father? Why, He is repeating word for word the prayer you just prayed. Only it's better now, it's stronger and it makes more sense. That's right! The vow and the promise you just uttered is being re-spoken into the ear of God.

He cleans up our prayers and perfumes them with His superior knowledge and love. He knows just exactly what the Father wants to hear and how to best present your petition. Have you been praying long for a certain thing and not yet received an answer? Don't worry. If you do not succeed, Jesus will. When Jesus takes your prayer before the Father's throne, it cannot be dismissed. Jesus is God's Son and will prevail. Continue to pray! For Jesus ever lives to make intercession for us.

Prayer

Dear Lord Jesus, hear our prayers and reshape them. Perfume each word and present them to Your Father. There is no mediator in all this world like You. Thank You for being my intercessor. My prayers are never very good. They always need Your touch. They need to be spoken to God by someone who possesses great rank and authority, and that someone is You, dear Lord. I know that before I can say "Amen" to this prayer, that You will be speaking into Your Father's ear and heart. In my Intercessor's name, I pray. Amen.

Questions

- What is a mediator or intercessor?

- What makes Jesus qualified to be your "go-between?"

- Knowing this, should it encourage you to pray more or less?

Journal

_____

_____

_____

_____

_____

September 12

I am the vine; you are the branches. If a man remains in me and I in him, he will bear much fruit; apart from me you can do nothing. If anyone does not remain in me, he is like a branch that is thrown away and withers... If you remain in me and my words remain in you, ask whatever you wish, and it will be given you. This is to my Father's glory, that you bear much fruit, showing yourselves to be my disciples. (John 15:5-8)

Meditation   *Larry Sullivan*

The old preacher stood behind the well-worn pulpit in a one-room church building built by my grandfather and his father and brothers. The old pot-bellied stove sat in its prominent place, though there was no need for it on this hot summer Sunday. With a wide, sweeping motion of his hand, he drew the congregation's attention to the adjacent field, where large ears of corn were growing on long green stalks. "You can't grow watermelons on cornstalks," he said. "Nor can you pick blackberries off a cucumber vine." "Amen," said the congregation.

Everything bears fruit after its own kind, as everyone there knew, since they understood farming. Masterfully, he shaped his point. With God's spiritual nourishment, you bear the fruit of His vine: love, service, and the fruit of sharing Jesus the Savior with neighbors and associates. His point about Jesus the vine and Christians as the branches was driven deeply into my small boy's heart on that summer Sunday and remains to this day. Life without Jesus is really not life at all.

Larry Sullivan is the Assistant Director of the Strauss Institute for Dispute Resolution at Pepperdine University's School of Law, Malibu, CA.

Prayer

I am hurried and disconnected, O Lord, trying to pray but interrupted in my busy world. I have had many opportunities to think about You and meditate on Your glory, but only now I long to be still and focus on Your love. You are my life, the source of my strength. Without You, I become fearful and uncertain. O God, You are my peace, the motivation to carry out my purpose as a branch of the living vine, Jesus Christ. Thank You for loving me enough to listen to this prayer. In Jesus' name. Amen.

Questions

- How do you relate to Jesus as your vine?

- What do you do to care for yourself like a healthy branch, in order to bear good fruit?

- Are you willing to start today being open to God's direction in your life – to love, serve and share?

Journal

September 13

So then, King Agrippa, I was not disobedient to the vision from heaven. First to those in Damascus, then to those in Jerusalem and in all Judea, and to the Gentiles also, I preached that they should repent and turn to God and prove their repentance by their deeds (Acts: 26:19, 20)

Meditation   *Mark Brewer*

I was not disobedient to the Heavenly vision. What a wonderfully bold and gutsy thing to say in a Roman Tribunal when your life is at stake. But then again, Paul's entire life was driven by that vision. The vision birthed out of his meeting the Risen Christ on the way to fight against those who followed Him. God is in the business of transforming lives, and He seems to take great delight in bringing His glory and our good out of the messes we make of our lives. One of the tools Christ employs is the power of our visions. God mightily uses those deep dreams we hold in our hearts.

A vision is different than an idea. We all get buckets of ideas every day – some good, some bad. But a vision is the eyes of faith seeing, and responding to, what God is calling us to do. It's close to what developmental psychologists and some theologians call "The Dream." We all have within us The Dream that drives us on in life. This Dream is made up of certain elements or hopes we think make life worth living. The Dream is not so specific as a plan; and it's much more than a mere wish. The Dream provides the marching orders of our heart that drive us on in life.

Sometimes, the plans, hopes and goals we had lie broken and shattered at our feet. When these dreams are not submitted to God, the average person starts to live a life of bitterness and resentment. But Christ takes those shattered dreams and starts to weave them into a new pattern. When we have the courage to honestly evaluate our dreams in the light of Christ, we see clearly that the thing we thought would make life worth living was only a bad reflection of our longing for God. Paul can stand before those who have the power of life and death over him and declare – without flinching – the vision he has seen. He knows he belongs to Christ and nothing will ever change that fact.

Mark Brewer is Senior Pastor at Bel Air Presbyterian Church in Bel Air, CA.

The Dream

Prayer

Precious Heavenly Father, thank You for placing in each of our hearts a rich and unique dream of what life can be. Praise Your Name, for You have been honest with us and never promised the entire dream would be fulfilled in this short earthly life. But thank You that Your Hand is holding us up as we journey through this life together. Give me the courage to dare to dream Your dreams. Give me the grace to help others live out their dreams. To the glory of the only One I truly yearn for, Jesus my Savior – it is in His wonderful name I pray. Amen.

Questions

- For you, what are the elements or hopes that would make life worth living?

- What are some dreams that just don't seem to be happening right now?

- How does God exchange His vision of what life can be for your plans and ideas?

Journal

September 14

Therefore we do not lose heart. Though outwardly we are wasting away, yet inwardly we are being renewed day by day. (II Corinthians 4:16)

Meditation   *Dudley C. Rutherford*

They say that getting old is not for sissies. The body gets older and weaker day by day. No hand can stay the clock of time. All of us are wasting away day by day as the Bible declares. But the wonderful truth is that the soul can grow stronger with every passing day. While we grow more infirm physically, we can become stronger in the Lord. The Apostle Paul surely knew that even at age 68, he was a stronger Christian than he had ever been before. Not only should mental wisdom come with age but spiritual wisdom as well.

Maybe you got a late start in your walk with Jesus. If so, you can do those things that will enable you to grow tall and strong for the Lord. One is never too old to start a private prayer time with the Lord. It's not too late to start studying His word and to begin serving others in a selfless way. Yes, we are all getting older and weaker each day, but thanks be to Him, we can prosper and flourish spiritually. We all know folks who are physically frail of body but great athletes for the Lord.

Bumps and Bruises

Prayer

My precious Lord, I know I'm not getting any younger. I have had my share of bumps and bruises. But I also know that with Your help and Your Spirit, I can become a better Christian. I so want to be a good Christian now, but I want to be a far better Christian when I am old and infirm. Help me, dear Father, to spiritually mature as You bless the longevity of days. I pray in Christ's name. Amen.

Questions

- In what ways will your body begin to waste away?

- What things can you do to grow stronger spiritually?

- Why is spiritual health so much more vital than good physical health?

Journal

_____

_____

_____

_____

■ September 15

But the widow who lives for pleasure is dead even while she lives.

(I Timothy 5:6)

Meditation   *Dudley C. Rutherford*

This verse, along with others, teaches us that we can be alive and yet dead at the same time. When the space shuttle Columbia exploded and scattered over the fields of East Texas, it was so obvious that something had gone tremendously wrong. Experts have suggested that the tiles on the left wing were damaged during lift-off. The opinion was expressed that even if we had known instantly about the damaged tiles, nothing known to man or science could have brought them safely home. They were up there for days, working, sleeping, eating and laughing, but knew not that the flight was doomed from the start. They were alive, they were so alive, but in reality they were dead.

I want to give that a spiritual application. If you are awake, alive and conscious now and you are not a Christian, and you are not growing in the Lord, and if you are serving self and not Christ, then no matter what else you are doing in life, I say in all loving-kindness, you are on a doomed journey. Without Christ, there is no safe landing. Will you, at this moment, commit your heart to Christ in very real way?

Prayer

Gracious Lord, I thank You for the peace and the security and the promise of a safe landing with Christ. Give me the wisdom not to deceive myself, but let me come to You right now in renewed and complete surrender. I know that if I have You I have everything, and that if I don't have You I have nothing. Bless me as I now pray in Jesus' name. Amen.

Questions

- How can one be dead and alive at the same time?

- What do you consider a safe landing?

- How does a person know for sure they are saved?

Journal

September 16

Let us not become weary in doing good, for at the proper time we will reap a harvest if we do not give up. Therefore, as we have opportunity, let us do good to all people, especially to those who belong to the family of believers. (Galatians 6:9-10)

Meditation   *Mark Miller*

It was opening day of little league baseball, and we were making our way through the parade route. Since I coach my son's team, I rode with the boys on our float. We were having a great time – enjoying the festive atmosphere, waving and throwing candy to those who came to watch. As we approached a couple of kids standing on the sidewalk, one of the boys said, "Hey guys, don't throw them any candy." He repeated his challenge, directing it specifically toward one of the boys who is a definite leader on our team. "[Name], don't throw them any candy!" One thing I've observed about children is that they can be both cruel and loving.

Before I intervened, I saw the young man ignore the request and throw some of his candy toward the kids. Teammates followed his example, as did the one who wanted to ignore them. Obviously, I was very proud of this young man for his actions and told him so later. It's not just kids who make choices in how they treat others; adults do too! We size them up and decide whether they will receive our attention and love. Paul says the Christian life involves much more than teaching the word and giving our material possessions; it also involves doing good to *all* people. As we grow in our love of God, may it overflow in love for others.

Mark Miller is Senior Pastor of Greencastle Christian Church in Greencastle, IN.

Prayer

Father, please forgive me when I fail to look at people as You look at them. Forgive me when I fail to take the opportunities You give me to do good to all people. Forgive my selfishness and pride, and please help me to remember that all people are precious in Your eyes. May I choose to let Your light shine through me, instead of listening to the voices encouraging me to do otherwise. Thank You for not treating me as I deserve, but allowing me to experience Your grace and love. In Jesus' name. Amen.

Questions

- Do you have a tendency to ignore people who aren't like you or who are "different" in some way?

- When was the last time you did something nice for your neighbor?

- Will you give away some of your candy as God gives you opportunities today or in the coming days?

Journal

September 17

Search me, O God, and know my heart; test me and know my anxious thoughts. See if there is any offensive way in me, and lead me in the way everlasting. (Psalm 139:23-24)

Meditation   *Kay Norris*

Several years ago, while doing a study on the book of James, I realized my walk with the Lord was not where it should be. There was so little peace in my heart, and I craved the applause of man more than God. I began to pray Psalm 139:23-24 every day with total sincerity. I wanted to be the Godly woman people thought I was, but my heart truly needed a searching and cleansing.

About a month into this prayer, God revealed so many things I thought were hidden even from Him. How silly of me to think He didn't notice. The pain of realizing He did notice and so did others brought me to tears for nearly two months. While God continued on a daily basis to reveal one offensive way after another, I thought my heart would break.

Then the most glorious thing happened: I was renewed of mind, soul and spirit. I now desire to hear the applause of God, not man. My heart yearns to serve whenever and wherever He chooses, and the need to "fight" for my rights and recognition are no longer necessary.

The joy of the Lord is truly my strength and my happiness, and the pain of a thorough heart search has brought me into a closer walk with Him and a new ministry of helping others "see the light" of total surrender.

Kay Norris is the Women's Ministries Director at Shepherd of the Hills Church, Porter Ranch, CA.

Heart Search

Prayer

Thank You, Lord, for revealing to me what needed to be changed in my life and attitude. The joy and peace that comes from surrendering all to You far outweighs anything the world has to offer. Continue to work in me daily; show me my offensive ways and give me strength to make changes and help others. And thank You for the people and ways You used to bring me back into a right relationship with You. In Jesus' name. Amen.

Questions

- Does your heart need a "check-up"?

- Do you lack peace and joy in your life? If so, why do you think that is?

- Are you looking for worldly recognition… or God's?

Journal

September 18

I put this in human terms because you are weak in your natural selves. Just as you used to offer the parts of your body in slavery to impurity and to ever-increasing wickedness, so now offer them in slavery to righteousness leading to holiness. (Romans 6:19)

Meditation   *Dudley C. Rutherford*

I've had for many years a dog named Sunday. Sunday is an animal. That's all she is. The word animal and animate comes from the same root word. Sunday is not inanimate like a mountain or rock; she moves. She does a lot of moving. What does Sunday live for? Three things basically. She wants to eat, sleep and play. That's about it. It's never crossed her small mind to pray or go to church. She knows nothing about giving.

What a tremendous difference between a man and an animal. Many folks live like animals. Their main ambition is to eat and sleep and have a little fun. When this happens, a man has stooped from the high level of moral and spiritual living to the low plane of mere physical existence.

A writer once told of the death of a soldier: "He was a low character – had a foul tongue, mouthing the most blood-curdling profanities and boasting of the vilest, unclean escapades. Whenever on leave he became drunk and frequented the lowest dives. He gambled and cursed, drank and caroused. He finally died in one of his drunken brawls." The author of the article, in commenting on his death, wrote this striking, sobering sentence: "I'm not sorry he died; I'm only sorry he never began to live." When we live only on the level of the barnyard, we are not living. When we live like animals, we are of little value to God, our world, or ourselves.

A Dog Named Sunday

Prayer

Dear wonderful God, I never want to live the low life: a thankless ingrate, a human animal or a practicing prodigal. I want to refrain from squandering my immortal soul on things that so quickly pass and fade away. Help me to do good things for others and for Your cause and Your Kingdom. Help me to think of the needs of this lost world, long before I consider my need to eat, sleep and play. May I stay in Your word until I live on a level far above the barnyard. In Jesus' name I pray. Amen.

Questions

- What are some of the main differences between man and animal?

- In the best definition, when did you begin to live... really live?

- How should one go about learning to live on a higher plane?

Journal

_____

_____

_____

_____

_____

September 19

Praise be to the God and Father of our Lord Jesus Christ, the Father of compassion and the God of all comfort, who comforts us in all our troubles, so that we can comfort those in any trouble with the comfort we ourselves have received from God. (II Corinthians 1:3-4)

Meditation — *Dudley C. Rutherford*

Midnight is normally the darkest hour of the twenty four. It is farthest from sunset and longest from sunrise. It signifies that hour most removed from light in either direction. Our midnights can have a very definite effect on us. It all depends on our attitude toward them and our use of them. They can make us stronger or weaker, better or bitter. We must master them or they will master us. So the question: Are you mastering your midnights or are your midnights mastering you?

Jesus is called "The Light of the World." He himself said, "I am the light." John said, "God is light, and in him is no darkness" (I John 1:5). Paul declared, "We are not of the night" (I Thessalonians 5:5). In this present world, it seems conclusive that there is a constant war between light and darkness, good and evil, blessing and cursing, sunshine and rain, roses and thorns. A battle rages between the forces of darkness and the armies of light. In the future life, a separation will be made. In Heaven all is light and "there is no night there" (Revelation 21:25; 22:5). Hell is described by Jesus as a place of "utter darkness" (Matthew 8:12). There are three attitudes we can take toward our midnights. We can oppose them bitterly, accept them stoically, or welcome them happily. The last is the Christian's answer to personal midnights. We master them. Our midnights can become stepping stones to higher levels of service, rather than stumbling blocks to lower living.

Prayer

Father above, I want Jesus, The Light of the World, to fill my life. I want to master life's last midnight: death itself. I yearn to live in the eternal light of God's perpetual sunshine. I am so grateful that in Christ I now have found great joy even in deep sorrow. I have found much sunshine after the rain, and springtime after every winter. I put my trust in You. I dare not trust another. In Your name, the matchless name of Christ, I pray. Amen.

Questions

- Describe a spiritual midnight.

- If you don't master your midnights, what will they do?

- What are three attitudes toward midnights?

Journal

_____

_____

_____

_____

■ September 20

And pray in the Spirit on all occasions with all kinds of prayers and requests. (Ephesians 6:18)

Meditation   *Jon Weece*

About 15 years ago, I took 50 high school students from Kentucky to New York, where together we would teach the Bible and do service projects for children. After we arrived in New York, we took the subway. Imagine 50+ Kentuckians on the subways of New York. It was great, except for the one time we got totally lost, and I do mean *totally* lost. We found ourselves beneath the mammoth world of New York City in a maze of concrete tunnels, and we had no idea how to get where we needed to go. Though we were in a large group, we felt alone, abandoned and scared to death.

Then the greatest thing happened. We circled the wagons and prayed. Now that prayer was mainly for the benefit of the students, who were getting a bit tense. But to be honest, that prayer was also for the adult leaders who were downright worried. We told God we were totally lost and felt alone. We asked for patience and wisdom to get home safely. We reaffirmed our trust in Him.

When we opened our eyes after the prayer, one of the students noticed we were right in front of the very exit we needed to get to the bus that would take us home. We were in the right place the whole time, but the unfamiliar surroundings had distracted us so much that we couldn't find our focus. Our time of prayer allowed us to do that: to stop and refocus.

Jon Weece is the Senior Pastor of Southland Christian Church in Lexington, KY.

Prayer

Sing this song if you know it: "You Are My King"

I'm forgiven, because You were forsaken
I'm accepted, You were condemned
I'm alive and well, Your Spirit is within me
Because You died and rose again.

Amazing love, how can it be
That You my King would die for me
Amazing love, I know it's true
And it's my joy to honor You

Questions

- When was the last time you felt alone?

- What should you pray if you feel alone?

- What assurances and promises has Jesus made to you?

Journal

_____

_____

_____

_____

■ September 21

Jesus said to them, "My Father is always at his work to this very day, and I, too, am working." (John 5:17)

As long as it is day, we must do the work of him who sent me. Night is coming, when no one can work. (John 9:4)

Meditation   *H. Dean Rutherford*

One of the strange paradoxes of Christianity is that we worship an all-powerful God who keeps repeating, "I have need of you." In this thrilling text, Jesus is testifying that He is a replica of His Dad in that He never stops working. The clarion call of our Master is ever to roll up our sleeves and get to work. We who are dogmatic in declaring salvation by grace have sometimes been hesitant to endorse a gospel message of work. We have been scared to death that man might forget that we are saved by God's great grace.

That is a legitimate fear! But the grace of our God is not simply and exclusively receiving the unmerited favor of God. Receiving God's grace includes the power that prompts us to be as gracious to others as He has been gracious toward us. We are duty-bound by our Chief Commander to be gracious to those who could never merit our graciousness, any more than we could merit God's favor. The true evidence that we are His children of grace is that we are gracious toward others.

James, our Lord's brother, makes it clear that we are not saved by our works, but he insists that we are not saved if we do not work. James teaches that the true faith that saves is the faith that works. Our text tells us that if we are to be like God and like Jesus, then our lives will reflect His shining attributes, one of which is *working*.

Are You Working?

Prayer

Dear Father, we know You need us. We don't mean to sound conceited, but we know that even though You own everything, yet You once borrowed a boat, a donkey, a stable, a grave and an upper room. We acknowledge that Your great Kingdom will soon be paralyzed unless the Church goes into action. We know You are no aristocrat, that You are a common laborer. You did not just create this world but You also have remained on the job to sustain it. Help us to get the hint, the command and work while it is day. In Christ's name, I pray. Amen.

Questions

- What work do you do for Christ and His Church?

- Are you saved by grace or by your works?

- Why does such a powerful God need you?

Journal

_____

_____

_____

_____

_____

So do not worry, saying, "What shall we eat?" or "What shall we drink?" or "What shall we wear?" For the pagans run after all these things, and your heavenly Father knows that you need them. But seek first his kingdom and his righteousness, and all these things will be given to you as well. (Matthew 6:31-33)

Meditation   *Dudley C. Rutherford*

One day, our Lord was standing near a tree and a black crow landed in the tree. "I feed that raven," Jesus said. "If I can feed him, I can feed you. So don't worry. Please. Consider the ravens." One day while our Lord was talking, a small sparrow landed on a fence. "I care for that sparrow. If even one sparrow falls to the ground, I know it and care about it. If I care for them, I certainly care for you. Consider the little birds."

One day, our thirsty Lord stopped at a well and drew some water to drink. He looked around and said, "I am the living water, the living fountain that never runs dry. Consider the water." One day, our Lord was eating some bread. He looked at his men and said, "I am the bread of life. Consider the bread." Walking through a door of a house, He stopped and said, "I am the door. If you are going to go anywhere, you must go through me. Consider the door." One day our blessed Savior was walking through a beautiful garden. He looked at the lilies dressed in full regalia, and said, "Consider the lilies. They toil not, neither do they spin yet I say to you that Solomon in all his glory was not arrayed like one of these. If I can paint and clothe the lily, I can surely take care of you. Consider the lilies."

Jesus is saying to us today, "Look around. Consider how I take care of lesser things. Don't you know I will care for you?"

From Ravens to Lilies

Prayer

Dear Lord of life, thank You for reminding me again that You care for the birds of the air and lonesome flowers of the fields and all the things of life. I know that if You care for these lesser forms of creation, which do not have Your Spirit, and do not possess a soul, that You will more than provide for all my needs. Help me to be more child-like in my faith and have complete trust in You and Your caring love. In Christ's name, I pray. Amen.

Questions

- What proof do you have that Jesus cares for you?

- Should Christians and pagans worry about the same things?

- What should you seek first that will guarantee other blessings?

Journal

_____

_____

_____

_____

But if serving the LORD seems undesirable to you, then choose for yourselves this day whom you will serve, whether the gods your forefathers served beyond the River, or the gods of the Amorites, in whose land you are living. But as for me and my household, we will serve the LORD.

(Joshua 24:15)

Meditation   *Marshall Hayden*

When I live a life worth living, I have to take sides. I can't change uniforms and loyalties in the heat of battle. It's not always easy. Nobody pretends that it is. It requires courage, and the confidence that any pain I might have to experience is a price worth paying in order to be loyal.

In college, I had an experience that exposed an unflattering streak in several of us. The night before the big basketball game against the state college team across town, in response to some of our fellows having "borrowed" their mascot, several of the fraternity boys came to visit our campus. A brief fight ensued, and it started to look pretty good for us. Then I grabbed the wrong guy, who left me with a broken tooth and a smashed lip. The police came, and the fight was a short one. But on game night, some of their ruffians stormed the court and swiped the buffalo head from our cheerleaders. Boys on both sides of the stands emptied into the tunnels. As we were running through, we met the enemy. They said, "Which way did they go?" And we said, "That way." The second fight never happened.

Now, in the case of a potential fistfight over a team's mascot, cowardice might not be a bad idea. But when it comes to Godliness, a little song says it well. "One door, and only one, and yet its sides are two, inside and outside. On which side are you?"

Marshall Hayden is Senior Pastor of Worthington Christian Church in Columbus, OH.

Borrowed Mascots

Prayer

Dear Father God, in our gratitude, we think of the song that says, "I am satisfied with Jesus. He has done so much for me." And its last line says, "But the question comes to be, as I think of Calvary, is my Master satisfied with me?" Your Son is the answer to any question we might have about whether or not You are on our side. Our commitment today is to be – and to let others see us be – on Your side. We pray to You through Him. Amen.

Questions

- What one thing will you do today to show God that you are serving Him?

- Does your neighbor know whose side you're on?

- What is something you need to "lose" and something you need to "gain" to make your loyalty clear to yourself?

Journal

■ September 24

> *Then Jesus said to his disciples, "If anyone would come after me, he must deny himself and take up his cross and follow me. For whoever wants to save his life will lose it, but whoever loses his life for me will find it."*
>
> *(Matthew 16:24-25)*

Meditation   Dudley C. Rutherford

Great one-day sales! Bargains galore! Win the sweepstakes, a bingo game or the lottery. And what about all the TV programs like, *Who Wants To Be A Millionaire?* We all want something for nothing. How about those horse races or the dog races or football games? Gambling can be bad. It exploits the human nature. It glorifies selfishness: to get something you haven't earned from someone who doesn't want you to have it. It emphasizes laziness and dishonesty. I saw a huge sign in front of a church near a racetrack that said in bold letters: "For a sure thing, bet on Jesus."

Every person is betting his life on something. Every one of us is risking his life on some goal. The unbeliever is betting his life and risking his soul that there is no God, that the Bible is not inspired and true. The sinner is betting his soul that his present pleasure is worth the risk of his eternal loss. When Jesus called his followers, they risked their all on Him. They bet that He was the Messiah, the Son of God. They didn't bet small, either; they bet their homes, boats, their families, their jobs and their very lives. And look how they won and what they won! Dear friend, you can literally bet your life on Jesus. You can invest every penny, every hour and every treasure you possess in Him and His church, and you'll get it all back with a million percent increase. Please, bet your life on Jesus. You'll win big!

You Bet Your Life

Prayer

Dear wonderful God, I want to be on the winning side, the winning team. I am thankful to be one of the millions who have bet their lives on You. May we not be like the prodigal son who went into a far country and squandered his money, time, health, talents and his very life on those unrighteous, riotous things. I want to bet my life that You are the pearl of great price, the lily of the valley and the true rose of Sharon. I pray this sincere petition in the saving name of Jesus. Amen.

Questions

- What happens if you try to lose your life?

- What happens when you try to save your life?

- Is it a bargain if you gain the world and lose your soul?

Journal

> *Do not be deceived: God cannot be mocked. A man reaps what he sows. The one who sows to please his sinful nature, from that nature will reap destruction; the one who sows to please the Spirit, from the Spirit will reap eternal life. Let us not become weary in doing good, for at the proper time we will reap a harvest if we do not give up. (Galatians 6:7-9)*

Meditation   *Dudley C. Rutherford*

Our God has carefully placed physical laws in the universe. The law of gravity is one such example. If you step off a skyscraper, you are going to fall. That law can be ignored but it cannot be denied. God also has many spiritual laws that are irreversible. One such law is that no one can fool or mock God.

There are three definite laws of sowing and reaping. One, we always reap *what* we sow. If we sow potatoes, we will reap potatoes. Likewise, if we sow lust or greed, we will reap lust or greed. Two, we will always reap *more* than we sow. Much more. God says it, and that settles it! No farmer would plant one kernel of corn if he only reaped one kernel. Not much profit in that. Sow a few kernels and you will reap thousands and thousands. We need to be careful what seed we sow, because it is going to come back in multiplied numbers. Hosea said, "For they have sown the wind, and they shall reap the whirlwind" (Hosea 8:7). The third law is that we reap *later* than we sow. God seldom repays us for sin today. Payment comes on a delayed basis. Read Ecclesiastes 8:11.

An atheist farmer wrote the local editor and bragged that he didn't go to church on Sunday. He boasted that he worked, plowed, planted and reaped on Sunday and that every October his crops were bigger than his Christian counterparts. The editor wrote back: "God doesn't always settle his accounts in October." It's true!

Prayer

Dear Father of us all, help me to remember that You have placed spiritual laws in my world, and if I begin to sow sinful seeds, I will reap what I sow, and reap more than I sow, and always reap later than I sow. Help me also to remember that if I sow spiritual seeds, I will reap what I sow, and reap more than I sow and reap much later than I sow. Help me to not be weary in well doing, for in due season I will reap a great harvest for You and for me. I pray this in the name of Jesus. Amen.

Questions

- What are the three laws of sowing and reaping?

- Have you read and memorized Ecclesiastes 8:11?

- Why should you not be weary in well doing?

Journal

_____

_____

_____

_____

I have been reminded of your sincere faith, which first lived in your grandmother Lois and in your mother Eunice and, I am persuaded, now lives in you also. (II Timothy 1:5-6)

Meditation   *Matt Proctor*

Got discouragement? Timothy did. He was a young pastor in ancient Ephesus— shy, sick, alone and overwhelmed. His fire was fading, so his mentor Paul wrote to stir the embers of his faith. How? By reminding him of his heritage. "You can't quit, Timothy. Remember your grandmother's faith, and your mother's? My investment in your life? You've been given a legacy to honor, a story to continue, a heritage to uphold."

To celebrate our anniversary, my wife and I recently watched our wedding video. I was amazed at how slim and handsome I once was! I was so young… and foolish, selfish, ignorant of how to truly love. Remembering our first year of conflict, I wondered how we ever made it. As the video rolled, I spotted my wife's grandparents. We were married on their 65th wedding anniversary, a special day they allowed us to share. I saw my grandparents in the video, married 46 years at the time. There were my wife's parents at 40 years of marriage and my parents at 24 years, and I remembered: That's how we made it. Difficult as it got, we knew we couldn't quit. We'd been given a heritage to uphold.

Who has invested in your life? Whose example spurs you on? When you're discouraged, remember those who've passed the torch to you. Let it rekindle your faith, and don't quit!

Matt Proctor is President of Ozark Christian College in Joplin, MO.

Prayer

Dear Father, thank You for the faith of those who've gone before us – family, friends and mentors whose lives have shaped ours. Thank You for the heroes of Scripture and Church history, whose lives stand in stirring testimony to Your faithfulness. Since we are surrounded by such "a great cloud of witnesses," let us run with perseverance the race marked out for us. Let those who someday come behind us find us faithful. I pray this in the name of Him who endured the cross and finished the race marked out for Him. Amen.

Questions

- In whose footsteps is God calling you to follow?

- How did your spiritual heroes endure difficult times?

- What is the heritage you are leaving for others to uphold?

Journal

_____

_____

_____

_____

_____

> *If anyone considers himself religious and yet does not keep a tight rein on his tongue, he deceives himself and his religion is worthless.*
>
> *(James 1:26)*

Meditation   *Dudley C. Rutherford*

The story has been told many times about a small boy who had a bad temper. His Father gave him a bag of nails and told him that every time he lost his temper, he must hammer a nail into the back of the fence. The first day the boy had driven 29 nails into the fence. Over the next few weeks, as he learned to control his anger, the number of nails hammered daily gradually lessened. He discovered it was easier for him to hold his temper than to drive those nails into the fence. Finally the day came when the boy didn't lose his temper at all. He told his father about it, and the father suggested that the boy now pull out one nail for each day he was able to hold his temper.

The days passed and the young boy was finally able to tell his father that all the nails were gone. The father took his son by the hand and led him to the fence. He said, "You have done well, my son, but look at the holes in the fence. The fence will never be the same. When you say things in anger, they leave a scar just like this one. You can stab a person with a knife and pull it out. It won't matter how much honest regret or remorse you have or how many times you say, "I'm sorry," the wound is still there.

A verbal wound is as bad as a physical one. Please read and carefully study at length the third chapter of James. It is so needed and worthwhile.

Twenty-Nine Nails

Prayer

My Father and my God, I have long sensed that talking about others was not a good thing for my soul, but now I have some idea about the literal evil it can carry to my heart and how easily it sets on fire the very course of nature of my life. Help me to remember that each critical remark I make leaves a scar, both on the heart of the giver and the receiver. I must get better at keeping my negative opinions to myself and to be more considerate of others. I pray for help in the name of Jesus Christ. Amen.

Questions

- Can you be a good Christian and still talk critically about others?

- What part of the body brings the most evil?

- Ask someone who will be honest with you if you have a problem controlling your tongue or temper.

Journal

_____

_____

_____

_____

_____

September 28

Blessed are the meek, for they will inherit the earth. (Matthew 5:5)

Meditation   *Dudley C. Rutherford*

As the Roman legionnaires marched down the boulevards of Israel and flexed their mighty power, Jesus was in the shadows insisting the meek shall inherit the earth. In a world where every last thing is measured and gauged by power, Jesus keeps repeating the meek will come out on top. Can the followers of Christ really buy that line? Can we, by faith, swallow that? Our destiny depends on our ability to risk total meekness.

That's exactly what it takes to live the Christian life! Only the strongest among us can turn our cheeks to be hit again. Only the stoutest Christians can sincerely pray for God to bless their enemies. Only the toughest souls can walk the second mile on every occasion. Only the stalwart can joyfully find hope during difficult circumstances. If one would reduce everything our blessed Savior taught while on earth, it would parlay into a three-and-a-half-year sermon on meekness and poverty of spirit.

A word of warning: The meek person is not a spineless person. He is not someone without power; indeed, he possesses all power. He simply refuses to use it on self. How do you get the power to live a meek, surrendered life? Spiritual calisthenics is the answer! Prayer, service, Bible study, constant rehearsal and practice of surrender. A word to the wise: Pride has a way of ruining everything.

The Meek

Prayer

Almighty God, I come to You today with a greater understanding of my life's purpose. I am to live a meek and surrendered life, that others can see in me Your true power to change a stubborn soul. I know it takes great strength to live a meek life and I know that You are the only source for such power. May I always remember that I gain by losing, that I get up by getting down, that I get by giving, and that I become powerful by remaining weak. In Christ's name I pray. Amen.

Questions

- How does God make foolish the wisdom of this world?

- Who will inherit the new earth, Heaven itself?

- How does a person get this power to live a surrendered life?

Journal

September 29

Not many of you should presume to be teachers, my brothers, because you know that we who teach will be judged more strictly. (James 3:1)

Meditation   *Barry Cameron*

Did you hear about the Ft. Lauderdale, Florida firefighter who took his neighbor's cat some 15 miles out into the country… to the Everglades? I'm reasonably sure his intent was finding the furry friend some large, lizard-like acquaintances. Evidently, the cat used the fireman's truck bed as a litter box.

The cat's owner said she believes the firefighter should be fired. "He's a firefighter, and I think it's horrible that a firefighter, who ought to be taking it out of a tree, is dumping a cat."

What do you do when someone does the opposite of what they're supposed to do? Especially someone in society we're supposed to be able to trust, like a firefighter, a high-ranking official in the Boy Scouts, a priest, professor, police officer, teacher, congressman, CEO or even the president?

The Bible is unequivocal that spiritual leaders are held to a higher standard even when the world winks at wrongdoing, condones what God condemns and periodically provides a pass to those who pervert their positions of trust.

The good news is most firefighters and leaders can be trusted to faithfully carry out their duties on a daily basis, with little fanfare and lots of class. The bad news is that occasionally you'll find people in positions of leadership who can't be trusted and shouldn't be followed.

When bad leaders take you for a ride, more often than not, you rarely make it back to where you were before. Thankfully, and miraculously, Mr. Kibbles did.

Barry Cameron is the Senior Pastor of Crossroads Christian Church in Arlington, TX.

Kitty, Kitty, Kitty

Prayer

Lord, help me to be a leader people can trust - to always do the right thing. Help me to be a person of integrity and honor. Help me to always represent You and Your word with consistency and character. Above all, help me to always follow You as closely as I can and help me to lead others to You. In Jesus' name. Amen.

Questions

- Why should the issue of trust be so important to you?

- Are you sometimes tempted to compromise?

- How can you make sure you're a leader others can follow?

Journal

_____

_____

_____

_____

And whatever you do, whether in word or deed, do it all in the name of the Lord Jesus, giving thanks to God the Father through him... Whatever you do, work at it with all your heart, as working for the Lord, not for men, since you know that you will receive an inheritance from the Lord as a reward. It is the Lord Christ you are serving. (Colossians 3:17, 23-24)

Meditation   *Dudley C. Rutherford*

The powerful Scottish pastor, Ian McClearen tells of visiting a woman in his congregation. As he walked into her house, she was using the corner of her apron trying to stop some tears of remorse that were falling from her eyes. "Why do you cry so hard, Mrs. McBrien?"

"Because I have done so little for Jesus. You see, pastor, when I was just a wee little girl, I promised Jesus that I would do everything I could for Him, and I have done so little."

"Mrs. McBrien, haven't you lived the Christian life?"

"Oh, yes, I certainly have."

"Well tell me what you have done?"

"Well, I've only washed clothes and cooked and washed dishes and made beds. I've done all these things for years, but I have done so little for Jesus."

"But, what about your boys?"

She said, "We've got four boys: Matthew, Mark, Luke and John. Matthew and Mark are in China doing missionary work. Luke is preaching in Africa. John is still at home but he wants to join his brother in Africa."

The famous preacher said, "Do you mean to tell me that when you evaluate your life, you describe it as only cooking, sweeping and washing? My dear Mrs. McBrien, when we get to Heaven, I'll gladly swap my mansion for yours, for somehow I believe yours is going to be much nearer the throne."

Dear Christian, please reread the above Scripture and know that whether you are preaching or washing dishes, all Godly effort is for our blessed Lord. We serve God, not man!

Prayer

Dear Heavenly Father, help me to remember that when I take the garbage out or when I am on my knees in prayer, that I am likewise serving You. Help me to remember that as a Christian, sweeping floors or washing dishes is just as important as preaching. Help me to understand that working in the church nursery is just as important as preaching or baptizing. Let me do everything with all my heart and do it unto the Lord Jesus. In His matchless name I pray. Amen.

Questions

- If you are to be a servant, what kind of servant should you be?

- If you are a true Christian, which is more important: sweeping or preaching?

- When you fix your neighbor's flat tire, who are you serving?

Journal

■ October 1

And the peace of God, which transcends all understanding, will guard your hearts and your minds in Christ Jesus. (Philippians 4:7)

Meditation   *Dudley C. Rutherford*

Look carefully at this passage. What Paul is saying here is that the peace of God not only transcends all understanding; it also transcends all events, all things, all cancers, all car crashes, all failures and misfortunes. And it will so guard your heart and mine that no problem or setback can invade the sanctuary of your soul. It's true!

This is the great secret of the Apostle Paul: Let your fundamental joy come from within. Let your fundamental joy come from spiritual achievement. Don't be happy if you get a new car. If getting a new car makes you happy, then you will become unhappy again as the car gets old. Don't be happy if you get a new job. One of these days, you will have to give that job up to younger and more willing hands, and you'll become unhappy all over again. Don't be happy because the sun is shining. You'll become unhappy when the clouds appear. Make your happiness about inward things and not outward things.

Rome may separate the imprisoned Apostle from his friends, from his bed, from his comforts, from his food and from his freedom, but Rome is absolutely powerless to separate the Apostle from his God. Listen to what Paul says about this in Romans 8:38: "For I am persuaded, that neither death, nor life, nor angels, nor principalities, nor power, nor things present, nor things to come, nor height, nor depth, nor any other creature shall be able to separate us from the love of God, which is in Christ Jesus our Lord."

Prayer

Dear God of all peace, help me today to so surrender my heart to You that a perfect peace will occupy the throne of my heart. I empty myself and commit to walk in Your ways. May I learn to be happy about eternal things and things that lead others into Your Kingdom. I pray this wholeheartedly in the name of Christ Jesus. Amen.

Questions

- How many things does the peace of God transcend?

- If you are happy when you get new things, what must eventually happen?

- Name some things that can't separate you from God.

Journal

■ October 2

Woe to those who call evil good and good evil, who put darkness for light and light for darkness, who put bitter for sweet and sweet for bitter. (Isaiah 5:20)

The Lord is slow to anger and great in power; the LORD will not leave the guilty unpunished. His way is in the whirlwind and the storm, and clouds are the dust of his feet. (Nahum 1:3)

Meditation   *Wayne Smith*

Following back surgery in 1971, it was necessary that I remain horizontal for three weeks. I grew bed-weary, yielded to temptation and watched a soap opera, *Days Of Our Lives*. I made a feeble attempt to explain what I saw. However, Marge said what I thought I saw wasn't really what I saw. She explained there were deeper issues. What I thought I saw was a fellow named Bill having an affair with Laura, his brother's wife. While they were embracing, Bill's brother's child, Mike, age nine, came upon his mother Laura and Bill kissing. He was so upset that he rushed from the scene and was struck by an automobile. The problem in this marriage was not only unfaithfulness, but also that Mike was not the son of Mickey, who was his mother's husband. He was the child of Bill, an uncle, and Laura didn't know that Bill knew. However, God knows "even the hairs of our head are numbered."

This nation is crying out for judgment. "Whatsoever a man sows, that he shall reap." The sexually promiscuous, the unfaithful spouse believe their actions take place in a vacuum. Actions have consequences, and we will be held accountable. If the above holds any similarities to your life, take the first step today… that first and right step of Godly sorrow that leads to repentance.

Wayne Smith is the former Senior Pastor of Southland Christian Church in Lexington, KY.

Prayer

Gracious Heavenly Father, I am convicted by the text and have enough maturity to believe You honor those who honor You. I simply ask that You would give me the strength to conquer my pride and yield to Your will. I have not walked in the light, because I have enjoyed the darkness. However, I do not want to die the way I have lived. I am unworthy, but I pray that Your saving grace would include me this day. In Jesus' name, I pray. Amen.

Questions

- Do you think the "soaps" reflect real life in America?

- If your priorities are not right, will this affect the next generation?

- What do you think the following statement means: The darker the night, the brighter the light?

Journal

_____

_____

_____

_____

_____

> *Everything comes from you, and we have given you only what comes from your hand. (I Chronicles 29:14)*
>
> *The earth is the LORD's, and everything in it, the world, and all who live in it. (Psalm 24:1)*

Meditation   *Dudley C. Rutherford*

Get the stewardship habit! Get the tithing habit! Good habits are like an anchor: they will hold you safe in any storm. Science maintains that somewhere deep within our souls, our cells, our nerve endings, our protoplasm, our complicated molecular makeup, every action we commit leaves a tiny pathway. Ever sit in the same place in church or in a theater? Sure, and do you know why? Your brain has memorized your action and choices, and it gives you a chance to act again without too much thought. I've read that to avoid Alzheimer's, we should put on our belt, or tie our shoes, or brush our teeth not using the hand we've trained, but the other one.

Bring all this over into the spiritual world. Get the tithing habit! May I say I have tried to tithe my entire life? I'm in partnership with God. Let me also say I've tithed for so long that I no longer think about it. Tithing doesn't hurt me one little bit. It's a habit. It's a good habit that the Lord wants each of us to possess. Please don't start thinking that the food you eat is yours, or the home in which you live is yours, or the pet you have is yours. Everything belongs to the Master. The Bible says of Christ, "For in him were all things created, all things have been created through him, and unto him" (Colossians 1:16). He's the landlord and we are His trustees. Get the tithing habit.

Stewardship Habit

Prayer

Forgive me, dear Father, when I sometimes start thinking I have carved out a living on my own strength and talent. Your Bible reassures me that all things, everything belongs to You. You not only created all things; You made them for Yourself. And that includes me. I want to be honest. I want to be a square shooter with You. Help me from this moment forward to start giving You the first dime out of every dollar. I want You to be able to say of me, "He was a good and faithful servant." I pray in Your holy name. Amen.

Questions

- What can good habits do for us?

- Who made and owns your car, your house and your time?

- Finish this verse: All things were created by him and _____?

Journal

_____

_____

_____

_____

_____

_____

_____

In the year that King Uzziah died, I saw the Lord seated on a throne, high and exalted, and the train of his robe filled the temple. Above him were seraphs, each with six wings: With two wings they covered their faces, with two they covered their feet, and with two they were flying. And they were calling to one another: "Holy, holy, holy is the LORD Almighty; the whole earth is full of his glory." (Isaiah 6:1-3)

Meditation   *Dudley C. Rutherford*

The story has been told of a wonderful oil painter named Joseph Turner who had some friends over and they insisted on viewing the artist's masterpieces. Turner directed the men to sit in a pitch-black room for ten minutes. When he called them out of darkness to his gallery, he explained that the darkness was necessary to empty their eyes of the common glare before they could appreciate the true colors of his artistry. When we pray, we should bow our heads and shut our eyes to the sights and sounds that cloud our vision of the holy God that we serve. Proper preparation for prayer creates a perfect darkroom in which we can develop the true color of God's greatness.

Have you ever so shut out the world and its noise and light and prayed to the extent that you were constrained to call out: "Holy, holy, holy is the Lord Almighty?" Have you ever envisioned Him to the point you wanted to cry out, like Isaiah did, "Woe is me! For I am undone; because I, a man of unclean lips, and I dwell in the midst of a people of unclean lips; for mine eyes have seen the King, the Lord of hosts." When we see God in all His brilliance and holiness, it becomes a mirror in which we see our own sinful blemishes. If I compare my life with another person's, I won't look too bad. However if I compare my life with the true holy God in all His glory, I would look like a small candle outshined by the brilliance of the noonday sun. Oh friend, let me encourage you to pray to the point you can see Jesus in all His perfection and glory.

Prayer

Dear Holy and Majestic God, forgive me when I have lavished my affection on heroes, athletes, stars and family members and others who bring mostly disappointment. Forgive me that I haven't placed You high on the throne of my heart and worshipped at Your feet. May the fact that You are seated high above the earth in all Your splendor serve to remind me of my own sinfulness and my utter need of dependence upon Your love and forgiveness. In the strong and saving name of Jesus, I pray. Amen.

Questions

- Have you read the sixth chapter of Isaiah?

- When was the last time you envisioned the Glory of God?

- Seeing His perfection reflects what about you?

Journal

_____

_____

_____

_____

_____

■ October 5

We have not stopped praying for you and asking God to fill you with the knowledge of his will through all spiritual wisdom and understanding, that you may live a life worthy of the Lord and may please him in every way: bearing fruit in every good work, growing in the knowledge of God. (Colossians 1:9b-10)

Meditation   *Jim Dorman*

Many years ago my wife, Phyllis, our three children and I moved to Flagstaff to partner with God in the creation of a new local church. We were full of anticipation for the wonderful adventure God had set before us. We were ready for the wonderful events God would bring into existence, and we found ourselves occupied with the various expectations that starting a new ministry brings. We were not as prepared, however, for the challenges life and ministry would bring to our doorstep.

One day, I was sharing some of these challenges with a visiting prayer consultant. She asked me to identify the names of people I had asked to pray for my family and me. I told her that I believed I would be able to eventually withstand the onslaught of God's enemies and the situations I was experiencing. She then asked me a very penetrating question: "Are your wife and children able to withstand the lack of protection as well as you are?"

That question led me to realize that neither my children, my wife nor I were able to face the challenges of life or ministry without the protection, encouragement, growth, productivity and strength that comes from the prayers of people who seek God's best for my life, relationships and ministry. I have had people praying for my family and me daily since that meaningful encounter.

Jim Dorman is Senior Pastor of Christ's Church of Flagstaff in Flagstaff, AZ.

Meaningful Encounter

Prayer

Good morning, Father! It is great to be in Your presence once again! Thank You for the wonderful opportunities I have to share my love, concern, challenges and the needs of other people with You. Thank You for Your involvement in my life. I appreciate the ways You guide me to live life more and more like Jesus. Thank You for the opportunities I've had to minister to other people and for the successes You have brought to my efforts. I look forward to learning more about You each and every day. I pray this in Jesus' name. Amen.

Questions

- What challenges are you or your family facing now that have led you to prayer?

- Who does God want to join you in praying for these issues?

- Who would God have you begin to pray for on a daily basis?

Journal

_____

_____

_____

_____

For the eyes of the LORD range throughout the earth to strengthen those whose hearts are fully committed to him. You have done a foolish thing, and from now on you will be at war. (II Chronicles 16:9)

The one who calls you is faithful and he will do it.
(I Thessalonians 5:24)

Meditation — H. Dean Rutherford

Our Christ refuses to be ignored! He haunts the human race. Men have tried for twenty long centuries to escape Him, to elude Him, to discredit Him, to ignore Him, and yet after all their endeavors He pursues them still. Nearly 2,000 times in the Bible God says, "Come." The Bible is not only a bleeding book but also a pleading book. Whether civilization climbs the steep ascent of Heaven or plunges down to the abyss of hell, Christ will still be pleading for you. The world may flaunt His laws and trample His matchless name in the dust of oblivion, but his dogged love won't quit.

Francis Thompson in his famous poem, "The Hound of Heaven," worded it so wonderfully well. The first few lines describe what so many are trying to do today:

"I fled Him, down the nights and down the days;
   I fled Him, down the arches of the years;
      I fled Him, down the labyrinthine ways
        Of my own mind; and in the mist of tears
          I hid from Him..."

We can flee from Him, but Jesus, like a bloodhound, won't turn back. One can, like Pilate, wash his hands of Him, and deaden and drug his soul into spiritual slumber. Yet irresistibly and inexorably, He always comes back, as our Judge, our Redeemer, our Tormentor and our Savior. The gentle and steady pressure of the Almighty's hand is ever knocking at your heart's door. He is there now. What will you do with Him? How will you answer? He will not go away. He will not be ignored. He will not be denied.

Relentless Love

Prayer

Dear Lord of Life, thank You for Your dogged pursuit of my soul. Anybody else would have given up a long time ago. If it wasn't for You, I'd be lost today. I have so many times fled from You and turned away from You, but still You stalk me with Your relentless love. I can't help but wonder if You ever tire in Your task of wooing me and winning me. This day, this very day and this very hour I re-surrender my heart to You and pledge anew my love. In Christ's name, I pray. Amen.

Questions

- What does I Thessalonians 5:24 say God is faithful to do?

- Can you relate how God reached out to you?

- Do you think it's possible to outrun and outlast God?

Journal

■ October 7

They asked each other, "Were not our hearts burning within us while he talked with us on the road and opened the Scriptures to us?" Then the two told what had happened on the way, and how Jesus was recognized by them when he broke the bread. (Luke 24:32, 35. Read Luke 24:13-35)

Meditation   *Dudley C. Rutherford*

Doggedly and dejectedly, on that first Easter morning, Cleopas and his friend were walking from Jerusalem to Emmaus, a seven-mile trek. No two hearts were ever more disillusioned because they had pinned their hopes and dreams on Jesus, and to their knowledge He was still buried in His tomb. As the two crestfallen disciples of Jesus trudged toward home, they were joined by a third party. The third man inquired as to why they were so downcast. They blurted out the news that their Christ was executed three days earlier and ended up on a cross and not a throne!

Jesus chided them for their lack of knowledge about the Scriptures. Jesus said in effect, "Did not the Christ have to suffer these things and then enter his glory?" (verses 25-26). As they plodded along, they reached Emmaus and begged Jesus to stay and have dinner with them. Then another miracle took place. While they reclined at supper, their hearts and deepest souls were illuminated as they recognized their visitor to be the risen Christ. On an odyssey of great joy, Cleopas and his nameless friend raced back to Jerusalem to tell the other disciples of their miraculous discovery.

Friend, Jesus has been walking beside you for a long time now. Have you recognized Him? Have you given Him first place in your life? Are you serving Him? Jesus was born in Bethlehem but is He born in you? True, He arose from the dead, but does He live in your heart? Please take a closer look at Him.

Prayer

Thank You, dear Lord, for appearing to me so many times. Especially those times when I was not expecting You or thinking about You. You have been walking beside me for a long time now and my prayer is that I shall rediscover You, pause and dine with You and gaze into Your blessed face. I want to break bread with You and commune often with You, and always be aware of Your presence. Help me to stay on this Emmaus road of discovery. In the strong and wonderful name of Christ, I pray. Amen.

Questions

- Why were these two men so disheartened?

- Have you read Luke's 24th Chapter?

- Do you recognize Him and dine with Him everyday?

Journal

■ October 8

If we confess our sins, he is faithful and just and will forgive us our sins and purify us from all unrighteousness. (I John 1:9)

Meditation   *Murray Hollis*

I was standing in the hot sun in the middle of the prison yard, which was well-known turf for the inmates in the Cell Block F. While surrounded by men who told me of sentences ranging from 81 days to life plus 20 years, I engaged in a discussion with an alert-looking young man named Tom who told me of the tragic night of his accident. He described the horrific crash, and through tears, he told me of the death of the young boy in the other vehicle. On that night, he had been affected by alcohol, which caused him to collide with the other driver, and now he was to be separated from his wife and two children for up to three more years. Freedom from prison might be in his future, but he said freedom from the haunting reality that he was responsible for the death of a child might never come.

The words naturally came to me: "You can confess your sins, Tom, and turn to the Lord for forgiveness." However, did my words fall on ears made deaf by the massive weight of his guilt? We are all guilty of many sins, but may we never be guilty of denying the freedom-producing power of the forgiveness of Almighty God. If therefore the Son shall make you free, ye shall be free indeed. (John 8:36).

Murray Hollis is the Senior Pastor of Southwest Christian Church in Temecula, CA.

Prayer

Father God, in the name of my Lord Jesus, I ask You to bring complete assurance of forgiveness to my sometimes guilt-ridden mind. Take away the thoughts that would imprison me again for sins already forgiven. I trust You for the unquestionable grace and only ask for freedom from any residue of doubt that might give the "deceiver" a foothold. Thank You, Lord! Amen.

Questions

- What specific things do you need to confess and ask forgiveness for today? (Sins of commission or omission)

- What is the Biblical connection between repentance, confession and forgiveness?

- Must you *feel* forgiven to *know* that you *are forgiven*?

Journal

For none of us lives to himself alone and none of us dies to himself alone. If we live, we live to the Lord; and if we die, we die to the Lord. So, whether we live or die, we belong to the Lord. (Romans 14:7-8)

Be very careful how you live - not as unwise but as wise, making the most of every opportunity because the days are evil. (Ephesians 5:15-16)

Meditation   *Dudley C. Rutherford*

If you are not a Christian, time is your biggest enemy. If you are a Christian, you have a totally different perspective. Clocks or calendars do not hamper or threaten the Christ we serve. Regardless of facelifts and all forms of cosmetic surgeries, one cannot stay the hand of time. The true Christian is not caught up in the spectacle of racing against the calendar. It is only the unsaved who are paralyzed by the anxiety of watching the moments fly by, with no sign or symptoms of repentance. The passage of time doesn't bother or burden the Christian one bit! He knows that time, like his money, talent and strength are simply opportunity tools on loan from God, and that everything we possess is to be used in the service of our timeless Christ.

Time, or the lack thereof, cannot hold the whip over the believer. The Christian can sing that song I used to sing as a boy: "This world is not my home, I'm just a passin' through! My treasures are laid up somewhere beyond the blue. The angels beckon me from Heaven's open door, and I can't feel at home in this world anymore."

Read the above Scripture once more. It's saying the days are evil because they can end in a split second. They are evil because they are not promised or guaranteed. The clock can overtake us and catch us unprepared. Time is always unsure. The sure promise of God is judgment. The Bible states this: "Just as a man is destined to die once, and after that, face judgment..." (Hebrews 9:27).

Your Biggest Enemy

Prayer

Dear Father of mine, we thank You for the march of the relentless years. For it teaches us that we need to be prepared at every moment. None of us knows our future schedule or Yours. Please help me to rebuke and resist the idler within me, who begs for me to waste the precious hours I have left in which to live for You. Let me remember that You are eternal and that eternal life has been prepared for me. I ask this prayer in the strong name of Jesus. Amen.

Questions

- Why is it so important for the non-believer to come to Christ today?

- How many minutes is a man guaranteed to live?

- Man is promised to die and then what happens?

Journal

■ October 10

The LORD is my shepherd, I shall not be in want... You anoint my head with oil; my cup overflows. Surely goodness and love will follow me all the days of my life, and I will dwell in the house of the LORD forever.

(Psalm 23:1, 5-6)

Meditation   *Dudley C. Rutherford*

This 23rd Psalm has been used at more funerals than any other passage of Scripture. David starts out the Psalm by saying, "The Lord is my shepherd, and I shall not be in want." In the fifth verse he explains that the shepherd has a large sheepcote, or cage with one narrow door. The sheep come in for the night and pass through the door as the shepherd examines each sheep, running his skilled hands all over the sheep looking for cuts or lacerations. Finding some, the shepherd will dip his hand in the vat of oil and rub it over that affected area and by morning the cuts were usually healed. David adds that the vat of healing oil (cup) overflows. Jesus has enough healing oil to cure the whole world.

Then David adds in verse six, "Surely goodness and mercy shall follow me all my days." Forgive my wild imagination, but I see two sheepdogs that are trained to help the good shepherd. Their names are Goodness and Mercy. And then the dramatic declaration at the conclusion, "And I will dwell in the house of the Lord forever." This infers that if we allow Jesus to be our Good Shepherd in this life, and if we follow Him, we will someday enter Heaven. Come to the Shepherd and those two sheepdogs of His, Goodness and Mercy, will follow you all the way home.

Two Shepherds

Prayer

Dear Great Shepherd, thank You for guiding me in the paths of righteousness. I have never really wanted for anything. There have been times when I was sure I was in need, but You knew better than I did. At times, I am tempted to run away and stray. But I thank You that You have thus far guided me safely. I thank You for the presence of Your goodness and Your mercy. Every time I look around, there they are. I renew my trust in Your leadership today. In the name of Jesus, I pray. Amen.

Questions

- Why did a shepherd need oil?

- What is the meaning of the overflowing cup?

- Be honest: have goodness and mercy followed you?

Journal

_____

_____

_____

_____

_____

Each one should use whatever gift he has received to serve others, faithfully administering God's grace in its various forms. If anyone speaks, he should do it as one speaking the very words of God. If anyone serves, he should do it with the strength God provides, so that in all things God may be praised through Jesus Christ. To him be the glory and the power for ever and ever. Amen. (I Peter 4:10, 11)

Meditation   *Murry Whiteman*

Jesus said, "Go and tell all men about the Kingdom." Many of us freeze up at sharing our faith. I have discovered our Father has provided a key to men's hearts.

Our Father has given gifts to us all – passions, if you will. I have found that when you share a passion to do something with another, be it fishing, gardening, sports, painting, decorating, helping, reading, etc., you have an open door into their hearts. Both of you are speaking your heart's language. And in the course of events, it is easy to share the biggest "passion" of your life: Jesus.

Instead of trying to attack someone who is wearing heart armor, who is not open to you, share a passion. As they open their heart to you, there will come a time to plant the Gospel.

In speaking with fellow artists, where we speak the same language, when asked why I help or am caring or have hope, I share that Jesus has made me so. No set message, just what God has done for me. It works everywhere: as I've coached sports, visited hospitals, helped neighbors or gone fishing. Everywhere people speak the language of passion, and their hearts are open to speak the same language. Try it!

Murry Whiteman is a member of Discovery Church in Simi Valley, CA.

Prayer

Father, as I am going about my life, help me share my heart with others. You created me specially as I am and gifted me to have passion. I ask that I don't hide from what You made me; rather, that I rejoice in the doors my abilities open for me and the hearts I can touch for You. Thank You for the "key" of passion, and show me the joy of sharing all You have gifted me to be. Thank You that You meant for *all* to have a part in harvesting for Your Kingdom. In Jesus' name. Amen.

Questions

- Are you practicing one of your passions regularly and thanking the Father that He made you this way?

- Have you experienced the joy of sharing with another open heart what you love?

- Have you thought about or asked Jesus to show you how to use your passion (gifts) to find open doors into someone's heart?

Journal

_____

_____

_____

_____

■ October 12

Jacob replied, "First sell me your birthright."
"Look, I am about to die," Esau said.
"What good is the birthright to me?"
But Jacob said, "Swear to me first."
So he swore an oath to him, selling his birthright to Jacob.

(Genesis 25:31-33)

Meditation   *Dudley C. Rutherford*

Esau was like many in our day. "He knew the price of everything and knew the value of nothing." Sounds like America. We pay a ballplayer $25 million a year, while violinists, biochemists and teachers struggle financially. Sure, Esau sold his birthright and forfeited all the wealth and blessings of being the oldest son in the family. Spiritual things didn't matter to Esau. "Eat, drink and be merry for tomorrow we will die." Esau did snare a headline over in Hebrews 12:16: "See that no one is godless (profane) like Esau, who, for a single meal, sold his inheritance rights as the oldest son." The true definition of godlessness or profanity is to treat something God calls sacred with careless abuse.

Oh, dear heart! Are you profaning your life? Your life is very sacred. It is the prelude to eternity. It is the warm-up before the opening curtain. It is the practice before game day. It is the overture to the concert. This short life is not all there is. Your life is a sacred thing to God. It cannot be duplicated or counterfeited. We get only one chance at it. You can still decide for God. There is still time. You haven't gone too far yet. The final page of your life story has not yet been written. If Esau were here today, he would say to us, "I was a sellout. Don't make my horrible, fatal mistake. Live for God. Get into God's Word and God's Church and live your life to bring glory to God."

A Bowl of Chili

Prayer

Dear Lord of Heaven and earth, I know that I am still living, still breathing and that I still retain my mind, senses and faculties. I know I haven't gone too far yet and that there is still time for me to avoid Esau's great miscalculation. Help me to write the final page of my life's story and to write it well. I don't want to sell out my soul to a Christ-less world that cares nothing for me. Help me to make this day the kind of day that would bring honor to You and salvation for me. I plead these causes in the name of Jesus. Amen.

Questions

- What did Esau trade for a bowl of chili?

- Why was this such a bad decision?

- Is it too late to make a decision to change the course and direction of your life?

Journal

_____

_____

_____

_____

■ October 13

Come, all you who are thirsty, come to the waters; and you who have no money, come, buy and eat! Come, buy wine and milk without money and without cost. Why spend money on what is not bread, and your labor on what does not satisfy? (Isaiah 55:1-2)

Meditation   *Dudley C. Rutherford*

Dr. Clovis Chappell, one of the South's most gifted and beloved preachers of yesteryear, told of the first Christmas Program he attended as a boy in the small local church. The tree stood bright with candles and loaded down with presents. Santa Claus pranced happily among the people, distributing presents to those whose names were called. There was a young, feeble-minded man there, a hired hand on somebody's farm looking at the tree with eager eyes. His name had not been called and his face was growing downcast, when suddenly Santa Claus took down the largest box on the tree, looked at it and called his name. A look of radiance came into his poor, simple, blank face as he reached out his hands for the box. With nervous fingers, he untied the string and opened it; and then anticipation gave way to pitiful despair. The box was empty. Somebody had played a trick on the most underprivileged person in the village.

It is a terrible story. This old world is full of empty boxes, and we've all taken turns playing the fool. What is there in the glittering things we reach for and spend our energy to get? We spend our lives chasing after mirages. We reach our hands out and ask for empty boxes. "Give me the goods," we cry and grasp them, only to discover they were phantom goods. "I must see life!" "I must taste life!" and it wasn't life at all; it was just a pitiful staring into empty boxes. We must understand that only in Jesus do we find life that matters.

Prayer

Dear God, forgive me for chasing that pot-of-gold at the end of the rainbow that was never there in the first place. Forgive me for chasing mirages. Forgive me for majoring in minors. Forgive me for emphasizing things of little worth, and neglecting the things of eternal value. Forgive me for my weak moments, when I think if I can only have this or buy that, I will then be satisfied forever. I know there is only one thing in this world that brings real and lasting satisfaction, and that is *You*. In Your name, I pray. Amen.

Questions

- What is laboring for bread that does not satisfy?

- Name some things you've pursued that did not satisfy.

- Name some things you know will satisfy and bring joy.

Journal

■ October 14

Dear friends, now we are children of God, and what we will be has not yet been made known. But we know that when he appears, we shall be like him, for we shall see him as he is. Everyone who has this hope in him purifies himself, just as he is pure. (I John 3:2, 3)

Meditation

During the past year I had the blessed privilege of being at my father's bedside when his spirit soared out of his body to be at home with the Lord. In the days preceding his departure, I whispered in his ear with great emotion, "You're at the threshold of a new beginning, dad….you have a great future before you!" Many who are reading this can probably relate to losing someone near and dear. Although the pain is intense as we separate from our loved ones, this very pain is often the only force dynamic enough to make us shift our attention from this temporary existence to the greater reality of eternal life. As we recognize more of the faces in the crowd gathering on the other side, how reassuring it is to contemplate the great reunion that will take place when we pass through our personal corridor of death into life everlasting. The very thought of reuniting with our family and friends brings joy inexpressible! Yet this passage contains a promise that transcends inexpressible joy. For the Apostle John declares, "…we shall be like Him…." When we "see Him as He is," every single person on the other side will be more like Jesus than ever before. "Everyone who has this hope in Him purifies himself, just as He is pure!"

Ultimate Reunion

Prayer

Father in Heaven, thank You for bringing us into Your forever family and calling us Your children. Thank You for providing the Way to keep us pure. When we begin to feel dirty and soiled from our earthly focus, we give You permission to do whatever it takes to help us "fix our eyes on Jesus" our source of eternal life. Please fill us so that we will always keep our eyes on the prize! And Lord, give us the passion to bring others to the ultimate reunion. I love You and want to share Your love! In Jesus' name. Amen.

Questions

- What did Jesus say about those who do God's will? (Matthew 12:48-50)

- What dramatic change will occur when we see Him as He is? (I John 3:2)

- Can you think of the person for whom you have the most intense devotion? Now, try to imagine a place where that extreme love exists for every person you meet. You've just contemplated one facet of Heaven!

Journal

■ October 15

Just as each of us has one body with many members, and these members do not all have the same function, so in Christ we who are many form one body, and each member belongs to all the others. (Romans 12:4-5)

Meditation   *Bobby Braswell*

October 15 marks the first official day of college basketball practice. At the beginning of the first day of practice, we will huddle together and I will ask one of our players to quote the Thought of the Day. I have used the same thought on the first day of practice every year: "Isn't it amazing what can be accomplished when no one cares who gets the credit?" I use this quote because it is my desire to implant the clear message that the success of our season will depend on selflessness and teamwork.

The Apostle Paul, in his letter to the church at Rome, was reminding the believers that it was important for them to work together with a spirit of unity. One of my main objectives as a coach is to make sure each player understands his role on the team; what talent each has that will help our team function better. More importantly, they need to understand that the role they play, no matter how small or insignificant it may seem, is vital to our team's success. Once they know their roles, it's important that they accept them and execute them to the best of their ability.

This is true for the Church today. God has blessed each of us with specific gifts that He expects us to use in building up His Church. In order for the Church to be truly effective in doing God's work, each of us must learn what our God-given gifts are, accept them and execute them in our daily lives with a spirit of unity. If we don't, the Church will never function as effectively as God intended it to. There's plenty of work to be done. It's time to break from the huddle and get to it!

Bobby Braswell is the Head Men's Basketball Coach at California State University, Northridge.

586

Prayer

Heavenly Father, help me to understand what it is that You need me to do in Your Church. Help me to understand, accept and execute Your plan with a spirit of love and unity. Lord, help me to remember that whatever I do, in word or in deed, that I do it in Your name and for Your glory. Thank You for my church family. Thank You for my gifts. In Jesus' name. Amen.

Questions

- What are your special gifts and talents?

- Have you accepted these gifts?

- How can you use them to build up the Body of Christ?

Journal

■ October 16

In my Father's house are many rooms; if it were not so, I would have told you. I am going there to prepare a place for you. And if I go and prepare a place for you, I will come back and take you to be with me that you also may be where I am. You know the way to the place where I am going.

(John 14:2-4)

Meditation   *Dudley C. Rutherford*

A sick man turned to his doctor, as he was preparing to leave the examination room and said, "Doctor, I am afraid to die. Tell me what lies on the other side." Very quietly the doctor said, "I don't know." "You don't know? You, a Christian man, do not know what is on the other side?"

The doctor was holding the handle of the door, on the other side of which came a sound of scratching and whining, and as he opened the door a dog sprang into the room and leaped on him with an eager show of gladness.

Turning to the patient, the doctor said, "Did you notice my dog? He's never been in this room before. He didn't know what was inside. He knew nothing except that his master was in here, and when the door opened he sprang in without fear. I know little of what is on the other side of death, but I do know one thing: I know my Master is there, and that is enough. And when the door opens, I will pass through it with gladness, and with absolutely no fear. "Now faith is the substance of things hoped for, the evidence of things not seen" (Hebrews 11:1).

Prayer

Dear Lord, thank You for this very day and thank You for that coming day in the future when we shall be privileged to dwell with the One who paid for sins on Calvary's cross. I am confident there will be many wonderful and exciting things in Heaven, but the best thing about it will be that You will be there. Help me to so live for You that I will not let that day carelessly slip from my grasp. In Christ's name, I pray. Amen.

Questions

- How many rooms are in the Father's house?

- Who will be the main attraction of Heaven?

- How would you describe Heaven?

Journal

_____

_____

_____

_____

_____

■ October 17

For all have sinned and fall short of the glory of God, and are justified freely by his grace through the redemption that came by Christ Jesus.
(Romans 3:23-24)

Meditation   Cameron McDonald

Hypocrisy is one of the main reasons many non-believers cite as to why they do not want to go to church. I remember when I was growing up, one of my favorite CDs was DC Talk's Jesus Freak album. Arguably, the best song on the CD started with this intro written by Brennan Manning: "The single greatest cause of atheism in the world today is Christians who acknowledge Jesus with their lips, and then walk out the door and deny Him with their lifestyle. That is what an unbelieving world simply finds unbelievable!"

That serves as a great reminder that, as Christians, we have to constantly guard our witness. On the other hand, we must be firm with those who use this as their scapegoat for not attending church. Someone once said we should ask that person, "If a hypocrite stands between you and God, look and see which one is closer."

That's true. If a person doesn't do very well performing Hamlet, you wouldn't say Shakespeare was a horrible writer and not worth reading. On the same level, if a Christian doesn't do very well acting like Jesus, that does not mean Jesus is not worth following. We are to follow Christ only, not people who claim to be Christians, not people who say they have an incredible relationship with Him. We are to follow Jesus as best we can, and we will be judged accordingly.

Prayer

Heavenly Father, probably what most of us hate about hypocrites is that we know in our heart of hearts that we are also hypocrites. We understand that we are not perfect and we hate that about ourselves, but would You give us the strength and wisdom to understand that Jesus is all the perfection we need? Father, thank You that when You look down at us, You don't see all of our disgusting, sinful imperfections. When You look at us, You see the perfection of Your Son Jesus Christ who is living inside us. Father, keep me aware that I need to be constantly on guard, because people don't view us as individuals but as institutions. Father, we represent Your Son Jesus; give us the strength to be worthy of the name that we bear. In Jesus' strong name. Amen.

Questions

- Have you ever been a hypocrite?

- Be honest: in light of all the hypocrisy scandals by so-called religious leaders today (i.e., Jim & Tammy Faye Bakker, Jimmy Swaggart or the numerous allegations about Catholic priests), have you been tempted to turn your back on Christianity?

- Read Luke 18:10-14 and then journal your thoughts.

Journal

_____

_____

_____

_____

Jesus said to her, "I am the resurrection and the life. He who believes in me will live, even though he dies." (John 11:25)

Meditation   *H. Dean Rutherford*

Four days had passed since a stone had been placed across the entrance of the cave where Lazarus' body was buried. Upon seeing Jesus, Martha and Mary each made the confession, "If You had been here, my brother would not have died." Yet we know from the story that Jesus intentionally avoided coming prior to Lazarus' death. Jesus made the reason for His delay very clear when He said, "…for your sake I am glad I was not there, so that you may believe."

As astounding as this miracle was for the eyewitnesses that day, the intense passion of Jesus is that the resurrection of Lazarus becomes your reality too. In this story, we have dramatic assurance that Jesus not only has the power of life, but He also has the power of resurrection. It is one thing for each of us to be given life in our mother's womb, but it is quite another dynamic to be brought back from the dead and made alive. Yet that is exactly what happens when we become Christians. As the Apostle Paul said, "God… made us alive in Christ when we were dead in sin" (Ephesians 2:5). Indeed, Jesus longs to personally demonstrate His resurrection power to the people who are witnesses to your life. Jesus calls you by name and repeats the question, "Do *you* believe this?"

Do You Believe This?

Prayer

Heavenly Father, thank You for creating me and blessing me with life here on this earth. Thank You even more for making me alive in Christ when I was dead in sin. Awaken within me a desire to grow in my comprehension of the resurrection power that You have available for me today! May I never be content to hear the story of Lazarus without understanding that I too am the walking evidence of Jesus' resurrection to the 21st century. Empower me to be as vibrant a witness today as Lazarus was so many years ago. In Jesus' name. Amen.

Questions

- Why did Jesus wait until Lazarus had died before coming to Martha and Mary?

- What phrase above meditation explains how you are considered dead?

- What event symbolically unites you to the resurrection life of Jesus? (See Romans 6:4ff)

Journal

■ October 19

> *Fix these words of mine in your hearts and minds... Teach them to your children, talking about them when you sit at home and when you walk along the road, when you lie down and when you get up. (Deuteronomy 11:18-19)*
>
> *Train a child in the way he should go, and when he is old he will not turn from it. (Proverbs 22:6)*

Meditation   *Dudley C. Rutherford*

These words are directed to every son or daughter that is now reading this. I want you to pretend for a moment that I am your father and mother, because I am going to say to you what I know they want to say to you. If you want to remember Mother's Day, or Father's Day, God bless you, and if you don't, God bless you anyway. If you want to remember us at Christmas, on birthdays or anniversaries, God bless you, and if you don't, God bless you anyway.

What do we want from you? We want you to take everything we are. We want you to take everything we have. We want you to take our money, our labor and our toil. We want you to take our blood, sweat and tears. We want you to take our health, our hopes, our dreams and our entire lives. We want you to take and take and keep on taking, only for Jesus' sake and be the best Christian man, the best Christian woman that God can possibly make out of you.

That is all we want. That is all we ever wanted. We don't care whether or not you excel as an athlete or make straight A's. We don't care whether you are popular or not. We just want you to take everything we have and use it for Christ. We want you to walk with the Lord. We want you to be like Jesus! Can you? Will you?

What Parents Want

Prayer

Dear Father, I want to be the best son or daughter my parents ever had. I want to honor them with the rest of my life, in service and dedication to You. I want to honor You with the rest of my life and I know that in so doing, it will bring honor and respect to them. Thank You, Lord, for being my Father and having patience with me while I learn to be Your humble and obedient child. In Jesus' name, I pray. Amen.

Questions

- What do parents want most from their children?

- What is the promise for those who train a child right?

- What is the best way to teach a child to follow Christ?

Journal

_____

_____

_____

_____

■ October 20

Meditation   *Dudley C. Rutherford*

Of course, that's the question of the ages! That's the one question you and I must answer. Kierkegaard was right when he said there were only two possible answers: to believe in Him and accept Him, or else to be "offended" in Him. To try to settle somewhere in between is a slap in His face. To present to Him some sort of lip service and routine discipleship is an insult to Him. He is God. He really is God! Do you think casual church attendance, going to church only when you feel like it, giving to Him only what you think you can afford to do without... do you think that is a proper response to Him?

Come on! Get real! Jesus is not just some inspired teacher. We dare not think of Jesus as just a beautiful man whose compassion toward the poor and the downtrodden was admirable. He died for you and me on that cross. He shed His sinless blood to pay for your sins. He is not merely a good example. What we do with Jesus depends upon who we think He is. If I accept Him as God then personal, behavioral and moral consequences are demanded from me. One cannot exclaim, "He is God" and then spend more on hair care than on getting His message out. Today, Jesus is asking us, demanding us to get into the Church and help wake it up. He is asking us again: "What will you do with me?"

Prayer

Dear Father, I have settled in my heart the answer to that lingering question: What shall I do with Jesus? I am going to put You on the throne of my heart where You belong. I am going to serve You and try my best to be Your true representative here on earth. I am going to make a difference in my church and in my neighborhood. People will be able to observe that I belong to You and You belong to me. I ask this prayer in Your sacred name. Amen.

Questions

- What's the one question we all must answer?

- What does it mean to be lukewarm?

- At what level is your commitment to Christ?

Journal

■ October 21

The Lord is my shepherd, I shall not be in want. He makes me lie down in green pastures, he leads me beside quiet waters, he restores my soul. He guides me in paths of righteousness for his name's sake. (Psalm 23:1-3)

Meditation   *Paul S. Williams*

Some people enjoy a laser-like focus. Not given to introspection, they are "doers," always building a better light bulb, planting a better garden, creating a bigger company. They know their calling and are true to it. But not everyone enjoys such a clear focus.

There are times when we feel lost, standing under the dark canopy of a giant forest with no sense of the four cardinal directions, while a cacophony of voices screams into our ears, "Do this with your life, my friend."

Such times can be terrifying, but we must understand, lost is a place too. The Psalmist encourages us to stand still in such moments of uncertainty. It's all right to stop scurrying hither and yon. It's all right to lie down in green pastures beside still waters for a spell. It doesn't matter if everyone is yelling, "Here! Look here! Come over here! I have your answer!"

The truth is that no one has your answer. Only you have your answer, and it will come in its own time. You must listen for it. You will hear God in the quiet: "Stand still. *I am* not lost. You must wait. Wait until you have eyes to see My footprints, ears to hear My whisper and a heart to sense My presence. *I am* not lost, friend. Stand still."

Paul S. Williams is Editor-at-Large at the Christian Standard and President of Orchard Group, a church planting agency in the Northeast.

Prayer

Dear Father, help me to remember that You are not mine to possess but that I am Yours to be possessed. And help me to understand that when I am lost, that is when I am the most open to hear Your sweet voice leading me through the valley of the shadow of death. Give me ears to hear Your calling, then give me faith to walk in obedience. In Jesus' name. Amen.

Questions

- What decision are you faced with today?

- How does a person clearly hear the voice of God?

- Are you living a life of complete obedience?

Journal

Peace I leave with you; my peace I give you. I do not give to you as the world gives. Do not let your hearts be troubled and do not be afraid.

(John 14:27)

Meditation   *Dudley C. Rutherford*

Jesus must have startled His listeners when He talked about the peace He possessed. They all knew Jesus was hated, beaten and whipped. He faced more problems and crises than a turkey on Thanksgiving Day. Strange but true, Jesus had peace and serenity in all situations. Even on the cross, with His blood flowing, His pain and fever mounting, Jesus still had great peace as He prayed for His enemies: "Father forgive them, for they know not what they do."

Of course, we shouldn't think that peace of mind would free us from problems. Difficult situations and all tests are necessary for good growth. The only way to obtain this perfect peace is to become like Jesus. We must develop a mindset that will allow us to turn from worry to complete trust and dependence upon Him. Peace is not the absence of conflict. It is the presence of Christ embedded deep in our hearts. Paul was also a wonderful example of perfect peace. He was beaten, shipwrecked, forsaken, abandoned, tortured and left for dead, and in the midst of it all he could say, "Be of good cheer." John the apostle, stranded on the Isle of Patmos, could exclaim, "This is the victory that overcomes the world." If these fellows can find peace in the midst of such storms, it is surely available to us all. Thomas À Kempis wrote, "All men desire peace, but few desire the things that make for peace."

Prayer

Dear precious Lord, You said You would keep me in perfect peace if I keep my mind on You. Let me learn to so trust and depend upon You, so that in the face of severe adversity or raging loss and conflict, I may be like my Master and have perfect peace. For I know that submission to You will soon provide a perfect peace. In Christ's name, I pray. Amen.

Questions

- Is the absence of war peace?

- Name three examples of perfect peace.

- How do you obtain this perfect peace?

Journal

In the same way, I tell you, there is rejoicing in the presence of the angels of God over one sinner who repents. (Luke 15:10)

Meditation   *Dudley C. Rutherford*

In this wonderful chapter of Luke 15, the Bible states in red letters that there is joy in Heaven when a sinner repents. This is what is important to God and to all others who are in Heaven. The angels did not shout when man discovered the radio, for in Heaven they had been hearing the music of the spheres. The new television principle did not cause a ripple in that perfect realm. They had known about that from the foundation of the world. When NASA sent rockets to the moon and landed men thereon, this caused no stir in that perfect city. Centuries before, God had placed a moon around the earth, two around Saturn and eleven around Jupiter. The discoveries of laser beams and wireless technology didn't garner a single headline in Paradise. The invention of the computer, with its vast capacity of stored knowledge, did not cause any excitement in Heaven, for Jesus who is the wisdom of God has had perfect knowledge from the foundation of the world. But I have come to say that they still strike up the band in Heaven when a human being, made in the image of God, gets tired of the hog pen of sin and heads for the Father's house, arms and heart. And all God's people said? "Amen!"

Heaven's Band

Prayer

Dear Father of all fathers, forgive me when I get to thinking that soul-winning and soul-witnessing are not the most important agendas in Your eternal Heaven. Give me the courage and the holy boldness to talk about You to everyone I know. Help me to do something that will make all of Heaven shout and rejoice. Forgive me for thinking of my own problems, when I possess the serum (Jesus) for people's lost souls. In Your blessed name, I pray. Amen.

Questions

- Take the time to read the three parables of Luke 15.

- What emotion is present at the close of each of these three stories?

- Can you name a person you have helped lead to Jesus?

Journal

■ A Tribute

Before you turn the page to read the next devotion, I want to pay tribute to my dear friend, Dr. Scott Bauer.

On Friday, October 24, 2003, Dr. Scott Bauer, Senior Pastor of The Church On the Way, went to meet the Lord. He was 49 years of age and had experienced an aneurysm at the conclusion of the church's Wednesday night service. The next morning, I received a phone call and an urgent request for prayer. Little did I know that the next day, Scott would be in the presence of our Lord and Savior. The following words I penned that week, which I now share with you, as a tribute to an awesome man of God.

*   *   *   *   *

In a whirlwind week, it seems almost impossible that Scott is no longer with us. While writing the words, "Life is but a vapor" for a sermon I was to preach this weekend, the phone call came that I wished was a dream and not reality; that Pastor Scott was on life support. Knowing in my heart that Scott and I were bonded together by the size and scope of our responsibilities, and sensing that we were both in the same foxhole fighting the enemy at hand, the news of his condition weighed heavily upon my mind. The two churches we pastored, The Church On The Way and Shepherd of the Hills Church, were anchors in the valley in which we lived and worked. Neither of us ever thought we deserved these positions. In fact, we talked on several occasions that we were only able to do our jobs by the grace of Jesus Christ. The task at hand was beyond our abilities, but we were always available and more than willing to be used of God as He desired. Although we grew up in different denominations, we were one in Christ. I was his biggest fan and he was mine. Whenever we spoke, he expressed his love and his protocol of praying for me every week.

We both envisioned working side by side in this valley for the next 15 to 20 years. We hoped our churches, encouraging one another, would be the lighthouses for the people of our valley. There was never a single ounce of rivalry or competition. I wanted him to succeed and he wanted me to succeed. For you see, Scott had a Kingdom vision to see the world won to Christ. Very rarely have I ever known anyone to have such zeal and fervor for the Lord. I pray that his life and purpose will never erode from our memory. He influenced everyone with whom he came into contact and sought to draw them into a closer walk with the Master. He loved the church. He loved his wife. He loved his children. He loved his family. He loved his Jesus.

There have been many evenings I have cried myself to sleep thinking of my dear friend, and there are many mornings I have awakened only to cry again. Am I sad for Scott? Only in that he truly loved his place of anointing. That he was doing exactly what God had planned for him. Always gracious, forever encouraging, sincerely burdened to build the Lord's Kingdom here on earth. He was God's man for God's appointed time at The Church On The Way.

To say I have struggled with his graduation into glory would be an understatement. Don't get me wrong; he is in his Heavenly home and he is happier now than he's ever been before. But forgive me for being so selfish. I wish my good friend were still here.

Scott, my dear friend. Thank you for your friendship, for the camaraderie that we shared. You truly were my Jonathan. You will never, ever be replaced. We will see you soon. The time we will be apart is short.

If Scott could tell us anything, he would say these four lines that I first heard from a fellow minister named Wayne B. Smith:

Grieve not for me
Nor let one teardrop fall
What you dream of I can see
and friends 'tis worth it all.

Scott, thank you for continuing to make a difference in my life and church.

Dudley C. Rutherford

■ October 24

I have come to bring fire on the earth, and how I wish it were already kindled! (Luke 12:49)

Meditation   *Scott Bauer*

Gusts of wind and raging flames terrify those who live near the hillsides and mountain passes of Southern California. The harder the wind blows, the higher the flames go. And the flames can't be contained. The same thing happened on the day of Pentecost – not destructively, but with the same power. Winds of ferocious intensity and flames that still haven't been stopped began to overtake our world. And now, 20 centuries later, the world burns with the work of God!

But the Bible also talks about those who would rather be "warmed" by the fire than ignited by it. Peter denied the Lord while "warming himself" by the fire. James 2 warns us about compassion that only talks a good game without addressing people's needs. Revelation 3:16 ominously pronounces judgment on those who are "lukewarm" in their faith in Christ.

As believers, some have felt the breeze of the Spirit and been content to live with only the warmth of embers that remind them of what once burned brightly in their lives. Others have only come to be "warmed" by the flames.

It is not God's way to allow us the comfort of being warmed without the demand to be filled with His Spirit and set on fire to reach with His love. Begin *today* to seek for and experience a fresh gust of wind and a new outbreak of fire in your life. The wind is blowing – and the Lord has already lit the match!

Scott Bauer is the former Senior Pastor of The Church on the Way, Van Nuys, CA.

Prayer

Dear Heavenly Father, Your Word says that Your mercies are new every day… as is Your fresh oil, daily bread and fire! I want that, Lord! I ask that You pour out Your fire on me. In every area of my life, I ask that You fan the flame, ignite the spark, kindle a blaze in me. Don't let me become comfortable with what You have done in my life in the past. Urge me; press me always toward my future and what You want to do next. I love You, Lord! Ignite something new in me today! In Jesus' name. Amen.

Questions

- Are there areas in your life where you are only being "warmed"?

- Has the Lord been pressing you out of your comfort zone?

- What point of action is He asking you to take?

Journal

The Lord is not slow in keeping his promise, as some understand slowness. He is patient with you, not wanting anyone to perish, but everyone to come to repentance. But the day of the Lord will come like a thief. The heavens will disappear with a roar; the elements will be destroyed by fire, and the earth and everything in it will be laid bare. (II Peter 3:9-10)

Meditation   *Dudley C. Rutherford*

Someone is always predicting the end of our world. Many times, cults and preachers have stepped forward and made some bold prediction of Christ's second coming. Those cult members have sold their houses and furniture, gone out on a mountaintop and prayed and waited, and came back home embarrassed, chagrined and disappointed. They should have known better. They should have read the Bible. The certainty of Christ's coming is sure; His exact time is uncertain. Jesus plainly said in Matthew 24:36, speaking of His return to earth, that "No one knows about that day or hour, not even the angels in Heaven."

Jesus warns us of the unexpected suddenness of his return: "For as the lightning comes from the east and flashes to the west, so will be the coming of the Son of Man" (Matthew 24:27). It will be the greatest, grandest surprise in all history. Even the angels are going to be shocked. Imagine! But every Christian will be celebrating with an incredible excitement. The homecoming of brave soldiers from the battle lines of a war will hold no comparison to this thrilling reunion. The closing breath of our Lord in the Bible, His closing salutation was, "Yes, I am coming soon." Then John tacks on his hearty, "Amen." "Come, Lord Jesus." This should be the reverberating echo of every Christian heart.

Unexpected Suddenness

I know You are coming back, dear Lord, for me. I don't know when that day and hour will be. But I intend to be faithful, waiting and ready for that big reunion of the centuries. I can't imagine how You are going to make everything happen, but I trust You. I am not only trusting You with my time, my money, my heart and my life; I am trusting You with my future; I am trusting You for all time and eternity. Bless me to be faithful, and in Jesus' name, I pray. Amen.

Questions

- Who knows for sure when Jesus will return?

- Do the angels have some idea of this date?

- What is the last word, the last recorded promise of Jesus?

Journal

_____

_____

_____

_____

_____

Like a city whose walls are broken down is a man who lacks self-control.
(Proverbs 25:28)

Meditation   *Randy Gariss*

A tale of two cities: one with walls and one without. In both towns, they store their winter grain and keep their homes. In both towns, the dreams are the same. But in one town, the dreams will never come to be. The grain will be stolen, the houses will be pillaged and the children will become slaves in another man's household. All of this, because of the absence of walls.

The most dangerous person on the face of the earth is not the scoundrel. The scoundrel is soon found out for what he or she is, and is quickly dismissed. No, the most dangerous person on the face of the earth is the well-liked, well-intentioned man or woman who lacks self-discipline. They want the right things for their life and the lives of those they love. They speak with heartfelt passion about the core values of their life and their love for the Lord. But their personal lack of self-discipline means that most everything important to them will be stolen.

The absence of self-discipline means that those values are not protected… and what is not protected is eroded by time and temptation. The man who betrays his wife and children means well, but his lack of self-discipline meant he never really carried out the things that mattered, and no one could really count on him. The woman who had the affair never dreamed of such a thing. But the lack of self-discipline left her vulnerable to the cold winds that can blow through a soul.

Do you want to love the Lord and love your family? Build within your life the walls of self-discipline.

Randy Gariss is Senior Pastor of College Heights Christian Church in Joplin, MO.

Prayer

Lord, I do not want to live the life of a fool. I want to be a person whose life is reliable for Your sake. May Your people be safe with me! May my family be safe beside me! Lord, convict me and confront me with the truth about my life. Where I lack reliability, break my heart. May I confess what is broken. And then, Lord, would You, by Your Spirit and the accountability of others, help me rebuild the walls of my life. O God, may I be found in Your sight as "faithful in the little," that You can safely entrust me with Your dreams. Amen.

Questions

- Where do you have holes in the walls of your life? Where do you lack self-discipline?

- Do you believe God can help you change? Or do you intend to "play victim" to your own weaknesses for the rest of your life?

- Who are the two or three Godly individuals you need to confess to and then ask to help hold you accountable for the first areas of change?

Journal

■ October 27

When the people heard this, they were cut to the heart and said to Peter and the other apostles, "Brothers, what shall we do?" Peter replied, "Repent and be baptized, every one of you, in the name of Jesus Christ for the forgiveness of your sins. And you will receive the gift of the Holy Spirit." (Acts 2:37-38)

Meditation   Dudley C. Rutherford

Everybody in the world ought to love Jesus and therefore everybody in the world ought to be baptized. Water baptism by immersion is a command of Jesus Christ. It is a command, dear heart, not a suggestion. I've seen it happen several times... No sooner does a person give his life to Christ than the devil proceeds immediately to talk him out of obeying this plain command of our Savior. The lover of Christ has no choice but to obey. Excuses such as failure to understand all the great Christian doctrines, or delay to see if one can live the Christian life, or other theological and dilatory tactics are not permitted by the Bible. Believers must be immersed at once!

The first Gospel sermon preached in the New Testament (Acts 2:38) had the audience crying out at the end, "What must we do?" Peter, filled with the Holy Spirit, replied, "Repent and be baptized, every one of you." That's awfully clear to me. When I meet someone who doesn't want to be baptized, I don't preach to that person a sermon on baptism; rather, I preach a sermon on repentance. When you stand in that water, you look like Christ on the cross; when you go under the water, you look exactly like Jesus being buried; when you rise from the water, you look just like Jesus coming back to life. You are powerfully testifying that you believe Jesus died and was buried and rose again! You do love Him, I know! Please obey Him in this if you have not already done so.

Prayer

Dear Crucified but Risen Lord, You are more than worthy of my deepest love. You are more than worthy of my best obedience. I want to drop all arguments and excuses and simply obey You in child-like faith. I am not only willing to be immersed, but I am also willing to try and obey all the other things You have commanded. I want to tell and show the whole world that You died, and came back from the grave to pay the penalty for my sins. I am not ashamed of Jesus, and in His name, I pray. Amen.

Questions

- Is water baptism a command or a suggestion?

- How long after conversion should you wait to be baptized?

- Your baptism is a pantomime of what great event?

Journal

■ October 28

Meditation   Dudley C. Rutherford

Even Jesus, with His superior mind and His perfect knowledge of the human heart was surprised. This is one of the few times that Christ had a look of shock on His face. The failure to give thanks stung Him like a lash. The treachery of Judas, his kiss, hurt Jesus more than the whips of Pilate's soldiers. A forgotten birthday can hurt sometimes more than a whipping. "Thanks" is still one of the world's best *pain-relievers*. We live, move and have our being in a world of sickness, poverty, shame and death; a kindly thought and gracious word from you could be the very strength that helps someone to endure.

Anybody can be an unthankful sinner. It takes a real person to be a Christian. Anybody can die. It is this business of living that takes hard work. The acid-test of whether Calvary and its power is working in your life is if you're good to bad people; if you serve the unthankful; if you smile in the midst of frowns; and if you hold your faith in others undimmed and your trust in God inviolate. When we fail to be thankful, when we "turn our noses up," we snub the Cross of Calvary. Would you, this day, write some letters or make some phone calls of appreciation? Could you, this day, start to look for the good and the best in others? If so, it would not only make a great deal of difference in their lives but in yours as well.

Thank You

Prayer

Thank You Lord for all the ways You bless me every day of my life. I don't want my life to be "all about me." I want my life to be all about You and others. I know how it hurts when I do something for someone else and there is no response of gratitude. I know it must hurt You when I fail to respond to Your countless mercies every day. Help me to realize that most people are having a tough time in life and that my encouragement might make a difference in their struggle. In Jesus' name, I pray. Amen.

Questions

- What do you think happened to the other nine?

- What is a good offering we can give the Master?

- Do you consider yourself to be someone who expresses gratitude easily?

Journal

_____

_____

_____

_____

■ October 29

Today I am reminded of my shortcomings. (Genesis 41:9)

If we claim to be without sin, we deceive ourselves and the truth is not in us. If we confess our sins, he is faithful and just and will forgive us our sins and purify us from all unrighteousness. (I John 1:8-9)

Meditation   *Dudley C. Rutherford*

We have all done a little housecleaning. Spiritual housecleaning is also a wonderful exercise. When we fail to clean our souls, like our homes, they become littered and cluttered. Like ships, we need to enter dry-dock now and then and have the old barnacles scraped off. A sin may seem small but a few of them together can clog and stifle our souls. Let me suggest some Biblically-defined causes for a dirty soul:

1. Talking too quickly. The Bible reads, "Everyone should be quick to listen, slow to speak and slow to become angry" (James 1:19). We all have had to choke while eating our own words. Humble pie has a bitter taste.

2. Finding fault in others. We appoint ourselves prosecutor, jury and judge. We condemn and execute. That requires less effort, brains and strength than to simply help. James 4:12 reads, "Who are you to judge your neighbor?"

3. Letting "things" crowd our lives. Jesus spoke often about the cares and worries of this life (Matthew 13:22). If we are too busy to serve Him, we are simply too busy.

4. Nursing a grudge. Jesus has much to say about this in Matthew's 6th chapter. A grudge can soon become a malignant cancer that gnaws away at the soul.

So, Mr. Preacher-man, what shall we do about our faults? Confess them and forsake them! James had this in mind when he said, "Therefore confess your sins to each other and pray for each other so that you may be healed" (James 5:16).

Housecleaning

Prayer

Just as You warned us "little foxes can spoil the vines" (Song of Solomon 2:15) even so, little sins can destroy our determined efforts to serve the Lord. Help me, dear Lord, to stop judging and stop talking about others. Help me to stop faultfinding and letting the cares and worries of this life fill my heart. This moment, I want to confess and forsake my sins and make this a day of "beginning again." In the matchless name of our forgiving Savior, I pray. Amen.

Questions

- How often do you think you sin?

- What two things should you do about your faults or sins?

- Name three Biblical causes for your sins.

Journal

_____

_____

_____

_____

_____

■ October 30

For since in the wisdom of God the world through its wisdom did not know him, God was pleased through the foolishness of what was preached to save those who believe. (I Corinthians 1:21)

So then, let us not be like others, who are asleep, but let us be alert and self-controlled. (I Thessalonians 5:6)

Meditation   *Dudley C. Rutherford*

Snoring through sermons is so common that jokes abound concerning this oddity. A pastor was preaching when a loud snoring sound interrupted him and the pastor shouted, "Someone wake up Fred!" A voice was heard in reply: "Pastor, you wake up Fred, you're the one that put him to sleep."

Sleeping in church is nothing new. Our Puritan churches here in America and elsewhere used to have some stern fellow with a long pole bop you on the back of the noggin if you nodded off. Admitting that many of my sermons deserve some snoring, I have a point to make. All of us often sleep through some of God's most compelling sermons. Walking by a flower, listening late at night to some distant siren, a stately pine tree, a chest pain, a flowing stream can be a superior sermon. God expects us to sharpen our spiritual antennae not just in church but at every sight we see.

There are graphic lessons and sermons from God everywhere. We all need to regularly be in church and hear preaching – good or bad. Thankfully God can survive loudmouth, foolish preaching as well as some polished exhortation from the pulpit (I Corinthians 1:21). But He also loves for us to observe His countless messages that come from life, nature and experience. God is a phenomenal communicator, if we will only look and listen. No wonder the Bible keeps repeating, "He who has ears to hear, let him hear what the Spirit says."

Prayer

Dear wonderful Savior, thank You for preaching. I thank You that someone preached to me. Preaching not only got me started, it keeps me going. Thank You for the many messages You have preached to me through life's experiences. Please keep preaching to me every way You can, for if anyone needs it more than me, I can't imagine who it would be. Help me to so live that my life would be one of Your sermons to others. In Christ's name, I pray. Amen.

Questions

- Preaching may look foolish but God uses it to do what?

- Name some non-verbal sermons you've observed.

- Is your life, and your love for Christ, a sermon to someone?

Journal

_____

_____

_____

_____

■ October 31

I tell you the truth, all the sins and blasphemies of men will be forgiven them. But whoever blasphemes against the Holy Spirit will never be forgiven; he is guilty of an eternal sin. (Mark 3:28-29)

Meditation   *Dudley C. Rutherford*

Many have asked, "What is the unpardonable sin?" or "Have I committed the unpardonable sin?" Let me answer in the clearest terms: If you have *any* longing in your heart for God, any concern at all for your soul, you have not yet committed the sin that can never be forgiven. That is the unpardonable sin: to so reject and deny the light of God and His Son's Gospel plea, that it no longer makes the slightest impression on your soul. Have you ignored Him so many times that all Gospel appeals rush into the gutter of forgetfulness and bitterness?

It is not that one reaches a point where God can no longer forgive; it is that one reaches a point where he no longer wants forgiveness! Barclay, the great Scottish scholar puts it like this: "If he for long enough shuts his eyes and ears to God's way, if he for long enough turns his back upon the messages which God is sending him, if he comes to a stage when his own evil seems to him good, and when God's good seems to him evil, then he has committed that sin." If you have even a faint desire to serve Him, you have not committed that sin; no matter how calloused or hidden or disguised that desire may be. At this very moment, do you hear God calling to you? If so, you haven't crossed that line – yet. You haven't gone too far – yet. There is still room at the cross for you.

The Unpardonable Sin

Prayer

God of many calls, I know You are dealing with me again, right now. I've tried to stifle many of Your clarion calls for my repentance and salvation. I don't want to play any longer this game of spiritual Russian roulette. I want to make my way to the mercy seat of Christ. No more half-hearted attempts at surrender but a full and complete surrender today, while my heart is still touchable and tender. In the forgiving name of Jesus, I pray. Amen.

Questions

- What is the unpardonable sin?

- Have you committed it as long as you still have spiritual desire?

- What would it take for you to commit this unforgivable sin?

Journal

> *Do not be anxious about anything, but in everything, by prayer and petition, with thanksgiving, present your requests to God. And the peace of God, which transcends all understanding, will guard your hearts and your minds in Christ Jesus. (Philippians 4:6-7)*

Meditation   *Dudley C. Rutherford*

The true Christian can always find something for which to be thankful. Let me show you four snapshots from the Bible and life.

Snapshot number one has five thousand hungry people gathered with no food. Jesus is standing in their midst and is wanting to feed them. This might have been His time to whine because He has so little with which to work. Instead of griping, He lifts up His eyes to God and offers thanks (Mark 6:41).

A second snapshot has Christ at the table with His twelve disciples. It's the Last Supper and so much seems to be going wrong. Instead of complaining, Jesus takes bread and gives thanks (Luke 22:19).

A third picture is Paul on board a ship in the midst of a 14-day storm. Every heart on board is terrified but Paul stands up, takes bread and gives thanks to God (Acts 27:35).

A fourth snapshot is a little band of pilgrims who have just come to America. During that short time, half of their families have perished. They are facing a hard New England winter with savages all around them. In spite of their hardships and bleak future, they band together and kneel in prayer to thank God for His blessings. The Christian can always find something of value from the Lord. Don't ever quit. Don't ever give up! Don't count what you don't have. Count what you still have.

Four Snapshots

Prayer

My Lord and my Savior, as I read Your Bible, I can see where I can always find something over which to be grateful. Forgive me for those many times when I have had only my own comfort in mind and had not the faith to see Your plan and will working in my life. I'm still a weak Christian, but I would like to think I'm gaining more spiritual insight that will allow me to see good in every situation of life. I ask these things in the name of my Savior, Jesus Christ. Amen.

Questions

- Can you name a situation where no thanks should be given?

- Are there some things you should be anxious over?

- Who do you turn to when you're discouraged?

Journal

■ November 2

All authority in heaven and on earth has been given to me.
(Matthew 28:18)

Now to him who is able to do immeasurably more than all we ask or imagine, according to his power that is at work within us.
(Ephesians 3:20)

Meditation   Glenn Kirby

Sometimes we feel weak, and sometimes we feel like we don't know what we should be doing. When you feel weak, remember that Jesus said all power and authority has been given to Him. Then Paul said that same power is at work within us. We may feel weak, but we need to remember we are not alone. God's power in us will give us new strength!

When we feel that we don't know what we should be doing, we must remember that God promises to give all of us wisdom when we ask for it. We don't have to feel uncertain. God wants us to know His direction and His guidance. That's why Paul told us in Romans 12, "Therefore, I urge you, brothers, in view of God's mercy, to offer your bodies as living sacrifices, holy and pleasing to God - this is your spiritual act of worship. Do not conform any longer to the pattern of this world, but be transformed by the renewing of your mind. Then you will be able to test and approve what God's will is--his good, pleasing and perfect will." When you are having difficulty distinguishing what it is that God has called you to do, go back to the basics, resubmit your life as a sacrifice to Him and read His word for the renewing of your mind. And when you read it commit it to heart and memory, soak it up and it's amazing how God's will becomes clear. That's why the hymn writer wrote, "Turn your eyes upon Jesus, look full in his wonderful face, and the things of earth grow strangely dim in light of His glory and grace!"

Glenn Kirby is the Senior Pastor of West Valley Christian Church, West Hills, CA.

Prayer

Lord, help my weakness to become Your strength, because of Your power working within me. Lord, help my uncertainties to become certain because of Your wisdom. I know that You are working in me to make me more complete. I want to be strong and certain for You. Please help me. In Jesus' name, I pray. Amen.

Questions

- What weaknesses are you dealing with right now?

- What uncertainties are you dealing with right now?

- What help has God promised you in your weaknesses and uncertainties?

Journal

November 3

Meditation   *Dudley C. Rutherford*

I've always been a slow learner. Sometimes, however, I do learn some things… usually the hard way. I don't know whether you could profit from my experiences or not. Let me state just a few of them. Being a preacher for 30 years, here are some of the basics I've discovered:

1. I can't accomplish anything overnight except a good night's sleep.

2. Thirty years ago, I wanted to get to know all the great pastors. Now my goal is to get to know Jesus far better.

3. It's a lot harder to live a good sermon than it is to preach one.

4. If I spend my time meeting other people's needs, God will send somebody to meet my needs.

5. One of life's greatest joys is to be loved by people who know all your weaknesses and still love you.

6. The great secret to living, preaching or just about anything else I can think of is prayer, prayer and more prayer.

Experience

Prayer

Dear Father, I know I can count on You. You will never leave me or forsake me. You are my helper. Forgive me for the many instances when I have thought I was on my own, and that You were somewhere far, far away. Help me to live each day, knowing that no risk is involved when I step out in faith and live for You. If my heart is right and I'm living for You, what can man do to me? Bless me, in Jesus' name. Amen.

Questions

- What lessons do you learn from the above Scripture?

- Which of these six points is something you needed to hear?

- Can you ever name a time when God wasn't by your side?

Journal

November 4

It saves you by the resurrection of Jesus Christ, who has gone into heaven and is at God's right hand—with angels, authorities and powers in submission to him. (I Peter 3:21b-22)

And if I go and prepare a place for you, I will come back and take you to be with me that you also may be where I am. (John 14:3)

Meditation   *Dudley C. Rutherford*

Going to Heaven is like going home. You see, Heaven is not primarily a place but a person. Oft times I am away from home on revivals or speaking engagements or conventions. I don't like being away from home. When I do go home, I don't walk into the house and run to the silverware drawer and pull out the silverware and say, "Oh, I have really missed you." I don't run to the drapes or the TV and say, "Oh, how I have missed you." I seek out my beloved wife and put my arms around her. She is our home. She is my home.

One of these days, when this life is over and God sees fit to take me out of this life, I will know I am home, not because I will stand on streets of gold, or because I can see the gates of pearl or a crystal sea of glass; I will know I am home because I will stand face to face with the person of Jesus Christ. Heaven is not primarily a place; it is primarily a person. I heard of an old preacher who used to say, "If I can just get a peek of Jesus, a glimpse of Jesus through a keyhole every 1,000 years, that will be Heaven for me."

Lonely For My Jesus

Prayer

Dear Lovely Lord Jesus, I look forward to going to Heaven because I shall get to see the Captain of my Salvation. I know that in Your divine presence all things will be well and good and safe. I don't deserve to be in the same place with You, but I will be grateful and inspired just to know that You are there. Thank You for going to prepare a place for me. I ask these things in the name of my eternal Savior, Jesus Christ. Amen.

Questions

- How would you explain Heaven?

- What is the first thing you'll do there?

- Who do you expect to see?

Journal

_____

_____

_____

_____

> *Now a man came up to Jesus and asked, "Teacher, what good thing must I do to get eternal life?" "Why do you ask me about what is good?" Jesus replied. "There is only One who is good. If you want to enter life, obey the commandments." "Which ones?" the man inquired. Jesus replied, "Do not murder, do not commit adultery, do not steal, do not give false testimony, honor your father and mother, and love your neighbor as yourself."*
>
> *(Matthew 19:16-19)*

Meditation   *Rick Rusaw*

Not long ago, I was in New York City along with my wife and some good friends. We decided to see the Broadway show, *Moving Out*, which has a number of Billy Joel's songs strung together in a storyline. When we purchased our tickets, we didn't realize they were for "obstructed view" seats. We could hardly see anything. About ten minutes into the show, I leaned over to Diane and said, "You know, I don't really have any interest in this. I think I'll go." When I didn't get the response I wanted, I agreed to stay for the rest of the show.

As the show ended, in walked Billy Joel to celebrate the second anniversary of the show's opening. The audience didn't know he was coming. We moved from our obstructed-view seats so we could watch him give a 15-minute performance. It was a highlight of our trip – and I would have missed it had I gotten my way earlier and left the show.

These obstructed-view seats happen to us sometimes, don't they? We want to see something but we don't get to see it. Something gets in our way. Sometimes, when we gather together, we bring a lot of stuff – the stuff going on in our lives, the things that have happened to us in the past week. Some have been good things, some bad. Sometimes, this stuff blocks our view and keeps us from seeing God, and from hearing from God.

What is Jesus saying here: "You don't want to miss what's coming, but you've got to get a different vantage point." I'm convinced that if you and I are going to see God, we've got to change seats.

Rick Rusaw is Senior Pastor of LifeBridge Christian Church in Longmont, CO.

Obstructed View

Father, our goal in life is to see you, Lord often times in a world full of clutter and chaos it is difficult to get a clear view of who You are and what Your will for our lives truly is. Father, today I ask that you allow me to get a different vantage point, so that I will be able to see Your will for my life more clearly and so that I can make a difference for Your Kingdom. In Jesus' name. Amen.

Questions

- In your everyday life, has there been a time when you are tempted to check out of what God has called you to do and leave the show early?

- How can you begin to make the seat you're in less obstructed?

- Where does your motivation come from to stay in your seat and not miss what is coming?

Journal

_____

_____

_____

_____

_____

■ November 6

Meditation   *Dudley C. Rutherford*

Death is such an important experience. You will have but one chance to die. How do you intend to approach it? Will you whine and beg? Will you try to sheepishly offer some bribe? Will you look for a place to run and hide? Will the curtain come down on a complete failure, or will you, like Paul, bring the audience to their feet with, "I have fought a good fight, I have finished my course, I have kept the faith."

You cannot decide when or where you will die, but you can decide how you will die. What will it be like when time has run out and eternity is about to begin? How will things look to you then? Will you be proud of your profanity and stagger into eternity with yet one more foul word upon your lips? Will you still be cursing the preacher, the doctor, your boss or your mother? Will you call for another round of drinks and try to laugh your way into the next world? *How will you handle the big scene*? After you've burned the candle of your life for Satan, will you then blow the smoke of a misspent life in the face of the Eternal Judge?

Death for the Christian is the supreme moment. He knows he has not believed and obeyed in vain. This is the Christian's coronation hour. It is the crucible of all his lifelong faith. Death for the sinner is a busy hour. Those last minutes are always crowded. Don't wait until all the answers have been checked, and the report cards and grades are final and have all been recorded. Prepare now; begin today to get ready for that hour.

Prayer

Dear Father, like all those who have gone before me, I know I have to die and face You. Help me to live my life, that when I come to that climactic moment, I will not be ashamed or afraid. I want to be confident in that hour. Not confident in my works but confident in Your power to keep Your Word in saving a poor lost sinner who trusted You in simple child-like faith. Help me today to prepare for tomorrow. I ask these things in the name of Jesus. Amen.

Questions

- What is the charge you are to keep?

- You should keep that charge until when?

- How many more years are you promised here on earth, before you die and stand at the Judgment?

Journal

_____

_____

_____

_____

_____

November 7

My help comes from the Lord, the Maker of heaven and earth. He will not let your foot slip— he who watches over you will not slumber; indeed, he who watches over Israel will neither slumber nor sleep. The Lord watches over you— the Lord is your shade at your right hand; the sun will not harm you by day, nor the moon by night. The Lord will keep you from all harm— he will watch over your life. (Psalm 121:2-7)

Meditation   H. Dean Rutherford

Now, that is just the kind of Lord I need. Somebody who will watch over my life and never once fall asleep. I hate to confess this, because it says something about me as much as it says about others. But I have to admit that I have some friends who have let me down. They have gone to sleep on me. Once in a while, my kids have disappointed me. My own children have gone to sleep on me. My wife, one of the great women of all time, has let me down. I must agree that I have let her down too.

And while I'm at it, I might as well admit that I have let myself down on more than one occasion. I sleep a lot. I sleep on the job. I sleep when my children are trying to tell me something. I sleep when someone who really needs me cries out for my extra time and attention. I can be a world-class sleepwalker. Okay! I'll admit it right now: I'm a sleepy Christian. But I have a God who never slumbers or sleeps. He never turns His head or diverts His attention even for a moment. He stays awake all the time. He never tires. He never yawns. In fact, while He's standing guard, I've never seen Him flinch or blink. He is just the God I need to watch over my life. I'm so glad He doesn't get tired or frustrated watching over me.

Sleepless Jesus

Prayer

Dear lovely Lord Jesus, You are just the kind of God I need. 24/7! That describes You perfectly. I am oft times fickle and forgetful. I not only sleep and slumber, but I sleep and slumber when I should be wide-awake doing Your will and way. Thank You for never sleeping. It only serves to remind me that the world, the flesh and the devil, who want my devotion, sleep all the time and care not one bit about my good, well-being or salvation. Thank You, my sleepless Jesus. In Your name, I pray. Amen.

Questions

- Name some times you have fallen asleep.

- What does that mean, He never sleeps?

- If you truly and fully serve Him, will He allow your feet to slip?

Journal

> *Peace I leave with you; my peace I give you. I do not give to you as the world gives. Do not let your hearts be troubled and do not be afraid.*
>
> *(John 14:27)*

Meditation   *Roger Storms*

It was the end of November 1996. Our 15-year-old son was slipping away in death after a five-year struggle with disease. He was an amazing young man with an indestructible attitude. He celebrated life every day. *Fun, family, friends* and *faith* filled his life. He never wanted pity – only to be treated with respect and normalcy. He accepted Jesus as his Savior and was a dedicated follower of Christ.

During a particularly bad health day, when he had been vomiting all day long, he weakly looked up from his bathroom "perch" and said, "I don't know how anyone who doesn't know Jesus could handle this!"

So on this November day, I asked my bedridden son how he was doing. He replied, "Okay." At this point, his near coma-like state usually resulted in one-word sentences. So I asked, pointing to my head, "Not up here," then pointing to my heart, "How are you doing here?" Then with eyes clearer than I had seen in weeks, and with the strong voice I hadn't heard in a while, he declared, "I'm not afraid, Dad!"

These were the last words he was ever able to speak. Within the next two weeks, he lapsed into a full coma and entered Heaven.

Life comes at us hard sometimes. Satan's greatest ploy is to fill us with fear. Jesus can take that away. I hope that you know the joy of living the *"No Fear!"* life.

Roger Storms is Senior Pastor of Chandler Christian Church in Chandler, AZ.

I'm Not Afraid, Dad

Prayer

God, sometimes I'm afraid. I fear my past creeping up and embarrassing me. I'm afraid of my future being difficult. I'm afraid of letting You down, letting others down and letting myself down. My fears often keep me from reaching out, reaching around and reaching up. Help me to know that as Your child, there is no fear when I'm holding Your hand. You'll never let me go or let me fall. Hold me closely, so I too can say every day, even on my last day, "I'm not afraid." In Jesus' name. Amen.

Questions

- What do you fear the most?

- How has fear hindered you from living the abundant life Jesus came to give you?

- What are three things you can do to live the *"No Fear!"* life?

Journal

■ November 9

Meditation   *Dudley C. Rutherford*

Someone once said the Colorado River has shown what can be done "just by keeping at it." It was the constant flow of that great river that carved out one of nature's most spectacular masterpieces. Life is not a 100-yard dash; it is rather a 26-mile marathon. Are you keeping at it? William Carey, one of the most successful missionaries the world has ever known, said these words toward the end of his life: "If after my death anyone should think it worthwhile to write about my life, I will give you a criterion by which you may judge its correctness. If that writer gives me credit for being a plodder, he will describe me justly. Anything beyond this will be total exaggeration. I can plod. That's all I can do. I can persevere in any definite pursuit. To this I owe everything."

One cannot accomplish all things by perseverance, but very little can be accomplished without it. The author of the Book of Hebrews said we should "run with perseverance the race that is set before us" (Hebrews 12:1). God doesn't usually ask us to climb some impossibly steep mountain to prove our devotion, but He does require that we live a day-by-day faithful life of devotion to Him. I would hope that someone could someday say that about me: "He was a plodder; he never quit; he never gave up; even when storms came and all seemed so futile, he plodded on."

Plodding Along

Prayer

Dear Lord in Heaven, don't keep me from discouragement or failure. Just let me be faithful through all the events of my life. Whether through the rain or the sunshine, I want to be steady. I pray that no one will ever have the right to say, "He just gave up; he quit when he should have stayed in there and fought at least one more battle." Help me to be one of those plodders that occupy such a large part of Your Church and Your Bible. I ask all this and more in the name of Jesus Christ. Amen.

Questions

- How can you live so that your labor is not in vain?

- What are some things that should shake your faith, according to Paul?

- Would you consider yourself to be a "plodder"?

Journal

November 10

Peace I leave with you; my peace I give you. I do not give to you as the world gives. Do not let your hearts be troubled and do not be afraid.

(John14:27)

And he will be called Wonderful Counselor, Mighty God, Everlasting Father, Prince of Peace. (Isaiah 9:6)

Meditation   *Dudley C. Rutherford*

Some of our popes are called "The Pontiff" or by the Latin title, "Pontifex Maximus." They acquired this name from some of the early Roman Emperors. The word "pons" means "bridge." "Maximus" means the highest or best. A practical definition for "Pontifex Maximus" would be a "supreme bridge builder." When Caesar Augustus called himself the "Pontifex Maximus," he wanted the entire world to perceive he was so powerful, charismatic, wealthy and able that he could cross any ocean, span any chasm, solve any problem or bring true and lasting peace to any conflict. The truth is, Caesar Augustus was not much of a bridge builder. He left the world in far worse shape than when he assumed office with his new title. His legacy was one of confusion and despair.

Having said all this, there really is a true Pontifex Maximus, and His name is Jesus. My Jesus can build bridges between the rich and the poor, the educated and the ignorant, the tyrant and the slave, the Jew and the Gentile. He can take down any wall. He is the only builder I know that can build a bridge out of hell that leads to Heaven. He can build you a bridge out of this world into His saving presence. Won't you invite this builder of peace into your life today, if you haven't already done so?

Prayer

Thank You, dear Lord, that You are truly the only genuine bridge builder in the world. Thank You for building a bridge over my sins, and my lostness, and the poverties of my soul. Thank You for building a bridge for me to someday get out of this world and spend all eternity with You. Help me to try and build bridges of love and invitations to my friends and acquaintances, so that they may also learn to walk this bridge of redemption. In Jesus' name, I pray. Amen.

Questions

- Does the world have a different definition of peace?

- What were some of the prophesied titles for Jesus?

- How is Jesus the real Pontifex Maximus?

Journal

_____

_____

_____

_____

_____

Teach us to number our days aright, that we may gain a heart of wisdom. (Psalm 90:12)

Meditation   *Rubel Shelly*

Although all of us sometimes manufacture problems for ourselves and others, by putting off until tomorrow what could be done today, there is another abuse of time that seems even more pervasive among people I know. That more common desecration of time is *frenzied hurry*.

One person's constant hurry becomes others' stress. The compulsion to "get it done" quickly degenerates into tasks getting priority over relationships. Then one begins to wonder about the absence of peace and joy and contentment with life.

Time is God's gift, and life is not to be abused with frantic haste. What of the spiritual value of living in the present? Playing games with your children, giving them undivided attention, paying attention to people in the midst of your busy life. Prioritize them while still meeting deadlines and being productive.

Neither frantic busy-ness nor careless inattention honors God's gift of time. Instead, we need to make God's time holy by being aware of those with whom we are sharing it.

Rubel Shelly is the Senior Minister of Woodmont Hills Church of Christ in Nashville, TN.

Prayer

Holy Father, please teach us the path of honoring You by valuing one another. Let us learn to invest our precious time where it matters the most, in Jesus' name. Forgive me, Lord, when I get wrapped up in the busy-ness of life and fail to treasure the more important things, such as family, church, friends and the invaluable Word of God. Lord, help me to live my life in such a way that it would bring glory to You. In Jesus' name. Amen.

Questions

- Which is your greater threat: procrastination or being too frantic?

- Do you owe any apologies for bulldozing anyone yesterday?

- How will you redeem at least 30 minutes today for a relationship you value?

Journal

The LORD does not look at the things man looks at. Man looks at the outward appearance, but the LORD looks at the heart. (I Samuel 16:7)

But as for you, be strong and do not give up, for your work will be rewarded. (II Chronicles 15:7)

Meditation   H. Dean Rutherford

Do we really have heroes? Yes, there are millions of them. But they are not the ones you might first consider. There are heroes on distant, forgotten battlefields, fighting for our liberties and for people they will never know. There are research workers in laboratories, feverishly working against some dread scourge of disease. There are many faithful teachers, tireless doctors and Godly preachers. There are many heroes in life. The ones that grab Heaven's headlines, though, are the ones we seldom think about. The real heroes are not the Michael Jordans, or Tiger Woodses, or the rock stars or the movie actors.

That unnoticed single woman down the street who works hard all day, every day, and gets her kids to school and church – you know, the one whose husband walked out on her? Now that's a hero. The elderly gent next door, who is now left all alone as the lengthening shadows of life creep in, but he remains faithful to his vows and his God. That, my friend, is one of God's heroes. That 80-year-old lady in the nursing home whose mind is partially gone, but she keeps trying her best to survive. Her best can't be very good, but it is good enough for God. God's heroes are those who attend the task before them and do it with little complaining. And they do it in faith, as if it were being done only for God.

Prayer

Father above and beyond all else, be glorified in my work. Thank You for my life. All of my life! All the parts I like and the parts I don't like and the parts that bore me. The mundane and the trivial parts too, Lord. Thank You for the task of living that You have set before me. May I so do my job, that others can see the beauty and faithfulness of Christ Jesus in me. In Christ's name, I pray. Amen.

Questions

- In your opinion, what makes a person a hero?

- Who are some of God's best heroes?

- Who are some people considered to be heroes that may not be heroes?

Journal

November 13

> *And if the Spirit of him who raised Jesus from the dead is living in you, he who raised Christ from the dead will also give life to your mortal bodies through his Spirit, who lives in you. (Romans 8:11)*

Meditation

At Calvary, God, in crimson garments dressed, courted and wooed our love. There, at the intersection of the ages, Christ put away sin by the sacrifice of Himself. There, God, the Father of the clouds (Job 38:28) allowed Him to thirst who came to remove the moral thirst of mankind. There, God, who clothes the valleys with corn (Psalm 65:13) and feeds the young ravens when they cry, left Him naked under the darkening sky and answered not His cry. But He died. Die, He did. No man was ever deader. But there came a day when Jesus resumed His power and regained His influence, and reasserted His sacred grandeur. He "arose a victor from the dark domain, up from the grave He arose!"

Oh, dear heart, be not hard to convince, nor slow of heart to believe. Be not stubborn of will, nor foolish of mind. Let not your heart be so set upon this world and its deceptive charms that you have no eyes or ears for the world to come. Live no longer in the uncertainty of delayed decisions. Look unto Christ on the cross, crucified for your sins. Look unto Christ raised from the dead for your justification. Yes, look and live! "Believe on the Lord Jesus Christ and all that it implies and you shall be saved." Don't shy away from the truth by telling yourself, "It's all too complicated for me." Believe Him and trust Him today, in child-like faith.

Prayer

Remind me, Father, that my home is not in this world but in Your eternity with You. I love and thank You that in reality, I am already a citizen and an inhabitant of Your eternal world. Thank You for proving to me that You have power over death, hell and sin which gives me strength to overcome all the obstacles that Satan puts before me. I place anew my complete trust and future in Your strong hands. In Christ Jesus, I pray. Amen.

Questions

- What powers did Christ defeat?

- Is there a sense in which you are already living in eternity?

- How does Jesus give you victory?

Journal

> *Here I am! I stand at the door and knock. If anyone hears my voice and opens the door, I will come in and eat with him, and he with me.*
>
> *(Revelation 3:20)*

Meditation   *Rusty George*

When my wife and I first moved to California, we decided to rent a house rather than buy. We found a wonderful house owned and managed by a lovely couple that lived down the street. This was their only rental and it was also their retirement investment. So, the house was very precious to them.

At Christmas-time my wife and I thought it would be good to invite this couple over for dinner, and tell them thanks once again. Our house was decorated, candles were lit and soon the doorbell rang. We greeted each other, we exchanged hugs, gifts, and we sat down in the living room before the meal.

I then noticed one of the Christmas candles I lit had spilled over the side, and hot red wax was pouring down the white fireplace and hearth. I was mortified, thinking of how I was staining this man's fireplace right before his eyes! So I ran over and sat down in the wax, covering it up. While sitting there dealing with second-degree burns, I played through my mind how he might react: "How could you be so careless?" or "There goes your deposit!" Every vision in my head was an unhappy landlord letting me have it.

I think we have that expectation when we pray sometimes. We are afraid to approach God, because of the mess we've made of the life He's entrusted to us. But did you notice what He says in this verse? He stands at the door and knocks. If we invite Him in, He says He will come in to eat and reside with us.

Imagine if my landlord had walked over to me, put his arm around me and said, "I see the wax. We'll deal with the cleanup later. In fact, I'll help you fix it. But for now, let's eat!" I think that's exactly what God says to us.

Rusty George is Senior Pastor of Real Life Church in Santa Clarita, CA.

Knock, Knock, Knock

Father, I want to invite You in to eat. I'm honored You are knocking. I'm honored You don't force Your way in. I'm honored You want to spend time with me. I confess to You my preoccupation with all the messes I've made in my life. But I recognize that we'll deal with that later. Right now, in these moments, I want to be just with You. I want to hear Your words and know that You hear mine. Thanks for dining with me. In Jesus' name. Amen.

Questions

- What is Jesus saying to you over dinner?

- Which words from the Bible is He telling you?

- What do you want to tell Jesus, knowing you have His undivided attention?

Journal

■ November 15

Meditation   Dudley C. Rutherford

How close are you to Jesus? How close are you supposed to be? The difference between Christianity and all the other religions is that we are to have a living, personal relationship with Jesus. I never get over the metaphor and analogies that Jesus uses to describe how we are joined together with Him and with each other. In John 15, Jesus says He is the vine and we are the branches – how close is that? In I Corinthians 12, Jesus is the head of the body and we are the members. In Ephesians 5, Jesus is the bridegroom and we are the bride. How close should that be?

Nearly every time Jesus speaks, He has something to say about His Church and His people as a loving, close, harmonious, caring, bonding relationship. Jesus said, "By this all men shall know that you are My disciples, that you have love for one another." I would like to suggest that you read these several passages on unity and love that I have given you. We are supposed to be very close with Jesus and very close with our brothers and sisters in Christ.

Prayer

Dear wonderful Friend and Savior, I sometimes forget that loving You and worshiping You is not enough. I know as I read these Scriptures that I am to have a personal relationship with You. I am supposed to walk each hour of each day hand in hand with You. You are not just someone for me to cry out for when I am in trouble, but You and I are supposed to be best friends. I know any failure is on my shoulders, not Yours. Help me to be Your close friend. In Christ's name, I ask. Amen.

Questions

- According to Paul, what clothes should you wear?

- What does Paul say your most important garment should be?

- What are some Biblical metaphors describing your relationship with Christ?

Journal

■ November 16

Not long after that, the younger son got together all he had, set off for a distant country and there squandered his wealth in wild living.

(Luke 15:13)

Meditation   *Dudley C. Rutherford*

Emerson said the story of the prodigal son is the greatest story in or out of the Bible. There is a phrase in that haunting parable which Jesus taught that has always caught my attention. It says the young man went into a far country or a distant country. Years ago, I used to think the far country was some place out in the Western United States at the turn of the last century; a place where bawdy outlaws roamed and dust was a foot deep in the streets. Later, I thought the far country might just be a place Kipling describes as "where the trails run out into the deep and stop." But I have learned the deeper meaning. The far country is anywhere and anytime a person walks away from God.

I've had businessmen come into my office and make a wrong decision, and as they left my office, I knew in my heart they were walking into a far country. I've seen people walk out of church refusing to submit to God, and I well knew they were walking into a distant country. A far country is anywhere a person makes a move or decision that takes them away from God. The far country might only be a step or two, but once that journey begins, it may take years to come back home. I've learned that the far country is anytime a person travels outside the will of God.

Prayer

Dear God in Heaven, I want to be near You. I want to feel the nearness of Your presence. Don't ever let me slip or slide into that distant country. I know in my more serious moments that every step away from You is a step away from happiness and hope and salvation. I know I need to fly dead-reckoning back to Your side and stop flirting with the world and its alluring calls. Keep me out of that far country, I pray in Jesus' name. Amen.

Questions

- Where is the distant country for you?

- What temptations are you facing today?

- How willing are you to start back home today?

Journal

> *Pray that out of his glorious riches he may strengthen you with power through his Spirit in your inner being, so that Christ may dwell in your hearts through faith. (Ephesians 3:16-17a)*

Meditation   *Shan Rutherford*

On a Friday in March 2005, Brian Nichols was on trial for rape and confinement in Atlanta, Georgia. He took a gun from a corrections officer and shot three people to death in a matter of seconds, including a judge, a court reporter and a deputy officer. He fled the 7th floor and made his way to the parking garage. Stealing a car, he fled. A massive search began all over the Atlanta area and state of Georgia. Later that day, he stole a truck and murdered a customs official in his yard. That evening, he waited in the parking area of an apartment complex, where he forced 26-year-old Ashley Smith by gunpoint into her apartment.

This young widow and mother was bound hand and foot and placed in her bathtub. After a few hours, she was released. She asked Brian if she could read. He agreed, and she went to her bedroom and got the Bible and the *Purpose Driven Life* by Rick Warren. She read to him, told him it was a miracle to have escaped the courthouse, and that perhaps God had a purpose for him to share the Bible in prison. After seven hours, he released her. Some said God was in that apartment. Some questioned why God was not in the courthouse. Rush Limbaugh observed that God isn't necessarily in places, but in people, and God was in Ashley Smith!

Shan Rutherford is Senior Pastor of Greenwood Christian Church in Greenwood, IN. and the uncle of Dudley C. Rutherford.

Where Is God?

Prayer

Almighty God and Father, I need You in my life each day to be the person You want me to be. I want to be ready, like Ashley Smith, for whatever comes into my life. Help me, Father, to open my heart and mind to You today and be the witness You want me to be. I know there are many people who are lost, and they need to see Jesus in me. In Jesus' name, I pray. Amen.

Questions

- Does Christ dwell in your heart though faith?

- Would you be ready to witness to a person as Ashley Smith did?

- Have you given much thought to why God placed you on earth?

Journal

So he got up and went to his father. But while he was still a long way off, his father saw him and was filled with compassion for him; he ran to his son, threw his arms around him and kissed him. (Luke 15:20)

Meditation   *Dudley C. Rutherford*

Most of you remember that story of the prodigal son. The boy took his dad's money and went into a far country and wasted his life, and devoured his living with harlots, but in that hog pen of stinking manure he came to his senses and said, "I will arise and go to my father." So he arose and headed home. Meanwhile, back home the dad sat there on the front porch looking for that boy. And when Dad saw him coming down that dusty road, he ran to meet him. Old age loses pain and feebleness when sons are coming home.

This is the only picture we have in the Bible of God running. The servants hear the commotion and they come running down the road toward this scene of compassion. But dad says, "Stop, turn around, go prepare the fatted calf for a feast, bring me a new robe for my returned son, and bring him a royal ring for his finger. For my son which was lost has come home."

You see, this is a story not so much about the son as it is about the father. It's the father in this story who is the great lover. I know some of you are saying, "Well preacher, I've sinned so much, for so long, God could never forgive me. God knows I'm such a pretender and sinner, the Father could never forgive me." He not only can forgive you, He will run and fall on you and hug you and kiss you before you can get the words of confession out of your mouth.

Prayer

Dear Lord, I know You are the world's greatest lover and forgiver. I have always known that You will meet me more than halfway. Help me today to say goodbye to that far country and head back home to the Father's mansion and His open arms and warm kisses. I can almost hear Your footsteps as You race toward me with a smile of love and forgiveness. In Jesus' name, I pray. Amen.

Questions

- What emotion does God have for returning sinners?

- What kind of a speech will you have to make if you return?

- Is this story more about the son or the father? Why?

Journal

> *In a flash, in the twinkling of an eye, at the last trumpet. For the trumpet will sound, the dead will be raised imperishable, and we will be changed. For the perishable must clothe itself with the imperishable, and the mortal with immortality. (I Corinthians 15:52-53)*

Meditation   *Dudley C. Rutherford*

Said the brave doctor to the pensive parents: "Your precious daughter is desperately ill. We have done all we can do. There is no cure. I'm afraid there isn't much time left." After a few days of serious soul-searching, the parents decided they should tell their daughter she was going to die. "After all," they reasoned, "she is ten years of age. She became a Christian and was baptized when she was seven and she possesses a great faith."

On a late afternoon, as she lay in her bed looking out her window and realizing that things were so terribly wrong, the suffering father sat beside her and held her hand. He said: "Honey I need to talk to you about something that is very, very difficult for me to discuss with you. Honey, we have prayed and prayed and prayed for God to heal you, but it must be that He wants to take you to Heaven to be with Him." The young girl, with a heart full of faith, courageously asked, "Daddy, what do you think death will be like?" The dad cleared his throat and said to her, "Oh darling, it will be easy and so exciting. God will simply and quietly send a happy train to get you and take you to Heaven where He lives with all His angels." Then the girl asked with depth of soul, "Daddy, do you think Jesus will be there to meet me?" "Oh yes, He will. I know He will. And what's more, Mom and Dad will soon be there on the very next train."

The Next Train

Prayer

Remind me, Heavenly Father, that this old world is not my home; I'm just passing through. I am aware and grateful for the fact that I am not only going to some day be in Heaven with You, but that I am already a citizen, an inhabitant of Your eternal world. Your great grace amazes me and prompts me to do my best to live for You and to tell others about You. I know You'll be there to meet and greet me. In Jesus' name, I pray. Amen.

Questions

- What will happen when the trumpet sounds?

- Your perishable body must be transformed into what?

- In what sense are you already an inhabitant of Heaven?

Journal

> *Then the Israelites, all the people, went up to Bethel, and there they sat weeping before the Lord. They fasted that day until evening and presented burnt offerings and fellowship offerings to the Lord. And the Israelites inquired of the Lord. They asked, "Shall we go up again to battle with Benjamin our brother, or not?" The Lord responded, "Go, for tomorrow I will give them into your hands." (Judges 20:26-28)*

Meditation   *Shane Womack*

Have you ever felt like giving up on the battle? Have you ever lost a battle God wanted you to fight? Such was the case of the Israelites in the midst of a bloody civil war.

God had clearly instructed the ten tribes of Israel ("sons of Israel") to attack the tribe of Benjamin for tolerating homosexuality (see Judges 19, 20:1-18). The sons of Israel should have easily defeated Benjamin, in that they outnumbered them 400,000 to 26,000. However, Benjamin prevailed mightily in the first two skirmishes. In fact, Benjamin killed 40,000 of the sons of Israel in those two battles. Devastated and confused, the sons of Israel asked God whether they should even try for a third time. This time, however, the Israelites fasted that day until evening (verse 26) and also held a worship service. When God saw the fasting and worship, He promised them a victory and deliverance the next day.

Sometimes, God grants victory if we fast and worship. I recall a man named Brad, whose unbelieving wife was stubborn to the Gospel. We assigned prayer coverage to Brad for his wife's salvation for a month, to no avail. Finally, our men's group fasted seven days for Sandra's salvation. On the seventh day, Brad had a conversation with his wife about Christ. She started reading, praying and attending church. Sandra gave her life to Christ.

Shane Womack is Senior Pastor of Knott Avenue Christian Church in Anaheim, CA.

The Good Fight

God, help me to fight the good fight without giving up. Help me to be a prayer warrior even if things aren't going very well. I believe You are all-powerful and sovereign. Grant me victory as I fast and worship. Even though the enemy has prevailed, I ask that You grant deliverance by tomorrow. Forgive me for questioning You on whether or not I should surrender and give up. Show Yourself strong and bare Your mighty arm today. In Jesus' name, I pray. Amen.

Questions

- What spiritual battle are you fighting but not winning?

- Would you consider fasting and worshiping before the Lord until you receive the deliverance and breakthrough you desire?

- Who are the lost souls, lost neighbors, lost countries, lost relatives, etc., you might be willing to "fast and pray" into salvation?

Journal

_____

_____

_____

_____

■ November 21

For physical training is of some value, but godliness has value for all things, holding promise for both the present life and the life to come. This is a trustworthy saying that deserves full acceptance. (I Timothy 4:8-9)

Meditation   *Dudley C. Rutherford*

How many of you have ever been tempted by God in the best sense? Have you ever been tempted to be a missionary? Have you ever been working at a job and felt the call to go into the ministry or some form of specialized Christian service?

Is there someone now reading this who has been content to be a lukewarm, mediocre Christian, and have felt the call to live a sold-out, totally dedicated life for our precious Lord? Is there anybody listening who will bet their life on God? If Christianity is anything, it is not a call to *play it safe*!

When I was a boy, every weekday evening a television show came on called *Star Trek*. I loved to hear the show begin. The starship Enterprise was being launched into outer space, and with some great background music, a voice would resonate, "To boldly go where no man has gone before!" The thing that worries me about our generation is that we are content to go only where everyone has always gone.

We all want to live in a gated community, drive a BMW and have a Jacuzzi. And yet, all the time God is saying, "Why don't you bet your life on Me? Why don't you step out and make some commitment that will take you out of your comfort zone? Why not start tithing or go soul-winning or make a ministry of visiting and helping the lost, the un-churched, the sick and the dying?" Will you step out in faith today?

Prayer

Dear Lord, I'm tired of being cautious when it comes to You and Your great purpose. I want to step out in faith and attempt something big for You today. Please enable me to think of the correct cross I should pick up and begin to carry for You. I'm spiritually tired of walking the same old safe, easy pathway. It does nothing for You and little for me. I want to bet my life on You this day. In Christ's name, I pray. Amen.

Questions

- Compare physical exercise versus spiritual exercise.

- When was the last time you were tempted in the good sense?

- What do you think it would take to get you out of your comfort zone?

Journal

_____

_____

_____

_____

_____

> *But he gives us more grace. That is why Scripture says: "God opposes the proud but gives grace to the humble." Submit yourselves, then, to God. Resist the devil, and he will flee from you. Come near to God and he will come near to you. Wash your hands, you sinners, and purify your hearts, you double-minded. (James 4:6-8)*

Meditation   *Dudley C. Rutherford*

There is an old legend about St. Peter escorting a man down the street of his hometown, and opening his eyes to things that were before invisible. They passed by a modern, liberal church, and one old devil was perched asleep high on the church roof. Later, they walked by a house in which an elderly lady was in her closet and on her knees in prayer. The roof of that house had a hundred demons on top, sweating and breathing deep. The man asked St. Peter, "Why did that church we walked by only have one demon watching it while that lady's house had a hundred demons?" St. Peter replied, "Well, it only takes one devil to watch over a backsliding, worldly congregation. But when that woman got on her knees, that roof wasn't large enough to hold all the demons needed."

If we are intent on doing wrong or doing nothing, we probably won't get much attack or attention from Satan. But once we get serious about living "all out" for Jesus, Satan will attack, attack and attack again. However, once Satan can plainly see we aren't going to heed him and go back into the world, he will leave us and go to someone else, where he thinks he can do some good. Or should I say "bad"?

An Old Legend

Prayer

Dear God of my life, help me to live such a holy life for You, that old Satan himself can see there is simply no chance of my turning back, and that he will soon get discouraged by my faith and go away. Help me from this day forward to so resist the devil, to have faith and love so strong that he will flee from me, allowing me to have a more consecrated walk. I pray in the strong name of Jesus. Amen.

Questions

- How do you get Satan to leave you alone?

- Why does Satan keep trying to get you?

- What are some keys to having victory over the things of this world?

Journal

> *No one has ever seen God, but God the One and Only, who is at the Father's side, has made him known. (John 1:18)*
>
> *Jesus answered: "Don't you know me, Philip, even after I have been among you such a long time? Anyone who has seen me has seen the Father. How can you say, 'Show us the Father?'" (John 14:9)*

Meditation   *Steve Moore*

Baby boomers may remember the childhood television show, *Romper Room*. As a closing ritual to each edition, the host would look into a mirror and call out names: "I see Billy, and Susie. I see Linda, and Johnny." But the host could not actually see the children who were watching the television program. It was merely an idea. John, the apostle, rightly clarifies that no human can see the total God in physical form. God's appearance is an idea.

Yet Jesus asserts to His friend, Philip, that God could be seen if one watched the living of Jesus. Jesus apparently meant we humans could see the attributes, character and nature of God through the actions of Jesus. The claim that Jesus made to Philip is the claim God wishes every disciple would make to his family, friends and neighbors: "He who has seen me has seen the Father." This is not to be a boastful claim, but rather a claim that takes seriously the human challenge. Those of us who have "been so long with" Jesus have the privilege of integrating the attributes of God into human flesh.

Steve Moore is Senior Pastor of Cherry Lane Christian Church in Meridian, ID.

Romper Room

Prayer

Holy yet gracious Father, forgive me for the days I settle for Satan's lie that I am "only human." Remind me all day long that I know You, I have been with You and You can be seen in my human life. It is a privilege to know Your nature, and I am honored that You have confidence in me to demonstrate Your appearance in my world. Fill my life with Your qualities, so that my neighbors will know Your glory. In Jesus' name. Amen.

Questions

- What would happen if the total God were reduced to someone the human eye could behold?

- What qualities of God would you like the world to see through you?

- Explain the privilege you feel it is to display to the world what God "looks like."

Journal

_____

_____

_____

_____

"My son," the father said, "you are always with me, and everything I have is yours. But we had to celebrate and be glad, because this brother of yours was dead and is alive again; he was lost and is found."

(Luke 15:31-32)

Meditation   *Dudley C. Rutherford*

It's a terrible thing to be lost. I have been lost in many ways. I have been intellectually lost, as I have gone off on some tangent and chased some foolish idea, only to become more confused. I have been morally lost. Some temptation hits me and I am tripped up to the place that I stumble, and then one sin leads to another and I find myself down to the level of the swine. I have been geographically lost. I was sure I knew where to find a particular address or the location of my misplaced car keys. But the greatest loss is spiritual loss… and a greater loss than that is to be lost and know you are lost.

The prodigal son was lost in all these ways and more. Do you know what his greatest sin was? It wasn't the fact that he had wasted his father's money or that he had run from responsibility. It wasn't his drunkenness or carelessness. His primary sin, his greatest sin, was that he broke the relationship with his old dad. Every wrong he did was but the trampling of his father's love. By breaking the relationship with his father, he had committed the matrix sin from which all others were born. The essential curse of every trip into a far country is separation from God.

Prayer

Dear wonderful, patient, forgiving God, how I thank You for Your earnest patience in waiting for me to come home. The one sin I don't ever want to commit is that chief sin of breaking away from Your strong loving arms. Help me to know that our relationship can only be broken by me and my unwillingness to forsake my old ways and start for the Father's mansions and the Father's open arms. I ask these things in Christ's name. Amen.

Questions

- What are some different ways to be lost?

- What is the worst state of being lost?

- What is the best way to return home, spiritually speaking?

Journal

_____

_____

_____

_____

■ November 25

Make sure that nobody pays back wrong for wrong, but always try to be kind to each other and to everyone else. Be joyful always; pray continually; give thanks in all circumstances, for this is God's will for you in Christ Jesus. (I Thessalonians 5:15-18)

Meditation   *Dudley C. Rutherford*

I read about a man in the Wall Street district of New York who was walking into his office building one morning. As he walked by, he noticed a young girl on a pay phone. He proceeded to go on upstairs. He looked out an hour later and she was still on the phone. Rather curious, he went to lunch and couldn't help but notice she was still on the phone. An hour later, he came back from lunch. Still she was talking on the phone. By now he couldn't get any work done; he just stared out the window at what seemed to be the world's longest phone conversation.

At four in the afternoon, he just stomped down there and waited for her to get off the phone. Finally! She hung up and came out! He said to her, "Young lady, forgive me; I know it isn't any of my business, but who in this world have you been talking to so long?" "My boyfriend," was her casual reply. "But how could you talk to anyone for seven hours?" "It was easy. In fact, I'm going home now and we are going to talk some more."

Oh, dear heart, how long has it been since we had a half-hour conversation with our eternal lover, Jesus Christ? A great wise man said, "You can't keep praying and sinning at the same time. You'll soon give one of them up, but not both!" Let's give up sinning and start praying continuously.

Prayer

Dear wonderful Savior, I want to contact my Lord and stay on a more intimate basis. I flirt with the world far too often, thinking that Your love will overcome my indifference. I come back to Your throne again today to start a new life of devotion and Bible study. If I can spend time talking with friends and strangers, I can surely find time to talk with the One who purchased my sins at Calvary. Thank You for Your command to pray continually. In the name of My Lord Jesus, I pray. Amen.

Questions

- How often should you pray?

- Under what circumstances should you give thanks?

- Why do you think you can't keep sinning and praying at the same time?

Journal

_____

_____

_____

_____

_____

> *Finally, brothers, whatever is true, whatever is noble, whatever is right, whatever is pure, whatever is lovely, whatever is admirable—if anything is excellent or praiseworthy—think about such things. (Philippians 4:8)*

Meditation   *Kaylene Idleman*

While parked in my car, I overheard a young woman – very distraught – crying to her husband about the "fender bender" she just had. It was the third one in less than a year. Pretty much spoils the day! She probably thought, "I should have taken a different route." "It wasn't all my fault." "Life isn't fair." We've all been consumed with thoughts of gloom and doom. Much of our focus is on occurrences that come and go. Other times, serious, life-changing, mind-boggling thoughts call for constant attention.

The discipline of controlling our thoughts is so worth our time and effort. The first challenge is to answer, "What am I thinking right now?" We often don't realize how much mental energy we are spending on one or two dominating concerns. They drain us of our joy. They can cause us to be depressed, anxious and negative. Except for the times such a focus is productive, choose to dwell on things that are "excellent or praiseworthy."

Once you realize what is consuming your thoughts, deliberately replace a thought by 1. Quoting a Scripture or, 2. Offering a prayer, giving that area of your life to God to bless, to use or to heal. You have thereby removed the debilitating thought; instead, you are continually filling your mind with the Word of God or with laying it before the Lord.

Kaylene Idleman is the wife of Ken Idleman, Chancellor of Ozark Christian College in Joplin, MO.

Thought Life

Prayer

Father, may my mind and my heart be filled with Your word. Make me over again today, that I may think Your thoughts and follow Your ways. I give You the worries and cares of this world and ask You to fill me with Your peace and joy. May You be honored through it all. Amen.

Questions

- What concerns are consuming your mind today?

- What Scripture verses answer or assure you in these areas?

- Are you willing to take on the discipline of controlling your thoughts?

Journal

_____

_____

_____

_____

_____

November 27

> *Children, obey your parents in everything, for this pleases the Lord. Fathers, do not embitter your children, or they will become discouraged.*
> *(Colossians 3:20-21)*

Meditation   *Dudley C. Rutherford*

This is for dads. You moms are free to read this but it really is intended for fathers. I remember when I started preaching, there was a time when I heard my dad and others say, "Dudley, when you start having kids, when you get a family of your own, you will be a much better preacher." I thought, "How ridiculous. What does having children have to do with being a good preacher? What do these old 'fuddie duddies' know about preaching? Besides, Pop's got more kids than he can count and he's no Billy Graham yet!"

I didn't understand then but I understand now. I never did realize, I never did know the love of God until I became a father myself, until my heart reached out to my own precious children. I learned that when my children do wrong, really bad things, I am at a loss. I have not many options. I can talk with them and pray with them and of course forgive them.

It is so true! Children can teach a preacher a lot about the love of God. I have some understanding how God is put on the spot when I sin and why He is so committed to dealing with me. I also have a better understanding about God's ability to love and forgive at the same time.

Prayer

Thank You, dear Lord, for giving to me my precious children. They teach me something every day about my difficulties in dealing with waywardness and disobedience. Every day, I learn how to love and teach and forgive. Help me to be stern when I should be, and super-forgiving when that need arrives. Thank You for Your love and patience in dealing with me. May I be able to pass Your love on to others. In Jesus' name, I pray. Amen.

Questions

- What do children teach you about God and how He deals with you?

- When children do wrong, what should your response be?

- How should a parent punish a child when he or she does wrong?

Journal

■ November 28

O Lord, you have searched me and you know me. You know when I sit and when I rise; you perceive my thoughts from afar. You discern my going out and my lying down; you are familiar with all my ways. (Psalm 139:1-3)

Meditation   *Dudley C. Rutherford*

These Psalms of David's repentance (51 & 139) are spectacular. For example, David writes, "Lord, You know every time I sit down. And You know every time I stand up."

Once, I was knocking and the woman of the house came to the door. I guess she figured that since I was a preacher, I was against smoking. So as she talked to me, she held her hands in back of her. She did hide the cigarette but she couldn't hide the smoke. From where I was standing, it looked like her head was on fire. I felt like Moses standing before the burning bush. She didn't hide the cigarette, and the truth is we can hide nothing from God.

The New Testament tells us that Jesus marks the fall of every sparrow. Does anybody know what the sparrow population is? Yet God attends every sparrow's funeral. Does anybody know the combined number of hairs on the heads of those who live in your city? Our Lord knows. Talk about knowing everything! In this wonderful chapter, David says, "Where can I go from Your Spirit? Where can I flee from Your presence? If I go up to the heavens, You are there; if I make my bed in the depths, You are there." David says, "Lord, I don't want to get away from You, but even if I did, where could I ever go that Your Spirit cannot follow?"

Prayer

Dear all-knowing Father, I am amazed at Your care and Your perfect knowledge. You know the number of hairs on my head and You read my every thought. Help me to so live that I won't have to come to the end of the way with remorse and regret. Knowing I can hide nothing from You makes me want to come clean and be ever honest with You and myself. If I will only come clean, Your Word promises (I John 1:9) that You will forgive me. In the Master's name, I pray. Amen.

Questions

- Is there anything God doesn't know about you?

- Where can you go to get away from God?

- How would you define repentance?

Journal

_____

_____

_____

_____

_____

Therefore, there is now no condemnation for those who are in Christ Jesus, because through Christ Jesus the law of the Spirit of life set me free from the law of sin and death. (Romans 8:1, 2)

Meditation   *Tim Winters*

Growing up on a farm in mid-western Illinois, I always looked forward to crop season. It was a time filled with working alongside my dad after school and on weekends preparing the soil, planting the seed and caring for the corn crop. A very important part of that process involved cultivating the crop to keep weeds from growing between the rows. Many an evening and Saturday were spent sitting on a John Deere tractor, listening to country music as I drove up and down fields for hours, pulling an eight-row cultivator behind the tractor. Since it was an eight-row cultivator, if you got off the row, you would eliminate eight rows of corn at a time.

My dad taught me that the surest way to stay on a row was to focus straight ahead while driving the tractor. However, regardless of my dad's advice, I was always tempted to look behind me to make sure everything was okay. Without fail, every time I looked back, I would get off-track and wipe out endless rows of corn. For the rest of the summer, as we watched the crop grow, I could look at big empty places in the field and remember that is where I did not focus straight ahead, but instead turned to look back at what was behind. Oftentimes today, I find myself doing the same thing in my Christian walk. I find myself tempted to not look straight ahead and stay focused on the fact that I am "in Christ," and instead to turn around and look back… which gets me off-track every time.

Tim Winters is Executive Pastor of Shepherd of the Hills Church, Porter Ranch, CA.

Plowing and Cultivating

Prayer

Today, God, my desire is to stay focused straight ahead, focused entirely on bringing glory to Your name in whatever I do. Wherever I go, to whomever I speak in any and all encounters today, may I bring glory to You, God. Bless me with the strength and determination to stay focused straight ahead, even when I am tempted to look back and be pulled off-track. Help me to live and to focus on the now and how I can serve You and Your people today. In Jesus' name. Amen

Questions

- What are some things in your life that tend to cause you to look back, rather than to stay focused ahead?

- What are some warning signs you have missed in the past that would indicate you are getting off-track?

- What does the phrase "in Christ" mean to you, and how can you keep that foremost in your mind?

Journal

_____

_____

_____

_____

_____

■ November 30

Do not worship any other god, for the Lord, whose name is Jealous, is a jealous God. Do not make cast idols. Redeem the firstborn donkey with a lamb, but if you do not redeem it, break its neck. Redeem all your firstborn sons. No one is to appear before me empty-handed.
(Exodus 34:14, 17, 20)

Meditation   *Dudley C. Rutherford*

This marvelous passage teaches us that God is jealous over the misuse of time, talent and money. He is jealous of our time. We have 168 hours a week to live. The richest man in America doesn't have a second more. I know God must say, "He spends 20 hours a week watching television, 40 hours at work, and two hours at most in My house with My people. Why won't they spend more time in My Word, more time on their knees, more time trying to reach someone in My name?"

These verses also say that God is jealous of our talent. I think God says, "Those young people sing worldly songs; why won't they sing songs about Me? They sing in the school choir; why won't they sing in the church choir?" I think God looks at businessmen and says, "They go to work and wheel and deal, make executive decisions, write large checks. At work, they think big and act big. Then they turn around and come to church and exercise extreme caution. They have talent and creativity, and yet they come to church and ride the brakes." Then God says, "I wish they would support My Kingdom financially. Most of what I give them, they won't give back. They can't give back sunshine, air or water. The little they can give back, a portion of their money, they won't even do that. Even after I have promised to repay them, to take their gift and bless it and multiply it, they still won't give."

Jealous

Prayer

Dear God, I had forgotten that Your name was Jealous. I get so wrapped up in what I am doing, where I am going and what I think I need, that I often fail to think of Your broken heart over me. Give me the grace to sit down and figure out how much of my time, talent and money belongs to You. Forgive me for keeping so much of what You have given me. I want You to be proud of me, not jealous of me. Thank You for Your deep love. In Christ's name, I pray. Amen.

Questions

- What does it mean to you that God is a "jealous" God?

- What are some specific things over which God is jealous?

- Many things you can't give Him. What *can* you give Him?

Journal

_____

_____

_____

_____

December 1

Out of his mouth comes a sharp sword with which to strike down the nations. "He will rule them with an iron scepter." He treads the winepress of the fury of the wrath of God Almighty. On his robe and on his thigh he has this name written: KING OF KINGS AND LORD OF LORDS.

(Revelation 19:15-16)

Meditation

There never was another who was a human child as well as a divine Son. There never was another who in Heaven had no Heavenly mother, and on earth had no earthly father; who was wounded by Satan and yet crushed Satan. There never was another who was divinely appointed the Savior of men and yet was crucified by men. There never was another who was the judge of men, yet was led as a felon and criminal from one tribunal to another. There never was another who was killed, dead and buried, and yet lived. There never was another who was born 2,000 years after Abraham and yet said, "Before Abraham was, I am." There never was another who saved others, yet He could not save Himself. There never was another who had no sin in Him, but had all sin on Him. There never was another who was the King of all kings and the King of all glory, yet wore no crown except a crown of thorns.

No other had been like Him and no other will ever be like Him, for He stands alone, august and supreme. He is the paragon of all virtue, knowledge, power and love. He truly is the King of all kings and the Lord of all lords.

There Never Was Another

Prayer

Dear lovely Lord Jesus, I forget how wonderful and powerful and perfect You are. I get so careless in my daily living that sometimes I forget that I do belong to the King of all kings. Let me, one more time, praise the name that is above every name. Your sovereignty and Lordship are all I need, and may I never take my eyes or focus off You. In that name, the name of Christ, I pray. Amen.

Questions

- Who is the King of all kings?

- Has any great person ever approached Him in greatness?

- Should the realization of this truth weaken your faith or give it more strength?

Journal

■ December 2

"Lord, if it's you," Peter replied, "tell me to come to you on the water."
"Come," he said. Then Peter got down out of the boat, walked on the
water and came toward Jesus. (Matthew 14:28-29)

Meditation   *Dudley C. Rutherford*

I know you might not agree with me on this, but hear me out. There are times
when I wish I had faith like that. I think we need some more recklessness. We
need to simply believe God and step out in faith. I think as individuals and as a
Church, we need to be bolder. We need to attempt the impossible. Sometime,
somewhere we need to get out of the boat. I confess, I get a little weary of
feeling like I'm in the boat all the time.

Remember when Gideon took only 300 men to defeat an army of 135,000
Midianites? I think somewhere in that battle, there was a tingle up his spine.
His heart was beating fast, and some sweat drops were falling from his forehead.
I think he was saying, "I may die, but this is worth the risk!"

Remember when Peter and John were put in jail and beaten so many times when
the Church was new? I honestly think they said something like this: "Man, we're
bleeding and hurting, but this is living! This is excitement! This is what life is
all about. We're laying our necks on the line. We are risking everything!"

Prayer

Lord Jesus, I'm tired of never attempting anything very big in Your name. I know You're the same God that has given victory to so many others, and I ask You to give me victory too. Help me today to set a goal, a big goal for You, and with Your help to reach that goal. I want out of the boat. I want to walk on water. I want to be used by You. I want to do something that can only be explained by Your power. I pray earnestly in Christ's name. Amen.

Questions

- What does "getting out of the boat" mean?

- Why have you never attempted anything big for the Lord?

- Will you pray to be used by God in a mighty way?

Journal

This is what he showed me: The Lord was standing by a wall that had been built true to plumb, with a plumb line in his hand. And the LORD asked me, "What do you see, Amos?" "A plumb line," I replied. Then the Lord said, "Look, I am setting a plumb line among my people Israel; I will spare them no longer. The high places of Isaac will be destroyed and the sanctuaries of Israel will be ruined; with my sword I will rise against the house of Jeroboam."

(Amos 7:7-9)

Meditation   *Mont Mitchell*

Several years back, as our new church was experiencing growth, we began the process of preparing for our first permanent Ministry Center facility. Our church plant had been meeting in a local elementary school, and we were thrilled with the prospect of soon being in "our own place." During this process, a well-intentioned individual suggested we could save a great deal of money if we tried to do some of the work ourselves. We agreed to tackle the building of the interior walls of the facility. Looking back, I'm not sure it was that great of a decision. But I have to admit, I learned a great deal. One of the things I learned was the necessity of the walls being straight, true and plumb. Without this precision, everything else could potentially be off. Doors might not hang right, windows could be off and even ceiling grids might be affected. Each day that I assisted in the process, I was intrigued by one of our guys who had a plumb line.

The plumb line is a simple and basic builder's tool. A weight is attached to a line that is held against a wall to measure its vertical trueness. In eighth-century Israel, skilled builders constructed walls as they do today and used a plumb line to ensure their accuracy. But when God measured the morality of Israel's society, it was shown to be so far from true that the whole construction had to be torn down. I often wonder, as God looks at our world today, how far off might we be from His "plumb?" And then I ask you, "If God measured the morality of your life, how true are you?"

Mont Mitchell is the Senior Pastor of Westbrook Christian Church in Bolingbrook, IL.

Plumb Line

Prayer

Dear Father, thank You so much for giving us a straight direction in which to head. In a world built on foundations of shifting sand, may we construct our lives with Your eternal plumb line and build in trueness! May I immerse myself in the truth found in the Word of God. I pray that I will align my life to the Biblical principles and help me not to look at anything but You. In Jesus' name. Amen.

Questions

- What does our world use today to measure standards of morality and ethics?

- How "plumb" or "off-plumb" is your life right now?

- What can you do, starting today, to get your life in line with Christ?

Journal

■ December 4

For to me, to live is Christ and to die is gain. If I am to go on living in the body, this will mean fruitful labor for me. Yet what shall I choose? I do not know! I am torn between the two: I desire to depart and be with Christ, which is better by far. (Philippians 1:21-23)

Meditation   *Dudley C. Rutherford*

Many years ago, a young couple named John and Betty Stam went deep into the interior of China to be missionaries. They had one young daughter named Priscilla. Communist bandits entered their camp one night and cut off the heads of John and Betty Stam. Only the little daughter Priscilla lived, to be brought back to America. So many folks in their home church said, "What a tragedy; what a shame; what a waste of talent and young life." I can well imagine some people thought, "Oh, if John and Betty had known the terrible cost, I wonder if they would have gone to China." Fortunately for us, we have the answer to that question. For in the flyleaf of her Bible, Betty wrote the following words the day before her decapitation:

"Lord, I give up my own purposes and plans, all my own desires, hopes and ambitions and accept Your will for my life. I give myself, my life, and my all, utterly to You to be Yours forever. I hand over to Your keeping all of my friendships, my love. All the people whom I love are to take second place in my heart. Fill me and seal me with Your Holy Spirit. Work out Your perfect will in my life, at any cost, now and forever. 'To me to live is Christ and to die is gain.'" Philippians 1:21 Elizabeth Alden Stam, August 3, 1935.

Prayer

Dear Lord, I want to be like this great woman of faith. I know I will probably never have the chance to die for You, but I know I have the command to live for You each day of my life. Forgive me, Lord, for being so complacent when others are so committed. It is my prayer that I would be willing to make my life count for You, O Lord. In His name, I pray. Amen.

Questions

- To live is Christ and to die is gain. What does that mean?

- How would you describe "living for Christ"?

- What causes a person to want to become a missionary?

Journal

_____

_____

_____

_____

December 5

Meditation   *Dudley C. Rutherford*

Who is this author? Who is this writer that demands we rejoice? Who is he to tell us to always rejoice? His name is Paul. He's a prisoner. His friends have all forsaken him. His home is a dark dungeon filled with dampness and the stench of death. He is at the complete mercy of others. He is awaiting trial. Then he writes, "The Lord is near." That is a direct reference to the second coming of Christ. Paul is saying that if we believe Christ may return to earth at any moment, how can we be upset about small things?

Suppose you knew you had just won the lottery for the tax-free amount of $142 million? You knew you would be paid in full tonight at midnight. All day, you receive bad news, such as, "A dog dug up your flower bed." Or, "Someone in the parking lot put a dent in your car fender." I've got a feeling nothing would bother you very much. Likewise, if we truly believe that our precious Lord may split the skies at any moment, take us to His eternal home and give us eternal and everlasting life, I think it would be very difficult to be worried or depressed. If you know that one of these days, you are going to die and live as long as God lives, that Heaven is your home and Christ is your Friend and Savior, it's going to be a difficult task to get you rattled or upset by something here on earth.

Prayer

Dear kind and ever-strong Savior, forgive me when I forgot that You are coming back soon. If I can just keep that fact in mind, my burdens will be placed in their proper perspective. I want to rededicate and renew my faith in You today. May I never forget that this could be the day. Oh, I feel better just thinking about that fact. In Jesus' name, I pray. Amen.

Questions

- How does Paul say you should deal with your problems?

- How does the certain second coming of Christ level your burdens?

- When do you think the Lord will return? Be careful how you answer this question.

Journal

_____

_____

_____

_____

_____

■December 6

> *Therefore encourage one another and build each other up, just as in fact you are doing. Now we ask you, brothers, to respect those who work hard among you, who are over you in the Lord and who admonish you. Hold them in the highest regard in love because of their work. Live in peace with each other. And we urge you, brothers, warn those who are idle, encourage the timid, help the weak, be patient with everyone.*
>
> *(I Thessalonians 5:11, 14)*

Meditation   Ray Cronkwright

In a certain meeting a number of years ago, the subject of church growth was being discussed. It was suggested that to reach out to the community, we could start a Christian day school. The leadership of the church was encouraged to pursue this specific task. It turns out the senior minister at that time had some firsthand experience with just such a project at a former ministry. The result some years later is in evidence with the presence of Hillcrest Christian School. Through this ministry, many young people have been given a great Bible-based education, and what is more, many have been led to accept Christ as their personal Lord and Savior.

What started as a dream is now a reality. It's amazing what a little bit of encouragement can accomplish. Remember that whenever someone has a dream to do something for God, it takes others coming alongside to support and encourage at every turn.

Ray Cronkwright is an elder at Shepherd of the Hills Church.

A Dream

Prayer

Our Father in Heaven, we pray that in many ways and with many interesting programs, we can reach out to the many people in this community. Give us the inspiration and the dedication we need to continue to expand the great work that is so much in evidence here at Shepherd today. These things we ask in Jesus' name. Amen.

Questions

- What areas of outreach can you pursue?

- How can you encourage others to volunteer?

- How can you become more effective in the areas you are involved in?

Journal

December 7

And we know that in all things God works for the good of those who love him, who have been called according to his purpose. (Romans 8:28)

Meditation   *Dudley C. Rutherford*

Yes, the Bible plainly says that all things work together for good to those who love God. It does not say all things are good. A fool knows better than that. Nature itself is trying to teach us this truth. For example, two of the most toxic, deadly elements on earth are sodium and chloride. Just a trace of either will kill you. But mix them together and you have table salt. Have you eaten any flour lately? How about a few raw eggs? You know, nearly all the ingredients in a cake are horrible-tasting. Flour, baking powder, raw eggs, salt and vanilla just do not taste good by themselves. But let a master cook blend all that together, and you have a wonderful cake.

Here is a life that's undergoing trouble: heartache, tragedy, setbacks and trials. None of that is good, but you let the Master blend all that together. God can make something sweet and eternal out of your circumstances.

A flower must be crushed before it can yield its perfume.
  God uses broken clouds to bring the rain
    Broken ground to grow the crops
      Broken seed to grow the plant
        And broken hearts to produce great people.

Prayer

Dear Lord Jesus, there are so many things that come into my life that I certainly didn't want or ask for. But I thank You for those things, because I know You can take them and mix them along with the other events of my life, and make something of eternal and exquisite beauty. When any hardship confronts me, may I know immediately that something good can come from this, since my life is in Your hands. In Christ's name, I pray. Amen.

Questions

- Is it just a few things – or all things – that eventually bring good?

- Can you see God working in your everyday life?

- How does God work for the good in your life, even if things go wrong?

Journal

_____

_____

_____

_____

_____

December 8

Consider it pure joy, my brothers, whenever you face trials of many kinds, because you know that the testing of your faith develops perseverance. (James 1:2-3)

Meditation   H. Dean Rutherford

According to legend, an Indian mother came to the Gautama Buddha, and asked for the restoration of her dead baby. He promised to restore the child, if she would bring him a few grains of rice from a home that had never known trouble. She began her journey with a light heart, but the weary months dragged into years, and she returned with her mission a failure. The Buddha had chosen this means to show her that heartache come to every home. This is only a legend, but it brings to our minds anew that God allows everyone to suffer.

Why does God permit suffering? For many reasons. Suffering today may bring glory tomorrow. Even though He doesn't cause suffering, He allows us to go through the fire so that we may be tested. The only way we are made better is through adversity. We are seldom made better in prosperity. No athlete can be at his best until he is disciplined; it's the same with Christians. Through our suffering, God also takes the ill-tasting ingredients of our lives and, like a master chef, adds them to the rest of the recipe, to make something beautiful and delicious.

Suffering Today

Prayer

Dear Father, You know so very much more about me than I know about myself. You know that if I got my way all the time, I would be so spoiled and independent from You, that I would surely drift far from my need of Your presence and power. Thank You for all the times things didn't go my way. You know best, and in the name of Jesus, I pray this prayer. Amen.

Questions

- Are you made better through prosperity or trials?

- What are a few reasons God allows you to suffer?

- Name a trial in which, when you view it in hindsight, you see how God grew and matured you.

Journal

■ December 9

> *By faith Noah, when warned about things not yet seen, in holy fear built an ark to save his family. By his faith he condemned the world and became heir of the righteousness that comes by faith. (Hebrews 11:7)*

Meditation   *Tom Ellsworth*

The low rumble of distant thunder and the cadence of the gently falling rain can be peaceful. But add crashing thunder, blowing wind and jagged streaks of lightning, and it becomes chaotic. What do you do when the storms of life batter you mentally, emotionally and spiritually?

Everyone faces storms. I love how Noah faced his. What a step of faith, to build this incredible boat in anticipation of the storm that was coming. Did you know that Noah's experience through the flood is the most precisely recorded year in the Bible? And did you know there are no less than 268 global flood legends from various ancient civilizations, with most being very similar to the detailed Genesis account? How do we account for such a permeating story if indeed nothing like that ever happened?

The emotional and spiritual storms will come… Will you be prepared when they rain down on your life? *Noah was not saved because the ark was so seaworthy, but because God is so trustworthy.* Noah built by faith, but God made the ark survive the storm; God made it a sanctuary from the chaos. If you too live by faith, God will sustain you through life's floods and make you an heir of righteousness.

Tom Ellsworth is Senior Pastor of Sherwood Oaks Christian Church in Bloomington, IN.

Old Noah

Prayer

Almighty Father, help me to trust in You when the storms around me seem overwhelming, when my struggles almost drown out my prayers, and when my faith founders in the flood. Only You can give me hope in the hopeless moments; only You can take me safely through the storm. Help me live my life by faith, that the righteousness of Christ might become my inheritance. If I can do that, then I will have no reason to be afraid. Lord, You are a very present help in a time of trial. Amen.

Questions

- What is the most difficult storm you are facing?

- How can you learn to live by faith when anxiety, worry and fear flood your mind and heart?

- What is the greatest lesson you can learn from Noah's experience that will help you be more obedient to God?

Journal

_____

_____

_____

_____

December 10

"Come, follow me," Jesus said, "and I will make you fishers of men."
At once they left their nets and followed him. (Matthew 4:19-20)

Meditation   *Dudley C. Rutherford*

The Bible says, "Let the redeemed of the Lord say so" (Psalm 107:2). We are supposed to be involved in telling other people about the Lord. Whenever we take the time to share Jesus, we, at that moment, become like Jesus.

Some years back, *The Denver Post* carried the story about a man who was walking along in a ghastly ice storm and nearly frozen to death. As he lay down in the snow to die, he spotted another man about to die. Instead of dying, he began to try and revive his newly found friend. And he did. *The Denver Post* carried this cryptic headline: "John Jones, Saving Others Saved Himself."

It is imperative that we learn to tell others about Jesus. "Oh preacher, that's not my gift." Then borrow it from someone else. "Oh preacher, I'm the quiet type." Then whisper it. A woman told me once, "Oh preacher, I can't get anyone to come to church." I said, "Aren't you the same person who had a Tupperware party after you went up and down the block, begging others?" I rested my case. If you say you can't get people to church, then I don't buy it, and I don't believe the Lord does either.

Prayer

Dear Lover of my soul, I'm so thankful that someone loved me enough to tell me about Jesus. Help me to love others enough that I might extend a warm, winsome, tender invitation to them. Please don't let me take for granted that someone else will do the work. Lord, as someone took the initiative to invite me, may I take the initiative to invite others. In Your Holy name, I pray. Amen.

Questions

- What does it mean to be a "fisher of men"?

- What principles in fishing relate to soul-winning?

- Which trait is more important in sharing your faith: ability or availability?

Journal

■ December 11

You have heard that it was said, "Love your neighbor and hate your enemy." If you love those who love you, what reward will you get? Are not even the tax collectors doing that? And if you greet only your brothers, what are you doing more than others? Do not even pagans do that? (Matthew 5:43, 46-47)

Meditation   *Dudley C. Rutherford*

I've got a feeling if Jesus were here today in the flesh, He would spend a lot of time in the nursing homes, in hospitals and in the poorer neighborhoods. If we called His home or office looking for Him, I think they would say, "He's not here right now. I think He's down at the city jail, and after that, He was headed over to the cemetery to comfort some folks at a funeral service." Oh, if Jesus were here today, I think He would spend a great deal of His time looking for some orphans, or helping children from broken homes deal with their broken hearts. If He were here, He would wash your car and clean your garage. He would carry your groceries. I know He would give you His time. That is what Jesus wants us to do. He wants you to spend your time trying to serve others.

A soldier in Europe during World War ll dove into a foxhole as bullets and bombs whistled overhead. There, in the bottom of the trench, he found a crucifix. He said to his chaplain, "How do you work this thing?" "You don't work this thing," the chaplain said. "Rather, this thing works you, and drives you to love and service."

Where Is Jesus?

Prayer

Dear precious Lord, thank You for setting the example of Your life before me. I now know how to live each day. I need to look for those folks I can bless and assist. I need to let others see You, dear Jesus, in me. As You have blessed me, I need to bless others. Help me to be selfless in every way and work diligently to reflect Your love to others. In the name of Jesus, I pray. Amen.

Questions

- If you just love those who love you, what is your reward?

- If you just love those who love you, who are you acting like?

- If Jesus were here today, where would you find Him?

Journal

_____

_____

_____

_____

▪ December 12

For this very reason, make every effort to add to your faith goodness; and to goodness, knowledge; and to knowledge, self-control; and to self-control, perseverance; and to perseverance, godliness; and to godliness, brotherly kindness; and to brotherly kindness, love. For if you possess these qualities in increasing measure, they will keep you from being ineffective and unproductive in your knowledge of our Lord Jesus Christ.

(II Peter 1:5-8)

Meditation   *Dudley C. Rutherford*

Last Sunday's newspaper carried a rather amazing story concerning heart attacks. From interviews with 32 patients who had suffered heart attacks, two medical doctors discovered that all but one admitted to having had a warning of some kind, but they had ignored the warning. You will notice I said the newspaper story was amazing, not surprising.

I am acquainted with dozens of people who have ignored the warnings of a much more serious type of heart trouble. There are countless Christians who realize they should be in worship on each Lord's Day, but they quiet the pangs of conscience by telling themselves it is really nothing serious. Failure to urge others to Christ. Failure to tithe, rather than spending it on one's personal pleasure. Failure to have one's children in Bible school. Nothing serious?

Don't take lightly that spiritual heartburn. God allows us to have that uneasy-queasy feeling when we go for days or weeks without personal devotions and prayer. The patients who suffered heart attacks refused to take the warnings seriously. So do most people with spiritual heart trouble. Even as you read these lines, are you trying to dismiss the aforementioned symptoms?

Prayer

The cure for my spiritual heart trouble requires that I seek out a physician. So I have come to You, the Great Physician. I don't want to risk growing away from You. I know in my more serious moments that my life is literally in Your hands. Whenever I drift away, I pray that Your loving reminders will cause me to repent and to return to You. I ask these things in the name of my Lord and Savior, Jesus Christ. Amen.

Questions

- Should you ignore serious warnings?

- Who is the Great Physician and how can He help you?

- Do you feel that you're drawing close to the Lord, or do you feel that you're drifting away?

Journal

_____

_____

_____

_____

_____

■December 13

In everything I did, I showed you that by this kind of hard work we must help the weak, remembering the words the Lord Jesus himself said: "It is more blessed to give than to receive." (Acts 20:35)

Meditation   *Wally Rendel*

Two weeks before Christmas, a lady walked into a men's clothing store in Lexington, Kentucky. She asked if they sold shoehorns. The owner, Harlan Logan, said they didn't, but he offered to give her a shoehorn. She gratefully accepted it.

Three weeks later, she came back to the store with her husband. She introduced herself, reminding Mr. Logan that she was the lady he gave a shoehorn to a couple of weeks before Christmas. He remembered her. The couple then proceeded to buy dress clothes. They shopped well past the closing time, with Mr. Logan waiting on them. When all was said and done, well after midnight, they had purchased over $36,000 worth of suits, ties, overcoats, trousers, belts, dress shirts and shoes. Seems incredible, but it really happened.

Once again, we are reminded of an old saying: "Big doors swing on little hinges." A simple act of kindness, the gift of a $2 shoehorn, returning such dividends. I am reminded of what Jesus said in Luke 6:38: "Give, and it shall be given to you. A good measure, shaken together and running over, will be poured into your lap. For with the measure you use, it will be measured to you."

Wally Rendel is the Senior Pastor at Southern Acres Christian Church in Lexington, KY.

Prayer

Dear Lord, thank You for Your abundant grace and mercy. Help me to see the many opportunities every day to express kindness. Remind me that I can never out-give You. I praise You for the greatest gift of all – Jesus Christ. I pray that I never will take for granted Your promise and Your assurances. Help me to be the little hinge on which You will swing big doors. I pray in Jesus' name. Amen.

Questions

- Is it easy or difficult for you to do simple acts of kindness?

- What is the end result of planting seeds of kindness?

- According to Luke 6:38, what happens when you give?

Journal

December 14

Do not be deceived: God cannot be mocked. A man reaps what he sows. The one who sows to please his sinful nature, from that nature will reap destruction; the one who sows to please the Spirit, from the Spirit will reap eternal life. (Galatians 6:7-8)

Meditation   *Dudley C. Rutherford*

Dwight L. Moody once said, "Suppose I meet a man who is sowing seed and ask, 'Hello, stranger, what are you sowing?'

'Seed.'

'What kind of seed?'

'I don't know.'

'Don't you know if it is good seed or bad?'

'No, I can't tell. It is just seed. That's all I know and I am busy sowing it.'

You would say that such a man was a first class lunatic, wouldn't you? But not half so mad as the man who goes on sowing for time and eternity, and who never stops to ask himself what he is sowing or what the harvest will be.

Many places in the Bible warn us that we are going to have to reap what we sow. If we tend to the things of the world, we will reap destruction. If we tend to the things of the Spirit, we shall reap of the Spirit and reap everlasting life. You don't plant corn and then harvest tomatoes; and you don't plant cotton and then reap okra. We are going to reap what we sow. And you get more than you sow. No farmer would plant one potato if he only reaped one potato. And you reap later than when you sow. You don't sow this morning and reap this afternoon. Those are the God-given laws of sowing and reaping.

God-Given Laws

Prayer

I know from reading Your word, and I know from observation that whatever I sow, I am bound to reap. Help me to sow righteousness, love, patience, obedience and understanding. Help me to sow every day. I know if I sow these things I shall, in due season, reap a great harvest for us both. I pray all this in His divine name. Amen.

Questions

- What are you sowing today?

- Why can't God be mocked?

- Can you name examples of God being true to His character?

Journal

_____

_____

_____

_____

■ December 15

Meditation   *Dudley C. Rutherford*

When anyone says, "I will not become a Christian today but I will tomorrow," they are saying one of four things:

1. "It is the right thing to do or I would never plan to do it."

2. "By saying 'tomorrow,' I am saying I recognize the change will be rather unpleasant and distasteful."

3. "By saying 'tomorrow,' I am saying I believe it will be easier tomorrow, or I would certainly do it today."

4. "By saying 'tomorrow,' I am saying I believe there is going to be a tomorrow for me."

If you believed that at midnight tonight, this very night, you would die, I know you would decide for Christ right now. If you are a Christian not living up to your vows, and you knew for sure you would die tonight, you would delay no longer. That tells God and the whole world you believe there will be a tomorrow for you.

Listen to what God says so directly to us in James 3:13-14: "Now listen, you who say, today or tomorrow we will go to this or that city, spend a year there, carry on business and make money. Why, you do not even know what will happen tomorrow. What is your life? You are a mist that appears for a little while and then vanishes."

Today or Tomorrow

Prayer

Dear Lord in Heaven, thank You for waiting on me all this time. I realize that the things I should accomplish for You in my life, I must be working on today. Help me to put aside all procrastination and all the excuses I have given myself, and begin anew for You right now. Your loving patience with me will not be wasted any longer. Amen.

Questions

- What day should you be saved: today or tomorrow?

- What would you do for Christ, if you knew this was your last day?

- Is Christ waiting on you today?

Journal

December 16

But seek first his kingdom and his righteousness, and all these things will be given to you as well. Therefore do not worry about tomorrow.

(Matthew 6:33-34)

Meditation   H. Dean Rutherford

The only things Jesus wants you to give up are those things that will ultimately destroy you if you don't. Jesus doesn't want you to be unhappy or bored. He wants to live eternally with you. Oh friend, listen; I say this with all the love of my soul. You don't have to go on sinning. You can choose. Starting today, you can make the right choice. You can start over again today. It will never be any easier than it is at this very moment. You can give up drinking, drugs, profanity and unfaithfulness to your church, to your wife or your husband. The only reason Jesus wants you to give up those things, is that He is afraid they will destroy you and *He* will miss out on living with you for all eternity.

"Oh pastor, that preaching on Satan and sin, that is so old-fashioned and so out-of-date." Yes, I know. It is old-fashioned. Air is old-fashioned but without it, men choke, gasp and die. Water is old-fashioned but without it, men go mad and insane. The noonday sun is terribly old-fashioned but take it away, and men soon wither and shrivel, choke and die. Food is old-fashioned but without it, men grow weak, pale, emaciated and die.

The Right Choice

Prayer

Dear Lord, I know You want more than anything else to spend eternity with me. I don't understand that, but I accept it because You said it was so. Help me to stop worrying so much about food, clothes, money and reputation, and start striving to be more like You; more mature in my faith and in my spiritual growth. In Christ's wonderful name, I pray. Amen.

Questions

- Is it okay to be old-fashioned?

- Do you believe Jesus wants you to be happy?

- Where does happiness come from?

Journal

■December 17

But You are holy, enthroned in the praises of Israel. Psalm 22:3

Meditation   *Jack Hayford*

Unquestionably, one of the most remarkable and exciting things about honest and sincere praise is taught here: praise will bring the presence of God.

Although God is everywhere present, there is a distinct manifestation of His rule which enters the environment of praise. Here is the remedy for times when you feel alone, deserted or depressed. Praise! Let this truth create faith and trust, and lead to deliverance from satanic harassments, torment, or bondage. However simply, compose your song and testimony of God's goodness in your life.

The result: God enters! His presence will live (take up residence) in our lives. The Hebrew word translated "inhabit" means to "sit down, to remain, to settle, or marry." In other words, God does not merely visit us when we praise Him, but His presence abides with us and we partner with Him in a growing relationship.

Today, let us invite God's presence into our immediate situation. He wants to come and abide where we are right now!

Jack Hayford is the President of the International Foursquare Church, Senior Pastor Emeritus of The Church on the Way and Chancellor of The King's College & Seminary in Van Nuys, CA.

Prayer

Father, right now I come to You offering You the praise You deserve. Life sometimes doesn't make sense, things do not always add up, but Lord, help me to turn to You and give You thanks and praise in all situations so that You can make sense of it all. When life seems to be closing in, when I am down to my last tear drop give me the strength I need to run to You, seek Your heart and will, and then give You the praise You deserve as the Sovereign of the Universe. In Jesus's name. Amen.

Questions

- The Bible tells us to consider it pure joy when we face trials of many kinds (James 1). In light of God's goodness, why should we consider trials joy?

- How does our praise invite God's presence?

- For what in your life are you thankful? Praise God for that now.

Journal

■ December 18

Do not be anxious about anything, but in everything, by prayer and petition, with thanksgiving, present your requests to God. And the peace of God, which transcends all understanding, will guard your hearts and your minds in Christ Jesus. (Philippians 4:6-7)

Meditation   *Dudley C. Rutherford*

Mrs. Billy Graham made a most interesting confession. She said, "If God had answered all my prayers, I would have married the wrong man seven times." When we pray, we should consider thanking God for not answering our prayers. And we should realize that if God has enough power to answer our prayers, He also must possess a superior knowledge to understand which prayers would be better unanswered. If you are a parent and have a four-year-old, for example, would you give him all he asks for? He would be ruined in no time at all. The next time you pray, try thanking God for unanswered prayers.

And something else: do you ever thank Him for things that didn't happen? More often we probably should say, "Thank you, Jesus, for the car wreck I didn't have this week, and the cancer I didn't get, and dear Lord, thank You for the fact that I'm not in some hospital room today. And Father, I don't like that job very much, but thank You that I didn't get fired. Thank You, Lord, that I'm not slowly starving like so many others in this world." Praying in the right way and for the correct things will soon change your "wanter." What percentage of our prayers are about our own needs and what percentage of our prayers concern the needs of others?

Unanswered Prayers

Prayer

Dear Precious God, thank You for not answering all my prayers. You know infinitely so much more than I do. Thank You for storms that didn't come my way. Thank You for the fact that even when things go wrong in my life, the good always outweighs the bad. Help me, Jesus, to spend a greater part of my prayer life concerned with the needs of others, because I know You are going to take care of me. I pray this prayer in Your righteous name. Amen.

Questions

- What are a few prayers you're glad God didn't answer?

- How much more does God know about you than you know about yourself?

- When God says "No," is that an answer to your prayer?

Journal

_____

_____

_____

_____

_____

December 19

On coming to the house, they saw the child with his mother Mary, and they bowed down and worshiped him. Then they opened their treasures and presented him with gifts of gold and of incense and of myrrh.

(Matthew 2:11)

Meditation   *Dudley C. Rutherford*

I laughed and laughed as I watched a comedian joking about Methuselah in the Old Testament. Methuselah was the oldest man in the Bible. God says he lived to be 969 years old. The comedian was impersonating Methuselah's brother when he exclaimed, "I'm glad that rascal brother of mine finally died. I really got kind of tired of trying to find him a new gift each year. In fact, I have to confess I've just been buying him socks for the last 600 years." Well, it's hard to find the right gift for any person. You want to give something that is useful and that will last. Christmas is a time for giving, and we all want to give something that will please and delight. Do you know what kind of gift the Lord wants from us? Nothing – absolutely nothing – takes the place of a consecrated Christian life devoted to Him. Why not give Him the ultimate gift this Christmas? You!

Prayer

Dear Lord of the manger, Lord of the Cross and Lord of our lives: Help me to give You the one gift that keeps on giving; the one gift that will make You and all Your angels delighted; the gift of my daily surrendered life to You. If I can do that, then I know I shall give new meaning to the phrase, "Merry Christmas." In Jesus' name. Amen.

Questions

- Why is Christmas a time of giving?

- What is the best gift you can give to Him?

- How can you share the "reason for the season"?

Journal

December 20

Meditation   *Cameron McDonald*

Each day is a gift from God. Not long ago, I had to leave my car in the shop overnight for some routine maintenance, so they provided me with a rental car. When I arrived at the rental car lot, they gave me a selection of cars, but for only a few extra dollars they could upgrade me. I thought by "upgrade" they were talking Yugo to Pinto. But they weren't. They said I could choose from a Mercedes, Cadillac Escalade or an Infiniti.

"Well, Mr. McDonald, would you like an upgrade?" I said, "Is the Pope Catholic?"

So I chose the Cadillac, and I have to admit that for the next 24 hours, I was living high. I became so attached to the car that I did not want to leave it. I drove it over to show it off to friends and then to family. I didn't realize you could become so attached to a rental. I even asked my wife if I could sleep in it.

Well, through many tears, the next day I returned it. I didn't say, "That's not fair. Who are you to take this car away from me? Why can't I have it a little longer?" I realized it was temporary and that it wasn't meant to last forever.

I think so many times we view this life as ours and not the Lord's. We think it's unjust for a person to die young, but when you look at your life as a rental, you put things in perspective. You learn to enjoy the time you have. You are more driven to accomplish your purpose in life when you understand that, at any moment, you might have to turn in the keys.

Upgrade Anyone?

Prayer

Father in Heaven, help us to not look at our lives as our own. Give us the wisdom we need to understand that each day is truly a gift from You. Please give us the strength we need to live each day to the fullest for Your Kingdom! May we always keep things in perspective and immerse ourselves in the truth that we belong to You. In Jesus' name. Amen.

Questions

- Have you ever been guilty of viewing this life as your own? When? Explain.

- When you begin to think of your life as a rental, what comes to your mind? What needs to be accomplished yet in your life?

- If you knew you would be gone tomorrow, who is the one person you would tell about Jesus? What are you waiting for?

Journal

But thanks be to God! He gives us the victory through our Lord Jesus Christ. (I Corinthians 15:57)

Meditation   *Mark Fugate*

Victory is an awesome thing. My little girl will see me watching a ball game, and invariably she will get in front of the television and become a cheerleader. Her favorite cheer is "that's all right, that's okay, we're gonna beat you anyway." She was with me once during a church softball game in which we were down 25 to 2 in the last inning. Sure enough, she stood up and yelled, "That's all right, that's okay, we're gonna beat you anyway." The other team did not listen to her, and it wasn't all right, and it wasn't okay; we got "killed."

This passage in I Corinthians speaks of the supernatural help available to the Christians. If there was any doubt about victory or where it comes from, it is made clear in this verse. Satan has been on the offensive, and many get discouraged because victory does not seem possible. Satan continues to come at our families and tries to rip them apart. He continues to get involved in school policy and mess with government officials. He is still trying to destroy the Church with division. But when he comes at us, we need to square our shoulders, sharpen our focus and cling to this promise of God: "That's all right, that's okay – we're gonna beat him anyway." Victory is ours, thanks to Jesus.

Mark Fugate is Senior Pastor of Bright Christian Church in Lawrenceburg, IN.

Victory In Jesus

Prayer

Our Father in Heaven, thank You for the victory that we have in and through Your Son. We are in constant need, Lord, of a reminder that "greater is He that is in us than he that is in the world." Life can be so difficult, Father, and that's why it's important for us to know that our victory has been secured. Who can mind the journey when we know the road leads home. Help us, Lord, to display to the world a victorious witness. And we offer our prayer in Jesus' name. Amen.

Questions

- What causes you to doubt the victory you have in Christ?

- What things keep so many from living a victorious Christian life?

- Did Satan consider the death of Jesus a victory?

Journal

_____

_____

_____

_____

_____

December 22

Why, O Lord, do you stand far off? Why do you hide yourself in times of trouble? (Psalm 10:1)

Meditation   *Raul Ries*

Like the Psalmist, there are times we feel as if God is absent in our daily lives. Sometimes when evil is all around us, we forget His promises to us. In times like these, we need to draw closer to God by following three important precepts. One: Trust in His Word. Just because we can't "feel" God doesn't mean He isn't right there with us all the time. His promises do not come and go depending on how we are feeling. Two: Take an inventory of your life. The loneliness you are feeling may be the direct result of your fellowship, or lack thereof with God. Three: Rebuke the devil. Satan loves to take advantage whenever we feel like this, and he specializes in making us feel guilty. When this occurs, we must immediately rebuke him and he will flee.

We have the assurance of God's Word and power through the Holy Spirit to overcome all of our fears and troubles. Scripture says you will have trials, but it also says God is faithful. We have the Lord to watch over us and lead us into all truth. So next time you feel all alone, call upon His name, because He cares for you and will answer you. Take some time today to be alone with Him. Share your heart, and let Him know how much you love Him.

Raul Ries is Senior Pastor of Calvary Chapel in Golden Springs, CA.

Prayer

Lord, please be by my side. Lead me, guide me and fill me with Your Holy Spirit. Lord, I believe all Your promises, and I will wait on You to fulfill them. Lord, You always keep Your Word and replace our loneliness with Your presence. Instead of me looking to others, I pray my gaze and attention will always be on You. You are the Rock of my salvation. In Jesus' name. Amen.

Questions

- Do you know who your enemy is?

- Do you know how much God loves you?

- Do you know how to use God's Word for your defense?

Journal

_____

_____

_____

_____

December 23

And there were shepherds living out in the fields nearby, keeping watch over their flocks at night. An angel of the Lord appeared to them, and the glory of the Lord shone around them, and they were terrified.

(Luke 2:8-9)

Meditation   *Dudley C. Rutherford*

Did it ever occur to you why God first appeared to the shepherds and made His first announcement to them? It was only a pretty story to me, until I learned the deeper meaning. These shepherds, to whom the angels appeared, were not just ordinary shepherds. They may have been temple shepherds. They were professionals. If you had lived in that ancient day and wanted to make a sacrifice, you were not permitted to bring your own lamb; you had to instead buy one from one of these expert temple shepherds who had a corner on the market. So when Christ appeared in the manger, the angels appeared to these men first, to let them know they were out of a job.

God was downsizing! The coming of the real Christ, the real Lamb put these shepherds out of business. God was saying to them, "If you want to see a real lamb, go to the manger. There is my Lamb from now on. We are shifting gears; we are going into a new era. No more sheep killing. We are moving from the shadow to the substance; we are shifting from the figure to the reality. You are out of a job. You are now standing in the ranks of the unemployed. And my little Lamb, yonder in the manger, will grow to die on the cross."

Shepherds

Prayer

Dear wonderful Lord, I'm so very glad You spoke to those temple shepherds, and that we do not have to go to Jerusalem and sacrifice a lamb to have our sins covered. Our true Lamb, Jesus Christ, sacrificed His life for me. If You had not died for me, I would be forever dead in my own sins. Thank You, Lord, for Your greatest of all Christmas gifts: the gift of Your self-sacrifice. In Jesus' name, I ask. Amen.

Questions

- Do you think the shepherds were afraid when the angels appeared to them?

- What was the message given to the shepherds?

- Of all Christ's gifts, which is the greatest?

Journal

■ December 24

While they were there, the time came for the baby to be born, and she gave birth to her firstborn, a son. She wrapped him in cloths and placed him in a manger, because there was no room for them in the inn. (Luke 2:6-7)

Meditation — *Dudley C. Rutherford*

Then it happened. It must have been a beautiful night when the shepherds reclined on the slope of the hill, watching their flocks by night. I can imagine the atmosphere was prophetic on that night. The sky seemed as if it had been washed for the occasion, and the stars seemed as if they had been burnished for this holy event. The clouds floated by like a silver fleet from an infinite sea.

Then all of a sudden, a star of peculiar brilliancy detached itself from its sister stars and swung down over the earth like the pendulum of a clock. The shepherds were shaking and quaking with fear. But God, seeing their frenzied hearts, sent down one of Heaven's best choirs to allay their fears. "Fear not, for behold we bring you good tidings of great joy. For unto you is born this day a Savior, which is Christ the Lord!" And they rushed to the manger and observed that the Infinite had become an Infant. Salvation was now wrapped in swaddling clothes. God was in gunnysacks. The almighty God, the Creator of the world was only 20 inches long in the arms of Mary.

Prayer

O dear Christ of Christmas, thank You for coming into our world. We are mindful that You, in one sense of the word, so miraculously entered our world, yet in another way entered our world so commonly. Even at Your birth, You showed Your God/man nature. We do not understand much, but we do know You love us and You came to save us. Help me to be what You would have me to be. In Christ's name, I pray. Amen.

Questions

- Why were the shepherds afraid?

- Why was the unusual star there in the first place?

- Explain Christ's dual nature.

Journal

_____

_____

_____

_____

_____

December 25

You are the light of the world. A city on a hill cannot be hidden. In the same way, let your light shine before men, that they may see your good deeds and praise your Father in heaven. (Matthew 5:14,16)

Meditation   *Dudley C. Rutherford*

One of my favorite preachers related this: "Years ago driving in early January on our way to church, a family had left its outdoor Christmas lights on. I griped, and asked out loud, 'Why doesn't that fellow take his lights down? Good grief, my wife would have made me take them down.' A few weeks later I was still complaining, 'Good night, if he can't take those lights down at least he could turn them off.' Then the local newspaper published a story that made me feel mighty small. The family who lived there had a son, who was in the Gulf war, and has a very sensitive job and was required to stay there long after most of our boys had come back home. The young man had hoped to be home by Christmas but it was obvious he wasn't going to make it. His folks wrote him a letter and promised their brave son that they would leave the Christmas tree up and leave on all the outside lights. They promised they would not turn them off until he returned home from operation Desert Storm."

When we stay faithful to Christ, when we engage in prayer, Bible study, Communion and soul-winning, we are leaving the lights on until Jesus returns to claim His own. Be steadfast, be faithful and leave on all the lights. Let others see Jesus in you.

Christmas Lights

Prayer

Dear Lord of Life, please help me to remember to leave on the lights until You come back for Your bride. I'm not sure of the day or time or season You are going to return, but whenever that happens to be, I want to turn on every light I can for Jesus and His Church. I want to be found faithful, waiting and ready for my Savior's return. I pray this request in the strong name of Jesus. Amen.

Questions

- How does a person let their light shine?

- How does God get the glory when you shine your light?

- Is living for Jesus a seasonal thing for you?

Journal

_____

_____

_____

_____

December 26

Both the one who makes men holy and those who are made holy are of the same family. So Jesus is not ashamed to call them brothers. He says, "I will declare your name to my brothers; in the presence of the congregation I will sing your praises." And again, "I will put my trust in him." And again he says, "Here am I, and the children God has given me." (Hebrews 2:11-13)

Meditation

Turning back a few pages from yesteryear, I well remember that my church office was always a little hidden or concealed. If you wanted to see me, you couldn't just come to my office and barge in and say, "Hi." Instead, you had to go through the receptionist's office and then past some secretaries and look for an unmarked door. The church was kind enough to do all that to grant me a measure of privacy while I tried to study. I was well protected. However, I remember my small children would simply walk into the receptionist's office, walk right past the secretary, open the unmarked door without knocking and bounce across the room. They'd jump in a chair and say, "Hi, Dad." Those kids had a lot of nerve ignoring all that defensive protocol. But then again, they were family. They weren't guests or visitors, they were "flesh and blood."

Did you know that when you are in church or on your knees in prayer or at the Lord's table, you are not a guest? You are not a visitor. You are family! God's family. Christ's family. It's your home, and you have a special place at the table. You don't have to knock. You are not only welcome here in God's house and God's presence: you belong here!

Prayer

Oh Father, and You are our Father, thank You for calling all of us Your brothers and Your children. We thank You that in Your home and in Your dining room, there is a place, a plate for us at the dinner table. Thank You for including us in Your household. We never are so at home and feel so loved as when we enter Your presence, and gather with our brothers and sisters in Christ, in whose name, we pray. Amen.

Questions

- What does Jesus call you as a member of His family?

- Do you, as when you were a child, have a regular place at His table?

- Do you feel like "family" when you pray, read or commune?

Journal

_____

_____

_____

_____

_____

December 27

Love is patient, love is kind. It does not envy, it does not boast, it is not proud. It is not rude, it is not self-seeking, it is not easily angered, it keeps no record of wrongs. Love does not delight in evil but rejoices with the truth. It always protects, always trusts, always hopes, always perseveres.

(I Corinthians 13:4)

Meditation   *Vicki Ross*

Webster's definition of patient: Not hasty or impetuous.

I never thought in a million years there would be that one special person God would carve out for me, and me for him. The person who would love me for me, and me for him. Being patient is a funny thing. I remember how many of my loving, well-intentioned friends would try and set me up with who they thought was right for me. But I knew that if it ever were to be, God would be the provider with the one He so desired. I never was one to push, seek or even put myself out there.

As I grew older, I knew I wanted someone to share life with, but I had no idea how or when that would happen. About a year ago, I was talking with God and I said, "God, I surrender my singleness unto You. You know I am a great single - so keep me single if that is Your will. If You want me married, I surrender that unto You also. But please make sure I don't miss the one You may have for me, because Lord, You know how I am." After giving that to Him and not thinking about it much, six months later He brought the gift He prepared for me, in the form of a love relationship that is better than I could ever imagine, or even deserve on my own merits. Love is patient.

Vicki Ross is a member of Shepherd of the Hills Church, Porter Ranch, CA.

Love Is Patient

Prayer

Daddy, how awesome You are in keeping Your promises. You tell us to be patient and wait on You. You alone know exactly what I need. Because of Your faithfulness and unfailing love, I can depend on You to provide for all my needs, wants and desires according to Your will. Even in love, I have depended on You, and You have provided more than I ever hoped for. You've allowed me to experience a love that could only be produced by You; for that, I am truly grateful, and only deserving because of "whose I am and not who I am." In Jesus' name. Amen.

Questions

- Is the relationship you're in now God's will or your will?

- How can you surrender even your love life to God?

- Are you waiting in joyful anticipation for what God will provide for you, or do you get impatient and complain about how long it's taking?

Journal

_____

_____

_____

_____

_____

December 28

Meditation — Dudley C. Rutherford

The comedian Jerry Clower once told about a lady he knew who had 16 children. She lived near a construction site, where workers were putting a tar roof on a building. She lost one of her "youngins" and after a long hunt, she discovered he had fallen into a nearby 50-gallon drum of black roofing tar at the construction site. She reached down and grabbed him by the nape of his neck, took a long, careful look at him and put him back down. She said, "Boy, it would be a lot easier just to have another one than to try to clean you up."

I'm sure God must feel that way about us many times. It would be easier for God to create someone else than to try and clean us up. But He does clean us up. He lets us act on our faith and allows us, through His Spirit operating through His Word, to repent and start all over again. You do not have to keep living in the same old way. Let Him clean you up! Jesus is known as the God of the "second chance." He can clean us up to the point where we are "brand, spanking new."

Prayer

Dear God, please don't get tired of cleaning us up. We get so dirty so quickly. You've washed us many times before. But in these next few minutes of personal prayer and repentance, would You wash me again, scrub me and make me clean one more time? I want to commit to You today my desire for wholeness and holiness. That can only happen when I put my trust in You. In Jesus' name. Amen.

Questions

- Why is it difficult to be pure?

- How does Jesus cleanse us?

- Can you repent today of everything that should not be in your heart?

Journal

_____

_____

_____

_____

December 29

So he got up and went to his father. "But while he was still a long way off, his father saw him and was filled with compassion for him; he ran to his son, threw his arms around him and kissed him." (Luke 15:20)

Meditation   *Dudley C. Rutherford*

I know a mother who had six children. The kids were all pretty good kids. Someone asked her, "You've got six children. Which one do you love most?" What a question... but my, my, my what an answer. She thought a few moments and mused about which one she loved best. "The one who is away from home until he finds his way back. The one who is sick until he is well again. The one who hurts until his hurt disappears. The one who is lost and then is found."

Jesus' love is like that mother's love. Isaiah 66:13 says that God has a mother's love. Our Blessed Lord loves everybody – and everybody just the same. But I can't help but feel the ones He loves the most are those who today are hurting. He loves us all, but if your heart is hurting or hungering, if you are bruised or broken, if you are tired and weary and discouraged, Jesus is loving you right now the most. Jesus said, "Come unto Me all you who are weary and burdened and I will give you rest." (Matthew 11:28)

Prayer

Oh dear wonderful God above, we marvel again at Your immeasurable, matchless love. We can feel Your haunting love as we bow before You in prayer. We can feel Your Spirit brooding over us. We can sense Your great, sympathetic, mother-like heart healing our hurts. Bless us as we make contact with You again. In Jesus' name. Amen.

Questions

- What is the difference between a mother's love and a father's love?

- If He has a mother's love, then when does He love you the most?

- Can you trust Him with your life and all you have?

Journal

December 30

Consider how the lilies grow. They do not labor or spin. Yet I tell you, not even Solomon in all his splendor was dressed like one of these.

(Luke 12:27)

Meditation   *Dudley C. Rutherford*

Why did our wise God create flowers? The same reason we send flowers. Simply to say, "I love you." Since the beginning of the universe, when God said, "Let there be flowers," flowers have been everywhere. I have walked through a few of the flowers of Shenandoah Valley. I've gazed at the bluebonnets of Texas. Most of us have seen the magnolias and dogwoods of Georgia, the cherry blossoms of Washington, the tulip trails of Michigan and the poppies of California. Our God conveys His love each time you see a flower, or when you walk by a flower, drive by a flower or observe a flower in your own backyard. Each flower says, "I love you. From God."

Flowers are in the poor and in the ritzy sections of town. Flowers bloom in the yards of the illiterate as well as in the yards of the genius. They grow in China and Russia, Africa and California. Flowers are everywhere, and each flower is God saying, "I love you." Jesus Christ, the world's great master artist, painter, architect and designer, designs every petal, every variety, and paints every color and hue. No wonder the Holy Spirit called Jesus the "Lily of the Valley." The same hand that flung starry worlds from His omnipotent fingertips, the same hand that poured all the rivers from the crystal chalices of eternity, is the hand that painted the lily with His glory and perfumed it with His holy breath.

Flowers of the Field

Prayer

Father, there have been times when I have been lonely and discouraged. More than once, my heart has been broken. Some of my dearest plans and dreams have been shattered. But today, I am taking a new, long look at Your flowers. I realize now that if You can grow and feed and paint the lily, You can take care of me. I want to replace my full trust in You. In Jesus name, I pray. Amen.

Questions

- What does God do for the lily?

- Is God more concerned about you or a flower?

- Why should you trust all your future to Him?

Journal

■ December 31

Submit yourselves, then, to God. Resist the devil, and he will flee from you. Come near to God and he will come near to you. Wash your hands, you sinners, and purify your hearts, you double-minded. (James 4:7-8)

Meditation   *Dudley C. Rutherford*

Dr. James McConnell of Oklahoma City tells the wonderful story of when he was fishing years ago on the Missouri River. He looked up, and a few hundred yards downstream he saw a young boy standing at the end of a homemade fishing dock, looking at a mighty steamship coming down the Missouri River. It actually looked like the boy was trying to flag down the huge steamboat. Dr. McConnell said, "I just couldn't help it. I walked toward the lad and asked, 'What are you trying to do, son? You look like you're trying to get that huge ship to come over here and stop. You surely aren't fool enough to think you could stop that great ship with your little red flag. Why, that boat is so big it couldn't come over here if it wanted to.'" But the boy replied, "They'll stop all right, Mister. I ain't worried that they won't be stopping!" About that time, the huge ship took a sudden swerve and slowly made its way to the small homemade pier. The ship lowered a gangplank and the boy jumped up on it and ran up to the ship. Halfway up the gangplank, the boy look back at said, "I ain't no fool, Mister! My dad is captain of this ship. I ain't no fool!"

Do you want forgiveness of your sins? Wave your flag to Him now. Did you know that through prayer and repentance, you could summon our great captain and the ark of salvation? Don't sell yourself short. You are the captain's kid. Your dad owns and runs this ship. And the river too. Wave your flag and He'll come over to where you are right now.

Prayer

Dear God, my Father, please come here to where I am and allow me to board Your great ship of eternal life. I'm small and I'm weak, and the only credentials I have is that You love me. But I know, according to Your Word, if I will open the door of my heart, You will be my Lord and Savior. Thank You, Lord, for caring about little ol' me. I pray in Your Son's name. Amen.

Questions

- If you start toward God, will He meet you halfway?

- How does one get the devil to flee?

- Name some ways to draw closer to Him.

Journal

_____

_____

_____

_____

_____

Author List

Alan Ahlgrim - Pg. 92. Senior Pastor, Rocky Mountain Christian Church, Niwot, CO.

Greg Allen - Pg. 424. Worship Pastor, Southeast Christian Church, Louisville, KY.

Rick Atchley - Pg, 370. Senior Minister, Richland Hills Church of Christ, Richland Hills, TX

Curt Ayers - Pg. 342. Senior Pastor, Capri Christian Church, Naples, FL.

Rebecca Hayford Bauer - Pg. 420. Associate Pastor, The Church on the Way, Van Nuys, CA.

Scott Bauer - Pg. 606. Former Senior Pastor, The Church on the Way, Van Nuys, CA.

Chuck Booher - Pg. 66. Senior Pastor, Christ's Church of the Valley, San Dimas, CA.

Dean Bradshaw - Pg. 244. Teacher, Simi Valley High School and a coach at Hillcrest Christian School, Granada Hills, CA.

Bobby Braswell - Pg. 586. Head Men's Basketball Coach, California State University, Northridge.

Dennis Bratton - Pg. 336. Senior Pastor, Mandarin Christian Church, Jacksonville, FL.

Mark Brewer - Pg. 522. Senior Pastor, Bel Air Presbyterian Church, Bel Air, CA.

David Bycroft - Pg. 390. Senior Pastor, Tyro Christian Church, Tyro, KS.

Jan Caldwell - Pg. 38. Wife of John Caldwell, Senior Pastor of Kingsway Christian Church, Indianapolis, IN.

John Caldwell - Pg. 282. Senior Pastor, Kingsway Christian Church, Indianapolis, IN.

Barry Cameron - Pg. 554. Senior Pastor, Crossroads Christian Church, Arlington, TX.

Tony Campolo - Pg. 318. Professor of Sociology, Eastern University, St. Davids, PA.

Francis Chan - Pg. 168. Senior Pastor, Cornerstone Community Church, Simi Valley, CA.

Hongju Choi - Pg. 428. Senior Pastor, Everyday Church, Granada Hills, CA.

Ray Cronkwright - Pg. 692. Elder, Shepherd of the Hills Church, Porter Ranch, CA.

David Cruz - Pg. 396. Elder, Shepherd of the Hills Church, Porter Ranch, CA

John Derry - Pg. 288. President, Hope International University, Fullerton, CA.

Jim Dorman - Pg. 566. Senior Pastor, Christ's Church of Flagstaff, Flagstaff, AZ.

Tom Ellsworth - Pg. 698. Senior Pastor, Sherwood Oaks Christian Church, Bloomington, IN.

David Faust - Pg. 402. President, Cincinnati Christian University, Cincinnati, OH.

David Flaig - Pg. 414. Emerging Generation Pastor, Shepherd of the Hills Church, Porter Ranch, CA.

Heather Flaig - Pg. 124. Wife of David Flaig, Emerging Generation Pastor, Shepherd of the Hills Church, Porter Ranch, CA.

Mark Fugate - Pg. 722. Senior Pastor, Bright Christian Church, Lawrenceburg, IN.

Julie Gariss - Pg. 248. Wife of Randy Gariss, Senior Pastor, College Heights Christian Church, Joplin, MO.

Randy Gariss - Pg. 610. Senior Pastor, College Heights Christian Church, Joplin, MO.

Jim Garlow - Pg. 386. Senior Pastor, Skyline Wesleyan Church, La Mesa, CA.

Rusty George - Pg. 648. Senior Pastor, Real Life Church, Santa Clarita, CA.

Dave Hamlin - Pg. 354. Senior Pastor, Shelby Christian Church, Shelbyville, KY.

John Hampton - Pg. 472. Senior Pastor, First Christian Church, Canton, OH.

Bob Hastings - Pg. 116. Regional Sales Manager, Salem Communications, Glendale, CA.

Marshall Hayden - Pg. 542. Senior Pastor, Worthington Christian Church, Columbus, OH.

Jack Hayford - Pg. 714. President, International Foursquare Churches, Senior Pastor Emeritus, The Church on the Way and Chancellor, The King's College & Seminary, Van Nuys, CA.

Murray Hollis - Pg. 572. Senior Pastor, Southwest Christian Church, Temecula, CA.

Cam Huxford - Pg. 58. Senior Pastor, Savannah Christian Church, Savannah, GA.

Kaylene Idleman - Pg. 672. Wife of Ken Idleman, Chancellor, Ozark Christian College, Joplin, MO.

Ken Idleman - Pg. 492. Chancellor, Ozark Christian College, Joplin, MO.

Kyle Idleman - Pg. 504. Teaching Pastor, Southeast Christian Church, Louisville, KY.

Author List

Cal Jernigan - Pg. 196. Senior Pastor, Central Christian Church of the East Valley, Mesa, AZ.

Dane Johnson - Pg. 348. Pastor of Sports & Men's Ministry, Christ's Church of the Valley, San Dimas, CA.

Debbie Johnson - Pg. 100. Member, Shepherd of the Hills Church, Porter Ranch, CA.

Larry Jones - Pg. 378. Founder of Feed the Children, Oklahoma City, OK.

Milton Jones - Pg. 300. Senior Minister, Northwest Church of Christ, Seattle, WA.

Jane Kasel - Pg. 184. Member, Shepherd of the Hills Church, Porter Ranch, CA.

David Kendrick - Pg. 76. Superintendent, Hillcrest Christian School, Granada Hills, CA.

Larry Kerr - Pg. 508. Defensive Coordinator, UCLA Bruins Football Team.

Glenn Kirby - Pg. 624. Senior Pastor, West Valley Christian Church, West Hills, CA.

Victor Knowles - Pg. 324. Director of Peace On Earth Ministries, Joplin, MO.

Ed Kriz - Pg. 476. Former Pastoral Care Pastor, Shepherd of the Hills Church.

Greg Laurie - Pg. 276. Senior Pastor, Harvest Christian Fellowship, Riverside, CA.

Ken Long - Pg. 486. Senior Pastor, Northshore Christian Church, Everett, WA.

Craig Luper - Pg. 72. Executive Pastor, Crossroads Church, Concord, NC.

David Macer - Pg. 122. Adult Singles/LIFE! Groups Pastor, Shepherd of the Hills Church, Porter Ranch, CA.

Mike Maiolo - Pg. 308. Senior Pastor, Mission Viejo Christian Church, Mission Viejo, CA.

Cameron McDonald - Pgs. 60, 104, 232, 590, 720. Preaching Associate, Shepherd of the Hills Church, Porter Ranch, CA

Opal McLaughlin - Pg. 430. Friend of Dudley Rutherford.

Barry McMurtrie - Pg. 52. Senior Pastor, Crossroads Christian Church, Corona, CA.

Ben Merold - Pg. 16. Senior Pastor, Harvester Christian Church, St. Charles, MO.

Pat Merold - Pg. 466. Wife of Ben Merold, Senior Pastor of Harvester Christian Church, St. Charles, MO.

Mark Miller - Pg. 528. Senior Pastor, Greencastle Christian Church, Greencastle, IN.

Barbra Miner - Pg. 110. Member, Shepherd of the Hills Church, Porter Ranch, CA.

Mont Mitchell - Pg. 686. Senior Pastor, Westbrook Christian Church, Bolingbrook, IL.

Steve Moore - Pg. 666. Senior Pastor, Cherry Lane Christian Church, Meridian, ID.

Kay Norris - Pg. 530. Women's Ministries Director, Shepherd of the Hills Church,

Lloyd Ogilvie - Pg. 256. Former Chaplain of the US Senate, Former Pastor, First Presbyterian Church of Hollywood.

David Patrick - Pg. 418. Senior Pastor, Tri Lakes Christian Church, Branson, MO.

Dana Potter - Pg. 264. Elder, Shepherd of the Hills Church, Porter Ranch, CA.

James Price - Pg. 440. Senior Pastor, Diamond Canyon Christian Church, Diamond Bar, CA.

Matt Proctor - Pg. 548. President, Ozark Christian College, Joplin, MO.

David Reagan - Pgs. 144, 238. Director, Lion & Lamb Ministries, McKinney, TX.

Jim Reeve - Pg. 452. Senior Pastor, Faith Community Church, West Covina, CA.

Wally Rendel - Pg. 706. Senior Pastor, Southern Acres Christian Church, Lexington, KY.

Raul Ries - Pg. 724. Senior Pastor, Calvary Chapel, Golden Springs, CA.

David Roadcup - Pg. 156. Executive Director, Center for Church Advancement and Professor at Cincinnati Christian University, Cincinnati, OH.

Fred Rodkey - Pg. 172. Senior Pastor, Chapel Rock Christian Church, Indianapolis, IN.

Adrian Rogers - Pg. 44. Former Senior Pastor, Bellevue Baptist Church, Memphis, TN.

Vicki Ross - Pg. 734. Member, Shepherd of the Hills Church, Porter Ranch, CA.

Rick Rusaw - Pg. 630. Senior Pastor, LifeBridge Christian Church, Longmont, CO.

Bob Russell - Pg. 136. Senior Pastor, Southeast Christian Church, Louisville, KY.

Judy Russell - Pg. 270. Wife of Bob Russell, Senior Pastor of Southeast Christian Church, Louisville, KY.

David Rutherford - Pgs. 306. Senior Pastor, Northside Christian Church, Clovis, CA. and the brother of Dudley C. Rutherford.

■ Author List

H. Dean Rutherford - Pgs. 26, 46, 74, 80, 86, 98, 150, 206, 268, 304, 310, 364, 392, 422, 432, 460, 488, 506, 516, 538, 568, 592, 634, 644, 696, 712. Associate Pastor, Northside Christian Church, Clovis, CA. and the father of Dudley C. Rutherford.

Kerri Rutherford - Pg. 130. Age 9, is the youngest daughter of Pastor Dudley Rutherford.

Renee Rutherford - Pg. 408. Wife of Dudley Rutherford, Senior Pastor of Shepherd of the Hills Church, Porter Ranch, CA.

Shan Rutherford - Pg. 654. Senior Pastor, Greenwood Christian Church, Greenwood, IN. and the uncle of Dudley C. Rutherford.

Chris Seidman - Pg. 212. Senior Minister, Farmer's Branch Church of Christ, Farmer's Branch, TX.

Rubel Shelly - Pg. 642. Senior Minister, Woodmont Hills Church of Christ, Nashville, TN.

Brad Small - Pg. 24. Senior Pastor, Lakeshore Church, Rockwall, TX.

Wayne Smith - Pg. 560. Former Senior Pastor, Southland Christian Church, Lexington, KY.

Dave Stone - Pg. 360. Senior Pastor, Southeast Christian Church, Louisville, KY.

Roger Storms - Pg. 636. Senior Pastor, Chandler Christian Church, Chandler, AZ.

Larry Sullivan - Pg. 520. Assistant Director of the Strauss Institute for Dispute Resolution at Pepperdine University's School of Law, Malibu, CA.

George Taggart - Pg. 190. Member, Discovery Church, Simi Valley, CA.

Clark Tanner - Pg. 224. Senior Pastor, Beaverton Christian Church, Beaverton, OR.

Yvonne Vollert - Pg. 220. Women's Ministries Teacher, Calvary Community Church, Westlake, CA.

Jon Weece - Pg. 536. Senior Pastor, Southland Christian Church, Lexington, KY.

Murry Whiteman - Pg. 578. Member, Discovery Church, Simi Valley, CA.

Jud Wilhite - Pg. 480. Senior Pastor, Central Christian Church, Henderson, NV.

Paul S. Williams - Pg. 598. Editor-at-Large at the Christian Standard and President of Orchard Group, a church planting agency in the Northeast.

Don Wilson - Pg. 330. Senior Pastor, Christ's Church of the Valley, Peoria, AZ.

Susan Wilson - Pg. 362. Wife of Don Wilson, Senior Pastor of Christ's Church of the Valley, Peoria, AZ.

Carla Winters - Pg. 78. Wife of Tim Winters, Executive Pastor, Shepherd of the Hills Church, Porter Ranch, CA.

Tim Winters - Pg. 678. Executive Pastor, Shepherd of the Hills Church, Porter Ranch, CA.

Shane Womack - Pg. 660. Senior Pastor, Knott Avenue Christian Church, Anaheim, CA.

John Wooden - Pg. 200. Former Head Men's Basketball Coach, UCLA.

Ricky Woods - Pg. 446. Senior Pastor, First Baptist Church-West in Charlotte, NC.

Jim Wozniak - Pg. 458. Elder, Shepherd of the Hills Church, Porter Ranch, CA.

Gary York - Pg. 178. Senior Pastor, Eastview Christian Church, Normal, IL.

Alphabetical List of Devotions

■ Alphabetical List of Devotions

Alphabetical List of Devotions

Alphabetical List of Devotions

Bible References

Isaiah 5:20	560	Matthew 6:31-33	540
Isaiah 6:1-3	564	Matthew 6:31-33	142
Isaiah 9:6	640	Matthew 6:31-33	434
Isaiah 43:11	44	Matthew 6:33-34	712
Isaiah 52:14	286	Matthew 7:7-8	312
Isaiah 53:6	222	Matthew 7:13, 14	114
Isaiah 53:3	106	Matthew 7:22, 23	40
Isaiah 53:3, 4	274	Matthew 7:24, 25	266
Isaiah 53:4, 5	86	Matthew 7:24-26	250
Isaiah 53:5	286	Matthew 10:29-31	284
Isaiah 53:7	34	Matthew 11:28-30	70
Isaiah 55:1, 2	171	Matthew 13:30	376
Isaiah 55:1, 2	582	Matthew 14:28, 29	684
Isaiah 55:1-2, 6	490	Matthew 14:29, 30	308
Isaiah 58:11	270	Matthew 14:29-31	374
Isaiah 59:1, 2	352	Matthew 16:23	372
Isaiah 64:6	48	Matthew 16:24, 25	544
Jeremiah 17:10	338	Matthew 16:24-26	30
Jeremiah 18:5, 6	468	Matthew 18:20	484
Jeremiah 31:2	64	Matthew 18:3	236
Ezekiel 11:19, 20	444	Matthew 18:32-34	226
Hosea 2:15	336	Matthew 18:8-9	210
Amos 7:7-9	686	Matthew 19:16-19	630
Nahum 1:3	336	Matthew 20:28	344
Habakkuk 3:17-18	90	Matthew 24:30	514
Malachi 3:8	68	Matthew 24:39-42	84
Malachi 3:10	100	Matthew 24:44, 45	208
Malachi 3:8-10	442	Matthew 25:21	58
Matthew 1:1-16	440	Matthew 27:46	56
Matthew 2:11	718	Matthew 28:18	624
Matthew 4:19, 20	700	Matthew 28:19, 20	294
Matthew 5:14, 16	730	Matthew 28:19, 20	300
Matthew 5:43, 46, 47	702	Mark 2:3-5	332
Matthew 5:46-48	416	Mark 3:28, 29	620
Matthew 6:1	198	Mark 4:30-32	428
Matthew 6:24	368	Mark 4:30-32	242
Matthew 6:28-29	426	Mark 6:2, 3	228

▪ Bible References

Bible References

■ Be A Contributor!

Send in your own 200 word devotion and, if it is selected, you will receive a FREE copy of Romancing Royalty, Volume 2.

Format needed:

1. Bible verse
2. 200 word meditation
3. 75 word prayer
4. 3 study questions

Send all submissions to:

> Shepherd of the Hills Church
> Attn: Romancing Royalty II.
> 19700 Rinaldi Street
> Porter Ranch, CA 91326

OTHER BOOKS

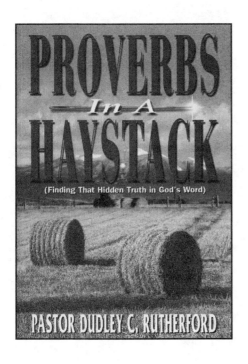

Available at:

www.callonJesus.com

Notes

Notes

Notes